THE PERSON AND THE SITUATION

For Stanley Schachter

About the Authors

Lee Ross is Professor of Psychology at Stanford University. He received his Ph.D. in psychology from Columbia University in 1969. He is coauthor with Richard Nisbett of *Human Inference* and coeditor with John Flavell of *Cognitive Social Development: Frontiers and Possible Futures*. He is a founder and one of the principal investigators of the Stanford Center on Conflict and Negotiation. His 1977 article "The Intuitive Psychologist and His Shortcomings" is the most widely cited article of the 1980s in social psychology.

Richard E. Nisbett is Theodore M. Newcomb Professor of Psychology and Director of the Research Center for Group Dynamics at the University of Michigan. He received his Ph.D. degree in Psychology from Columbia University in 1966. He taught at Yale University from 1966 to 1971. He is co-author, with Lee Ross, of *Human Inference*, with E. E. Jones, D. E. Kanouse, H. H. Kelley, S. Valins and B. Weiner of *Attribution: Perceiving the Causes of Behavior,* and with J. Holland, K. Holyoak, and P. Thagard of *Induction*. In 1982 he was the recipient of the Donald Campbell Award for Distinguished Research in Social Psychology.

THE PERSON AND THE SITUATION

Perspectives of Social Psychology

Lee Ross
Stanford University

Richard E. Nisbett
University of Michigan

Foreword Malcolm Gladwell

pinter
&
martin

The Person and the Situation: Perspectives of Social Psychology

First published by McGraw-Hill 1991
This edition first published in Great Britain by Pinter & Martin Ltd 2011

ISBN 978-1-905177-44-8

British Library Cataloguing-in-Publication Data
A catalogue record for this book is available from the British Library

Printed in Great Britain by TJ International Ltd, Padstow, Cornwall

Pinter & Martin Ltd
6 Effra Parade
London SW2 1PS

www.pinterandmartin.com

CONTENTS

Foreword

I still remember when I first read *The Person and the Situation*. It was in 1996. I had never taken any psychology courses in college, so the names Nisbett and Ross – not to mention Kurt Lewin and Solomon Asch – meant nothing to me. I didn't know what the Fundamental Attribution Error was. I had, from my days as a science writer at the *Washington Post*, a passing acquaintance with the *Journal of Personality and Social Psychology* and that was it. But by some happy series of coincidences I fell in love with psychology that summer, and started spending long afternoons at the New York University library, browsing through academic journals. I would find an article I really liked, and then read as many of the most interesting bits of the bibliography of that article as I could, and then the most interesting bits of the bibliography of those articles – and on and on, walking back the cat, as they say in the intelligence world. (You can kill a lot of afternoons at NYU library that way.) Anyway, the cat I kept finding at the end of those walks was *The Person and the Situation*. So one day, I sat down in one of the carrels at Bobst Library and devoured it in one sitting. And because I didn't have borrowing privileges, I photocopied it, front to back, in violation – I am now ashamed to admit – of every rule of copyright. I still have that bundle of pirated pages on my bookshelf. I hope Professors Ross and Nisbett will consider this foreword as partial reparation.

What is so special about *The Person and the Situation*? You will, in short order, discover the answer to that yourself, and it is not my intention to ruin the fun. But let me offer a few short personal reflections. This is an ambitious book. It might be, in fact, one of the most ambitious books that I (or I imagine you) will ever read. That is the first of its many virtues. It offers a way of re-ordering ordinary experience. It argues that when we perceive the actions and intentions of others, we tend to make mistakes. We see things that aren't there and we make predictions that we ought not to make: we privilege the "person" and we discount the influence of the "situation." It speaks, in short, to the very broadest questions of human perception.

I found this idea so disturbing and subversive that I think I have been wrestling with it ever since. Just the other day, for example, I gave a short talk at a gathering of sports-types on one of my favorite topics – professional quarterbacks. I argued that the idea that quarterbacks can be ranked – that there is such a thing as a good quarterback and a not so good quarterback and that we can say, with certainty, that, say Peyton

Manning is x number of points better than Brett Farve – is nonsense. A quarterback's performance is inextricably tied up in his situation: in the quality of the players around him, his coaches, the skills of his receivers, the plays call for him – and on and on – and in trying to extract some notion of quarterback quality from that jumble of factors we are making an error. (Actually, a Fundamental Attribution Error.) I was making the kind of argument that people make once they've read *The Person and the Situation*. Halfway through my talk I sensed that I wasn't getting anywhere, that my audience didn't much agree, and I suspect that's because most of them had not had the benefit of reading the *The Person and the Situation*. (The next time I will suggest that the organizers of the event invite Nisbett and Ross instead). That's a trivial example, I know. But that's my point. The genius of this book is that it will insinuate itself into the way you think about virtually everything – even Peyton Manning and Brett Farve. (If you care deeply about your professional sports team, by the way, I suggest that you buy an extra copy of this book and send it to the General Manager. I'm serious).

What kind of book is *The Person and the Situation*? It looks, I know, like an academic text. It has almost forty pages of references and indexes. (Walking back the cat, in this case, would take a very long time). It has figures and charts and references embedded in the text, the way that a serious book does. I'm guessing that a good number of those of you reading this are college students, to whom this book has been assigned. It would be a mistake, though, to put *The Person and the Situation* firmly in the academic category. We make that mistake too much, in my opinion, segregating ideas and books by virtue of provenance. The thing that struck me that day in the library – and will, I hope, strike you as well – is that *The Person and the Situation* has much more in common with an adventure story than a textbook. There is, on virtually every page, an insight or a little gem of research or an observation that will take you by surprise, and I defy you to predict, with any accuracy, where any chapter is ultimately headed. That is a tribute to the gifts and cleverness of Professors Nisbett and Ross. But it is also a tribute to the tradition that this book belongs to. Social psychology stands at the intersection between our eyes and the world in front of us, and helps us understand the difference between what we think we see and what is actually out there. If you have ever felt the excitement of putting on a pair of glasses for the first time, and seeing the world suddenly jump into focus, then you have some sense of what is in store for you in the pages ahead. You are in for a treat.

Malcolm Gladwell
March, 2011

Preface

A lot has changed in our field during the two decades since we wrote *The Person and the Situation*. There has been a huge growth in the visibility and appreciation of social psychological insights through the writings of skilled journalists like Malcolm Gladwell and those of prominent academicians like Dan Gilbert who have mastered the art of writing for the general public. We have also seen an explosion of interest in what has become known as behavioral economics, a discipline with obvious debts to the psychology of judgment and decision-making pioneered by Daniel Kahneman and Amos Tversky, and less obvious debts to the subjectivist tradition in social psychology. Indeed, we might say that behavioral economics, in its challenge to the rational markets model of traditional economics, and more specifically in its demonstration that responses to prospective gains and losses under conditions of uncertainty depend on the way they are "framed," is psychology with a "name change for business reasons."

Another notable development has been the flowering of cultural psychology, which has forced us to rethink what is natural or inevitable about social perception and interaction and what is a product of particular cultural contexts. There have also been heartening developments in applied social psychology – including the validation of theory-based interventions to serve stigmatized and disadvantaged students. An unexpected theoretical development has been a reawakening of interest in the impact of non-conscious or implicit process. But perhaps the most important development has been the waning of the classic "one-shot" experiment and the waxing of interest in longer-term, more dynamic influences on actions and outcomes of the sort that cannot really be captured in a single experimental session.

We resisted the temptation to revise our original chapters in light of these new developments. (A comprehensive review of new findings and directions in social psychology is available in the introductory chapter of the newest edition of *The Handbook of Social Psychology* authored by Ross, Lepper and Ward). However we thought it would be useful to our readers to add a brief "afterword" in which we comment on the ways in which these new developments build upon, and in some respects challenge, our original perspective on the person, the situation, and the cumulative contributions of social psychology in helping us to understand and influence human behavior.

We would like to acknowledge our publisher, Martin Wagner, for giving new life to our book, and for the opportunity not only to make it available to new readers but also to add some reflections on developments in the field over the two decades since its original publication.

Finally, we are extremely grateful to Malcolm Gladwell for his interesting new foreword and for his kind remarks about the book and its role in his own career. He gives us too much credit. It has been his skill as a writer, and his insight about our field, that accounts for his personal success and the resurgence of popular interest in our field. He is indeed an *outlier* whose efforts have created a *tipping point* for social psychology.

Lee Ross and Richard E. Nisbett
July, 2011

Preface to the first edition

A few years ago, when we both seemed to be spending an inordinate amount of time trying to explain why social psychology is worthy of governmental support, we began to think about distilling our understanding of our field and its most important intellectual contributions into a textbook. In fact, we discussed the possibility of organizing our text around such contributions – rather than around content areas such as aggression, attraction, and prejudice, or around traditional topics such as social perception, social influence, and intergroup relations. We soon became discouraged, however, when we talked to some successful publishers and authors and received their conventional wisdom about the requirements of the marketplace with respect to organization, breadth of coverage, and level of presentation.

Nevertheless, we continued to muse about a different kind of social psychology text, of which the classic 1952 text by Solomon Asch was perhaps the model, a book for colleagues as much as for students, one suitable for readers who wanted to know not only what social psychology was about but also why it might be important in addressing contemporary social, political, and intellectual concerns. We envisioned a slim volume that would be highly selective and focused in its treatment of topics, spelling out what we thought to be general, cumulative, and important, even if it meant omitting some topics normally included in traditional social psychology texts and adding some other topics that had long seemed critical and central to us, but had generally been left in the hands of personality theorists, social anthropologists, and sociologists.

At roughly the same time, we thought about two other potential writing projects of narrower focus. One project would have had us explain how our discipline, namely cognitive social psychology in the tradition of Kurt Lewin, is relevant to personality psychology and to the issue of behavioral consistency and predictability. We were intrigued by the discrepancy between lay beliefs in the predictive power of broad, stable personality traits (beliefs that all of us seem to find support for in our own everyday experience) and the cold, hard statistical results obtained from well-controlled empirical research implying that cross-situational consistency in behavior is largely illusory. A second project would have tried to link laboratory and applied traditions in social psychology, to explain the continuity we see between them, and to discuss the lessons that we believe the best of experimental social psychology holds for those who would, in Donald Campbell's (1969) terms, undertake "reforms as experiments." We wanted to write not only about dramatic and significant application successes but also about some famous "failures," that is, well-intentioned and even well-conceived social interventions that didn't work, or that produced results much less dramatic than expected or promised by the intervention advocates. We hoped to show how application successes and application failures alike contribute, and in fact dovetail, to drive home some of the most important lessons of mainstream theoretical and empirical social psychology.

After several years of continued discussion it became increasingly clear to us that the different projects we had been discussing were intimately related and could be addressed in a single volume written for the serious student of social psychology. The linkage was provided by our growing conviction that three contributions of social psychology are paramount. The first and most basic contribution concerns the power and subtlety of situational influences on behavior. In particular, what has been demonstrated through a host of celebrated laboratory and field studies is that manipulations of the immediate social situation can overwhelm in importance the type of individual differences in personal traits or dispositions that people normally think of as being determinative of social behavior. The second contribution is a refinement and, in a sense, a limitation of the first. It involves the need to take into account the subjective nature of situational influence, that is, to recognize the extent to which people respond to their own "definition" or "construal" of the situations that stimulate, and provide the context for, their behavior. The third contribution relates to Lewinian field-theory notions of "tension systems" and "quasistationary equilibria." These notions emphasize both the dynamic processes that constrain change and the dynamic consequences of change, both within social systems and within the cognitive system of the individual. Pressures to change one element or relationship within a system are often negated by homeostatic processes, and when change does occur, the results will often prove to be widespread throughout the system, "nonobvious" in character, and continuing until the system as a whole comes into balance.

Each of these contributions helps us to understand how lay intuitions about behavior are likely to go astray – sometimes with profound personal and social costs. For each contribution identifies a set of determinants of social behavior that actors and observers characteristically underestimate or fail to make adequate inferential allowance for in the conduct of their affairs. Understanding these three contributions, accordingly, becomes critical in addressing the two narrower topics that we had initially considered writing about. Through these contributions we develop a new and more sophisticated appreciation of the sources of both real and illusory consistency in social behavior. And through them, we come to appreciate the relationship between the celebrated triumphs of "situationist" laboratory research and the often-disappointing history of large-scale social intervention programs.

Once we realized how much our three long-contemplated projects had converged, the temptation to write became irresistible. And in our labors we found a bonus – a renewed pride in our field. We felt heightened respect for Lewin, Asch, and the other great social psychologists in the situationist, subjectivist, and field-theory traditions. We also felt more confident and less apologetic in defending the accomplishments and promise of our discipline.

As we survey the volume that has emerged from our efforts, we confess to some regrets and even some trepidation. In organizing our discussions so much around themes of situationism, subjectivism, and the dynamics of tension systems, we have been obliged to leave out, or address in cursory fashion, a great deal of praiseworthy research – notably, classic research on topics like attitudes and social relations that have played an important role in shaping the history of our field, as well as several strands of contemporary research in forensic psychology, health psychology, and business psychology that demonstrate our field's continuing capacity to make valuable applied contributions. We also have been obliged to make some flattering, but we hope not inappropriate, assumptions about the intellectual seriousness of our potential readers, in particular their willingness to explore complex ideas about personal versus situational determinants of behavior and their interest in relating the lessons of our discipline to important political, social, and even philosophical issues. But our overwhelming feeling is one of satisfaction in having written the type of book that we have long wished we had available to assign to the serious, critical student who asks, "What have we really learned from social psychology?"

So we offer this book as a kind of throwback to a golden age and as a tribute to our intellectual forebears. We offer it as a "stand tall and be proud" pep talk for our colleagues in general and for our younger colleagues in particular. We offer it as an olive branch and invitation to more fruitful intellectual dialogue with our friends in personality research (and also to our friends in anthropology and sociology who cluck, with some justification, about our parochialism). We offer it as a slim guide for nonpsychologists to the heart and muscle of our enterprise. And last, but not least, we offer it as an invitation to honor the great tradition of Kurt Lewin that links basic theory first to the analysis of socially significant real-world phenomena and ultimately to the task of effective social innovation.

Acknowledgements

This book is dedicated to our mentor Stanley Schachter. It was in working as his apprentices that we began to learn the lessons that we seek to articulate in this book – lessons about the power and subtlety of structural influences, about the critical role of subjective interpretation, and about the dynamics of tension systems existing within the minds of individuals and within social groups and institutions.

He, in turn, was passing on insights, suitably refined and enhanced, from Kurt Lewin, Leon Festinger, and other giants to whom we, and our field, are so indebted. The form in which we now offer these insights, and the focal points for our discussions of them, is different still, enriched by the contact we have had over a 20 year period with cherished colleagues and students at Stanford and Michigan.

Several people who contributed to planning, writing, and revising this manuscript merit special acknowledgment. They are Paul B. Andreassen, Daryl Bern, Lisa Brown, Judith Harakiewicz, Mark Lepper, Walter Mischel, Michael Morris, David G. Myers, Claude Steele, and Timothy Wilson. We also owe a large debt of gratitude to our secretaries, Fiona Anderson and Dorothy Walker, not only for their hard work, but also for their patience and good cheer. Special thanks are owed to Andrea Lawrence, who improved the manuscript in innumerable ways. Christopher Rogers and Curt Berkowitz of McGraw-Hill oversaw the production of the book with great skill and insight.

The following colleagues were requested to review earlier versions of the manuscript for McGraw-Hill and provided helpful comments and sugestions: John Dovidio, Colgate University; Melvin Mark, Pennsylvania State University; and Vaida Thompson, University of North Carolina.

Finally, we again acknowledge, with love and gratitude, the most important collaborators not in our work but in our lives, the *people* who make our personal *situations* so rich and satisfying: Judy, Joshua, Tim, Rebecca, and Katie Ross, and Susan, Matthew, and Sarah Nisbett.

Lee Ross and Richard E. Nisbett

CHAPTER 1
INTRODUCTION

Undergraduates taking their first course in social psychology generally are in search of an interesting and enjoyable experience, and they rarely are disappointed. They find out many fascinating things about human behavior, some of which validate common sense and some of which contradict it. The inherent interest value of the material, amounting to high-level gossip about people and social situations, usually ensures that the students are satisfied consumers.

The experience of serious graduate students, who, over the course of four or five years, are immersed in the problems and the orientation of the field, is rather different. For them, the experience is an intellectually wrenching one. Their most basic assumptions about the nature and the causes of human behavior, and about the very predictability of the social world, are challenged. At the end of the process, their views of human behavior and society will differ profoundly from the views held by most other people in their culture. Some of their new insights and beliefs will be held rather tentatively and applied inconsistently to the social events that unfold around them. Others will be held with great conviction, and will be applied confidently. But ironically, even the new insights that they are most confident about will tend to have the effect of making them less certain than their peers about predicting social behavior and making inferences about particular individuals or groups. Social psychology rivals philosophy in its ability to teach people that they do not truly understand the nature of the world. This book is about that hard-won ignorance and what it tells us about the human condition.

THE LESSONS AND CHALLENGES OF SOCIAL PSYCHOLOGY

As graduate students at Columbia University in the 1960s, working primarily with Stanley Schachter, we underwent the experience typical of students exposed to the experimental tradition in social psychology. That is, many of our most fundamental beliefs about human behavior, beliefs that we shared with most other people in our culture and that had remained intact or even been strengthened by our undergraduate courses in the humanities, were abruptly challenged in ways that have shaped our subsequent careers. An introduction to these challenges, which we offer below, provides a departure point for our discussion of the contributions of our discipline. Indeed, the remainder of our book represents an attempt to reconcile common sense and common experience with the empirical lessons and challenges that lie at the core of social psychology. In so doing, the book seeks to provide an overview of social psychology's primary scientific and intellectual contributions, one that serves to challenge, reform, and expand common sense.

The Weakness of Individual Differences

Consider the following scenario: While walking briskly to a meeting some distance across a college campus, John comes across a man slumped in a doorway, asking him for help. Will John offer it, or will he continue on his way? Before answering such a question, most people would want to know more about John. Is he someone known to be callous and unfeeling, or is he renowned for his kindness and concern? Is he a stalwart member of the Campus Outreach Organization, or a mainstay of the Conservative Coalition Against Welfare Abuse? In short, what kind of person is John and how has he behaved when his altruism has been tested in the past? Only with such information in hand, most people would agree, could one make a sensible and confident prediction.

In fact, however, nothing one is likely to know or learn about John would be of much use in helping predict John's behavior in the situation we've described. In particular, the type of information about personality that most laypeople would want to have before making a prediction would prove to be of relatively little value. A half century of research has taught us that in this situation, and in most other novel situations, one cannot predict with any accuracy how particular people will respond. At least one cannot do so using information about an individual's personal dispositions or even about that individual's past behavior.

Even scientists who are most concerned with assessing individual differences in personality would concede that our ability to predict how particular people will respond in particular situations is very limited.

This "predictability ceiling" is typically reflected in a maximum statistical correlation of .30 between measured individual differences on a given trait dimension and behavior in a novel situation that plausibly tests that dimension. This ceiling, for example, would characterize our ability to predict on the basis of a personality test of honesty how likely different people will be to cheat in a game or on an exam, or to predict on the basis of a test of friendliness or extroversion how much sociability different individuals will show at a particular social gathering. Now a correlation of .30, as we will emphasize later, is by no means trivial. Correlations of this magnitude can be quite important for many prediction purposes. But a correlation of .30 still leaves the great bulk of variance in people's behavior unaccounted for. More importantly, a correlation of this magnitude is a good deal lower than it would have to be to provide the type of predictability that most laypeople anticipate when they make predictions about each other's behavior or make inferences about others' personal attributes. Moreover, the .30 value is an upper limit. For most novel behaviors in most domains, psychologists cannot come close to that. Certainly, as we will see, neither the professional nor the layperson can do that well when obliged to predict behavior in one particular new situation on the basis of actions in one particular prior situation.

Despite such evidence, however, most people staunchly believe that individual differences or traits can be used to predict how people will behave in new situations. Such "dispositionism" is widespread in our culture. What is more, most of us, scientists and laypeople alike, seem to find our dispositionism affirmed by our everyday social experience. The challenge of accounting for this discrepancy between beliefs about everyday experience on the one hand and empirical evidence on the other hand is one of the most important faced by psychologists. We will deal with it at many points in this book.

The Power of Situations

While knowledge about John is of surprisingly little value in predicting whether he will help the person slumped in the doorway, details concerning the specifics of the situation would be invaluable. For example, what was the appearance of the person in the doorway? Was he clearly ill, or might he have been a drunk or, even worse, a nodding dope addict? Did his clothing make him look respectably middle class or decently working class, or did he look like a homeless derelict?

Such considerations are fairly obvious once they are mentioned, and the layperson, upon reflection, will generally concede their importance. But few laypeople would concede, much less anticipate, the relevance of some other, subtler, contextual details that empirical research has shown to be important factors influencing bystander intervention. Darley and

Batson (1973) actually confronted people with a version of the situation we've described and found what some of these factors are. Their subjects were students in a religious seminary who were on their way to deliver a practice sermon. If the subjects were in a hurry (because they thought they were late to give a practice sermon), only about 10 percent helped. By contrast, if they were not in a hurry (because they had plenty of time before giving their sermon), about 63 percent of them helped.

Social psychology has by now amassed a vast store of such empirical parables. The tradition here is simple. Pick a generic situation; then identify and manipulate a situational or contextual variable that intuition or past research leads you to believe will make a difference (ideally, a variable whose impact you think most laypeople, or even most of your peers, somehow fail to appreciate), and see what happens. Sometimes, of course, you will be wrong and your manipulation won't "work." But often the situational variable makes quite a bit of difference. Occasionally, in fact, it makes nearly all the difference, and information about traits and individual differences that other people thought all-important proves all but trivial. If so, you have contributed a situationist classic destined to become part of our field's intellectual legacy. Such empirical parables are important because they illustrate the degree to which ordinary men and women are apt to be mistaken about the power of the situation – the power of particular situational features, and the power of situations in general.

People's inflated belief in the importance of personality traits and dispositions, together with their failure to recognize the importance of situational factors in affecting behavior, has been termed the "fundamental attribution error" (Ross, 1977; Nisbett & Ross, 1980; see also Jones, 1979; Gilbert & Jones, 1986). Together with many other social psychologists, we have directed our attention to documenting this conjoint error and attempting to track down its origins. Every chapter of this book will discuss research relevant to this error. In Chapter 5 we will marshall the evidence showing how widespread the error is and try to explain why it occurs.

The Subtlety of Situations

There is another face to situationism. Not all situational factors prove to be powerful determinants of behavior, not even those that seem intuitively strong to both laypeople and social scientists. Some, in fact, prove to be astonishingly weak.

Nowhere is the weakness of apparently big situational factors more perplexing than in studies of the impact of various real-life events on important social outcomes. For some of these weak effects we can be grateful. For example, it turns out that in most cases the long-term impact of physical and sexual abuse suffered in childhood is relatively slight (Widom, 1989), as is the long-term effect of teenage pregnancy on a young woman's life outcomes (Furstenberg, Brooks-Gunn, & Morgan, 1987), and even the long-term effect of P.O.W. camp indoctrination (Schein, 1956). Unfortunately, apparently positive events sometimes also prove to be surprisingly weak in their effect. For example, the lives of major lottery winners seem to be influenced far less by their windfalls than most of us would predict, especially when we imagine how much our own lives would be changed by a similar windfall (Brickman, Coates, & Janoff-Bulman, 1978).

A more sobering example of the weakness of apparently large, apparently positive events is to be found in what is perhaps the progenitor of modern social intervention experiments, the Cambridge-Somerville study of delinquency described by Powers and Whitmer (1951) with follow-ups by the McCords (J. McCord, 1978; J. McCord & W. McCord, 1959; W. McCord & J. McCord, 1959). The subjects in this noble experiment (which we discuss at greater length in Chapter 8 on applications of social psychology) were both "delinquency prone" and "average" boys living in a lower socioeconomic status in a mostly Irish and Italian suburb of Boston in the 1940s. Some of the boys were assigned to an extremely ambitious and intensive experimental intervention condition in which, over roughly a five-year period, they were exposed to a wide variety of social, psychological, and academic supports. Thus counselors provided two home visits per month to work on personal and family problems. Tutoring in academic subjects was made available. Many of the boys received psychiatric or medical help. Contact with Boy Scouts, YMCA, or other community programs was facilitated, and a substantial number of the boys were given the opportunity to attend summer camps. Despite this intensive and apparently favorable intervention, however, the boys in this experimental, or "treatment," condition proved to be no less likely to become delinquent than those in an "untreated" control group. Indeed, follow-ups conducted 30 years after the end of the program suggested that treated subjects may actually have fared slightly worse as adults, for example, in terms of rates for serious adult offenses, than those subjects whose outcomes were merely monitored.

Follow-up research on the nondelinquent boys in the Cambridge-Somerville sample who received no treatment (Long & Vaillant, 1984) showed even more surprising noneffects – in this case, noneffects of apparently important social factors in the boys' family backgrounds. The boys were classified into four different categories depending on the degree of social health or pathology of their home life. At the lowest extreme were families with many serious problems – for example, an alcoholic or abusive father, a schizophrenic mother, a dependence on many social agencies for financial support, and so forth. At the opposite extreme were families that seemed for the most part to be models of the working poor

– fathers were employed, mothers were serving as homemakers, there was no obvious pathology and no dependence on social agencies. The life outcomes of boys in these different categories were then examined in a follow-up study 40 years later. On indicator after indicator – for example, income, mental health, prison incarcerations, suicides, and the like – the status of the subjects' home situation as children made little if any difference.

What do we learn from these spectacular noneffects? Certainly not that situational factors are unimportant in the world outside the social psychology laboratory. As we will see beginning in Chapter 2, many real-world effects turn out to be huge – from the dramatic personal changes wrought by immersing conservative young women in highly liberal surroundings (Newcomb, 1943), to the pronounced effect of competition on group conflict (Sherif, Harvey, White, Hood, & Sherif, 1961). Conversely, it is not only in the "real world" that situational factors and manipulations sometimes prove to be surprisingly small or nonexistent. It is the studies with detectable effects that get published, and the subset of the studies with large and unanticipated effects that become well known. The others languish in file drawers. We wish we had a dollar for every failed laboratory manipulation that social psychologists have designed with the confident expectation that the effects in question would be significant. What we have learned, in short, is that situational effects can sometimes be far different from what our intuitions, or theories, or even the existing psychological literature tell us they should be. Some factors that we expect to be very important prove to be trivial in their impact; and some factors that we expect to be weak prove, at least in some contexts, to exert a very large influence indeed. Accounting for our poor "calibration" as to the size of the effects produced by situational factors is a major focus of the education of the social psychologist and a chief concern of this book.

The Predictability of Human Behavior

When we, the authors, were undergraduates, we were assured that the sharply limited abilities of social scientists to make accurate predictions had to do with the relative youth of the social sciences. We no longer share such beliefs nor resort to such defenses of our field. We now believe that ours is not a particularly immature science and that we have, in fact, already discovered and documented some very important things about human social behavior. At the same time, we accept the fact that social psychology is never going to reach the point of predicting how any given individual (even one who is well known to us) is going to behave in a given novel situation. A corollary of this concession is that the application of social science knowledge is always going to be a risky business. When we try something new, even a new intervention that seems very reasonable on prior grounds, we are frequently going to discover that people respond quite differently than we had anticipated.

The roots of this fundamental unpredictability, we will argue, are very deep and perhaps akin to a source of similar unpredictability in phenomena in the physical and biological sciences (Gleick, 1987). We will consider this unpredictability issue further near the end of this chapter, and then return to it again at several other points throughout the book.

The Conflict Between the Lessons of Social Psychology and the Experience of Everyday Life

As we have seen, the evidence of empirical social psychology often conflicts sharply with what we "know" from everyday life. To be sure, we are sometimes surprised by the behavior of our fellow human beings, or by a genuinely unexpected act on the part of one of our children, or one of our friends, or some public figure. But for the most part the world seems an orderly, predictable place. It is extroverted Bill who dons the lamp shade at the party and not introverted Jill. Similarly, it is the pastor of the Church of the Good Shepherd who preaches charity and the Republican congressman from the wealthiest district in the state who preaches self-reliance and free enterprise. Moreover, soft answers do seem to turn away wrath. Sending a boy to do a man's job generally does result in disappointment. And, when it really counts, our best friends usually do come through for us, just as we had expected they would.

Earlier in their careers the authors seriously entertained the hypothesis that most of this seeming order was a kind of cognitive illusion. We believed that human beings are adept at seeing things as they believe them to be, at explaining away contradictions and, in particular, at perceiving people as more consistent than they really are. While we continue to believe that such biased processing of evidence plays an important role in perceptions of consistency, we now believe that the predictability of everyday life is, for the most part, real. At the same time, we believe that many of the principles and intuitions that people use to explain and predict behavior are unreliable. That is, people often make correct predictions on the basis of erroneous beliefs and defective prediction strategies.

We draw an analogy here between lay and professional physics. Lay physics (which is largely the same as Aristotelian and medieval physics) is undeniably mistaken in some of its main presumptions (Holland, Holyoak, Nisbett, & Thagard, 1986; McCloskey, 1983). In particular, lay physics, like lay psychology, errs in focusing on the properties of the object to the neglect of the field of forces in which that object exists. Moreover, the main interactional notion of lay physics – namely, the intuitive notion of "momentum" – is the utterly mistaken notion that a force applied to an object gives it a store of energy that gradually dissipates. The correct notion (that of inertia) requires that objects at rest remain at rest and that objects in motion remain in motion, unless some other force is applied. Nevertheless, lay physics does a perfectly good job of getting us through our days. In a world where air, land, and water all offer resistance or friction, the notion that objects somehow lose their momentum is good enough. Only when we step outside the normal haunts of daily life, for example, when we venture into a physics laboratory or into outer space, does our lay physics get us into serious trouble.

And so it is for social psychology. Our intuitive ideas about people and the principles governing their responses to their environment are generally adequate for most purposes of the office and the home; but they are seriously deficient when we must understand, predict, or control behavior in contexts that lie outside our most customary experience – that is, when we take on new and different roles or responsibilities, encounter new cultures, analyze newly arisen social problems, or contemplate novel social interventions to address such problems. When we go from being students to being professionals, when we bargain with a street vendor 5,000 miles from home, or when our community begins a new program to deal with crack addiction or homelessness, the inadequacies of lay principles are likely to be revealed.

Much of what we wish to do in this book involves describing how lay social psychology differs from scientific social psychology. In this task we will identify three principles as the major cumulative insights of our field – a kind of tripod that provides the foundation for our collective enterprise. The first principle concerns the power and subtlety of situational influences. The second involves the importance of people's subjective interpretations of the situation. The third speaks to the necessity of understanding both individual psyches and social groups as tension systems or energy "fields" characterized by an equilibrium between impelling and restraining forces. We will sketch these principles here briefly and then illustrate their application throughout the rest of the book.

THE TRIPOD ON WHICH SOCIAL PSYCHOLOGY RESTS

The Principle of Situationism

Our discussion of situationism in social psychology must begin with an introduction to Kurt Lewin, a German emigrant who came to the United States in the mid-1930s. His contributions over the next decade redefined the field of social psychology and continue even today to exert a profound effect on its major theoretical and applied traditions. Lewin's general theoretical formulation began with the familiar truism that behavior is a function of the person and the situation (or, in Lewin's terms, a function of the "life space," which includes both the individual and the individual's psychological representation of the environment). Despite the evenhandedness of Lewin's formulation, which cites the joint influence of situational and dispositional determinants of behavior, it was the power of the immediate social situation that was featured in his empirical work and that of his students. Lewin's particular concern was the capacity of situational factors, and social manipulations, to influence patterns of behavior that normally are seen as reflective of personal dispositions and preferences.

One provocative field experiment, for example, was conducted by Lewin, Lippit, and White (1939) at a time when the specter of Nazism was looming large for social scientists and for all humanity. The experiment featured a manipulation of leadership style to create authoritarian versus democratic group "climates" in recreation clubs (set up specifically by Lewin and company to conduct their study). This manipulation proved sufficiently potent to produce marked differences in the way that young male club members related to each other and to those with greater or lesser power. Scapegoating, submission to authority figures, and at times even expressions of hostility – in short, the disturbing complex of responses generally associated with the "authoritarian personality" (Adorno, Frenkel-Brunswik, Levinson, & Sanford, 1950) – could be either inhibited or promoted, the Lewinians showed, by a relatively short-term manipulation of the person's immediate environment.

Even more important, and illustrative of the tradition established by Lewin, was a series of studies employing the then-novel technique of "group decision making" to facilitate changes in consumer behavior, health practices, and work-place productivity (for example, Bennett, 1955; Coch & French, 1948; Lewin, 1952). These studies, which we will describe in more detail in Chapter 8 on application, brought to bear a fundamental insight of Lewin's that is now familiar to a generation of organizational psychologists and "training group" practitioners: When trying to get people to change familiar ways of doing things, social pressures and constraints exerted by the informal peer group represent the most potent restraining force that must be overcome and, at the same time, the most powerful inducing force that can be exploited to achieve success.

Thus the main point of Lewin's situationism was that the social context creates potent forces producing or constraining behavior. He was well aware that these forces were often overlooked in lay psychology and that their identification was to be a major task of scientific social psychology.

Indeed, Lewin explicitly noted the analogy we discussed earlier between the errors of lay social psychology and the errors of lay physics.

An equally important part of Lewin's situationism was a healthy respect for apparently minor but actually important details of the situation. He often called these "channel factors" because they referred to small but critical facilitators or barriers. Lewin recognized that behavior often is produced by the opening up of some channel (for example, by public commitment to a course of action, or by taking a halting first step in the direction of some new behavior) and sometimes is blocked by the closing of some channel (for example, by failure to formulate a specific plan to carry out a concrete action at an opportune moment).

An example of how Lewin's channel factors work was provided by Leventhal, Singer, and Jones (1965). Their experiment dealt with the familiar problem of translating good intentions regarding personal health practices into concrete and effective action. Their subjects were all college seniors who received persuasive communications about the risks of tetanus and the value of inoculation. All subjects, furthermore, were told where they could go to get themselves inoculated. Paper-and-pencil questionnaires revealed that the communication was quite effective at changing the beliefs and attitudes reported by the students. Nevertheless, only about 3 percent actually took the step of getting their tetanus shots. By contrast, when subjects who had received the same communication were given a map of the campus with the Health Building circled, and were also urged to review their weekly schedule to decide on a particular time and route to get them to the Center, the percentage of takers went up to 28 percent. Clearly, learning the relevant information about the disease and its prevention, and even forming a general intention to take the necessary steps to protect themselves, were not enough for most subjects. It was also necessary, apparently, for them to have a specific plan (and perhaps even a map) for getting there – or, in Lewin's terms, a ready "channel" through which intentions could lead to actions.

Of course, 28 percent may still seem like a disappointing percentage for "medical compliance." We suspect that an even more specific invitation and channel – for example, an invitation to "show up next Tuesday at 10:00 a.m. when your schedule suggests that you will just be coming out of your chemistry class, with an hour to spare before your 11:00 a.m. Psychology 1 course," – would have been even more effective in getting subjects on the path to the Health Center and to their tetanus inoculations. A similar point is made by many contemporary studies of the utilization of public health services. Attitudes and other "interesting" individual difference factors rarely do a very impressive job of predicting who will or who will not show up at the clinic or counseling facility. Instead, a more powerful predictor of usage is the mere distance of the individual from the closest service. Again, a simple channel factor tends to override all others in predicting who uses the services (Van Dort & Moos, 1976).

The channel factor principle, thus, is one key to understanding why some situational factors have bigger effects than might be anticipated and why some have smaller effects. Seemingly big interventions and campaigns that provide no effective input channel in the form of situational pressures, or no effective behavioral outlet channel in the form of clear intentions or plans, will generally produce disappointingly small effects. And seemingly small situational factors that operate on important input or output channels will often exert gratifyingly large effects.

The Principle of Construal

The second enduring contribution of social psychology, ironically, is one that challenges the theoretical and practical value of the doctrine of situationism. The impact of any "objective" stimulus situation depends upon the personal and subjective meaning that the actor attaches to that situation. To predict the behavior of a given person successfully, we must be able to appreciate the actor's construal of the situation – that is, the manner in which the person understands the situation as a whole. Construal issues are similarly important if our goal is to control or change behavior. Many well-intentioned, even well-conceived, social interventions fail because of the way in which they are construed by the targeted group (for example, as an insulting and stigmatizing exercise in co-option or paternalism).

As we will spell out in Chapter 3, situationism in social psychology has similarities to the situationism of the behaviorist tradition. Both traditions were impatient with the lay (and psychoanalytic) emphasis on the importance of individual differences and unique personal histories, and both emphasized the importance of the immediately impinging stimulus situation. But the social psychological and behaviorist traditions parted company long ago over the issue of construal. The avowed goal of the behaviorists was to specify objective stimuli and the associations formed between such stimuli and observed responses without any attempt to look inside the "black box" of the subject's mind. Social psychology, however, as Robert Abelson has put it aptly to us in conversation, was the one field of psychology that could never really be "behaviorized." Its most astute practitioners always understood that it is the situation as construed by the subject that is the true stimulus. This meant that theory was always going to have to focus on subjective interpretations of stimuli and responses as much as on stimulus-response relationships themselves.

As early as the 1930s, European psychologists, such as Piaget and F. C. Bartlett, offered discussions of the importance of construal processes and shaped research on the topic by introducing the notion of a "schema" –

that is, a knowledge structure that summarizes generic knowledge and previous experience with respect to a given class of stimuli and events and, at the same time, gives meaning and guides anticipation with respect to similar stimuli and events in the future. Aside from Lewin himself, social psychology's most convincing advocate of the importance of paying attention to the actor's definition of the situation was Solomon Asch (1952). In Chapter 3 we will discuss the nature of Asch's subjectivist orientation, especially as he applied it in interpreting the results of his own research and that of his contemporaries.

More recently, social psychologists, together with their colleagues in cognitive psychology and artificial intelligence, have focused again on what might be called the "tools of construal." Discussion of cognitive structures (schemas, scripts, models, social representations) and strategies (judgmental "heuristics," tacit rules of conversation), and their role in helping people make sense of the events they observe, have become ever more frequent. We ourselves have labored hard in that tradition, and wrote a book in 1980 that was in large part an account of the layperson's tools of construal and of their shortcomings for the various tasks of human inference.

In this book we will once again devote attention to how construal influences behavior and how construal works. But our primary concern here is not documenting that subjective construal occurs or that it matters in determining how people will respond to their environment. What we seek to establish is that laypeople consistently fail to make sufficient allowance for the role that construal plays in determining behavior, a failure with profound personal and social consequences. In particular, we will argue that people make three distinct but related errors about construal.

The first error is a failure to recognize the degree to which one's own understanding of stimuli is the result of an active, constructive process, rather than a passive reception and registering of some external reality. There is an old joke about the three baseball umpires who were discussing their work. The first says, "I call 'em as I see 'em." The second says, "I call 'em as they are." The third says, "They ain't no thin' till I call 'em." Our contention is that, like the second umpire, most people are philosophical realists, with little appreciation of the extent to which their own cognitive processes have contributed to their judgments. Insight into the interpretive nature of judgment such as that shown by the first umpire is rare, let alone the extreme subjectivism of the third umpire.

The second error is the failure to appreciate the inherent variability of situational construal. The way any two people interpret a given situation, or even the way a particular person interprets identical stimuli on two different occasions, is only imperfectly predictable and is always uncertain to some degree. Because people fail to recognize the extent to which others may construe situations differently from the way they themselves construe them, they tend to be overly confident in predicting other people's behavior. They may even be too confident in predicting their own future behavior when the context for that behavior is novel or ambiguous. We argue that people make behavioral predictions with a degree of certainty that would be warranted if, but only if, their construals were both perfectly accurate and perfectly shared by the actor in question at the moment that the actor behaved.

The third error concerns causal attributions for behavior. People fail to recognize the extent to which observed actions and outcomes, especially surprising or atypical ones, may prove to be diagnostic not of the actor's unique personal dispositions but rather of the objective situational factors facing the actor and of the actor's subjective construals of those factors. In effect, people are too quick to "recompute" the person (that is, to infer that he or she is somehow different from other ordinary people) and too slow to recompute or reconstrue the situation (that is, to infer that one's original construal of the situation was incomplete, or erroneous, or at least significantly different from that of the actor). Finding that Jane the librarian has cast away job and home for an opportunity with a travel agency in a distant city, we are too likely to assume that Jane is a far more adventuresome soul than we had assumed and too little inclined to assume that the new employment opportunity is much more interesting (or that additional but hidden constraints on Jane were more weighty) than we had recognized. Much of our own recent research has been concerned with documenting these three errors and pursuing their implications. This research is presented in Chapter 3 on construal and in Chapter 5 on lay personality theory.

The Concept of Tension Systems

Social psychology's third major contribution, and the remaining leg of the conceptual tripod upon which our field rests, is the principle that individual psyches, as well as collectivities ranging from the informal social group to the nation, must be understood as systems in a state of tension. The analysis of any given stimulus situation must include the recognition first that "behavior has to be derived from a totality of coexisting facts," and second that "these coexisting facts have the character of a dynamic field insofar as the state of any part of this field depends on every other part of the field" (Lewin, 1951, p. 25). No simple mechanistic laws relating particular stimuli to particular responses are possible, given that both are always embedded in dynamic contexts that alter and constrain their effects.

> . . . such phenomena as the speed of production in a factory are the result of a multitude of forces. Some forces support each other, some oppose each other. Some are driving forces, others restraining forces. Like the velocity of a river,

the actual conduct of a group depends upon the level (for instance, the speed of production) at which these conflicting forces reach a state of equilibrium. To speak of a certain culture pattern ... implies that the constellation of these forces remains the same for a period or at least that they find their state of equilibrium at a constant level during that period. (Lewin, 1951, p. 173)

There are three major contributions of the tension system notion. The first is that an analysis of restraining factors can be as important to understanding and anticipating the effects of a newly introduced stimulus as an analysis of the stimulus itself. The effect of introducing a new monetary incentive for production in a factory depends on the balance of forces maintaining production at the current level. If there is a group norm against overproduction or "rate-busting," the incentive may have little effect or even a reverse effect. The dynamic contest between opposing forces was nicely captured by Wolfgang Koehler's concept of the "quasi-stationary equilibrium." This concept implied that certain processes or levels, like the velocity of Lewin's river or the level of production in a factory, fluctuate within the confines imposed by certain constraining and impelling forces. The level can be easy to move up or down within certain relatively narrow limits, harder to move beyond those limits, and virtually impossible beyond still further limits. Furthermore, change in the system can be accomplished in two very different ways with rather different consequences. One can add or increase impelling forces (and thereby increase the tension in the system as the relevant restraining forces increasingly make their opposing influence felt) or one can eliminate or weaken the restraining forces that impede the desired change (and in so doing decrease the tension in the system). For example, it may be more effective to change group norms about rate-busting than to promise ever-higher incentives.

The second important point is the converse of the first. Systems sometimes stand balanced precariously on the cusp of change. We may return to the river analogy by noting some interesting facts about the Mississippi. Basically, the river meanders through its last several hundred miles before spilling into the Gulf of Mexico in a general course that could not be altered by any event of less than cataclysmic proportions. But its local course is subject to drastic alteration by remarkably trivial events. A person with a shovel can, at the right place, start a small cut that gets bigger and bigger until the whole river flows through the new channel and an entire curve of the river is obliterated. (This fact was an ever-present consideration to nineteenth-century owners of river-front property, who often hired men to shoot on sight any suspicious persons caught upriver in the possession of digging implements.)

The analogy between the flow of a river and both individual and social psychological processes should be clear. Quasi-stationary equilibria can be hard to change because of the balance of opposing forces that maintain, and in a sense overdetermine, the status quo. On the other hand, very dramatic and widespread changes in the system can sometimes result from the introduction or alteration of seemingly small and inconsequential forces. Thus, the third point arising from the notion of a tension system results from the linking together of the first two points. Like the principle of construal, the tension system principle helps us understand why apparently big situational manipulations sometimes have small effects and why apparently small situational manipulations sometimes have big effects. Big manipulations may fly in the face of, or even increase the strength and resistance of, even bigger restraining factors. Conversely, small manipulations may take advantage of the precarious balance of the system, or facilitate an important channel factor, moving the system by redirection rather than by brute force.

We may illustrate these notions by reference to the astonishing events in the East Bloc countries that are unfolding as we write this book. For the 40-year period from the end of World War II to roughly 1985, the level of most internal processes within these countries, as well as the level of most of their external relations, was held within limits that now seem to us to be rather narrow. For a time there would be extreme repression of dissent, followed by slight letups in repression; for a time there would be some toleration of entrepreneurial activities, and for a time almost none. Thaws and freezes in the Cold War relations of these nations with the West took place within a range that we now recognize as fractions of a degree centigrade. Such slight movements up and down of social processes are well understood as resulting from a state of quasi-stationary equilibrium. Impelling forces were being met by restraining forces of equal strength. Changes of level of various processes were correspondingly held to small magnitudes.

As events of recent years have shown, however, these systems, though in equilibrium, were at very high levels of tension indeed. Both impelling and restraining forces were at massive strength. Correspondingly, when channels were opened up, change occurred at breathtaking speed, and it is already clear that the world landscape will shortly be unrecognizable to those born in the first eight decades of this century.

These events also make a humbling point about predictability in a world composed of tension systems. If anyone in the West had predicted, say in 1984, that the political and economic systems of the Soviet Union might soon be transformed by a liberalizing revolution from the top, followed very shortly by the end of Party rule in virtually all the East Bloc nations, that person would have risked being labeled a fool or a dreamer. It was obvious to all sensible analysts that the East Bloc countries could be expected to move only glacially toward change. Indeed, the past four decades should have been adequate evidence for that point for anyone so naive as to doubt it.

The social psychologist who applied the tension system notions to the most impressive effect was Leon Festinger. Festinger (1954; Festinger, Schachter, & Back, 1950) recognized that individual human attitudes are best understood as existing in a state of tension in relation to the attitudes of members of the face-to-face groups to which each person belongs. People do not like the state of being in disagreement with their fellows, and when they discover that this is the case, three balance-restorative processes are instituted – attempts to change others' opinions so as to move them into line with one's own, receptivity to others' similar attempts to change one's attitude, and a tendency to reject others from the group to the extent that they refuse to move toward the central tendency of opinion in the group. Festinger derived many interesting social phenomena from the operation of these processes, which we will begin to discuss in the next chapter.

Festinger also regarded attitudes within the head of the individual as existing in a state of tension. Some attitudes support each other; some contradict each other. Contradictory attitudes exist in a state of tension, called "dissonance," which must be resolved. One attitude or the other must be changed until the system is restored to a state of balance (see Festinger, 1957; Aronson, 1969).

Festinger's most dramatic use of the tension system notion was for cases in which the two cognitive elements in conflict are an attitude and a behavior. This occurs when someone does something that follows neither from the attitudes the person holds nor from some extrinsic force such as the expectation of reward. Festinger showed that in such a situation people can be expected to move their beliefs into line with their behavior. Thus if someone is maneuvered into delivering a speech that happens not to reflect the person's prior beliefs, and if the person is paid little or nothing for doing so, the person's expressed attitudes move in the direction of the position taken in the speech. This movement is blocked if the person is paid a substantial amount for delivering the speech. In this case, giving the speech is highly consistent with the payment and the person recognizes the lack of relation between prior beliefs and what was said.

The dissonance theorists' analysis of dissonance and attitude change spearheaded what had perhaps been social psychology's most important contribution to the study of motivation, that is, exploring the significance of perceived personal responsibility and choice (see Aronson, 1969; Calder, Ross, & Insko, 1973; de Charms, 1968; Linder, Cooper, & Jones, 1967). Social processes unfold quite differently when people believe they have freely chosen their behavior, as a direct expression of their goals and attitudes, than when they believe the behavior was coerced or was under the control of extrinsic reinforcing agents. People who are paid to deliver a speech think of their behavior as unrelated to their beliefs and their beliefs remain unchanged; people not paid to give the speech presume that it was freely chosen and consequently feel compelled to realign their beliefs with their behavior. Factory workers ordered to carry out certain tasks in a certain order often function as inefficient automatons and sullen time-servers; the same workers asked to help design their jobs function as free agents with a stake in the success of the joint enterprise.

We will not give the tension system notion a chapter of its own, but we will refer repeatedly to it as we discuss the power of situations in Chapter 2, as we try to explain the bases of predictability of the social world in Chapter 6, as we explore culture and personality and try to understand the conditions of cultural change in Chapter 7, and as we analyze the fate of successful and unsuccessful social interventions in Chapter 8.

PREDICTABILITY AND INDETERMINACY

All three of the fundamental principles of social psychology speak in the most direct way to the question of prediction, both the ultimate predictability attainable by scientists and the typical level of predictability attained by laypeople in everyday life. We will be centrally concerned in this book with the ways in which the scientist and the layperson go about predicting behavior, what the limits of prediction may be, and how prediction can be improved. Let us anticipate our discussions of the two types of prediction we are concerned with.

Prediction by Social Scientists

We think that social scientists have been pursuing unrealistic goals of prediction. We may never be able to predict how particular people will respond to novel situations (either on the basis of personality assessments or on the basis of objective accounts of the situation). We also may never be able to predict how people in general or particular groups will respond to novelty. Situations are highly complex, and so are people's interpretations of them. One practical implication of this difficulty (discussed in more detail in Chapter 8) is that social remedies normally should first be tried out on a small scale. This applies even when the remedy in question has proved successful in some seemingly similar context. The surrounding matrix of situational forces and constraints may be subtly different, and the way people construe them may also be different, and the difference may be unanticipated by those planning and conducting the intervention.

We are neither apologetic about these limits to prediction nor distressed by their practical implications. They do not mean that we cannot effectively intervene to better the lives of individuals, groups, or society as a whole. The constraints merely indicate that there are limits to what is possible, and it may take some tinkering, using the best hypotheses of our science and the results of some careful pilot testing, before we can achieve those possibilities.

The other reason we are unapologetic is that the situation in the social sciences is not fundamentally different from the situation in the physical sciences. It has long been recognized that the laws of physics do not allow us to predict with much certainty where any particular leaf from a tree will fall. More recently, physical scientists have begun to recognize the limits of predictability in a variety of systems, such as ecological systems and weather systems. Although some effects are robust and highly predictable, others are extremely unstable. The term "butterfly effect" has been coined to describe small, unanticipatable perturbations that can have dramatic effects (Gleick, 1987). The whimsical name refers to a meteorologist's comment that a butterfly beating its wings in Beijing can, under the right circumstances, have a detectable effect on the weather in the midwestern United States a few days later. As a consequence of the extreme sensitivity of weather to local perturbations, long-range weather forecasting not only is not possible now but also, according to some scientists, will never be possible. A similar point can be made for ecologies. Sometimes the introduction of larva-eating beetles has just the desired effect of consuming all the targeted noxious insects. Sometimes the creatures introduced are immediately eaten by a predator and vanish. Sometimes the creatures become themselves a greater scourge than the one they were intended to replace.

Again, there is a real question as to whether such effects can ever be predicted with precision in highly complex, interactive, nonlinear systems. But the discovery and description of the sources of such inherent unpredictability, whether in the physical sciences or the behavioral sciences, is hardly a cause for apology. It is an important intellectual contribution with profound theoretical and practical implications.

Prediction by Laypeople

We are even more interested in the implications of social psychology's basic tenets for the layperson's predictions than for those of social scientists. We wish to demonstrate that, for reasons that make sense in terms of the three major principles we have outlined, lay predictions are often both wrong and too confidently made. To begin with, people are apt to have exaggerated notions about the strength of individual differences and the role such differences play in producing behavior. Some of the reasons for this are essentially perceptual. The continuity in Ralph's physical appearance and personal style (for example, his imposing stature, deep voice, steady gaze, and habit of clenching his fist to emphasize his words) may blind us to the lack of any real consistency in the degree of dependency or aggressiveness he shows across different situations. Other factors are more cognitive. Inconsistent data typically are assimilated in a way that produces illusions of past behavioral consistency. Our first impression that Ellen is friendly leads us to interpret her sarcastic response to Bill's whispered remark as jocular, or a justifiable reaction to what Bill must have said, or perhaps the result of pressures she has been under at work; but not as evidence that our earlier impression was wrong, and that Ellen is simply variable in her friendliness.

Beyond discussing such sources of illusory consistency, we will emphasize the extent to which uncertainty in the way particular individuals construe particular situations, and the difficulty in predicting such construals, necessarily limit the amount of observable cross-situational consistency that ever *could* be demonstrated. Ellen's friendliness, or lack of it, in particular social situations will depend on the way she labels those situations and resolves any ambiguity about the meaning of any behavior directed toward her.

At the same time, we will contend that people do, in fact, manifest considerable predictability of a sort that observers can perceive and make use of in their everyday social dealings. The apparent conflict between the lessons of formal research and the lessons of everyday experience, we believe, results from the investigator's reliance upon research strategies designed to disentangle the separate contributions of person and situation by exposing some sample of individuals to a fixed, and identical, set of situations. This strategy, despite several undeniable advantages for the theoretician, can lead us to ignore some important realities about everyday life. Foremost is the fact that in everyday experience the characteristics of actors and those of the situations they face are typically confounded – in ways that contribute to precisely the consistency that we perceive and count on in our social dealings. People often choose the situations to which they are exposed; and people often are chosen for situations on the basis of their manifest or presumed abilities and dispositions. Thus, clerics and criminals rarely face an identical or equivalent set of situational challenges. Rather, they place themselves, and are placed by others, in situations that differ precisely in ways that induce clergy to look, act, feel, and think rather consistently like clergy and that induce criminals to look, act, feel, and think like criminals.

We also will explore the implications of the fact that people sometimes feel *obliged,* even committed, to act consistently. This may be because of their social roles, because of the real-world incentives and sanctions that await those who honor or violate such roles, because of promises they make to others or even because of demands they place upon themselves. The net result of these influences is that we correctly anticipate a predictable social world, one with consistent, or at least coherent, actors. This result, moreover, is especially likely to be true in the domains that we care about most and in which we have the most experience.

Finally, it should be noted that both consistencies and seeming inconsistencies in behavior can sometimes be reflections of individual differences in the construal processes that people bring to their understanding of their social environments. Here we follow a strain in personality theory that has its origins in Freud, was developed by George Kelly (1955), and finds its modern fruition in work by Mischel (1973), Markus (1977; Markus, Smith, & Moreland, 1985), and Cantor & Kihlstrom (1987). Each of these theorists has contended that the key to a more powerful conception of individual differences is to be found in the enduring motivational concerns and cognitive schemes that guide attention, interpretation, and the formulation of goals and plans. An important consequence of this contention is that behavioral consistencies, where they are found, may not be well captured by traditional personality traits. That is, individuals may behave in consistent ways that distinguish them from their peers not because of their enduring predispositions to be friendly, dependent, aggressive, or the like, but rather because they are pursuing consistent goals using consistent strategies, in light of consistent ways of interpreting their social world (cf. Cantor & Kihlstrom, 1987).

In short, our overall thesis, developed in detail in Chapter 6, is that some of the layperson's most fundamental assumptions about personal consistency and predictability are validated by everyday experience, even though the basis for such consistency may be misunderstood by the perceiver. Thus, despite the demonstrable errors and biases of lay prediction, the world as it is experienced daily is, in fact, a reasonably predictable place. Lay psychology, like lay physics, generally gets the job done reasonably well using dramatically mistaken principles; and when it fails, it will generally be for reasons that rather deep principles of our discipline allow us to understand and sometimes even anticipate.

THE PROBLEM OF EFFECT SIZE

Implicit in our discussion to this point is that some effects are clearly big and some are clearly small, that some levels of predictability are demonstrably high and some are demonstrably low.

Consider our claim that demonstrating the power of the social situation has been one of social psychology's most important contributions, and that failing to demonstrate the power of classic personality traits or dispositional differences between individuals has been one of personality psychology's greatest frustrations. Implicit in such a claim is the suggestion that the relevant situation effects are in some obvious sense "big," and that the relevant person effects are in some obvious sense "small." It will be useful to offer some initial thoughts on the question of how to measure, or even to think more clearly about, effect size. This question turns out to be surprisingly controversial and difficult to answer; but we will do our best to begin shedding some light on it, because it is so fundamental to the concerns of this book.

Let us begin by noting that effects are big, or small, relative to something. For our purposes it will be sufficient to refer to three definitions of relative effect size, which we will call the statistical, the pragmatic, and the expectational.

Statistical Criteria of Size

In considering statistical criteria, we must begin by noting that effect size has very little to do with statistical significance. An effect of almost any size can be made to be statistically significant (that is, unlikely to have occurred solely by chance) merely by collecting a large enough number of observations. One of the authors had this point brought home with particular force in graduate school, when he opened the computer printout of analyses of a national survey, ran his finger down the column to the relationship he was particularly interested in, noted that the correlation was statistically significant at the conventionally accepted .05 level, and jumped for joy. His companion was required to note that the correlation the author was getting so excited about was .04 – a degree of relationship very close to zero. This trivial correlation was significant because the survey had well over a thousand respondents. Thus the author was right about this prediction – the relationship he proposed was there – but it was so weak that it could have no theoretical or practical significance.

A much more sensible convention for defining effect size was suggested by Cohen (1965, 1977), who suggested that the magnitude of experimental effects should be judged relative to the variability of the measure in question. Thus, by Cohen's criterion, a difference between two means that corresponded to a quarter of a standard deviation in the distribution of the relevant measure would be deemed small, a difference corresponding to half a standard deviation would be deemed moderate, and a difference corresponding to a whole standard deviation would be deemed large. This statistical definition, and other related ones, assess effect size relative to all nonspecified, "random" determinants of variability or, in other words, relative to "noise." The definition effectively finesses, in fact ignores, all considerations of the nature of the variable under consideration and the units of measurement involved. Therein lies both its major virtue and, as our discussion of the other two criteria will make clear, also its chief drawbacks.

Pragmatic Criteria of Size

The most telling objection to a simple statistical definition hinging on standard deviations is that in many cases we don't care in the slightest about some effects that would qualify as "big" by this definition or, conversely, that we care a great deal about other effects that would be termed "small" by this definition. Imagine, for example, that you are told that some exotic new drug can increase the survival time of people stricken with Smedley's Fever by 1.5 standard deviations. Interested at first, you then find out that Smedley's Fever is a virulent tropical disease to which untreated sufferers succumb after 40 hours on average, with a standard deviation of four hours. This means that the drug could prolong life for, on average, an additional six hours. If you next find out that the drug costs $10,000 per dose, your already diminished interest approaches the vanishing point. (On the other hand, the medical researcher who seeks to unravel the mysteries of this illness or related ones might jump at this clinically trivial improvement because it could hold clues that might lead to insights and advances that really would be big.)

Conversely, imagine the plight of a political candidate involved in a close contest. The candidate may be quite willing to spend a monumental sum on an advertisement or a campaign strategy that would influence the proportion of the total votes he or she would receive by less than one-tenth of a standard deviation [e.g., .05 of the votes cast, by the conventional formula whereby the standard deviation of a proportion (p) is equal to the square root of $p(1 - p)$ or, in other words, the square root of .5 x .5]. Most political pundits would agree that the effect of any advertisement or strategy that could produce a "five-point" swing in the vote should be termed "big." (It would have been big enough, notably, to change the results of roughly half of the American presidential elections in the twentieth century.) Similarly, as we will discuss in more detail in Chapter 4, a personality test that was inexpensive to administer and that could predict "only" 10 percent of the variance in some important outcome, could prove to be very valuable and "cost-effective" for many familiar assessment or prediction tasks, for example, for selecting people who are likely to be extreme on some dimension (see Abelson, 1985).

These examples demonstrate that utilitarian considerations almost inevitably influence our judgment about whether an effect is big or not. Effects are big or small relative to the obstacles that stand in the way of getting a particular job done, and relative to the importance of the job – that is, big or small in terms of their sufficiency for accomplishing specific objectives, and with reference to how much we care about those objectives.

Expectation Criteria of Size

Finally, and perhaps most important for our purposes, effects may be regarded as big or small relative to what we expected them to be. We may call this the expectation criterion because it involves changes in one's previous beliefs (or "Bayesian prior") with respect to some outcome or event. By this criterion, effects are big if the relevant data force big revisions in our expectations and in the theories that govern those expectations and effects are small if they force little or no change. It is worth noting in this context that very small effects (small, that is, by conventional statistical standards) can sometimes force us to rethink very basic and well-established theories – provided that we had a very well-grounded basis for expecting no difference at all, and provided that we had a very precise measurement technique for establishing whether there really was or was not any difference found.

Outcomes thus can be assessed in terms of their capacity to alter our subjective probabilities. When Senator Snort, who was expected to run fifth in the New Hampshire primary, manages to run second instead, we feel that he won a "big" fraction of the vote. When Governor Grump, expected to win the primary, comes in second instead, we may feel he won a "small" fraction of the vote. In both cases, we label the campaigns they conducted as "successes" or "failures" as a function of their effectiveness relative to our prior predictions and beliefs.

The judgments passed on social interventions and on the scientific theories on which they are based depend on how well they do relative to our expectations. Even a well-established theory may become ripe for re-examination when predictive chinks in its armor are discovered, and theories that are very implausible on their face gain substantial credibility when their progenitors make a prediction or two that are contrary to the received opinions of scientists but turn out to be correct. This final definition has an interesting and important consequence. Any experience, training, or even rhetoric that influences our expectations thereby influences both our assessments of the size of any given effect and our satisfaction or disappointment with the interventions that produced that effect. The positive effects of social interventions such as Operation Headstart (the preschool educational intervention program for disadvantaged children) and racial integration of schools are real enough, though not always statistically large. But in terms of the political and social science rhetoric of the era in which these interventions were introduced, and the resulting great expectations, the effects were widely dismissed as trivial and as grounds for de-emphasizing rather than maintaining and strengthening such programs in the future.

It should be noted that in this book when we speak of big situational effects, we normally will mean that the effects are big by at least two of these standards – statistical and expectational – and sometimes by the pragmatic criterion as well. When we speak of small dispositional effects, we normally mean that the effects are small by the same two standards – statistical and expectational – and usually by the pragmatic criterion also. When we speak of the effects of interventions and applications, we normally measure size by the pragmatic criterion alone.

When we compare effects, we will present results wherever possible in proportional form. Thus, in reporting the effects of experiments or interventions, we will report the proportion in the experimental condition and in the control condition who behaved in a particular fashion or who had a particular outcome. In reporting the differences associated with personality traits, we will compare the proportion above and below the median or at two standard deviations above the median versus two standard deviations below the median, who behave in a particular fashion. The proportional measure of effect size is, of course, associated with each of the three criteria of effect size, but only in a rough and highly variable way. Its great virtue is that it is a common metric readily understandable by everyone. Partly for this reason, it is the most efficient metric to use for estimating effect size by the expectation criterion. As we will see in Chapter 5, it is easy for people to convert their expectations about effect size to estimates of proportions, and then to compare these with actual proportions.

OVERVIEW AND PLAN OF THE BOOK

In summary, this is a book about the predictability and coherence of behavior as seen from the perspective of modern experimental and cognitive social psychology. We begin with the history of research suggesting that situational factors often prove to be more powerful determinants of behavior than the vast majority of US scientists and laypeople alike would have guessed. Implicit in this situationist lesson is the suggestion that people from different backgrounds, people with different beliefs, even people with apparently different personalities, must understand and react to some situations rather uniformly. In other words, there are at least some important respects in which human beings prove to be more alike than we generally reckon them to be.

At the same time, research and everyday observation constantly remind us that people often do differ dramatically both in their responses to particular situations and events and in the patterns of their everyday behavior. We will argue that the shared convictions that laypeople have about stable, consistent, coherent, and predictable individual differences are not always mere cognitive illusions. Rather, they are based, at least to a substantial degree, on the data of everyday experience. Far from disputing the existence or significance of individual differences, we will acknowledge them and then explore their bases and implications. More specifically, we will provide a "situationist" and "subjectivist" account of individual differences – one that gives heavy weight to the complex dynamics of social systems and to the role of construal processes. Our goal will thus be an account of individual differences that seeks to explain what kinds of differences are likely to exist and be important, when they are likely to be obscured, and when misinterpretations of such differences are likely to arise.

Beginning in Chapter 2 we will illustrate what we mean by the power of situational factors by reviewing some of the classic studies of social psychology. In that chapter we will focus first on group influences and then on the notion of channel factors as conduits and barriers that facilitate or inhibit behavior change. In Chapter 3 we will discuss the significance of construal processes. There we will reiterate the truism that construals vary among individuals and are significant determinants of social behavior. More importantly, we will stress the fact that people may characteristically fail to recognize and make allowance for the vagaries of construal, both in predicting their own behavior and in predicting and interpreting the behavior of others. The consequence of this failure is that people too frequently make wrong predictions about behavior and then compound their errors by explaining the discrepancy from expectations in terms of stable dispositions of the actor.

The next four chapters of the book deal explicitly with predictability of individual behavior. We begin in Chapter 4 by reviewing some major studies documenting the modest size of the cross-situational consistencies in the behavior of people exposed to a fixed set of situations – in particular, the consistencies in behavior seemingly relevant to classic personality traits like extroversion or honesty. We will then show, in Chapter 5, that these data are indeed surprising to people, that is, that lay beliefs in consistency and predictability are mistaken, both qualitatively and quantitatively, in ways that no refinements of measurement or definition can remedy. In Chapter 6 we will discuss what we believe to be the sources of real behavioral consistency and predictability, some of which involve individual differences in roles and other situational demands, and some of which do not involve stable individual differences at all. In Chapter 7 we will turn our attention to old but lately neglected questions of cultural effects on behavior, again highlighting the role of situations, construal, and tension systems. We will argue that different cultures, including identifiable local subcultures within modern Western societies, effectively place actors in different situations, expose them to different social dynamics, and lead them to habitual differences in construal that have real consequences for social actions.

In our eighth and final chapter we will speculate about the implications of the analyses of the preceding seven chapters for questions of intervention and social change. We will discuss some applied research that we think illustrates the value of the situationist, subjectivist, and tension system traditions discussed throughout this book. Our analysis seeks to explain why some kinds of interventions that one might expect to be powerful generally yield disappointing results, and why other, seemingly less powerful (and less expensive) ones may yield better results. This analysis helps illustrate the lessons that applied practitioners can learn from the best traditions of theoretically oriented social psychology, and the lessons that theoreticians can learn from the history of successful and unsuccessful applications. We believe it also offers important lessons for the layperson who attempts to apply social psychology in the conduct of everyday life, and in contemplating society's attempts to grapple with its most pressing social problems and challenges.

CHAPTER 2
THE POWER OF THE SITUATION

In Europe a few years ago, hundreds of angry British soccer fans attacked rival Italian fans and caused a wall to collapse, killing 39 people and injuring 400. Though we recoil from such behavior and denounce it, we do not understand it. We tend to assimilate such behavior to the case of individual aggression, failing to recognize that the situation that results in mob violence has properties that cannot be predicted from ordinary life situations or from knowledge of the life histories of the participants.

Indeed, it was these observations, as Allport (1954) noted in his classic review of social psychology's origins, that prompted social philosophers such as Tarde (1903) and LeBon (1896) to recognize the need for a level of analysis that goes beyond individual needs and traits. The mob situation, they noted, seems at once to energize the individual participants and to rob them of the rationality and sense of propriety that otherwise guide their behavior. Collectively, the actors willingly, even eagerly, behave in ways that would cause shame and embarrassment were they alone. We see contemporary demonstrations of "deindividuated" behavior in urban riots and racial harassment and, less ominously, in students' end-of-term revelries on the beaches of Florida and California; we also see them in New Orleans' Mardi Gras, Rio's Carnival, and similar celebration periods in which the devout traditionally can abandon customary constraints without fear of censure.

What accounts for such happenings? Is it simple excitement and arousal? Or is it the sense of anonymity, or the diffusion of responsibility, or the diminished likelihood of punishment? Or is it, as nineteenth-century social philosophers thought, that the mob somehow releases some mysterious source of energy? Teasing apart such determinants has continued to be a fascinating research topic (cf. Festinger, Pepitone, & Newcomb, 1952; Singer, Brush, & Lublin, 1965; Zajonc, 1965; Zimbardo, 1970). Whatever their origin, lynch mobs, marauding juvenile bands, and soccer fans run amok all powerfully illustrate the situational control of behavior. And when such events occur, they inevitably tempt us to commit the fundamental attribution error of explaining exclusively in dispositional terms what ought to be understood largely in situational terms. For few of us can contemplate such instances of collective abandon without feeling that neither we ourselves, nor our friends and neighbors, nor, for that matter, any other decent members of our society would have succumbed to the group influences. We believe, accordingly, that those who did succumb revealed thereby something irretrievably unbalanced and malevolent about their personal dispositions.

This chapter's review of classic studies of social influence and situational control will emphasize two themes: first, that social pressures and other situational factors exert effects on behavior that are more potent than we generally recognize, and second, that to understand the impact of a given social situation, we often need to attend to its subtle details.

SOCIAL INFLUENCE AND GROUP PROCESSES

Uniformity Pressures in the Laboratory: Sherif's "Autokinetic" Studies and the Asch Paradigm

We begin our discussion with a set of experiments that provides the best-known and probably the most compelling laboratory demonstrations of group influence and conformity – the famous experiments of Solomon Asch. It is ironic that these particular experiments have come to be cited as perhaps the ultimate demonstration of the individual's mindless surrender to the dictates of the group. For, at least initially, Asch sought to demonstrate precisely the opposite. In particular, Asch wanted to clear up what he believed to be a misconception fostered by an imaginative and seminal set of experiments conducted some years earlier by an unorthodox young psychologist named Muzafer Sherif, a recent immigrant to the United States from Turkey.

Sherif's "Autokinetic Effect" Paradigm. Sherif's experiments (Sherif, 1937) had been designed to illustrate the development and perpetuation of group norms. His subjects, believing themselves to be participants in a rather esoteric psychophysics experiment, found themselves seated in a completely darkened room with a pinpoint of light located at some distance in front of them. (They could not be certain of the exact distance; indeed, they were not even aware of the dimensions of the room. The absence of any such objective "frame of reference," in fact, was an important requirement for the demonstration to follow.) After a few moments of gazing directly at the point of light, the subjects suddenly saw it *"move"* and then disappear. Shortly thereafter, a new point of light appeared, moved, and again disappeared, a sequence that continued until a great many such "trials" had been completed. In reality, however, the stationary light only seemed to move, for the apparent movement was a perceptual illusion called the "autokinetic effect."

Sherif gave his subjects a simple task. On each trial they were merely to estimate how far the light had moved. When the task was performed by single subjects, these estimates were highly variable from one individual to the next (that is, ranging from an inch or so to several feet) and, at least initially, rather unstable from one trial to the next. However, when subjects performed the task in pairs or groups of three, the result was quite different. The subjects' estimates invariably began to converge, and a group norm quickly developed. Moreover, while different groups converged on quite different norms, the members of any particular duo or trio seemed reluctant to offer estimates that diverged substantially from the standard of their particular group. Lacking any objective basis for evaluating the appropriateness of individual judgments, the group members had substituted a social basis.

In one study Sherif introduced a confederate – something that no participant could have suspected in those innocent times when deception experiments were virtually unknown. This confederate, participating along with one naive subject, gave estimates that were either consistently much higher or consistently much lower than those typically made by subjects left to make judgments on their own. The subject quickly adopted the high or low standard of the confederate, a result showing that social norms did not have to evolve from the converging views of well-meaning but uncertain truth seekers; instead, they could be imposed by an individual who had no coercive power and no special claim to expertise or legitimacy, only a willingness to be consistent and unwavering in the face of others' uncertainty.

Additional results reported by Sherif and subsequent investigators further drove home this message. Once formed, regardless of whether imposed by confederates or arrived at by group convergence, autokinetic norms readily became internalized. Subjects would adhere to such norms even when their peers were no longer present to witness their judgments (and presumably, to approve or disapprove of them), and they would remain true to them even a year later (Rohrer, Baron, Hoffman, & Swinder, 1954)! Subjects would even remain true to *"old"* norms when they found themselves participating in new groups made up of peers who offered very different judgments. In fact, as Jacobs and Campbell (1961) showed many years later, autokinetic norms could be readily transmitted from one "generation" of subjects to the next. After each set of trials in this study, a fresh, naive subject was introduced and another retired, so that after a short while all the participants were new to the situation but nevertheless adhering closely to a group norm that had been handed down to them over several generations – long after the original imposer of the norm had passed from the scene.

Sherif's implicit message, however, was not simply that in the face of uncertainty or ambiguity people give weight to the judgments of their peers. Rather, it was that our most basic perceptions and judgments about the world are socially conditioned and dictated. And it was precisely this radical suggestion that Solomon Asch, long a student both of perception and of social influence processes (Asch, 1940), initially sought to challenge by replacing the "autokinetic" paradigm with an experimental procedure that now bears his name (Asch, 1951, 1952, 1955, 1956).

The Asch Paradigm. Upon their arrival at the laboratory, Asch's subjects, like Sherif's, were told that they were about to participate in an experiment on visual perception. Participating in groups of seven to nine persons, they were to undergo a number of trials requiring them to indicate which of three "comparison" lines displayed at the front of the room matched a so-called standard line. Each person answered in turn. As every undergraduate who has taken introductory psychology now knows, however, only one of the participants – the one designated to respond last on each judgment trial – was a naive subject. All the others were confederates of the experimenter whose judgments followed a prearranged script.

At the outset, participants were told that experimental considerations required that they not communicate with each other and that they make their judgments independently. But neither this instruction nor the other procedural details initially seemed very important because the judgments the subjects were required to make proved to be extremely easy – so easy, in fact, that they found the first couple of trials boring and a little pointless, as all nine participants, in order, repeated the "obvious" correct answer. Then, on the fourth trial, the subjects saw something very peculiar happen. Although this trial was no more difficult than the preceding ones, the first judge, with no hesitation or expression of indecision, offered a patently wrong answer. Instead of correctly "matching" the 1.5-inch standard line with a comparison line of the same length, this first judge opted for a comparison line only 0.5 inches long. (The remaining choice was 2 inches.) Inevitably, the subject's reaction was one of wide-eyed disbelief, a quick double check to make certain that the judge's response was as off-base as it seemed, and often a nervous giggle or some other expression of vicarious discomfort at his peer's folly. These feelings of disbelief and discomfort, however, were soon to be greatly heightened and to take on a different quality as the other group members all followed suit and repeated the same wrong answer. At last it was the lone subject's turn to answer and, in so doing, to decide whether to conform to the unanimous majority or to remain independent.

Before the experiment was over, there were to be (depending on the particular study) from 5 to 12 such "critical" conformity trials embedded within a total of 10 to 18 trials. Each critical trial confronted subjects with the same dilemma – either to conform, and thereby deny the evidence of their senses, or else to remain independent in the face of a unanimous, seemingly confident majority. Asch, it is worth noting, initially expected that the vast majority of his subjects would show the courage of their convictions (or at least the confidence of their perceptions) by remaining independent in the face of the unanimous majority. This expectation proved to be incorrect, however. Notwithstanding the simple and concrete nature of the perceptual judgment task, subjects typically manifested obvious conflict and discomfort, and not infrequently, they conformed. In fact, anywhere from 50 percent to 80 percent of the subjects (the actual proportion varied from study to study) yielded to the erroneous majority at least once, and overall, conformity occurred on over a third of all critical trials.

In follow-up studies, Asch quickly discovered two important facts. First, the size of the unanimous majority in his paradigm did not have to be particularly large. Indeed, Asch found that conformity rates did not decrease significantly when the number of confederates was reduced from eight to a number as small as three or four. (It is worth noting, in light of Sherif's earlier results, that a group consisting of a subject and two confederates prompted relatively little conformity; and when only a single confederate was employed, there was virtually no evidence of social influence at all.) On the other hand, the erroneous majority did have to be unanimous. When the target subject was provided with a single ally who remained independent, both the percentage of conforming subjects and the frequency with which they conformed dropped precipitously – even when the naive subject and the ally were confronted with seven or eight judges who all expressed a different opinion.

Although initially surprised, Asch was never tempted to conclude that basic perceptions of physical reality can be socially dictated. To defend his position, Asch pointed out that roughly a third of his subjects had never conformed at all, and that another third had defied the unanimous majority more often than they had yielded. More importantly, he insisted (using postexperimental interviews to buttress his case) that when conformity had occurred in the face of social influence, it was not because the subjects' perceptions had been altered. On the contrary, the subjects had conformed despite their private perceptions, either because they believed that their perceptions must be somehow wrong and those of the unanimous majority correct, or because they were unwilling to be a lone dissenter even when they were quite certain that the majority was wrong.

While Asch's interpretations were convincing and his follow-up studies enlightening, it was his basic empirical result – the willingness of so many individuals to deny even the unambiguous evidence of their senses rather than stand alone against the group – that captured the imagination of Asch's contemporaries and that continues to challenge us today. Social psychologists of the 1950s were quick to relate Asch's findings to the real world. The era was one of seemingly unprecedented political and social orthodoxy – of McCarthyism and loyalty oaths, of homogeneous middle-class suburbs and lockstep corporate culture. Few could have anticipated the conflicts and social confrontation that would begin with the Civil Rights Movement of the early 1960s and reach a climax in protests against America's role in the Vietnam War. Social critics of the 1950s complained about the relative paucity of dissent and the high price paid by dissenters. They lamented the loss of the independence and rugged individualism that they believed had characterized an earlier America; and they railed at the corporate and suburban blandness of the "man in the grey flannel suit" coming home each night to his well-scrubbed, right-thinking, consumerist brood. To such critics, the Asch experiment seemed to be a cautionary tale about the dangers of peer pressure.

Within the field of social psychology, especially among the Lewinians who were beginning to explore principles of group dynamics and social influence, the Asch experiments were employed as an argument about the potency of "pressures to uniformity." Substantial conformity could be shown to occur even in the Asch situation – a situation in which the ease and objectivity of the task and the relative absence of group power to reward or punish should have served to minimize conformity pressures. Therefore (so the argument went) could we not expect even greater conformity to occur in everyday situations in which ambiguous matters of opinion are discussed by group members who have reason to respect each other's judgment and fear each other's censure?

Like all classic experiments that challenge our intuitions and pre-conceptions, the Asch experiments prompt questions about generalizability and significance. Were Asch's results artifacts of the social psychology laboratory, irrelevant to the way social influence works in the real world? And even if they were not laboratory artifacts, what do they really teach us about the explanation, prediction, and control of human behavior?

It has long since been established that Asch's basic findings are not artifacts of a hothouse laboratory situation. We know, thanks to Stanley Milgram (whose own classic experiment will be explored in similar detail shortly), that the massive effects demonstrated by Asch do not depend on the use of college students, or even on the subjects' awareness that they are taking part in a psychology experiment. Milgram (1961) looked at the responses of adults who believed that they were being hired to test a new signaling system for jet airliners. In that context, the target subject was asked to judge the pitch of comparison tones relative to that of a standard tone. On a number of critical trials the target subject was faced with the prospect of conforming or remaining independent after the preceding judges (who, of course, were confederates of the experimenter) all matched the standard tone with one that seemed manifestly higher or lower in pitch. As in Asch's original experiment, the main finding was the high degree of conformity to the erroneous majority. This result, therefore, should effectively silence any skeptics who would insist that the Asch findings would not apply in real-world situations in which judges believe that their incorrect answers might have some consequences.

Questions about the broader theoretical significance of Asch's findings require a rather more complicated answer. We certainly know that massive conformity effects can be obtained with many other types of stimuli, including mathematical problems, general-knowledge items, and social and political judgments (Crutchfield, 1955). Indeed, follow-up studies to the original Asch experiments increasingly turned from the use of simple objective stimuli to matters of subjective interpretation and opinion. This was done because such judgments seemed more relevant to everyday conformity, because the studies were easier to do and more certain to yield large amounts of conformity, and because they somehow seemed less denigrating to the subjects. These studies demonstrated again and again that arbitrarily constructed groups, even ones that hold no long-term power to reward conformity or punish dissent, can exert potent conformity pressures.

On the other hand, the ease of demonstrating massive conformity should not prompt us to conclude from the Asch phenomenon that people are sheep, that they are somehow dispositionally inclined to join the majority chorus rather than allow their discordant note to stand out. Although more or less the conventional view of Asch's contemporaries, such a conclusion would reflect the fundamental attribution error we decry throughout this book. To rebut the "people are sheep" interpretation, we need only remind the reader, as Asch did, that most of his subjects, most of the time, did not conform. We also must note how drastically conformity in the Asch situation declined when the majority, even a very large majority, was not unanimous. Both of these results suggest that people often are quite willing to express a minority view. At worst, they find dissent difficult when they have no comrades who will do likewise. But we don't need laboratory findings to prove that people can and do dissent in the face of pressure to conform. We can all cite cases in which we ourselves, or others with whom we are familiar, have willingly expressed dissenting opinions – indeed, done so under circumstances where the potential cost of dissent would seem, at least at first consideration, to have been considerably greater than any that might have been anticipated by potential dissenters in the Asch situation.

The question of when, and why, people are willing to dissent was pursued by Ross, Bierbrauer, and Hoffman (1976), who analyzed the Asch situation in terms of the participants' causal attributions. Essentially, Ross and his colleagues argued, people who must choose between conformity and dissent almost always can cite reasons for their differing views. They can point to differences in goals, incentives, available information, or prior suppositions, differences that both would cause rational people to disagree and allow them to justify that disagreement. The Asch situation, by contrast, was unique in that it offered potential dissenters no way of accounting for their peers' apparently erroneous but unanimous judgment. To the subjects, the correct judgment appeared so obvious that only fools or mad people could err, and they had every reason to assume that the right answer appeared equally obvious to their peers. Accordingly, by dissenting, they ran the risk of appearing incompetent or even crazy. At best, their dissent promised to be as incomprehensible to their peers as their peers' judgments were to them. Their own dissent, in fact, would represent a challenge to the collective competence of their peers – a challenge one is particularly loath to offer when one's own ability to make sense of one's world suddenly seems to be in question.

To test this attributional analysis, Ross and his colleagues recreated a version of the Asch situation in which subjects made simple judgments about the relative lengths of two tones. They showed that subjects became much more willing to dissent on critical trials when there were different consequences for being wrong in one way than in the other. Subjects knew that on critical trials the apparently incorrect judgment, if it happened to be correct, would yield a high payoff for the individual who made it, whereas the apparently correct judgment would yield only a very low payoff. There was a substantial decrease in conformity in this situation. Ross and his colleagues argued that this occurred because the introduction of an asymmetric payoff matrix on critical trials provided a plausible explanation for the apparent disagreement. Subjects could reason that "their judgment, but not mine, was distorted by the prospect of a large payoff instead of a small one," or even that "they apparently thought it was worth playing a long shot; I don't." In other words, the introduction of the asymmetric matrix eliminated the most distinctive and potent feature of the Asch situation, which is the total absence of any suitable way for the naive subjects to explain the apparent discrepancy in perception.

Pondering the meaning of the Asch studies and of the factors that influence conformity remains a fresh and interesting activity even for psychologists long familiar with the work. But regardless of the interpretations preferred for the various findings by different psychologists, all are agreed that Asch's research represents one of the most stunning demonstrations we have of the remarkable power of situations to elicit behavior that most of us are sure we ourselves would never resort to – public conformity to the views expressed by others even when we privately hold utterly different views.

The Bennington Studies

A second classic set of social influence studies takes us outside the laboratory, and beyond the subtle details of particular experimental paradigms, to the familiar problem of political persuasion. As everyone knows, it is notoriously difficult to change someone's political views. Media campaigns do sometimes succeed, of course, but rarely if ever do they do so by altering the basic political views of the electorate. They may effectively showcase the candidate's personal vigor, capacity for leadership, or compassion; or they may take the low road and impugn the reputation of an opponent. But the fact remains that campaigns produce few genuine political conversions. Even the most artfully constructed rhetorical appeals rarely persuade conservatives to vote for candidates or ballot initiatives that they perceive to be liberal, or vice versa, much less persuade the voters to change their basic ideologies. In fact, most successful political campaigns do not even try to change the electorate's view. Instead, they try to win over the "undecided" vote, and then concentrate on identifying their supporters and making sure that they get out and cast their ballots on election day.

It is against this background of political wisdom, buttressed by the results of many empirical studies on the stability of voting habits (for example, Berelson, Lazarsfeld, & McPhee, 1954; Hyman & Sheatsley, 1947) and the more general failure of mass media campaigns to change social and political attitudes (for example, McGuire, 1986; Roberts & Maccoby, 1985) that we invite the reader to consider the results of the famous Bennington Study conducted by Theodore Newcomb in the late 1930s (Newcomb, 1943). The basic findings of the study can be summarized quite simply. Young women from predominantly upper-middleclass families entered Bennington College between 1935 and 1939, sharing the generally conservative Republican political views and voting preferences of their parents. Within a couple of years, after having been exposed to the Bennington milieu, the students' views and preferences had shifted far to the left of those of their family members and of most other Americans of their social class.

The results of a campus straw poll for the presidential election of 1936 offered particularly compelling testimony to these changes. In that year, President Roosevelt's reelection campaign faced challenges both from the Republicans who were critical of his liberal New Deal policies and from Socialist and Communist candidates who were enjoying con-siderable success in persuading Depression-weary Americans that even more radical changes were necessary. Among the first-year Bennington students, newly arrived on campus at the time of the election, over 60 percent supported the Republican (Landon), while fewer than 30 percent supported the incumbent Democratic President (Roosevelt), and fewer than 10 percent supported either the Socialist (Thomas) or the Communist (Browder). These voting preference percentages (including, remarkably, the nontrivial level of support enjoyed by the two radical candidates) reflected those of the students' affluent parents and others of their social class. Among sophomores, who had then been at Bennington a little over a year, the leftward shift was already quite evident. Landon and Roosevelt enjoyed roughly equal levels of support (43 percent), and the two radical candidates split the support of the remaining 14 percent. Among juniors and seniors the shift was even more dramatic. Only 15 percent supported Landon (the candidate favored by the clear majority of their parents), about 54 percent supported Roosevelt, and more than 30 percent chose one of the two radicals.

These voting percentages, along with many other measures collected by Newcomb over the four years of the study, illustrate that the social situation can produce a monumental shift in the basic social and political attitudes of a great many people – a change of the sort that is rarely produced in anyone by speeches, newspaper articles, or debates. It is notable, furthermore, that these changes occurred in the face of opposing family attitudes and values, and in the face of the sort of "objective" factors relating to economic self-interest and class interest that Marxist scholars emphasize so heavily. What is most remarkable of all, perhaps, is the degree to which the converts continued to show liberal preferences long after they had departed from Bennington. More than 20 years later, in the 1960 election, when John Kennedy received scant support from other well-to-do Protestant college graduates in the Northeast (30 percent is a generous estimate, according to Newcomb), roughly 60 percent of the Bennington 1935-1939 graduates voted for Kennedy. When asked to describe their present political views, over 65 percent said that on most issues they were "liberal" or "left of center," while only about 16 percent labeled themselves "conservatives," (the remainder described themselves as "middle of the road"). In short, political alliances continued to reflect the influence of the Bennington reference groups (Newcomb, Koenig, Flacks, & Warwick, 1967).

Newcomb's findings allowed him to offer a number of important observations about the Bennington environment and to test several specific hypotheses about social influence. We learn that the Bennington of the 1930s was an exciting, close-knit community, self-sufficient and isolated in important respects from the surrounding community. The professors were young, dynamic, politically liberal, and determined to increase the social awareness and involvement of the economically privileged young women they encountered inside and outside the classroom. Esprit de corps was strong, and there was clear evidence of group pressures to uniformity, in particular, pressures to the Bennington norms of liberalism and activism. Newcomb showed that politically active liberal students were more likely than conservatives to be chosen for friendship by others and more likely to be selected for positions of leadership and recognition. The liberals clearly formed a kind of ingroup, leading to a change in the student body that in some respects constituted a full-fledged social movement. For many, perhaps most, of the incoming students, their Bennington classmates came to be a primary reference group whose acceptance and approval was eagerly sought and whose values were internalized. For a minority, this did not happen; they remained aloof and largely unchanged in their attitudes, perhaps (as Newcomb suggests) because they remained tied to their families and were insulating themselves against possible conflict and disapproval.

Newcomb's analysis heavily emphasized the adaptive social function of the students' political conversions – that is, the relation of their newly adopted liberalism or radicalism to their desire for social approval. As Asch (1952) and others later observed, too little attention, perhaps, was given to cognitive aspects, for the Bennington students were obviously thinking, and talking, about the momentous events occurring in the world around them as America struggled with the Great Depression and the Nazis consolidated their power and prepared for war in Europe. It is not at all clear that just any political orthodoxy could have been so successfully imposed by the group and the opinion leaders who inspired it. But it is at least clear that the social situation at Bennington – group cohesion, relative isolation from competing influences, and, of course, pressures to uniformity enforced by the promise of social acceptance and the threat of rejection – was a necessary feature of the students' leftward movement. For the same world events and the same arguments about the need for greater social justice and economic reform had relatively little influence on siblings and peers who faced different social pressures within different social settings.

Separating the various strains of the Bennington story, and others like it – that is, exploring the nature of group pressures, the relevance of social isolation, and the sources and significance of group cohesiveness – became a major undertaking for psychologists of the 1950s. In field studies (notably Festinger et al., 1950; also Siegal & Siegal, 1957) and later in countless laboratory experiments (for example, Back, 1951; Schachter, 1951), new standards of sophistication and rigor were brought to bear, as psychologists demonstrated that they could successfully disentangle and investigate many of the complex social processes that occur in group settings. At the same time, however, Muzafer Sherif was hard at work on a set of field studies that could be traced to a very different intellectual tradition, and it is to these studies that we next turn our attention.

Sherif's Studies of Intergroup Competition and Conflict

Sherif's social influence studies derived from the ideas of an important nineteenth-century situationist whose impact on the social sciences was felt far less in psychology than in political science, economics, and sociology. The situationist in question was Karl Marx, who, over a century ago (Marx, 1859/1904), noted that "it is not the consciousness of men that determines their social being, but on the contrary, their social being that determines their consciousness" (p. 10). Mindful of this Marxist tenet, Sherif returned to the task of showing the social basis for individual perceptions and judgments, a task he had begun with his autokinetic effect studies a generation earlier. This time he undertook a classic series of field experiments on intergroup conflict.

The object of Sherif's three experiments (Sherif & Sherif, 1953; Sherif, White, & Harvey, 1955; Sherif et al., 1961) was a demonstration that intergroup hostility and negative perceptions are not inevitable consequences arising from the very existence of diverse social groupings. Instead, Sherif and his colleagues insisted, hostile sentiments and actions arise from intergroup competition for scarce resources and from other real or perceived conflicts of interest. Moreover, when intergroup relations become cooperative rather than competitive, and the actions of one group begin to further rather than to frustrate the goals of the other, intergroup relations may cease to be negative.

To test this situationist thesis, Sherif and company for a number of years undertook the task of running a summer camp in which they could manipulate the relationship between groups and then measure the resulting changes in intergroup sentiments and behavior. The essential features of their three best-known experiments were similar. The campers – all white, middle-class boys about 12 years old, who were unacquainted prior to the three-week session – found themselves assigned to one of two different cabins. In an initial phase of the study, there was little interaction between the two groups created by this assignment. Each group engaged in craft and sports activities (and developed the kinds of internal social structures and evolved the group symbols, rituals, jargons and other norms for appropriate behavior) that would be typical of any middle-class American summer camp. In a second phase, the groups were introduced to a series of intergroup contests (baseball, football, treasure hunt, and tug of war) with the promise of a trophy and individual prizes (for example, a new penknife) for those in the winning group, but nothing save frustration and dismay for the losers.

After the competition was over, and its effects on attitudes and be-havior had been documented, the third phase of the experiment began. Instead of vying for rewards that one group could gain only at the ex-pense of the other, the two groups now found themselves in a variety of circumstances in which they not only shared a single, "superordinate" goal but found that the goal could only be obtained by intergroup cooperation. In the most dramatic instance, the two groups, away on a joint outing, found that the camp truck had broken down. As a result, they would be able to return to camp for their noontime meal only if the truck could somehow be started – an outcome they accomplished by all pulling together on a rope attached to the truck's front bumper (the same rope, not coincidentally, that had been the instrument of their previous tug-of-war competition!).

The results of this short-term longitudinal field study were clear and compelling. While the physical separation of the campers into separate groups led to a network of in-group friendships, and even a tendency to rate one's own group somewhat more favorably than the other, it did not produce negative relationships between the two groups. Intergroup derogation and hostility began only when the groups competed for a scarce resource. Through informal observation, and through a number of cleverly designed little experiments presented as games, the investigators were able to demonstrate that the norm of peaceful coexistence vanished as the competition began and heated up. The two groups lost little opportunity to engage in name-calling, downgrading of each other's abilities, and even overtly displaying aggression. By the time the competition was over, the groups insisted they wanted nothing more to do with each other. During the same period, in-group solidarity increased, and physical toughness came to be more highly prized. In short, intergroup competition proved a sufficient condition for the rise of intergroup hostility. While cultural and observable physical differences between groups may facilitate hostility, Sherif concluded, differences of this sort were not a necessary condition for the development of such hostility.

Equally important, from Sherif's viewpoint, was the demonstration that intergroup conflict could be reduced by the introduction of super-ordinate goals and the initiation of cooperative ventures to achieve those goals. Once again, informal observations and mini-experiments illustrated the changes in sentiments and the development of friendships between erstwhile rivals and even former enemies. Sherif took particular pains to point out that such gains were neither immediate nor inevitable – the first cooperative ventures undertaken did not break down the "us" and "them" orientation of the groups. Sheriff also could not resist mentioning that mere informational campaigns, even those couched in appeals to moral values, were universally unsuccessful in reducing enmity. Sunday religious services that interrupted the period of competition with especially pointed appeals for brotherly love, forgiveness of enemies, and cooperation had no impact. The campers solemnly departed from the services and then, within minutes, returned to their preoccupation with defeating or harassing the detested outgroup. It was only changes in the type of interdependence existing between groups that produced a change in intergroup attitudes and behavior.

Social scientists of the 1950s could not miss the relevance of Sherif's demonstrations to contemporary problems of religious, ethnic, and especially, racial prejudice. His results offered encouragement to proponents of desegregation in housing, employment, and education and, at the same time, sounded a cautionary note about the value of "mere contact" – that is, contact without any cooperative pursuit (perhaps one should add *successful* pursuit) of shared goals (Cook, 1957, 1979, 1985; Deutsch & Collins, 1951; Gerard & Miller, 1975; Pettigrew, 1971, 1986).

It is worth noting that the last two decades have seen a rather intriguing challenge to at least one aspect of Sherif's theorizing. Henry Tajfel and his colleagues (Tajfel, 1970, 1981; Tajfel, Billig, Bundy, & Flament, 1971) have sought to demonstrate that "mere categorization" of people into different nominal groups, even in the absence of any close relationship among group members, can elicit favoritism toward ingroup members and discrimination toward out-group members. In one study, for example, children assigned to one of two "minimal groups" (on the basis of their alleged preference for the paintings either of Klee or Kandinsky) were given the task of allocating money to various ingroup and out-group members whose specific identity they did not know. The main findings from this study, which have been proven to be remarkably robust in conceptual replications conducted in several different countries, was a significant (albeit slight) tendency to reward in-group members more highly than out-group members. In other words, even the most arbitrary and seemingly inconsequential group classifications can provide a basis for discriminatory behavior. The findings of Tajfel and others have prompted critics to complain about artificiality (owing to the use of paper-and-pencil measures of reward allocation) and sparked heated debate about their real-world relevance and proper interpretation. (See review by R. Brown, 1986, pp. 543-551.) But these studies do suggest that the tendency to view the world in terms of "we" and "they," with at least a working hypothesis that "we" are somehow better and more deserving, is a rather basic aspect of social perception. They also suggest the anti-Marxist hypothesis that subjective aspects of social life, and not merely material, objective ones, can play an important role in social relations. We will return to this issue in Chapter 7, when we discuss the effects on social behavior both of the objective situation and of subjective aspects of culture.

Inhibition of Bystander Intervention

Some of the best and most interesting studies in the situationist tradition established by Lewin derive, at least initially, not from broad theories but from careful analysis of real-world events. The classic bystander intervention studies conducted two decades ago by John Darley and Bibb Latané provide perhaps the best-known examples of this tradition.

The 1960s were filled with events that made many feel that America's social fabric was unraveling. What caught the eye of Darley and Latané, however, was a rash of attacks on women in which no one came to the victim's aid. One such incident in particular received great national attention. Over a 30-minute period in Kew Gardens, a middle-class section of Queens, New York, a woman named Kitty Genovese was stabbed repeatedly by an assailant. Though she shouted for help continually during that time, and despite the fact (as police later were able to establish) that at least 38 people heard her and were aware of the incident, no one intervened in any way. No one even called the police!

The news media, never at a loss to explain human behavior, were unanimous in attributing the neighbors' lack of intervention to increasing alienation and apathy among dwellers in the megalopolis. Darley and Latané, trained in the situationist and subjectivist traditions of their field, thought otherwise. They hypothesized that in this incident, and in scores of others in which groups of bystanders failed to help victims of accidents, illnesses, or crimes (even in circumstances that would have exposed them to no danger or other significant costs), potential altruists had been inhibited not by indifference but rather by important aspects of the social situation. In particular, they had been inhibited by the presence of other potential altruists, and by their apparent failure to intervene in the same situation.

Group situations, Darley and Latané argued, can inhibit bystander intervention in two ways. First, and most obvious, is the dilution or diffusion of responsibility that each person feels because of the presence of others ("Why should I be the one to intervene, especially if no one else is? I'd be willing to do my share, but not to take on all the responsibility myself"). Second, and less obvious, is the construal or social definition problem to be dealt with in more general terms in our next chapter. That is, to the extent that there is ambiguity either about the nature of the situation or the nature of the appropriate response to that situation, the failure of other people to act serves to support interpretations or construals that are consistent with nonintervention ("it must just be a domestic dispute," or "she must not be hurt as badly or be in as much danger as she seems,"; or alternatively, "I guess this must be one of those situations where it's inappropriate, maybe even dangerous, to get involved, the kind of situation that prudent and sophisticated people steer clear of!"). In a sense, a vicious circle is initiated. The presence of other people inhibits quick intervention, and that initial lack of intervention supports definitions of the situation that make intervention seem unnecessary, unwise, or inappropriate, which in turn prompts further reluctance and delays, and so forth. By contrast, if the bystander is alone, and there is no one else to share the responsibility to intervene or to help define the situation, this vicious cycle never begins.

Darley and Latané undertook a number of studies to confirm the strongest version of this hypothesis – that is, that a victim's chances of receiving help would be greater if there were only a single bystander available than if there were a whole group of such bystanders. In one study (Latané & Darley, 1968), male undergraduates at Columbia were left to fill out a questionnaire either by themselves, with two other subjects, or with two confederates of the experimenter instructed to remain impassive and continue working when the subsequent "emergency" occurred. This emergency consisted of a stream of "smoke" that began to pour into the room through a wall vent, eventually filling up the entire room. While 75 percent of the solitary bystanders left the room to report the smoke, only 10 percent of the bystanders who participated alongside the two impassive confederates, and only 38 percent of the three-person groups, ever intervened in this way.

In another Columbia study (Latané & Rodin, 1969), individuals working alone on a questionnaire, individuals working in the presence of an impassive confederate, or dyads consisting of two naive subjects, heard what they believed was the sound of the female experimenter taking a bad fall on the other side of a movable room divider. Once again, most of the solitary bystanders (70 percent), but very few of the bystanders who sat next to an impassive confederate (7 percent), intervened to offer assistance. It also turned out that the victim would have fared better if she had been at the mercy of a lone bystander (70 percent intervention) than a pair of strangers (40 percent intervention).

Finally, in a New York University study (Darley & Latané, 1968), subjects heard someone whom they believed to be a fellow participant in an experiment feign an epileptic seizure while talking to them over an intercom system. When subjects believed they were the only listener, 85 percent intervened; when they believed that there was one other listener, 62 percent intervened, and when they believed that there were four other listeners, 31 percent intervened. Furthermore (as in both of the studies we've discussed previously), subjects who believed themselves to be the only potential intervener offered help more quickly. Indeed, by the end of the first minute of the feigned seizure, 50 percent of the solitary listeners, but none of those believing themselves to be only one of five listeners, had come to the assistance of the victim.

By 1980, four dozen follow-up studies had been undertaken – some using feigned emergencies in the confines of the laboratory, others exposing unwitting bystanders to simulated accidents, illnesses, or thefts, occurring in the streets, stores, elevators, and subway cars. And in about 90 percent of the comparisons, lone bystanders proved more likely to help than did people in groups (Latané & Nida, 1981). Moreover, as Darley and Latané had found in their seminal studies in the late 1960s, the victim's overall chances of receiving assistance often proved to be better if there was only a single bystander to rely upon than if there were many.

Follow-up interviews with subjects have also served to confirm the hunch that potential intervention situations, if at all ambiguous, are construed differently by group members than by lone bystanders. Potentially dangerous smoke pouring through a vent was interpreted as a leak in the air-conditioning or as vapors from a chemistry lab. Cries and moans of an accident victim became complaints and curses of someone who had probably suffered a mild sprain. The prospect of intervening now became "barging in," perhaps to the embarrassment of all concerned. Interestingly, it also appears that group situations may have inhibited subjects from noticing the emergency in the first place. Solitary students in the "smoke study" tended to glance around the room frequently as they worked on their questionnaires, generally noticing the smoke within five seconds. Those in groups typically kept their eyes on their work and didn't notice the smoke until it was quite thick – about 20 seconds after the first puff came through the vent.

The lesson of the Darley and Latané studies is not a difficult one to grasp, but it is sometimes hard to remember in the face of tales of "big city" life. In the movie *Midnight Cowboy* a naive young man comes from the range to the streets of Manhattan. Just off the bus, and walking through great throngs of people, he comes across a man lying on the sidewalk. He starts to reach down to see what's wrong with the man, then looks around him at the people walking past. They steer around the man on the sidewalk as they might avoid a log lying on a trail. The young man expresses surprise, then consternation, then shrugs his shoulders and goes about his business like the others.

One cannot witness such a scene without being reminded of one's own experiences of apathy and indifference in the megalopolis. But it should be helpful to ask oneself if New Yorkers, or Bostonians, or Philadelphians seem any less moved than their compatriots in Sioux Falls, Iowa, by the sufferings of stray cats, or by the fate of miners trapped in cave-ins, or by the plight of an abused and neglected child, or by the struggle of a young athlete stricken with a deadly variety of cancer. In our experience the answer is no. People are no more callous about such matters in one place than in another. To explain why urbanites walk around unfortunates lying in the street, or why they fail to investigate or call the police when they hear screams from an adjacent apartment, we need to look to the specifics of the relevant social situations, including, of course, the behavioral norms that are explicitly and implicitly communicated as these intervention opportunities continually present themselves.

Why Is Social Influence So Powerful?

Why are people so much influenced by the attitudes and behavior of other people, even of other people whom they do not know and who have no control over their lives? Some of the most interesting theoretical work of the social sciences has centered on answering this question by disentangling informational and normative aspects of social influence (Deutsch & Gerard, 1955).

Informational aspects of social influence. Other people are among our best sources of information about the world. If the animal in front of me appears to be a cat, then (almost surely) it is. But if the judgment in question is of some greater ambiguity than this, for example, how hard is this task I am about to undertake, or how capable am I of undertaking it, then the opinions of other people are usually valuable in arriving at a correct conclusion. If my opinion differs from yours, then I ought to consider yours simply on statistical grounds. Over the long haul, the average of the opinions of any two people is more likely to be correct than the opinion of either individual. To attend to the "base rate" of other people's opinions is only rational, and people who do this too little are aptly regarded as opinionated or reckless. Many of the experiments demonstrating dramatic social influence, including the Asch experiments, take advantage of this basic fact. We are not in the habit of ignoring the opinions of our fellows for the very good reason that they have proven in the past to be a helpful way of learning about the world. The state of disagreeing with others produces a discomfort that we need to resolve either by moving toward their position, moving them toward ours, or deciding that they are not a useful source of information for people who occupy our particular niche in the world.

An interesting implication of this derivation of conformity pressures is that it is not just majority opinions that should be influential, but minority opinions as well. Even if the holders of some view are not powerful, and not in the majority, their views are likely to have an influence on group opinions. And indeed, recent work by both Moscovici and his colleagues (Moscovici, Lage, & Naffrechoux, 1969; Moscovici & Personnaz, 1980) and Nemeth (1986) establishes that not all conformity is to majority opinion. Minority views often have an influence even when this is quite unrecognized by the majority. Such views enter the marketplace of ideas and may ultimately win even in the face of seemingly overwhelming opposition – especially if such views are expressed consistently and confidently.

Normative basis of social influence. A second reason that we attend to the views of our fellows is that we understand that movement toward group goals depends on a degree of unanimity about understanding of the situation (Festinger, Schachter, & Back, 1950). If all of us have different views about what the task is to accomplish and how to accomplish it, if in fact we even have different understandings of the meanings of the events we encounter, then collaboration and effective action are difficult or impossible. Largely for this reason, the opinion of the majority carries normative or moral force: To get along, go along; hang together or hang separately. Thus groups are punitive toward their deviates in part because they block group movement. Knowing that our disagreement can bring the wrath of our fellows, it is with great hesitation that we risk it. Better to yield in the interest of harmony, and fight only if sober reflection demands it.

Social influence and tension systems. As we noted in Chapter 1, the major theoretical treatments of social influence, especially those of Festinger (1954) and his fellow theorists (see Cartwright & Zander, 1953) are heavily influenced by Kurt Lewin's notions of tension systems. This is true both at the level of the group and at the level of the individual psyche.

Groups should be thought of as being in a constant state of tension produced on the one hand by requirements of uniformity and, on the other, by forces operating on individual group members that cause them to stray from the group standard. Individuals will have different sources of information about important topics and will construe this information in various ways. This will produce opinion deviance, which will be met with forces toward uniformity by the group. The group forces are toward an entropic, static state in which there is complete uniformity of opinion. Yet events and personalities will constantly be producing divergence from that state. When the divergence is great enough, the forces toward uniformity may actually produce fission of the group. Groups can tolerate only so much deviance with respect to important issues, and when the deviance exceeds that level, groups may socially reject, sometimes even officially expel, deviant members or subgroups (Schachter, 1951).

Individuals may also be thought of as tension systems in regard to their conflicts with the group standard. When one discovers a discrepancy between the group norm and one's own view, this creates a tension that must be resolved in one of three ways – influencing the group toward one's own views, opening oneself to influence so as to move one's view in line with that of the group, or rejecting the group as a standard for one's own opinions. In the event that it does not prove possible to move the group toward one's own view *and* the group is less than convincing on informational grounds *and* one is unwilling to reject the group, there is a powerful kind of tension recognized by many theorists of the 1950s, including Heider, Newcomb, and Festinger. Festinger called this tension "cognitive dissonance," a concept that he ultimately broadened to include tension produced by a variety of cases in which different sources pulled attitudes in different directions. In the case of social influence, the dissonance exists between one's own view and the views (as well as the conformity requirements) of the group. This dissonance is characteristically resolved in favor of the group's view, often not by simple compromise, but by wholesale adoption of the group's view and suppression of one's own doubts. The consequences of this sort of dissonance reduction are revealed in Irving Janis's (1982) well-known analysis of disastrous military and political decisions resulting from "groupthink." That is, loyal group members suppress their doubts about a planned course of action, thereby giving an illusion of consensus that in turn discourages believers and doubters alike from exploring flaws in the proposal and considering alternatives.

The tension system notion should be kept in mind as we consider the notion of channel factors in the next section. Channel factors are important because they release or redirect the energy in delicately balanced systems where there is tension between one or more motive states. Just which behavioral route, or which attitudinal state, is chosen is sometimes observed to be under the control of remarkably slight situational variations.

CHANNEL FACTORS

So far we have focused on one aspect of situationism – the power of various circumstances to elicit behavior that is surprising. The other face of situationism, implicit in much of the previous discussion, is that small differences between situations are often associated with very large behavioral differences. When we find an apparently small situational circumstance producing a big behavioral effect, we are justified in suspecting we have identified a channel factor, that is, a stimulus or a response pathway that serves to elicit or sustain behavioral intentions with particular intensity or stability. We now review three classic studies illustrating how channel factors can either facilitate or inhibit the links between general attitudes or vague intentions on the one hand and consequential social actions on the other. In each study, as we will see, the point is not simply that the relevant environmental manipulations produced significant change in some dependent variable measure; rather, it is the fact that the relevant effects were large and consequential – large relative to our expectations, large relative to individual difference factors that laypeople normally would expect to be the most important determinants of the behavior under investigation, and too large to be ignored by anyone whose goal is successful social intervention.

On Selling War Bonds

During World War II the U.S. government initiated a number of mass persuasion campaigns designed to encourage the purchase of war bonds to pay for the enormous cost of military operations. Social psychologists were asked to help increase the effectiveness of these campaigns, primarily by heightening the persuasiveness of the print, radio, and film appeals to the public. The Lewinian contribution to this effort took a somewhat different tack, one that proceeded from the insight that social influence depends not just on persuading people to hold particular beliefs, or even to develop particular intentions, but also on facilitating a specific, well-defined path or channel for action (Cartwright, 1949).

In concrete terms, this meant a change from relatively general appeals ("Buy War Bonds") to a more specific appeal ("Buy an *extra* $100 Bond"), and a stipulated time and place for doing so (for example, "Buy them when the solicitor at your workplace asks you to sign up"). The result, substantially because of this change in appeals (so Cartwright tells us), was a doubling of bond sales (from 25 percent of all wage earners to 50 percent). Perhaps most striking of all was the importance of direct personal requests. Although virtually all Americans heard the appeals and agreed that such purchases were desirable, and virtually all could name places where bonds could be bought (for example, at their bank or post office), fewer than 20 percent of wage earners purchased additional bonds in the absence of a direct, face-to-face appeal. By contrast, when asked to purchase another bond by someone who could sign them up on the spot, almost 60 percent put their names on the dotted line.

This lesson about the importance of channel factors has come to be appreciated more and more by contemporary persuaders. Increasingly, charities and businesses rely on direct telephone or door-to-door solicitations that force you to say yes or no, right there, without allowing you to consider the merits of their cause relative to others (or, more importantly, to turn your attention to other concerns without making any real decision at all). The increasing number of charity telethons offers another illustration. The telethon will, of course, prominently feature information about the disease or problem needing attention; and appeals that tug at the heartstrings and motivate you to care and to act will not be neglected. But the most distinctive and ubiquitous feature of the telethon is apt to be the single telephone number on the screen, and the continual plea from the heroic telethon host who looks you in the eye and urges you to "call that number now and make a pledge to our volunteers." Once you take that initial step by making the phone call, they take care of everything. In other words, they create a behavioral channel that very reliably transforms a long-standing but vague intention, or even a momentary whim, into a completed donation.

Christian evangelists show a similar sensitivity to the importance of channel factors. Instead of a vague and general appeal to change one's ways or to accept Christ as one's personal savior, the evangelist asks for a single concrete act at that exact moment in time, for example, to get out of one's seat and come forward as a sign of one's decision (after which a cadre of volunteers will lead the newcomers backstage and induce further acts of commitment). Successful evangelists, it is worth noting parenthetically, do not always rely only on channel facilitation. Some also make effective use of social influence techniques consistent with the message of the first half of this chapter. In particular, they employ models – explicitly instructed volunteers who immediately stand in response to the evangelist's appeal, thereby "getting the ball rolling" and making it more normative for others to rise to their feet (and, eventually, rather uncomfortable to remain seated).

Time to Be a Good Samaritan

We have already discussed the Darley and Latané demonstration that one apparently trivial feature of the social setting – the presence or absence of other people – can markedly influence bystander intervention. In a later study that we sketched in Chapter 1, Darley and Batson (1973) showed that another, seemingly even less consequential, feature of the social situation could exert almost as much influence on the potential bystander. Their experiment, they tell us, was inspired by the Good Samaritan parable, whereby the priest and the Levite, both important (and presumably busy) people, hurry by a stricken traveler leaving it for the lowly (and presumably far less busy) Samaritan to offer the necessary assistance. Reflecting on this parable, and deriving a decidedly situationist message from it, Darley and Batson decided to manipulate the "hurried" versus "unhurried" status of potential "Good Samaritans" – all of whom, by no means coincidentally, were students at Princeton Theological Seminary.

In an initial phase of the experiment, the young seminarians were told that they were to prepare themselves for a brief extemporaneous talk (which, for half of the participants, was on the Good Samaritan parable itself) to be recorded in a nearby building. After receiving directions from the experimenter, the seminarians in one condition were told "you're late; they were expecting you a few minutes ago, so you'd better hurry," while in the other condition they were told "it will be a few minutes before they're ready for you, but you might as well head on over." En route, the participants in both the "late" and "early" condition came upon a man slumped in a doorway, head down, coughing and groaning. As predicted, the late seminarians seldom helped; in fact, only 10 percent offered any assistance. By contrast, with ample time on their hands, 63 percent of the early participants helped.

Does this study prove that these seminarians were indifferent to worldly suffering, or that they placed the interests of the relatively high-status people waiting for them ahead of the lowly character who seemed to need their help? By now the reader should be able to anticipate that we think that these findings tell us little if anything about the personal dispositions of seminarians but a great deal about the situational determinants of altruism. Once again, incidentally, we suspect that some of the subtler details of the situational manipulation may have been important and would merit some emphasis. We suspect that the "late" manipulation employed by Darley and Batson not only made the young seminarians reluctant to stop, it also guaranteed that they would feel a little harried and nervous about their forthcoming talk – enough so, perhaps, to prevent them from paying attention to the victim. On the other hand, the "early" manipulation may have served to make the young seminarians walk more slowly, contemplate their surroundings more closely, and perhaps even welcome an excuse to tarry (rather than having to wait around awkwardly while the anonymous "they" got everything ready).

In Chapter 5 we will show that such situational influences tend to be far greater than most people are willing to predict. We can also note that scores of studies have probed additional situational determinants of altruistic behavior (and quite a few have looked for the personality characteristics of the altruist). The results of some of these studies have been fairly intuitive. Bryan and Test (1967), for example, showed that the presence or absence of altruistic "models" (peers who rendered the sought-after assistance in similar or identical circumstances) produced corresponding increases or decreases both in subjects' willingness to help motorists in distress and in their generosity when faced with a Salvation Army collection kettle. Other studies have produced more surprising, and often more complicated, results. For example, many studies have shown that mood inductions, either of "guilt" (Carlsmith & Gross, 1968) or "happiness" (Isen, Clark, & Schwartz, 1976; Isen, Shalker, Clark, & Karp, 1978) can markedly increase subjects' willingness to comply with requests for help or to show other altruistic behaviors. But none, we believe, can drive home the situationist message in general, and the importance of channel factors in particular, as pointedly as Darley and Batson's simple study. As we contemplate the earnest young seminarian (who, no doubt, has devoted in the past and will devote again in the future many hours to helping various types of unfortunates) almost literally stepping over a distressed victim as he hurries off to preach his sermonette on Good Samaritanism, we grasp an essential message of the Lewinian tradition: There but for the sake of a facilitating channel factor go we.

Effects of Minimal Compliance

The situationist perspective suggests social influence strategies quite different from the conventional approach of presenting persuasive appeals that address cognitive and motivational concerns. One of the most potent strategies, it has become apparent, consists of inducing people to take initial small, seemingly inconsequential steps along a path that ultimately will lead them to take much larger and more consequential actions. All of us, in fact, have had personal experiences that illustrate the relevant principle. We agree to help someone in some limited way or to undertake some small responsibility. But one thing somehow leads to another, and before we know it, we find ourselves deeply involved and reluctantly (occasionally, even willingly) devoting far more time, money, or energy to the endeavor than we ever had intended, ever would have predicted, or ever would have agreed to before becoming involved.

The principle in question, when applied by a skilled interpersonal manipulator, consists of first getting one's "foot in the door," that is, asking for a small favor or commitment (one that, in the context at hand, can scarcely be refused), and only then asking for the larger commitment or undertaking that constitutes the real objective. Jonathan Freedman and Scott Fraser (1966) illustrated this principle very elegantly in an experiment that has become a classic. Homemakers in a middle-class housing tract near the Stanford University campus were first approached by a person who asked them to do something relatively innocuous, that is, either to sign a petition or to place a small (3 inches square) sign in the window of their car or home promoting a noncontroversial cause (for example, safe driving). The vast majority of those approached, not surprisingly, agreed to this seemingly modest request. Two weeks later a second person visited the same sample of homemakers, and also called upon a control group sample who had not previously been contacted, to accede to a far more substantial, even rather unreasonable, request. He asked them to allow a large, crudely lettered, and decidedly ugly "Drive Carefully" sign to be installed directly in front of their house. As he made this request, he showed them a photo in which the ugly sign could be seen obscuring the front door of another house in the tract.

The results of this study were dramatic. Fully 76 percent of the subjects who had initially agreed to place a small auto safety sign in their window now agreed to place the big, ugly "Drive Carefully" sign in front of the house. By contrast, "only" 17 percent (actually, a surprisingly large percentage in absolute terms) agreed to erect the sign when there had been no prior foot-in-the-door visit. Interestingly, even when the issue pertinent to the subjects' initial compliance was irrelevant to the subsequent request (for example, when they initially had accepted a window sign, or signed a petition, that sought to "Keep California Beautiful"), the rate of compliance was close to 50 percent – almost three times the compliance rate in the control group.

Many subsequent studies have confirmed Freedman and Fraser's basic findings. For example, Patricia Pliner and her co-workers (Pliner, Hart, Kohl, & Saari, 1974) found that a sample of Toronto suburbanites became twice as likely to donate money to the Cancer Society after agreeing, a day earlier, to wear a lapel pin publicizing the forthcoming fund drive (an innocuous foot-in-the-door request that none refused). But the message of such studies should not be embraced too wholeheartedly. We know from subsequent research that not all big requests can be facilitated via foot-in-the-door techniques. In some circumstances (for example, when the initial request is large enough to make the individuals feel that they have "already done their share"), satisfying an initial request can make people more reluctant to comply with subsequent requests (Cann, Sherman, & Elkes, 1975; Snyder & Cunningham, 1974). By the same token, there are also circumstances in which people's refusal of an initial large request can render them easy prey to a second more moderate request – for example, when their refusal to aid a worthy cause motivates them to demonstrate, as soon as possible, that they are not hard-hearted or unreasonable (Cialdini et al., 1975). As always, contextual details, sometimes very subtle details, matter a great deal, and some talent (or better still, some pretesting) is required to figure out what kinds of initial requests are most likely to facilitate which kinds of later compliance. But the fact remains that careful use of initial commitments and other channel manipulations can lead people ultimately to take steps that no one, least of all they themselves, would have predicted from their previous behavior or from their previous expressions of their views.

Rather than attempting to offer any simple formula for using foot-in-the-door or other minimal compliance manipulations, we should consider briefly the explanation that researchers who employ them offer for their effectiveness. Basically, they argue either that the small acts of compliance motivate subjects to adopt attitudes consonant with such behavior (Festinger, 1957) or that these acts help to "inform" the subjects about the nature and degree of their heretofore unexamined and untested views (Bem, 1972). Whether the subjects rationalize their prior behavior, or simply use it as a clue as to their real attitudes and priorities, the result is a subsequent willingness to act accordingly, for example, to make further commitments or take further actions appropriate for one who holds those attitudes. We think that these cognitive explanations are correct, at least in part, but we think it is also important to emphasize that such explanations really explain very little unless they tacitly grant one of the central contentions of this chapter and of our book as a whole: People are prone not only to be influenced by situational factors but also to underestimate the extent of such influence (Nisbett & Ross, 1980; Ross, 1977). If they recognized that their compliance was elicited by situational pressures rather than freely chosen because it was consistent with their attitudes, they would not have to realign their attitudes to "sustain" the consistency.

Putting It All Together: Stanley Milgram and the Banality of Evil

In 1965 the moral philosopher Hannah Arendt announced her thesis that the Holocaust, or at any rate its day-to-day implementation, owed more to bureaucratic blandness and indifference than to sadistic pleasure in the suffering of the innocent. She came to this conclusion after watching the trial in Jerusalem of Adolf Eichmann, the man charged with overseeing the transportation of Europe's Jewry to the death camps. What she saw in the docket (in the bulletproof glass cage, actually – Israeli security was determined that Eichmann not be assassinated before facing his accusers) was a pasty, balding, middle-aged man whose defense was that he was merely following orders, and that he never cared much one way or the other about what happened to the people he transported to the camps in central Europe. Arendt was willing to believe that Eichmann was not a sadistic monster but a conformist without a cause, that he could as easily have been in charge of shipping vegetables, or more to the point, that many a vegetable shipper could have been induced to play Eichmann's monstrous role.

We share the suspicions of the social critic Alfred Kazin (1984) that Arendt may have too readily accepted at face value the only defense left to a man who could not plausibly deny either that he was who he was or that he did what he did. "Just following orders" has always been the defense of underlings who commit evil deeds in the name of the state. At the same time, we cannot help commending Arendt's willingness to resist the easier and more commonplace conclusion that heinous acts must be the product of heinous motives. For, as we have emphasized, the tendency to make unwarranted leaps from acts to corresponding dispositions is perhaps the most fundamental and most common failing of social inference. Whether Eichmann was a fiend, we do not know; that there were many Germans who were not fiends yet knowingly played a role in sending the victims of Naziism to their horrible fates, we do not doubt. It is certainly the case that many Nazi concentration camp guards led blameless lives, both before and after their horrible service (Steiner, 1980). To explain such complicity, therefore, we must assume the existence of a specific social and situational context that could induce ordinary people to commit extraordinarily evil deeds.

As it happens, at roughly the same time Arendt was developing her thesis about the banality of evil, Stanley Milgram was demonstrating it in his laboratory. As we described earlier, Milgram had previously done follow-up work on the Asch paradigm showing that people would conform to a unanimous majority even when they thought that they were testing airliner signaling systems. He had then gone on, using the same paradigm, to study cultural differences in conformity (and, in fact, to provide some support for the ethnic stereotype that the "contentious" French would show less conformity than the "more retiring" Scandinavians). These results, in turn, made Milgram wonder whether similar cultural differences would be manifested when the conforming response involved a potentially harmful action.

It was with this goal in mind that Milgram contrived the situation that now bears his name, a situation that originally was designed to be a "control" condition (in which people merely would be asked by the experimenter to do something that would presumably harm another person). This situation was intended to present no conformity pressures, but it nevertheless featured some very potent situational forces. In fact, the results of some pilot work using this situation to test ordinary Americans, a people supposedly rich in a cultural tradition of independence and distaste for authority, quickly switched Milgram's attention from conformity to obedience.

Milgram's subjects came from all walks of life. They were not impressionable college sophomores; rather (at least in his best-known studies), they were adult males of varied occupations who had responded to a newspaper advertisement soliciting participants for a study on learning to be conducted at Yale University. Let us now consider the details of Milgram's unfolding experimental scenario.

Upon their arrival, Milgram's subject meets another "subject," a pleasant-mannered, middle-aged man (who, unknown to him, is actually a confederate of the experimenter). The experimenter announces his interest in the effects of punishment on learning. He draws slips of paper from a hat to determine who will be the "teacher" and who the "learner" (a drawing rigged to make sure that the subject becomes the teacher and the confederate becomes the learner). The teacher's job, it is explained, will be to teach a series of word pairs to the learner. The teacher then watches as the learner is strapped into an electric-chair apparatus (to "prevent excessive movement," the experimenter explains). An electrode is taped to the man's wrist and electrode paste is applied to the skin (to "prevent burns").

The experimenter explains that the electrode is attached to a shock generator, and that the teacher's specific task will be to administer shocks to the learner (by pushing switches on the shock generator) every time the learner makes a mistake in recalling a word. The teacher is then led into an adjacent room, out of sight of the learner, and seated in front of the shock generator. On the generator, the teacher sees 30 lever switches, labeled in 15-volt increments from 15 to 450 volts, with accompanying descriptions of the intensities of shock, ranging from "slight shock" to "danger: severe shock." The last two switches, ominously, are labeled "XXX." The experimenter tells the teacher that he is to increase the shock level by 15 volts every time the learner gives a wrong answer. He assures the subjects that "although the shocks can be extremely painful, they cause no permanent tissue damage." The experimenter remains by the teacher's side, where he stays throughout the experiment that follows.

As the scenario unfolds, the learner indicates his answers by choosing from a list of four words and pressing a button that lights up one of four signals at the top of the teacher's shock generator. After the learner's first mistake, the teacher increases the shock – 15 volts, then another 15, and so on. The teacher's dilemma is heightened by the "feedback" he receives from the hapless learner. Initially, there are only verbal protests about the painfulness of the shocks, but the learner continues to participate. Then, when the shock level reaches 300 volts, the learner pounds on the wall in protest, and from this point on, no answers from the learner appear on the panel display in front of the teacher. The learner does, however, continue pounding after each shock is administered. Then even the pounding ceases.

Throughout the procedure the experimenter restates the teacher's duties. If the teacher looks to the experimenter for guidance, the experimenter says, "Please continue." If the teacher protests that the learner is no longer giving answers, the experimenter states that the failure to answer should be considered a wrong answer. If the teacher expresses a reluctance to continue or suggests that the learner's condition should be examined, the experimenter merely insists that "the experiment requires that you continue." If the teacher becomes really insistent, the experimenter announces, "you have no choice; you must go on." And if (but only if) the subject protests that he will not accept responsibility for harm that might be done to the learner, the experimenter assures him that "the responsibility is mine."

As all students of introductory psychology know (indeed, as most educated people in the Western world know, for Milgram's demonstrations have become part of our society's shared intellectual legacy; see Ross, 1988), this grim protocol was generally carried out to its conclusion. Most people (68 percent in the best-known variation) obeyed to the bitter end, beyond the "danger: severe shock" level, all the way to the final "450-volt, XXX" level.

This result confounded Milgram's own expectations and those of everyone else. Laypeople, social psychologists, and psychiatrists whom Milgram consulted all assured him that virtually no one would reach the highest levels of shock. The question that arose then, and that remains today, is why so many people obeyed so completely (or, alternatively, why so few people predicted the correct result). Even today we cannot read the results of Milgram's experiment without feeling that we have learned something very dire about our society in particular and the human species in generaL We find ourselves concluding that people are not only sheep (as Asch's earlier demonstration had suggested) but that they are also weaklings who cannot stand up to authority or, even worse, that they have a sadistic streak just waiting to show itself.

Some people react to Milgram's results with the reassuring conclusion that the subjects must have seen through the hoax and realized that the victim was not really being shocked. After all, "anyone" would know a respected institution like Yale would "never allow such a thing to happen." Milgram anticipated such objections, and he was determined that his results not be so easily dismissed. Accordingly, he replicated his study using a shabby office in a rundown section of Bridgeport, Connecticut – this time under the uninspiring aegis of an unknown "Research Institute." The dropoff in obedience proved to be relatively slight. He also took pains to invite skeptical social scientists to watch his procedure from behind a one-way mirror. All were shaken by what they saw, not only by the levels of obedience they observed but, frequently, also by the human anguish that accompanied it. As one scientist reported:

> I observed a mature and initially poised businessman enter the laboratory smiling and confident. Within 20 minutes he was reduced to a twitching, stuttering wreck, who was rapidly approaching a point of nervous collapse. He constantly pulled on his earlobe, and twisted his hands. At one point he pushed his fist into his forehead and muttered: "Oh God, let's stop it." And yet he continued to respond to every word of the experimenter, and obeyed to the end. (Milgram, 1963, p. 377)

Such reports not only allow us to dismiss the possibility that Milgram's subjects were merely going along with the experimenter's charade, they also allow us to discredit the potential explanation that people in this age of urban anonymity don't care what they do to strangers. The vast majority of Milgram's subjects, it seems clear, believed that what was happening was real, and most of them found it an agonizing experience. So why didn't they stop? Why didn't they just tell the experimenter where to go?

The answer appears to be that it was certain subtle features of Milgram's situation – whose influence tends to be unrecognized or underappreciated by all who read about or even personally witnessed that situation – that prompted ordinary members of our society to behave so extraordinarily. We cannot claim to have identified all these features, or to understand exactly how and why they interacted to produce so potent an effect, but we can outline a few of them which, not coincidentally, turn out to be some of the same situational influences and channel factors that we have discussed for other studies.

Milgram's own analysis began with the subject's implicit contract to do as one is told without asking why, faithfully serving the authority figure to whom one has willingly ceded responsibility. His analysis also stresses the gradual, stepwise character of the shift from relatively unobjectionable behavior to complicity in a pointless, cruel, and dangerous ordeal. The teacher, it must be remembered, did not obey a single, simple command to deliver a powerful shock to an innocent victim. At first, all he undertook to do was to deliver mild punishments – feedback really – to a learner who had willingly agreed to receive such feedback as an aid in performing his task. He also agreed, as did the learner, to a specific punishment procedure (that is, increasing the punishments by a fixed amount after each error), without ever imagining the full consequences of that agreement. It was only as the stepwise progression continued, and the shocks being administered reached alarming levels, that the teacher's psychological dilemma became apparent. In a sense, the teacher had to find a rationale (one satisfactory to himself, to the experimenter, and perhaps even to the learner) that would justify his decision to desist now when he hadn't desisted earlier, a way to explain why it was illegitimate to deliver the next shock when it presumably had been legitimate to deliver one of only slightly lesser magnitude just moments before. Such a rationale is difficult to find. Indeed, it is clearly available at only one point in the proceedings – the point at which the learner stops responding and thereby withdraws his implied consent to receive the shocks – and, significantly, it is at precisely this point that refusals to obey were most frequent.

There are also some additional, less obvious, features of the Milgram demonstration that we must recognize if we are to appreciate the subjects' view of their situation and their own behavior. In particular, it is important to note that relatively few of Milgram's subjects simply obeyed from beginning to end without ever questioning their orders or expressing any unwillingness to continue. While Milgram's research reports were not as precise as they should have been on this crucial issue, it is apparent that most participants did step outside the role of "obedient subject" to question the experimenter's wisdom in continuing, to urge the experimenter to check on the learner's condition, or to express their own reluctance. In fact, many subjects essentially said "I quit," only to be confronted with perhaps the most important yet subtle feature of the Milgram paradigm, the difficulty in moving from the intention to discontinue to the actual termination of their participation. Most of the subjects did confront the experimenter and even refused to continue, often quite forcefully. But nearly always they were backed down by the experimenter. ("The experiment requires that you continue." "You have no choice.") Indeed, the Milgram experiments ultimately may have less to say about "destructive obedience" than about ineffectual, and indecisive, disobedience.

A thought experiment will be helpful here. Suppose that the experimenter had announced at the beginning of the session that, if at any time the teacher wished to terminate his participation in the experiment, he could indicate his desire to do so by pressing a button on the table in front of him. We trust the reader agrees with us that if this channel factor had been opened up, the obedience rate would have been a fraction of what it was. The converse of this is that the absence of such a "disobedience channel" is precisely what condemned Milgram's subjects to their hapless behavior. In Lewinian terms, there was no well-defined, legitimate, channel that the teacher could use to escape from the situation and discontinue participation in the experiment; and any attempt to create such a channel was met with implacable opposition from an experimenter who, significantly, never even acknowledged the legitimacy of the teacher's concerns.

There is yet one more, still subtler and more elusive feature of the Milgram situation that may have been very important from the subject's viewpoint. The events that unfolded did not "make sense" or "add up" from the perspective of the subject. The subject's task was that of administering severe electric shocks to a learner who was no longer attempting to learn anything, at the insistence of an experimenter who seemed totally oblivious to the learner's cries of anguish, warnings about a heart condition, refusal to continue responding, and ultimately, ominous silence. What's more, the experimenter evinced no concern about this turn of events, made no attempt to explain or justify that lack of concern or, alternatively, to explain why it was so necessary for the experiment to continue. He even refused to "humor" the subject by checking on the condition of the learner. Unless subjects grasped both the nature of the deception and the real purpose of the experiment (in which case, presumably, they would have chosen to disobey in order to prove that they were not the sort to carry out evil orders in stolid, Eichmann-like fashion), there was simply no way for them to arrive at a stable "definition of the situation." And how does one respond when "nothing seems to make sense," when one's own understanding of the actions and outcomes unfolding around one obviously is limited or deficient? Few people, we suggest, would respond by acting decisively or asserting independence. Rather, they would become uncharacteristically indecisive, unwilling and unable to challenge authority or disavow role expectations, and highly dependent on those who calmly and confidently issue orders. In short, they would behave very much like Milgram's subjects.

We trust that the point of this detailed analysis of the Milgram demonstration is clear. We do not find evidence in Milgram's research that people are disposed to obey authority figures unquestioningly – even to the point of committing harmful and dangerous acts. (We've never found such slavish obedience forthcoming from the students or advisees whom we enjoin to keep up to date with their reading, take neat lecture notes, and to study for exams in an orderly and timely fashion – and it is not because they do not regard us as authority figures.) Rather, what Milgram offered was a pointed reminder about the capacity of particular, relatively subtle situational forces to overcome people's kinder dispositions. He also showed how readily the observer makes erroneous inferences about the actor's destructive obedience (or foolish conformity) by taking the behavior at face value and presuming that extreme personal dispositions are at fault. His studies also remind us that the task of understanding and interpreting behavior must begin with an attempt to appreciate the actor's understanding of the situation. It is therefore appropriate that our next chapter proceeds to consider general questions of situational construal.

CHAPTER 3
CONSTRUING THE SOCIAL WORLD

It was not social psychologists who heralded the situationist tradition in psychology. The pioneers were the behaviorists, led early in the century by John B. Watson, who wrote eloquently about the role that situational factors play in shaping human behavior. Watson's famous boast was that he could (through appropriate manipulation of environment and reinforcement history) ". . . make any child into a doctor, lawyer, artist, merchant-chief, and yes even a beggarman-thief, regardless of his talents, penchants, tendencies, abilities, vocations, and race of his ancestors" (1930, p. 82). The claim, of course, was not that "person" variables didn't matter in the determination of behavior; rather, it was that the "person" is simply the sum of the situational contingencies experienced in the past – contingencies that could be described objectively, and that provide a basis for precise behavioral prediction and control.

But the situationism of the behaviorists was bound up with their insistence that the inner workings of the human mind could not be the proper subject matter of a scientific psychology. They insisted on abandoning the nineteenth-century research strategy of having people introspect about subjective mental experiences. Instead, the new science of psychology was to concern itself exclusively with observable, quantifiable events – in particular, overt responses, observable environmental stimuli that provoked such responses, and objectively specifiable outcomes (for example, specific "reinforcements" relevant to well-defined biological drives) that were the consequences of such responses. All behavior, however subtle or complicated, was to be understood in terms of associations among stimuli, responses, and hedonic consequences, and in terms of generalizations made from one stimulus or context to another on the basis of similarity.

The behaviorists paved the way for many important theoretical and applied contributions in the exploration of classical and instrumental conditioning and, more generally, in the study of learning and motivation. But in the strategic decision to ignore subjective experience and concentrate only on objectively specifiable events, the behaviorists created a dilemma that has persisted for most of this century. While psychology had committed itself to a purely objective account of human behavior, our intuitions and experiences, and eventually our research as well, made it clear that much, if not most, everyday human behavior, especially social behavior, becomes explainable and predictable only when we know, or can accurately guess, the subjective interpretations and beliefs of the people involved.

SUBJECTIVIST CONSIDERATIONS IN OBJECTIVE BEHAVIORISM

Consider the following rather ordinary episode: Jane says to Bob, a young man she encounters at a sorority mixer, "Do you come to these things often?" He smiles and replies, "No, but I think I'm going to start coming *more* often." Clearly, the two people in this vignette have responded to relevant stimuli and their responses have had consequences. But to truly understand this episode, and especially to appreciate its implications for the two individuals' future behavior, we need to know how each of them perceived the overall situation and how they interpreted each other's responses. First, what were their subjective impressions of the mixer, and how did those impressions relate to their goals and expectations? Then, what meaning did they attach to each other's words (and to any nonverbal behavior accompanying such words)? Did Bob simply take Jane's question at face value, or did he believe it was an expression of her possible interest in him; and, if so, was such interest welcome or unwelcome? Similarly, did Jane interpret Bob's statement about attending future mixers as an indication that he is enjoying this one, as a pointed expression of his interest in her, or as just a charming but relatively meaningless conversational gambit?

No amount of specification of the objective details of the behavior in question, we argue, will allow us to predict the participants' future behavior. Only by knowing or correctly guessing the subjective meaning of the events could we determine why the individuals behaved as they did. Lacking such knowledge of the meaning of the stimuli and responses to the participants, we couldn't tell which specific responses had or had not been reinforced, nor how the episode will influence Jane's and Bob's subsequent responses to each other, to sorority mixers, and to other related social settings. Indeed, to understand fully the nature and implications of such social dramas, we need to bear in mind that people are not only trying to interpret each other's words and deeds, they are also trying to predict, monitor, and gently guide each other's *interpretations*.

The point of the sorority mixer vignette is a very general one. Whether we are disinterested scientific observers of such episodes or participants in them, we must attend closely to questions of subjective meaning. First, we must try to discern how the participants categorize the situation so that their past experience and current beliefs about the world can be brought to bear. Second, we must know what the participants believe about the contingencies between their actions and subsequent outcomes, that is, what likelihoods they attach to particular consequences and what they assume about the cause-effect relationships governing those likelihoods. In short, we must be aware that objective accounts of stimuli, responses, and reinforcements, and objective specification of the linkages among them, will rarely be sufficient for our purposes. We need to know how the participants themselves perceive these "objective" events, and what they believe about the relevant linkages among them.

It is no accident that Clark Hull, B. F. Skinner, and other learning theorists in the behaviorist tradition who exerted so much influence in the first half of this century found ways to effectively "finesse" such problems of subjective construal. First, in studying response acquisition and change, they relied primarily on rats and pigeons, organisms that we assume to be less disposed than humans to ponder the meaning of their environment. (And, in any case, whatever private ruminations these organisms might have about their private interpretations, expectations, or motives, they cannot tell us about them.) The stimuli employed by the investigators further discouraged questions about subjective meaning. The investigators worked almost exclusively with reinforcers that were clear and relatively invariant in their meaning to their subjects (for example, food pellets or drops of water presented to animals that previously had been made very hungry or thirsty, or noxious stimuli like electric shock, which all animals would try to escape) and with stimuli and responses that had no particular significance to the subjects (for example, lights, tones, lever pressing, and the like) until they became temporally associated with primary reinforcers.

When investigators in the behaviorist tradition did employ humans, they similarly avoided problems of interpretation or meaning. For example, they studied eye-blink conditioning by pairing a previously meaningless tone with the presentation of a puff of air to the subject's cornea (a stimulus to which an eye-blink was an innate or "unconditioned" reflex). Or they studied learning and memory by having subjects learn lists of nonsense syllables or mundane everyday objects, not by exploring their recollections of real-world events that would have a rich and varied significance for the different subjects.

Despite these strategies, and despite the learning theorists' successes in the laboratory, the limitations of such objectivist approaches became increasingly evident – especially to those learning theorists, and social psychologists, who concerned themselves with behavior outside the confines of the laboratory. In less sterile circumstances, where the stimuli presented are more complex, where behavioral options are less obviously tied to the satisfaction of innate drives, and where organisms are likely to hold theories based on their experiences with real-world contingencies, accurate behavioral prediction and control proved a more elusive goal. This was true even for pigeons, rats, and cats, as Martin Seligman (1970) pointed out in a revolutionary article near the end of the behaviorist hegemony in psychology. When psychologists attempted to condition stimuli or responses that had substantial prior meaning for the organism, they found that the "laws of learning" they had established with meaningless stimuli and primary reinforcers did not hold. Instead of smooth, gradual learning curves, investigators tended to find abrupt, even "one-trial" learning or sometimes, no learning at all. For example, cats can be taught to pull a string to get food, but they cannot be taught to lick their coats to get food, despite the fact that the latter response has a far higher "operant" or basal level of occurrence. Similarly, pigeons will die sooner than learn to *not* peck at a screen in order to get food.

Relativity in Judgment and Motivation Phenomena

Adaptation level. Unease on the part of psychologists about the radical behaviorists' insistence on defining input and output in purely objective terms had been growing for decades. The Gestalt psychologists had long been fond of showing that absolute judgments of stimuli were not possible and that stimuli were always judged relative to other stimuli. A favorite demonstration was to present a rat with two light stimuli, one brighter than the other, and to reinforce pressing the lever under the less bright light. Then, on the test trial, the animal would be presented with the originally reinforced light and one still less bright. An objectivist account would hold that the rat would have to choose the originally reinforced light. But, instead, the rat chooses the new stimulus. What the rat has learned is not "go for the 20-watt light" but "go for the less bright light" – a judgment that requires an active interpreter of information, not an automaton that simply registers objective physical properties of the stimuli to which it is exposed.

The tradition of studying the relativity of judgment gained prominence within American experimental psychology through the work of Harry Helson (1964). He showed that judgments of stimulus magnitudes were always relative – relative, that is, to currently or just previously encountered stimuli of a similar kind. Thus a weight is judged as heavier when it is examined just after exposure to several lighter weights than just after exposure to several heavier ones. Water of a given temperature is judged cold after the subject's hand has been resting in hot water for a time and is judged warm after the subject's hand has been resting in cold water. The judgment of a contemporary stimulus therefore is always a function of at least two important factors – the value of the stimulus measured objectively and the subject's "adaptation level" to stimuli of a similar sort.

Framing effects. The recognition of the relativity of judgment has become a dominant thread in modern cognitive psychology. Modern decision theorists, in particular, have noted that people seem far more responsive to the prospect of changes in their state than to the absolute level they might reach as a result of a given decision (Kahneman & Tversky, 1979). More generally, people are highly subject to "framing" effects. They judge costs and benefits of various actions, and experience various degrees of regret about choices, not with respect to final outcomes but with respect to comparisons that are implicit or explicit in the presentation of the problem (Tversky & Kahneman, 1981). Thus people tend to choose one action if they judge it in relation to a given arbitrary starting point of wealth and to choose another action if they are maneuvered into thinking about a different starting point of wealth. Recently, Kahneman and Miller (1986) have extended this point to apply to all of cognition. They argue that every stimulus recruits comparison stimuli from memory against which it is judged. For example, the vegetable soup you taste now is compared with the vegetable soup you had last week, the minestrone you had last month, the canned vegetable soup you had as a child, and so on. All these together constitute the "norm" in terms of which the present stimulus is judged. To a behaviorist, such a view stops little short of nihilism. Since each individual has a different history, different memories will be constructed for the reference frame. Nothing could be further from the behaviorists' dream of identifying stimulus properties objectively, without reference to the black box inside the subject's head.

The relativist view in psychology has been shown to have objective behavioral and motivational consequences of just the sort the behaviorist is honor-bound to respect. For example, Kahneman and Tversky (1979) have shown, in their prospect theory treatment of choice, that there is an asymmetry between loss and gain situations such that people are more motivated to avoid a loss of a given size than to gain an equivalent amount. Such a principle helps us understand why it is that people are often goaded into action less by the prospect of gain than by the prospect of loss. Thus American labor unions boast with justification about their past successes in winning better working conditions, higher wages, and shorter work weeks for their members; but labor historians tell us that union growth and union militancy in this country actually was spurred less by promises of gain than by the threat and experience of loss. In particular, the greatest period of union growth, and the most stormy epoch in the history of organized labor, came in the early part of the twentieth century at a time when the influx of jobless immigrants prompted employers to cut wages – secure in the knowledge that such wages, a relative pittance, would be acceptable to newcomers who were desperate for work and who had very recently escaped from far more adverse social and economic circumstances.

Comparison with the past. Another example of the motivational importance of comparative assessment involves the past. Thus people often speak nostalgically about the "good old days," or they give thanks that the "hungry 30s," the horrors of World War II, or the scariest days of the Cold War lie behind us. Such memories of the past exert an influence on the present. Soviet colleagues whose families survived the mass starvation and other horrors of the "Thousand Day" siege of Leningrad by Nazi forces during World War II assure us that for the two following decades their compatriots felt comparatively well-off, and disinclined to condemn their leaders – despite food shortages and other privations that Western visitors found intolerable and presumed to offer ample motivation for political protest.

One of the most interesting motivational implications of the relativity of judgment is that both happiness and unhappiness should be selflimiting to a degree. This is the strong suggestion of work by Brickman et al. (1978), who studied people whose life circumstances were drastically changed by good fortune or tragedy. He discovered that lottery winners were at first overjoyed at their new estate; but after a year or two they proved to be no more satisfied with their lot than the rest of us. People who became paralyzed through injury, or who struggled with life-threatening diseases similarly seemed to adapt to their circumstances. At first miserable or even suicidal, they eventually became about as happy as the average person.

Thus it appears that emotional and motivational states fluctuate in response to very immediate or "local" changes in people's circumstances, not to the absolute level of satisfaction of needs. The "poor little rich girl" of folk wisdom exists. She got that way because she compares her giant teddy bear of today with the pony of yesterday and finds it wanting.

Social comparison and relative deprivation. A second type of comparison that weighs heavily in people's subjective assessment of their state, and in their subsequent motivation and behavior, involves other people, in particular, other people they deem to be socially relevant to themselves. Social comparison processes in self-appraisal, and their motivational consequences, were a central theme in social psychology from the 1930s through the 1950s (see especially Festinger, 1954). Perhaps the best example in the literature is one of the oldest. Stouffer (1950), in describing the attitudes and sentiments of American soldiers in World War II, noted a rather surprising discrepancy in morale between black soldiers stationed in the South and black soldiers stationed in the North. The surprise lay in the fact that, notwithstanding the South's restrictive segregationist laws and social practices, black soldiers stationed there were more satisfied with their lot than were black soldiers stationed in the North (regardless, incidentally, of whether they themselves were Southerners or Northerners). The paradox is readily resolved, however, when we bear in mind the relevant sources of social comparison. That is, the black soldiers stationed in the South felt well-off because they compared themselves primarily with the Southern blacks they observed outside the military, who faced even harsher social and economic circumstances than the soldiers themselves. Conversely, black soldiers stationed in the North were unhappy with their lot because they compared themselves with peers outside the military, who then were earning high wages and enjoying unprecedented opportunities to work in factories and industries that previously had employed only whites.

The notion that people's assessment of themselves is inherently a comparative one is part of the grain of social psychology by now (Strack, Martin, & Schwarz, 1988). People believe themselves to be talented or untalented, rich or poor, healthy or unhealthy by comparison with others (Tesser, 1980). Indeed, by strategic choice of reference groups people can enhance their feelings of self-worth and cope better with adversity (Taylor, 1983). Teachers who distribute grades, bosses who assign raises, and physicians who treat diseases in different populations ignore this principle at their peril.

Some Nonobvious Motivational Consequences of Reward

Just as judgments about stimuli were shown to be inherently relativistic and subjective, other work showed that subjective construals of the relationship between response and reinforcer are also inherently a matter of interpretation. Such interpretations have significant implications for subsequent motives and behavior. The dissonance theorists, led by Leon

Festinger, took particular delight in tweaking the noses of the behaviorists. They did this by showing repeatedly that they could invert the effects of reward on behavior by manipulating the meaning the subject placed on the relation between the reward and the behavior that elicited it. One classic dissonance paradigm (Festinger & Carlsmith, 1959), for instance, paid subjects for telling a fellow student that a particularly tedious and mindless experimental task they had just completed (rotating pegs on a pegboard) was actually quite interesting. The subjects did so, at the request of the experimenter, in preparing the student to be the next participant to undertake the boring task. The finding was that subjects were more likely to "internalize" the message – that is, to decide that the task really had been interesting – when the payment in question was $1.00 than when it was $20.00 (which, in 1959, would have constituted a fair wage for a whole day of semiskilled labor).

From the viewpoint of dissonance theory, with its emphasis on cognitive balance and rationalization, it was not difficult to explain this result. Subjects receiving a mere $1.00 payment, it was argued, felt dissonance about agreeing to deceive their peers and about saying something publicly that was discrepant from their actual views. Accordingly, they reduced their dissonance in the one way left open to them, that is, by deciding that they really had found the task at least somewhat interesting. By contrast, subjects receiving a $20.00 payment needed no such mental gymnastics to handle the discrepancy between their private beliefs and their public behavior. The $20.00 payment provided a psychologically adequate justification for their lie. Consequently, they felt little residual dissonance, and had no need to adjust their subjective evaluation of the boring task.

The larger point of the Festinger and Carlsmith study has now been demonstrated literally hundreds of times, and the underlying motivational basis also has been demonstrated clearly (Cooper, Zanna, & Taves, 1978; Steele, 1988). Providing people with small incentives for acting as if they hold a given belief promotes greater change in the "rewarded" direction than providing them with large incentives. This, of course, is quite contrary to the spirit of conventional reinforcement theory, which leads us to expect that large rewards would be more effective in leading actors to adopt privately the preferences or beliefs that they were expressing overtly.

An even more challenging result for mainstream reinforcement theorists was provided by demonstrations that rewarding a given behavior can actually decrease its attractiveness and the likelihood of its future occurrence. Perhaps the best-known study of this sort was one conducted by Lepper, Greene, and Nisbett (1973). These investigators reasoned that if people undertook a task that they normally would have found quite interesting and enjoyable, but did so while expecting to be rewarded for their efforts, they might engage in a bit of private cognitive analysis complementary to that shown by subjects in the dissonance experiments. That is, they might decide that they had engaged in the relevant task in order to obtain the promised reward, and therefore come to view the behavior in question as less attractive in its own right. In other words, they would come to view such behavior as a means to an end rather than an attractive end in itself, and thereafter, in the absence of a prospect for reward, show relatively little inclination to engage in the task.

The results (which we will deal with in more detail when we discuss "applications" in Chapter 8) confirmed this intriguing hypothesis. Preschool children who were offered a "good-player award" to draw with magic markers – something they had done with great relish in the absence of any extrinsic incentive during an earlier test period – showed relatively little interest in the markers when they subsequently were introduced as an ordinary classroom activity. By contrast, children who had neither anticipated nor received a "good-player award" for playing with the markers showed no such decrease in subsequent interest. Nor, we should note, did children who had not anticipated any reward for their play but had received one anyway. Anticipated reward, it appears, had changed the children's subjective interpretation of the magic marker activity from something highly reinforcing in its own right to something that one does in order to get reinforced. In short, "play" had been subjectively turned into "work."

We should make it clear that conventional reinforcement theory was not really contradicted, or at least it certainly wasn't contradicted in any decisive or irrefutable way, by Lepper and his colleagues. Nor was it decisively contradicted by the Festinger and Carlsmith study (although the investigators in question did take great delight in inducing professional colleagues, steeped in conventional reinforcement theory, to predict the result opposite to the one actually obtained). What these social psychology experiments really did was to point out the limited scope of conventional, purely objective accounts of motivation and learning. These results challenged psychologists to take a new look at their discipline. They showed the necessity of viewing people as active interpreters of their environment and of their own responses to the environment.

THE CONSTRUAL QUESTION IN SOCIAL PSYCHOLOGY

"A man never steps into the same stream twice," the Greeks enjoined us to remember, because the stream is different and the man is different. William James rebelled against the mechanistic spirit of nineteenth-century psychology on just these grounds. He noted that ideas cannot be considered to be fixed and static, because they take on different coloration from the ideas by which they are surrounded and with which they are compared: ". . . *no state once gone can recur and be identical with what it was before*" *(1890/1948,* p. 154, italics in original). Consequently, "no two 'ideas' are ever exactly the same . . ." (p. 157).

Lawrence Barsalou (1987) has given this idea a modem interpretation and presented some interesting data in support of it. Barsalou argues that, "Rather than being retrieved as static units from memory to represent categories, concepts originate in a highly flexible process that retrieves generic and episodic information from long-term memory to construct temporary concepts in working memory" (p. 101). The common-sense assumption would be that a given individual's notion of such basic categories as "bird," "fruit," "vehicles," and "things to pack in a suitcase" would be a constant. But Barsalou has shown that there is a nontrivial degree of instability even in such familiar, often-used categories. Thus when he had subjects rate twice within a single month several exemplars of such categories, for example, "robin," "pigeon," "parrot," as to how typical they were of the concept, the subjects gave typicality ratings on the two different occasions that correlated with each other in the vicinity of .80. A correlation of .80 is, of course, a very high one; nevertheless, it falls substantially short of perfect predictability of the meaning of a category on one occasion from knowledge of its meaning on another. Moreover, the interpretation of any given complex situation requires the application of many categories, some of which are less clear-cut in their meaning than the simple ones examined by Barsalou. The likelihood that two literally identical situations will be judged the same on two different occasions therefore plummets rather rapidly as a function of complexity.

Barsalou also found that the correlation between any two subjects, all of whom were college students at the same university, averaged around .45. Thus agreement on typicality of exemplars, even for very common categories, is only modest.

These two findings are very important to arguments that we will return to repeatedly in this chapter and in this book. First, there is significant variability in a given person's construal of events, enough to lead us, just on the grounds of interpretive instability, to expect that there will be nontrivial variation in behavior across two objectively almost identical situations, to say nothing of the variation from one situation to another that is merely similar. Second, there is very substantial variability from one person to another in the meaning even of rather fundamental concepts. Hence, any two people are likely to interpret the same situation in somewhat different ways. We will argue that a great many important phenomena derive from the variability of construal within a person and from the differences in construal between people on any given occasion. Further phenomena of importance derive from people's relative ignorance of these two facts. We do not recognize the inherent variability in our own construal of events; hence we predict our own behavior with too great confidence. We similarly fail to recognize both the random (or at least unpredictable) differences between our own and others' construals of events and the systematic, stable differences. Consequently, we predict other people's behavior too confidently and, when confronted with surprising behavior on the part of another person, attribute it to extreme personality traits or to motivational differences between ourselves and the other person, rather than recognizing that the other person may simply have been construing the situation differently.

The insight that the same stimulus often can be interpreted in different ways by different people or by the same person in different contexts, and the recognition that the social scientist must therefore attend to subjective interpretations as well as objective measurements, has a long tradition within most of the major fields of psychology. Kurt Lewin (1935) consistently emphasized that the individual's "life space" must be characterized in a way that captures its (contemporary) subjective reality and personal significance. The Gestalt psychologists (for example, Koffka, 1935) gave similar emphasis to the subjective dimension, as did Brunswik's (1956) theories of social perception. Most notably of all, perhaps, the advice to focus on the patient's own subjective representation of events had been echoed by successive generations of clinicians – from Freud's (1901/1960) analysis of biases in perceptions and memory to Kelly's (1955) seminal discussion of "personal constructs." But the discussions of the construal problem that most clearly identified systematic factors contributing to variability and instability of meaning were provided by Solomon Asch – the investigator who conducted the famous conformity experiments discussed in Chapter 2.

Solomon Asch and the "Object of Judgment"

Asch's primary thesis was that people's responses to an object are often less reflective of their long-held attitudes and values than of the way they happen to construe the "object of judgment" on a given occasion. Asch illustrated this thesis in a memorable series of experiments and theoretical analyses that identified the sorts of factors that produce variability within and across people in construals of events.

Conformity and construal. The first phenomenon to which Asch applied his construal interpretation was social conformity. Conventional views of conformity held that people are influenced by the views of their peers because they seek acceptance and fear rejection by those peers. Without disputing such motives, Asch offered an additional, more cognitive, explanation. The responses of one's peers, Asch insisted, serve to *define* the object being evaluated. Such responses convey information about the way that object is understood by other actors, and offer at least a strong suggestion about the way it "ought" to be interpreted. Moreover, once one adopts the interpretation or definition offered by one's peers, one is likely to adopt their evaluations and ways of behaving as well.

Asch (1940) supported this argument with a very simple but compelling experiment. Two groups of undergraduates were asked to rank various professions in terms of their prestige or status. Included on the list was the profession of "politician." Before offering their own rankings, the subjects in one of the groups were told that a sample of their peers had previously ranked politicians more highly than virtually any other profession, while those in the other groups were told that their peers had ranked politicians at the bottom of the list. This manipulation of peer consensus, as expected, had a marked effect on the subjects' own rankings. But, as Asch confirmed with postexperimental interviews and questionnaires, this effect did not occur because subjects had changed their views either about politicians in general or about any specific politicians. Nor were the subjects trying to curry favor with their peers or escape censure, for they believed that the anonymous peers who had been the source of the earlier rankings would never meet them nor hear about their assessments. What the subjects' "conformity" reflected was the extent to which their peers' rankings had effectively dictated the meaning or construal of the term "politician." In the first group, where subjects conformed to a positive assessment, the term "politician" was taken by the subjects to refer to statesmen and celebrated national leaders like Jefferson or Roosevelt. In the second group, where subjects conformed to a negative assessment, the term "politician" had the connotation of corrupt political hack. In short, subjects did not yield to the judgments of their peers as much as they allowed their peers to dictate what it was that they were judging.

Construal of personal attributes. Once again using a very simple research paradigm, this time one in which subjects were given lists of personality traits and then asked to make various judgments about the person who allegedly possessed the traits, Asch attempted to show the influence of construal processes on impression formation. One phenomenon involved the seemingly disproportionate impact of certain "central" evaluation dimensions such as warmth versus coldness. Asch argued that the stimulus traits on his list (like virtually all isolated bits of information one possesses about a person) were susceptible to variable interpretation – and that the specific meaning or construal attached to particular items of information depended upon the more global impressions adopted by the subjects. Thus a seemingly straightforward descriptive term like "intelligent" would have very different connotations when construed in light of a positive global impression of warmth than when the same term was construed in light of a negative impression of coldness. In the former case, "intelligent" means something like "sensible, wise, insightful, and stimulating"; in the latter case, its connotation is closer to "cunning and scheming," or perhaps, "detached intellectual brilliance of a haughty, cynical, and inhuman variety."

Asch also offered a similar "construal" explanation for primacy effects in impression formation. Initial items on a trait list (like most formative experiences), he argued, lead us to develop tentative hypotheses that, in turn, dictate the way we construe or interpret later evidence. Accordingly, initial items of information exert disproportionate influence on judgments; and the same set of items presented in different orders gives rise to different overall assessments. In particular, positive pieces of evidence followed by negative ones produce more positive overall impressions than the same items of information presented in reverse order. This means that our construals of events are at the mercy of the often arbitrary sequence in which we encounter them. Having heard first about Joe's exemplary work for local charities and only later about his rather messy divorce, we like him and are rather sympathetic to his personal problems. Having heard first about the divorce and only later about the charitable work, we think he's a brute cynically trying to improve his image on the backs on the community's more unfortunate members. Thus, in contrast to critics who insisted that initial information has greater impact than later information because it receives more attention or is weighted more heavily (N. H. Anderson, 1974; Wishner, 1960), Asch insisted that the earlier information literally changed the *meaning* of the later information.

Construal and communicator credibility. Asch also applied his controversial change of meaning hypothesis in helping to illuminate the seemingly straightforward finding that arguments produce more attitude change in the people who read them when they are attributed to well-regarded (that is, attractive, trustworthy, or expert) communication sources than when they are attributed to poorly regarded sources. Conventional learning theory interpretations of this effect hinged on the fact that messages associated with attractive and highly credible sources would be attended to more closely, recalled more successfully, regarded as more accurate and reliable, and deemed more worthy of adoption by the recipient, than the same messages associated with unattractive, noncredible sources (Hovland, Janis, & Kelley, 1953). Asch, however, again offered a less conventional, and more "dynamic," hypothesis. As in the case of social conformity, he argued that the information about sources conveyed by the experimenter induces a change not in the "judgment of the object" but rather in "the object of judgment." The very meaning of the message, Asch (1948, 1952) insisted, changes as a function of the source to which it is attributed. Thus, to cite Asch's classic example, an assertion to the effect that "a little rebellion, now and then, is a good thing" is much more widely endorsed when attributed to Jefferson than to Lenin, because it has a different meaning in the former case than in the latter. When the statement comes from Thomas Jefferson, it conjures up images of honest farmers and tradespeople throwing off the yoke of corrupt and indifferent rulers. When it comes from Lenin, the images (at least to Americans) are quite different – a revolutionary reign of terror in which mobs run amok and harsh new authoritarians take the place of the old oppressors. Given these differences in construal, it is hardly surprising that the rebellion championed by Jefferson is endorsed more enthusiastically than the one championed by Lenin.

Partisanship and Perception

Asch's studies convinced most social psychologists that construals can readily be manipulated, and that such manipulations can have profound effects on people's judgments. A few years later, a classic study by Albert Hastorf and Hadley Cantril (1954) showed that motives can exert the same effects. In this study, Dartmouth and Princeton football fans both viewed the same film of a particularly rough gridiron struggle between their respective teams. Despite the constancy of the objective stimulus, the opposing partisans' assessments of what they had viewed suggested that they "saw" two different games. The Princeton fans saw a continuing saga of Dartmouth atrocities and occasional Princeton retaliations. The Dartmouth fans saw brutal Princeton provocations and occasional measured Dartmouth responses. Each side, in short, saw a struggle in which their side were the "good guys" and the other side were the "bad guys." And each side thought this "truth" ought to be apparent to any objective observers of the same events.

Thirty years after the Hastorf and Cantril classic, research undertaken by Lepper and Ross and their colleagues focused again on the divergent construals of opposing partisans. Lord, Lepper, and Ross (1979; see also Nisbett & Ross, 1980; Ross & Lepper, 1980) showed that two opposing partisan groups respond to the same body of mixed and inconclusive evidence by increasing the strength and polarization of their respective beliefs. This polarization effect, it seemed, occurred because the subjects in both partisan groups tended to accept evidence supportive of their own position uncritically, while at the same time critically scrutinizing and "explaining away" evidence that was equally probative but that ran counter to their position. Thus, both proponents and opponents of capital punishment who were asked to read a mixed package of evidence about the deterrent value of the death penalty came away with their views strengthened. Both sides took comfort from the evidence in support of their position, and both sides had no trouble seeing the flaws in evidence for the opposing view.

Building on these results, Vallone, Ross, and Lepper (1985) reasoned that the same biases in assimilation of evidence should influence the reactions the partisan groups have to third parties who offer evaluations, or even summary reports, of any evidence relevant to the dispute. Specifically, the partisans should perceive even maximally objective or evenhanded evaluations – and those who offer them – as unfairly biased and hostile.

This prediction of a "hostile media" effect was borne out in studies examining partisan responses to media coverage of the 1980 and 1984 presidential elections and to television news coverage of the 1982 massacre of civilians in Lebanese refugee camps. Data from the latter study, which presented pro-Arab and pro-Israeli viewers with videotapes of network newscasts, were particularly compelling. On measure after measure there was virtually no overlap in the evaluations offered by the two partisan groups. Pro-Arab and pro-Israeli viewers alike were convinced that the other side had been favored by the media, that their side had been treated unfairly, and that these biases in reporting had reflected the personal interests and ideologies of those responsible for the programs.

Interestingly, the results of this study suggested a type of disagreement that had not been anticipated (but one that perhaps should have been expected on the basis of the earlier Hastorf and Cantril classic). Rather than simply disagreeing about whether the tone and emphasis of the newscasts were appropriate in view of the immediate facts and long-standing history of dispute, the two partisan groups seemed to disagree about what they actually had seen. Thus both pro-Arab and pro-Israeli viewers of the same 30-minute videotapes reported that the other side had enjoyed a greater proportion of favorable facts and references, and a smaller proportion of negative ones, than their own side. Both groups also believed that the overall tone, emphasis, and message of the videotapes was such that it would lead neutral viewers to change their attitudes in a direction favorable to the other group and hostile to their own. Interviewing these subjects and hearing their comments, in fact, made one wonder whether they had seen the same newscasts (to say nothing of the same Mideast history), just as interviewing Hastorf and Cantril's subjects made one wonder if they had seen the same game.

The same conceptual analysis that applied to partisan evaluations of news coverage can be applied to partisan evaluations of proposed plans to deal with problems that the media cover. Imagine how the pro-Arab and pro-Israeli viewers in the hostile media study would have evaluated the efforts of some "nonpartisan" group that tried to fix blame, suggest punishments, or propose measures to avoid such tragedies in the future. Better still, imagine how they would respond, not to thirdparty initiatives, but to proposals offered by the other side. Any proposal that seems equitable and forthcoming to the partisan group offering it would likely seem inequitable and self-serving to the partisan group receiving it – both because the two sides are apt to differ in what they believe to be "fair" (in the light of their divergent views of history and what the important issues are) and because they are apt to differ in the way they construe the specific terms and overall balance of the proposal itself. There is, however, an additional construal bias that comes into play in bilateral negotiation, and it constitutes a further barrier to conflict resolution. The very act of offering a proposal might lessen its attractiveness, and perhaps even change its meaning, to the recipient.

A series of studies by Stillinger, Epelbaum, Keltner, and Ross (1989) tested this "reactive devaluation" hypothesis. One such study took advantage of a conflict between the Stanford University administration and various campus groups demanding that Stanford divest itself of all holdings in American companies doing business in South Africa. The particular focus of the study was on student responses to various compromise proposals that would have stopped short of total divestiture but nevertheless signaled the University's opposition to the racist apartheid policies of the South African regime. Two such compromise proposals were of particular interest: One was a proposal that the University immediately divest itself of stockholdings in companies that had been specifically linked to the South African military, to the police, or to apartheid practices in the workplace (that is, a proposal for "partial" divestiture); an alternative was a proposal that the University specify a two-year deadline for major reforms in the apartheid system, after which total divestiture would follow if the reforms in question had not occurred (that is, a proposal for a "deadline"). When students were simply told (accurately) that the University was considering both proposals, along with many others, the two proposals were rated to be about equally satisfactory and significant. When the students were led to believe that the University was about to ratify one of these two compromise proposals, however, the reactive devaluation phenomenon was apparent. That is, when the University was purported to be ready to enact the partial divestiture plan, a clear majority rated this concession to be less satisfactory and significant than the nonoffered alternative of a deadline for total divestiture. Conversely, when students were told that the University was about to propose a deadline plan, the clear majority rated this plan as less satisfactory and significant than a plan for immediate, albeit only partial, divestiture.

The final chapter in this research story was written a few months later, when the University at last decided to take action against apartheid by approving a plan rather similar to (but somewhat more comprehensive than) the partial divestment plan that had been attributed to it in the earlier study. As it happened, the investigators learned the details of this plan before it was made public. Accordingly, they were able to measure the partisan students' evaluations of its provisions twice – first, before the announcement, when it could be described as merely one of several hypothetical possibilities, and then after the public announcement, when it was no longer hypothetical. As predicted, the students' ratings of the University's plan decreased significantly from the first evaluation to the second; and also as predicted, partisans soundly criticized the University's plan as "token" and "too little too late."

These studies allow us to see the first step in a process that is all too likely to promote distrust and misunderstanding in the negotiation process (Ross & Stillinger, 1991). The party offering the compromise proposal is bound to be disappointed, and even resentful, when its proposal meets a cool reception and its concessions are dismissed as trivial or even self-serving. The party responding coolly is apt to be similarly chagrined when its response provokes accusations of bad faith. What both sides fail to recognize, of course, is the extent to which the other side is responding to a subjectively different, and decidedly less appealing, proposal.

The Tools of Construal

Beyond recognizing that the construal process occurs, and that construals are apt to differ from one person to the next and from one judgment context to the next, social scientists have long sought to understand the construal process itself. The great sociologist W. I. Thomas (Thomas & Znaniecki, 1918) talked about the influence of the individual's unique life history in defining that individual's personal and social reality (see also Ball, 1972; Schutz, 1970). The symbolic interactionists (for example, Goffman, 1959; Mead, 1934) discussed the processes by which situational definitions are "negotiated" through social interaction. Farr and Moscovici (1984) have argued that such discourse creates "collective representations" of objects and events that are shared by the members of a given society. And the role that culture, subculture, and even gender play in creating construal differences and resulting misunderstandings has been commented upon frequently by psychologists, sociologists, and anthropologists alike (Abbey, 1982; D'Andrade, 1981; Forgas, 1976; Shweder, 1991; Triandis, 1972; Waller, 1961). It has been modern cognitive psychologists, however, who have done the most to document the process by which perceivers, in Bruner's (1957) famous words, "go beyond the information given."

Two related aspects of the construal process have received particular attention. The first aspect involves labeling or categorizing – that is, deciding on the kind of object, person, or event one is encountering, and hence forming expectations about specific characteristics or properties one is likely to experience. The second aspect of construal involves the resolution of ambiguity – that is, the filling in of gaps in information, and the possible reinterpretation of information that seems incongruent with the label or category one has assigned. Propagandists and other would-be manipulators of public opinion understand the importance of these two aspects of construal. Labels like "freedom fighter" versus "terrorist" are chosen not only to evoke overall positive or negative affective responses but also to encourage us to make additional inferences, consistent with the connotations of those labels (that is, virtuous, self-sacrificing patriots versus cruel, anomic psychotics) that will heighten our sympathy or distaste. The labels that spokespersons use to frame public debate about abortion, public funding of medical costs, and preferential hiring of minorities (i.e., reproductive *freedom* versus *murder* of the fetus, health *insurance* versus *socialistic* medicine, *affirmative* action versus *discrimination* against nonminorities) are similar attempts to manipulate our judgments by controlling the way we construe the particular objects of judgment.

In recent years cognitive psychologists have speculated about the types of "knowledge structures" that underlie and direct the construal process. Particular emphasis has been given to structures that capture our generic knowledge and understanding not just of static objects and categories (trees, cars, houses, birds, and the like) but also of dynamic event sequences. The term "schema" (Bartlett, 1932; Piaget, 1930) was the earliest, and remains the most popular, term used to describe such dynamic knowledge structures. For example, the child learns a "conservation schema," or set of rules, that tell the child what to expect about changes in quantity of material as its shape changes. More recently, the provocative term "script" (Abelson, 1981; Schank & Abelson, 1977) has come into use to capture our understanding of the ways in which people in many familiar settings play well-defined roles and choose from among specified behavioral options (for example, the *restaurant* script, the *birthday party* script, the *university lecture* script, and so on). The notion underlying the script concept is that predictable, even ritualistic, interactions occur between people who are attempting to satisfy their needs with as little social stress and cognitive strain as possible.

The details of different types of knowledge structures need not concern us here, only the sorts of work they accomplish. It is now well documented by researchers that by employing preexisting schemas and other knowledge structures, the social perceiver is permitted to make inferences and judgments with heightened ease, speed, and subjective confidence. To the extent that we employ knowledge structures that are generally accurate in their generic representation, and to the extent that we refrain from employing them too quickly, broadly, or "mindlessly" (Langer, 1989), the consequences of schematic processing are entirely salutary. Time and energy are saved, rumination and doubt are reduced, and nothing important is lost. But there is an obvious cost to our reliance upon the scripts, schemas, and other knowledge structures that help us interpret our world. When the cognitive representations we happen to choose or are led to employ turn out to be inaccurate in important respects, or when we employ them inappropriately (two almost inevitable problems whenever we venture into new social or intellectual terrain), the results are far less salutary. We are bound to make errors in interpretation or judgment, and we are apt to be slow both in recognizing that our preconceptions were wrong and in learning the lessons offered by our new experiences. Thus rapid and easy understanding as well as persistent, painful misunderstanding; warranted confidence as well as overconfident stubbornness; the capacity to be enlightened and informed as well as the capacity to be manipulated and misled are intimately related, indeed complementary, consequences of the tools that we all rely upon to construe our social environments. (See reviews by Cantor & Kihlstrom, 1987; Fiske & Taylor, 1990; Hamilton, Dugan, & Trolier, 1985; Markus & Zajonc, 1985; Nisbett & Ross, 1980; Petty & Cacioppo, 1985; Rumelhart, 1980.)

For present purposes, what is most important about these various tools of construal is that they are carriers of both individual differences in interpretations of events and of instability of interpretation over time within the same individual. Just which knowledge structure is elicited, as well as the precise contents of knowledge structures representing particular aspects of the world, differ from person to person and from occasion to occasion.

THE ATTRIBUTION PROCESS

One particular type of subjective construal became a central concern of both theoretical and applied social psychology in the 1970s. This is the causal attribution process that people engage in as they attempt to understand the relation between social situations and behavior, and the relation between behavior and outcomes. There is a set of related attribution tasks, including inferences about the relative importance of various causal factors, inferences about the personal characteristics and capacities of the people we observe (including ourselves), and predictions, based on these attributions, about the likelihood of various future actions and outcomes. Such subjective interpretations, it is clear from research, have extremely important consequences in terms of objective behavior.

Whether one's concern is a laboratory rat's "decision" about the wisdom of continuing to press a lever in the absence of continuing reinforcement, a college sophomore's decision about whether to take an advanced chemistry course after earning an A in the introductory course, or an employer's decision about whether to offer encouragement or criticism to a salesperson whose sales have fallen off in recent months, it is the decision-maker's perceptions about the causes of relevant past events that will determine the decision.

Normative and Descriptive Principles of Causal Attribution

In 1967, Harold Kelley, building on the work of many investigators, including Heider (1958), de Charms (1968), and Jones and Davis (1965), brought the topic of attribution to the center stage of social psychology, where it has been ever since. Kelley's approach was novel in that it was both normative and descriptive. He proposed a set of principles or decision criteria that would promote accurate attributions, and he further suggested that people generally are guided by these principles. These normative and descriptive principles, not coincidentally, were closely analogous to the principles of statistical analysis commonly employed by scientists and statisticians when they perform an "analysis of variance." Thus Kelley suggested that in trying to understand why a person acted in a particular way, one calls on one's knowledge of or guesses about the way the person has acted in other similar situations (distinctiveness data), the way the person has acted in the same situation in the past (consistency data), and the way other people have acted in the same situation (consensus data). Cause is then attributed to the factors with which the effect seems to "covary." For example, in trying to decide why John liked the new thriller playing at the Bijoux (that is, deciding whether this film is really worth seeing or whether John's response merely tells us something about his tastes), we consider how John and other filmgoers have responded on past occasions to this film, and to lots of other films. We then observe whether it is John or this particular film that is most strongly associated with positive reviews. If John raves about all films, or at least all "thrillers," or if other filmgoers have been unenthusiastic about this particular film, we are disinclined to think that John's rave tells us very much about the film's quality. If, on the other hand, John rarely offers raves (especially to thrillers playing at the likes of the Bijoux), or if other filmgoers share John's enthusiasm for this particular film, we start making plans to go to the Bijoux next Saturday.

Kelley (1972) proposed a second attribution principle to supplement this covariation rule, one that could be employed in the case where one possesses no information about the actor's response to other related stimuli or about the responses of other actors to this particular stimulus.

This principle involves discounting any particular cause or explanation to the extent that one can discern the presence and possible influence of other potential causes. Thus, if John tells us that he loved the film at the Bijoux, we discount the quality of the film as a potential cause of his praise to the extent that we can think of other plausible reasons for his response (for example, the fact that he gets a commission on every ticket sold, or the suspicion that he wants us to go to the Bijoux next Saturday so he can get a ride home from his job at the fast-food restaurant next door).

Not surprisingly, researchers (for example, McArthur, 1972; Orvis, Cunningham, & Kelley, 1975) have been able to show that people can and often do use information about covarying causes and effects and about competing causal candidates in much the way that Kelley predicted. However, it has been the *exceptions* to accurate, or at least normatively sound, attribution practices on the part of the layperson that have attracted most attention and controversy in subsequent research. One particularly important set of biases constitutes the fundamental attribution error. This is the tendency for people to overlook situational causes of actions and outcomes in favor of dispositional ones. We will discuss these biases (Nisbett & Ross, 1980; Ross, 1977) later in this chapter and in great detail in Chapter 5. First, however, we must discuss some important research and theory suggesting that similar attribution processes, and similar attributional biases, may take place when the individual whose actions are being interpreted, and the individual doing the interpreting, are one and the same.

Attributions Regarding the Self

The notion that people strive to understand the causes of events in the world around them using the best cognitive tools at their disposal is scarcely controversial. It is far more controversial, and far more surprising, to suggest that people use the same inferential tools and are susceptible to many of the same errors and biases when it is their own feelings and actions that they are trying to understand. Two lines of work that went on simultaneously in the 1960s converged on this important idea about self-perception and self-attribution.

Schachter and Singer's "attribution" theory of emotion. In 1962, Stanley Schachter and Jerome Singer published a famous paper offering a startlingly new theory about emotion. Their contention was that people's subjective emotional experiences – that is, the way they label their feelings and the way they respond to triggering stimuli – may not depend strictly on the nature of their internal physiological state. Such sensations, Schachter and Singer argued, tend to be too diffuse and nonspecific to give rise to our diverse emotional experiences. Instead, emotional experience and emotional behavior depend on the inferences we make about the causes of our arousal. If the most plausible source of our arousal is a slapstick movie we are watching, we feel amused or happy and we laugh. If the most plausible explanation for our arousal is the snarling Doberman Pinscher running at us, or an insulting comment about our ancestry, we feel, respectively, afraid or angry, and act accordingly. And if the most plausible source of the same clammy palms, racing heartbeat, and rapid shallow breathing is an attractive member of the opposite sex, we feel sexual attraction. But if the most plausible explanation for these physiological symptoms is provided by a physician's warning that such symptoms are common side effects of the adrenaline injection we have just received, we feel no real emotion, and show no inclination to act emotionally.

While many contemporary theorists would challenge Schachter and Singer's ideas about the lack of physiological specificity in emotional experience, few now would deny that we can be led to mislabel our feelings and to reach erroneous conclusions about the source of such feelings. There is also considerable evidence that people who are undergoing an emotion-provoking experience may feel and act less emotional if they are led to attribute their bodily symptoms to a source that is nonemotional. Thus subjects who received a "drug" (actually a sugar-pill placebo) that they believed would make them feel aroused, just before undergoing a series of increasingly intense electric shocks, found those shocks less painful than control condition subjects, and actually tolerated four times the amperage before indicating that their pain threshold had been reached (Nisbett & Schachter, 1966). Similarly, subjects who had just taken a pill that they believed would make them feel aroused proved to be more willing than control subjects to cheat in grading their own exams – presumably because they misattributed to the drug the arousal that was actually produced by the prospect of cheating or by the prospect of getting caught (Dienstbier & Munter, 1971).

Bem's "attribution" theory of self-reported attitudes. At roughly the same time that Schachter and Singer were claiming that people label their emotions on the basis of plausible causal attributions, a young social psychologist named Daryl Bem was offering essentially the same thesis about the way people label their attitudes and beliefs.

Bem (1967, 1972) argued that people make inferences about their attitudes, and their preferences and personal dispositions as well, by examining their overt behavior and the context in which it occurs – just as they would in making such inferences about other people. Thus, one responds to the question, "do you like brown bread?" by reasoning, "I guess I do; I'm always eating it, and no one is forcing me to do so." Or one responds to the question, "do you like psychology?" by saying,

"I must like it; I take psych courses all the time and it isn't even my major." Bem's radical thesis, and the many self-perception experiments it eventually inspired, suggests that actors, like observers, may inappropriately infer personal attributes instead of recognizing the extent to which their behavior has reflected situational pressures and constraints rather than enduring traits or dispositions. More generally, it implies that people may be obliged to figure out the causes of their overt behavior – just as Schachter and Singer's work implies that people are obliged to figure out the causes of the covert feelings of arousal – using the same types of theories and evidence that they would use in making judgments about other people, with little if any "privileged access" to the cognitive processes and events that underlie such responses. As we will see next, there is ample evidence that people often are as much in the dark about the causes of their behavior as Bem's thesis implied.

Awareness of mental processes. Why are the results of dissonance and arousal attribution studies so surprising? A little thought reveals that it is because one does not typically observe oneself engaging in the cognitive processes postulated to underlie the effects in question. That is, one does not observe oneself changing one's attitudes to bring them into line with behavior. And one does not observe oneself taking into account the origin of a state of arousal in deciding how to feel about the situation in which the arousal takes place. Nevertheless, countless experiments leave us with no choice but to assume that such high-level mental activity does go on outside of awareness.

How general is such unconscious, high-level processing of information? Nisbett and Wilson (1977) argued that it is very prevalent indeed. In fact, they argued that there is no direct access to cognitive processes at all; instead, there is access only to the ideas and inferences that are the outputs resulting from such processes. Some processes, such as the algorithms for solving well-formed problems, have verbal concomitants that may accompany and track the processes, and thus we may be quite accurate about the way we reached a judgment or conclusion. (For example, "I recognized that this must be a conservation of energy problem and applied the appropriate formula.") But for many problems, especially novel ones involving social judgment, there is very little conscious representation of underlying cognitive processes. Thus, for example, when subjects were asked to rate applicants for a job, they were no more accurate in reporting on the factors that affected their appraisal than they were in reporting on the factors that affected someone else's appraisal. Jack's reports about what influenced his judgment were no more accurate for his judgments than they were for Pete's. Similarly, college women were no more accurate in reporting the factors that caused day-to-day shifts in their own mood than they were in predicting what factors affected another woman's mood (Weiss & Brown, 1977). Indeed, they showed no net accuracy at all in their causal reports either for themselves or for others. People have theories about what effects their judgments and behavior just as they have theories about all kinds of social processes. These theories, rather than any introspective access to mental processes, seem to be the origin of people's reports about the influences on their judgment and behavior. Moreover, many of these theories are demonstrably poor ones. (See Wilson & Stone, 1985.)

The generalization that we have little access to our cognitive processes carries over to the main concerns of this chapter, as we will see in the next section. Although we are aware of some construal processes of conscious speculation about the causes of someone else's behavior, for example – we are unaware of other construal processes. What feels like direct perception of the stimulus is often highly mediated by construal processes that lie outside the purview of consciousness. It therefore feels like we "call 'em as they are," rather than "as we see 'em." This lack of awareness of our own construal processes blinds us to the possibility that someone else, differently situated, might construe the same objects in a different way. When we find that someone else has appraised the stimulus differently from the way we have appraised it, we leap to conclusions about unusual dispositions or strong motives on the part of the other person. These often erroneous conclusions could be avoided if we were aware of the major role of construal processes, and of the variability inherent in them. People sometimes construe the same object differently because they view it from different angles, rather than because they are fundamentally different people.

FAILURE TO ALLOW FOR THE UNCERTAINTIES OF CONSTRUAL

Like Solomon Asch, we have suggested that when people differ in their perceptions or behavior, the divergence may reflect differences not in the "judgment of the object" but in the construal of just what "the object of judgment" is. One of the most important consequences of this state of affairs is that when people make incorrect inferences about situational details, or fail to recognize that the same situation can be construed in different ways by different people, they are likely to draw erroneous conclusions about individuals whose behavior they learn about or observe. The real source of difficulty does not lie in the fact that human beings subjectively define the situations they face, nor even in the fact that they do so in variable and unpredictable ways. Rather, the problem lies in their failure to recognize and make adequate inferential *allowance* for this variability and unpredictability. In the remainder of this chapter we will illustrate how this failing has been at the heart of inferential and attributional shortcomings that have preoccupied social psychologists and cognitive psychologists over the past two decades. Once again we will take the liberty of focusing on phenomena that we have dealt with in our own research (Nisbett & Ross, 1980; Ross, 1990).

The False Consensus Effect

In a study of attributional shortcomings, Ross, Greene, and House (1977) asked subjects to read descriptions of a series of hypothetical situations, each of which posed a choice between two response alternatives. For each situation, subjects indicated what their own response would be, estimated the commonness of their own and the opposite response alternative, and assessed the degree to which each alternative would permit strong and confident inferences about the personal dispositions of people making that choice. One scenario, for instance, described the following dilemma:

> As you are leaving your neighborhood supermarket, a man in a business suit asks whether you like shopping in that store. You reply quite honestly that you do like shopping there and indicate that in addition to being close to your home, the supermarket seems to have very good meats and produce at reasonably low prices. The man then reveals that a videotape crew has filmed your comments and asks you to sign a release allowing them to use the unedited film for a TV commercial the supermarket chain is preparing. Would you agree or refuse to sign the release? (Ross et al., 1977)

The principal finding, which was termed the false consensus effect, involved the tendency for people to rate their own particular choice in the dilemma as more common, and less reflective of personal dispositions, than the alternative. Thus people who thought they would sign the release also assumed that most ordinary people would do likewise and that the minority who failed to do so would probably be unusually shy or distrustful. People who thought they would not sign assumed that refusal would be the majority response and that the minority who agreed would be unusually gullible or exhibitionistic.

This phenomenon is similar to one that has been called "egocentric attribution." Reports of findings resembling this false consensus effect had appeared sporadically in the social perception and attribution literatures (Holmes, 1968; Katz & Allport, 1931; Kelley & Stahelski, 1970). Generally, the interpretations offered for such phenomena had been motivational, centering on peoples' need to feel that their behavioral choices are rational and normative. Ross and colleagues suggested that a more cognitive process also might have played some role. The situational descriptions to which subjects had responded, it was noted, necessarily left a lot of details and contextual information to the subjects' imagination. Inevitably, different subjects would resolve ambiguities, fill in details, in short, construe the hypothetical situations, in different ways; and in so doing, they would be on their way to showing the false consensus effect.

Consider, for example, what is not specified in the brief description of the hypothetical supermarket encounter: What exactly did the "man in a business suit" look like, and how exactly did he make his request? (Was he a fast-talking huckster wearing a pinky ring, or a pleasant, clean-cut chap whom one would hate to disappoint?) How were you dressed at the time? (Were you in sweaty jogging togs, or in a snappy new outfit?) And what, exactly, did you say, and how did you say it? (Were you fluent and witty, or inarticulate and a little silly?) Beyond these details of content and context, there are questions of prior experience. (Have you seen commercials of this sort in the past, and if so, what did you think of the people who appeared in them?) There is also the question of your thoughts and feelings at the time of the request. (What kind of mood were you in, and what else was going on in your life?) What specific ideas were invoked by the request and by the context in which it occurred? (Did you experience fears about "being exploited," adhere to norms about helping out someone who is "just doing his job," feel joy or dread at the notoriety of "being seen on television?") Obviously, some readers of the scenario would fill in more of these unspecified contextual details than others. But the way in which you happen to resolve such ambiguities would influence not only the hypothetical response you specified for yourself, but also your estimates of consensus and your assessment of the "meaning" of the two possible responses.

The fact that ambiguities exist in written or oral accounts, and the likelihood that they will be resolved differently by different individuals, is rich in its implications – especially in a world where so much of the knowledge we have about each other's actions does, indeed, come secondhand. But the issue of semantic ambiguity raises a question about the generality of the false consensus effect. That is, does it occur only for hypothetical secondhand descriptions and reports, or does it also occur in our evaluations of real actions that we personally experience? To answer this question, the investigators conducted a study that forced subjects to face a real dilemma, make a real choice, and then offer consensus estimates and personal attributions about individuals who purportedly had responded to the same dilemma. While participating in what they thought was a study on "communication techniques," subjects were asked if they would be willing to walk around campus for 30 minutes wearing a large sandwich-board sign bearing a simple message (EAT AT JOE'S) so they could record the responses of their peers to this "unusual communication technique." The experimenter made it clear to subjects that they could easily opt out of the sandwich-board study (and sign up for some later study) even though he obviously would prefer that they agree to participate. At that point, he asked them first for their own decision, then for estimates about the probable decisions of other students in general, and finally for some trait inferences about a pair of individuals who had allegedly agreed or refused to participate when given the same choice as the subject.

This "real" dilemma confirmed the findings of the questionnaire studies. Overall, subjects who agreed to wear the sandwich-board sign estimated that 62% of their peers would make the same choice. Subjects who refused to wear the sign estimated that only 33% of their peers would comply with the experimenter's request. "Compliant" and "noncompliant" subjects also disagreed about the relative diagnosticity of agreement versus refusal to wear the sandwich board on the part of two specific peers. As predicted, compliant subjects made more confident and more extreme inferences about the personal characteristics of the noncompliant peer, while noncompliant subjects made stronger inferences about the compliant peer.

The sandwich-board study shows that the false consensus effect does not pertain only to estimates about hypothetical responses to vaguely described scenarios. Real situations, like hypothetical events, generally can be construed in variable ways. Thus subjects who imagined that their sandwich-board adventure would prompt ridicule from their peers, or who anticipated that the experimenter would accept their refusal to participate with equanimity, or who construed the overall situation as a test of their conformity tendencies, likely would refuse to wear the sign. They also would tend to assume that people who acquiesce under such circumstances would have to possess unusual or extreme personality traits. By contrast, subjects who imagined that their peers would applaud their good sportsmanship, or who imagined that their refusal to participate would meet with incredulity and scorn from the experimenter, or who construed the overall situation as a test of their "uptightness," would likely agree to wear the sign. And they, in turn, would tend to assume that it was individuals who refused to cooperate under such circumstances who were the "odd ducks," and whose behavior had to be explained in terms of their traits.

An interpretation of the false consensus effect in terms of construal, it should be reemphasized, requires more than the simple assumption that different people construe a given situation in different ways. It depends on the additional assumption that in doing so they fail to recognize or fail to make adequate inferential *allowance* for the fact that their peers may construe the "same" situation quite differently. The contention here is that people fail to recognize the degree to which their interpretations of the situation are just that – constructions and inferences rather than faithful reflections of some objective and invariant reality.

Overconfident Social and Personal Predictions

Studies of behavioral prediction conducted by Ross and his colleagues over several years provide evidence that people are prone to express more subjective certainty in the predictions they make about each other's responses than is warranted by objective assessments of their accuracy. In studies of social prediction (Dunning, Griffin, Milojkovic, & Ross, 1990), this overconfidence effect was evident regardless of whom the subjects were asked to make predictions about (that is, roommates or individuals interviewed in anticipation of their prediction task) and regardless of the type of prediction items employed (that is, responses to hypothetical dilemmas, inventories of past behaviors and habits, or responses to contrived laboratory situations). Whether predicting a roommate's decisions about participating in the annual dormitory play or about choosing a major, or predicting if someone they just interviewed will want to comb his hair before having his photograph taken, or if he will choose to subscribe to *Time* magazine rather than *Playboy*, the accuracy levels that subjects achieved rarely approached the confidence levels they expressed.

Even more significant, perhaps, was the fact that in the predictions people made about their *own* academic choices, social preferences, and recreational activities, they showed the same type of overconfidence (Vallone, Griffin, Lin, & Ross, 1990). In other words, not only when subjects made predictions about the responses of people they knew well (that is, roommates) but even when they made predictions about the responses of the people whom they knew best (that is, themselves), subjects overestimated the certainty of the outcomes they were predicting. Overconfidence proved to be most dramatic, furthermore, in the case of predictions in which subjects knowingly or unknowingly went against the relevant response base rates – that is, when they predicted that a particular actor, or even they themselves, would respond in a way that differed from the most frequent behavior of their peers (and, presumably, from the dictates of whatever situational pressures and constraints govern the behavior of people in general).

The overconfidence effect in personal and social prediction cannot be traced to a single cause or underlying mechanism. Like most interesting and robust phenomena, it no doubt has many determinants. Indeed, erroneous predictions, and undue optimism on the part of those making such predictions, may reflect virtually the whole range of human inferential shortcomings and biases that investigators have documented over the past decade, from ignorance about particular statistical principles (such as regression to the mean), to general misconceptions about the predictive power of dispositional factors relative to situational ones (Dawes, 1988; Kahneman, Slovic, & Tversky, 1982; Nisbett & Ross, 1980; Ross, 1977). Nevertheless, as we have reflected upon the results of these studies, and upon real-world instances of misplaced certainty in prediction, we have come increasingly to appreciate the extent to which overconfidence arises from people's failures to understand the role of construal processes in producing their appraisals of situations.

There are two different aspects to the construal problem that produce overconfidence in social prediction. First, to predict a person's response to a given situation – even a person whom one knows very well and has been able to observe in a wide variety of previous situations – one usually must know or correctly infer the details of that situation, in particular, those features of the context that help determine the relative attractiveness of the available response alternatives. Second, beyond knowing such objective features of the situation, one must discern the meaning of the situation from the private perspective of the actor. Uncertainty either about objective features of the situation or about their subjective construal by the actor increases the difficulty of prediction and the likelihood of error. And the failure to recognize or make adequate *allowance* for such uncertainty makes it likely that one will also fail to reduce appropriately the confidence one places in one's predictions.

That people are indeed very insensitive to their imperfect ability to construe situations with high accuracy when lacking details was shown by a series of studies by Griffin, Dunning, and Ross (1990). In these studies, subjects were asked to read about situations and then make predictions about the way they or other people would behave in those situations. Subjects were just as confident in their predictions when they had no real basis for assuming that their construals were correct as when they were instructed to assume that all their interpretations were exactly correct.

Situational Construal and the Fundamental Attribution Error

Often people give us a capsule description of some event – for example, that "Jane yelled at her two-year-old in the supermarket" or that "John donated blood last Thursday" – without telling us about relevant situational factors and contextual details. We may even personally witness the relevant behavior but be left to imagine or construe features that may have been critical in their influence – for example, what Jane's two-year-old might have done in the preceding hour and how the child may have responded to milder rebukes in the past, or whether John's office might have set itself a blood donation quota to which everyone but John had already contributed.

In such cases we are usually too ready to assume a person has traits corresponding directly to the type of behavior that was exhibited, without reconsidering one's construal of the situation facing that person in light of the response. The implications of such naive dispositionism are perhaps clearest in cases where one learns that a person of presumably ordinary character has behaved in a way that seems exceptional – exceptional, at least, given our current construal of the situation. In such cases, we contend, observers are overly disposed to "recompute" the person, that is, to abandon the assumption that the person is probably quite average and begin searching for dispositions that would explain the behavior in question. What observers are insufficiently disposed to do, we argue, is to recompute the nature of the *situation* – that is, to consider ways in which the situation (either the objective situation or the person's subjective construal of it) might have been different from what we had assumed, different especially in ways that would make the relevant behavior less surprising and less reflective of extreme personal dispositions.

An experience of one of the authors drives this point home. A colleague who perennially taught an upper-level undergraduate methods class was reputed to give very high grades in the course as a routine matter. Upon finding out about this, the author began looking for an explanation in the colleague's personality. A need to pander to student opinion, perhaps? A misguided egalitarianism? It is important for the sake of the illustration to note that the author had no good prior reason to assume that this colleague, rather than any other colleague, possessed such traits. A short time later, the author himself taught the course. He found the students to be an unrepresentatively talented bunch who threw themselves into original and ambitious laboratory projects with energy and zeal. In appropriate response to this situation, he, too, gave very high grades!

Thus lay dispositionism is reflected in the failure simply to withhold judgment about the individual – that is, to assume that one's prior construal of the situation was probably inaccurate in some nontrivial way, and to assume further that a more accurate construal would make the actor's behavior seem less exceptional and, hence, less revealing of exceptional personal characteristics. What we are proposing, in essence, is a lack of attributional *conservatism* or, in cases where the dispositional inferences made on the basis of one's initial construal of the action and situation would be negative, a failure of attributional *charity*. In taking seemingly exceptional behavior at face value, and in failing to entertain the strong possibility that such behavior reflects the influence of exceptional pressures and constraints (including ones that are not presently apparent or ones that arise from the particular subjective meaning of the situation to the actor), the ordinary social perceiver is guilty of the same folly as the intuitive statistician who pays too little heed to base rates or averages. Both overestimate the informativeness of the "exceptional" observation; and both fail to give appropriate weight to the fact that exceptional traits simply are much less common than unexceptional ones. This tendency, which lies at the heart of the fundamental attribution error, helps keep alive a belief in powerful, consistent, individual differences in social behavior and in underlying personality traits (Nisbett & Ross, 1980; Ross, 1977). In the next chapter we examine empirical evidence concerning the predictive value of classic personality traits. Then, in Chapters 5 and 6, we explore in detail the discrepancy between lay beliefs and this empirical evidence.

CHAPTER 4
THE SEARCH FOR PERSONAL CONSISTENCY

An important thesis of the preceding three chapters has been that when people are called upon to interpret the events that unfold around them, they tend to overlook or to make insufficient allowance for situational influences. This tendency, we argued, is especially likely to mislead people when they are confronted with behavior that is surprising or extreme, in other words, behavior that would prompt the situationist to search for extreme or extenuating circumstances that might account for such behavior. A related thesis involves the layperson's failure to recognize the importance of subjective interpretation, that is, to realize the extent to which behavior can be predicted and understood only in light of the actor's own construal of the situation providing the context for such behavior.

If people slight the importance of objective situational factors and subjective construals, to what do they attribute the behavior they observe? And on what do they base their predictions about future behavior? The answer we get both from research evidence and from everyday experience is that people are inveterate dispositionists. They account for past actions and outcomes, and make predictions about future actions and outcomes, in terms of the person – or more specifically, in terms of presumed personality traits or other distinctive and enduring personal dispositions.

In this chapter we review evidence concerning the explanatory and predictive power of personality traits such as extroversion, honesty, and dependency. What our review highlights, however, is their apparent lack of power – at least when evaluated in the harsh light of standard correlation coefficients determined in well-controlled research settings. These statistical results, it is important to note, were quite surprising both to the investigators who did the research and to the field of psychology as a whole, just as they are likely to be surprising to most students who learn about them in the classroom. Indeed, in their own way, the results in question have proven to be just as challenging to intuition, just as inviting of skepticism, and ultimately just as provocative in their implications as the results of the classic studies we have cited to demonstrate the power of the situation. What is the source of this widespread surprise and skepticism? We suspect that these reactions can be traced to the fact that professional psychologists draw heavily on essentially the same intuitive theories and reflect upon essentially the same types of everyday social experiences as do laypeople. And the theories are wrong and the experiences are misleading in some very important respects.

We begin this chapter with a quick sketch of the intuitive dispositionist theories that first gave rise to the fields of personality theory and personality assessment, and that continue today to influence conceptual analysis and research. Then we proceed to some unsettling empirical evidence and to various empirical and logical rebuttals of that evidence. We close the chapter with our assessment of the "consistency controversy" that has been at the very heart of personality psychology for over half a century. Chapter 5 offers a more detailed look at lay views about personal consistency and predictability. The chapter also explores the origins of lay dispositionism and discusses various cognitive, perceptual, and motivational processes that may encourage such dispositionism. Chapter 6 takes a very different tack in addressing the relationship between the empirical evidence and the impressions we all commonly derive from everyday social interaction. It argues, essentially, that lay beliefs about the consistency and predictability of behavior have a basis in the reality of social life, although that reality may owe much less to the impact of commonly conceived personality traits than most laypeople realize.

AN OVERVIEW OF CONVENTIONAL THEORIES OF PERSONALITY

Theories of personality, those of the layperson and those of the academic psychologist alike, generally proceed from two basic assumptions about human behavior, both of which seem to be demanded by everyday social experience. The first and most basic assumption is that many, and perhaps even most, stimulus situations in the social sphere provoke distinctively different responses from different people. Indeed, it is the observation of such diversity in response that prompts lay and professional psychologists alike to postulate dispositional differences in the first place. The second assumption, equally congruent with everyday social experience, is that individuals display a substantial degree of consistency, and hence a substantial degree of predictability, in responding to different situations. Putting these two assumptions together gives us the core proposition of lay dispositionism – that is, that the variability in responses we witness when different people react to a given situation is a reflection not of randomness or indeterminacy but of the distinctive and enduring personal attributes that the various actors bring to that situation.

The labors of the personality researcher, accordingly, begin with a pair of related tasks – identifying the major behavior-determining attributes of people in general and finding ways to measure these attributes in individuals. A later, more theoretical, task for the personologist is to discover regularities in the ways in which specific attributes relate to each other in determining the structure of personality. Last but certainly not least come questions of personality development and change. How do individual attributes first develop, and then endure or become transformed as a consequence of the individual's experiences and the interpretations placed on those experiences?

These tasks generally have been undertaken with the conviction that while there were formidable methodological problems to be overcome, the basic soundness of the theoretical assumptions underlying the investigation could not be seriously doubted. It seems obvious to any observer, theorist as well as layperson, that people differ in their responses and in their underlying personalities. And it seems almost as obvious that people's behavior across different situations shows the imprint of who they are and what they are. People seem to differ strikingly from each other in the friendliness, honesty, dependency, impulsivity, and so on, that they manifest over time and across different situations.

Experience further seems to suggest regularities in the organization of personality. Attributes seem to form distinctive, organized clusters, so that it is reasonable to talk about extroverts, sociopaths, authoritarians, Machiavellians, mama's boys, bon vivants, and countless other personality "types." Indeed, if consistent diagnostic attributes did not exist, it would be hard to explain why speakers of our language find it useful to coin and perpetuate the hundreds, even thousands, of dispositional terms that we all recognize and use. In one early study, Allport and Odbert (1936) reported finding over 4,500 such terms in a contemporary edition of *Webster's Unabridged New International Dictionary*. With another half century of shared social experience to enrich our outlook, and all kinds of seemingly new personal lifestyles to contemplate, the list has further inflated to include beatniks, hippies, yuppies, supermoms, liberated women, bag ladies, and scores of other types. It is hard to imagine that this rich descriptive vocabulary could gain currency if it made no contact with regularities in observed behavior.

Finally, experience and intuition encourage us to see a basis for individual differences. We frequently see similarities between children and their parents that, depending on one's view about "nature versus nurture," suggest the influence either of heredity or of the values that parents express in their words and deeds. Few adults would deny that their own outlooks and ways of dealing with the world have roots in their early social experiences and in the social models to whom they have been exposed. Thus we not only see distinct personality traits and types, we often can also explain why they exist and even why the individuals in question could hardly be otherwise.

In short, within our Western culture at least, both everyday experience and the wisdom of our sages seem to encourage the set of conventional dispositionist views that shapes the research agendas of personality researchers. Over the years these researchers have developed elaborate taxonomies of personality traits and types – some inspired by specific theories about personality structure and development (notably psychodynamic theories), some inspired by analysis of the way ordinary laypeople understand and use trait terms, and a precious few even inspired by statistical analyses of actual response data. Researchers have also developed literally thousands of assessment instruments, ranging from simple self-report and self-description questionnaires dealing with particular traits or behaviors to subtle projective tests (like the Rorschach) and giant omnibus inventories (like the Minnesota Multiphasic Personality Inventory) for analyzing and quantifying personal attributes and higher-order clustering of such attributes.

Whatever its original inspiration, the net result of the traditional personologist's empirical and intellectual labors is a view of individual differences that is entirely compatible with, and in fact seems essentially an elaboration of, conventional lay views about the dimensions of personality and social behavior. At the top level of generality we are likely to see one dimension or factor corresponding to extroversion-introversion, a second corresponding to agreeableness-disagreeableness, and a third corresponding to emotional stability-instability (for example, Eysenck, 1967; Norman, 1963). Other broad factors that emerge from some studies include dominance-submissiveness, conscientiousness-unconscientiousness, and cultured-boorish (for example, Digman & Inouye, 1986; Norman, 1963). At a lower level of generality than the broad factors are found the traditional traits per se. Thus, under the broad rubric of extroversion (versus introversion) would be found the traits of talkativeness (versus silence), sociability (versus reclusiveness), adventurousness (versus cautiousness), and frankness (versus secretiveness). Under the broad rubric of agreeableness would be found such trait descriptors as good-natured (versus irritable), cooperative (versus negativistic), and so on.

Many studies have been conducted to show that people agree quite well about what personality dimensions and specific traits are most useful in capturing the differences among themselves and among different actors. People also show significant levels of agreement in the traits they assign to particular individuals. And there is considerable stability over time in the assessments people give of both their own personality traits and those of their peers. Finally, trait ratings based on self-reports and peer ratings alike have been shown to predict actual behavior in everyday life as well as in the laboratory. Nevertheless, as we indicated in introducing the concerns of the present chapter, there lurks in the research evidence a long-standing problem and a challenge to the shared dispositionist convictions of layperson and professional alike, one that we now explore in some detail.

THE SCIENTIFIC FINDINGS AND THE DEBATE

Given the "obviousness" of individual differences in personality, the sophistication of the researchers, and the sheer volume of research that has been done, the layperson might reasonably anticipate, even fear, that personality measurement and behavioral prediction have been perfected to a high degree – that assessment instruments and formulas exist that permit reasonably precise and accurate predictions about the behavior of particular actors in particular situations. The facts, however, largely belie any such expectations. To be sure, investigators have been able to show statistically significant correlations between behavior measured in one situation and behavior measured in another situation. And personality scales of every sort have yielded statistically significant correlations both with other assessment instruments and with objectively measured behavioral outcomes. The problem, and ultimately the challenge to personologists, has been one of effect size, or more specifically, the discrepancy between observed levels of cross-situational consistency and the levels anticipated by our widely shared dispositionist theories. Indeed, although the relevant correlations have been significantly greater than zero, and therefore have offered proof that person variables do account for some of the variance in observed behavior, they have been low enough to make the degree of consistency and predictability in behavior less striking and less informative than the degree of inconsistency and unpredictability.

After over half a century of research, there is no "classic" dispositionist demonstration to rival Asch's conformity experiments, or

Milgram's obedience experiments, or Freedman and Fraser's foot-in-the-door experiments, or even Newcomb's field study of social influence at Bennington. That is to say, there are no famous studies in which stable personal attributes, either as measured by the investigator or as revealed in the record of past behavior, have proved to be markedly better predictors of behavior than academicians or even laypeople had anticipated. Nor do any studies show that seemingly small and subtle individual differences, whether measured by personality inventories or by any other means, produce large and reliable differences in overt social behavior. On the contrary, and as we now will describe, the existing literature on behavioral consistency and predictability has generally provided more ammunition for the critics of conventional personality theory than for its proponents.

The Challenge of 1968

The year 1968 was a watershed for personality research. It was in that year that both Walter Mischel and Donald Peterson, in independent literature reviews, pointed out that the predictability of individual responses in specific situations is quite low – low enough, in fact, to call into question the most basic assumptions about behavioral consistency shared by laypeople and personologists. Mischel's (1968) personality assessment text in particular seemed to shake the field of personality to its very foundations. The aftershocks continue today, despite the fact that Mischel's initial contribution was simply to summarize some facts that were well known to most researchers. Perhaps the most important of these facts was that the average correlation between different behavioral measures specifically designed to tap the same personality trait (for example, impulsivity, honesty, dependency, or the like) was typically in the range between .10 and .20, and often was even lower. This means, in terms of the percentage comparisons we have used to convey magnitude of effect, that there is almost no gain in accuracy of prediction about situation 2 by virtue of knowing how someone has behaved in situation 1. If the correlation is, say, .16 between friendliness in any two situations, this means that knowing that Jane was friendlier than Ellen in situation 1 increases the likelihood that she will be friendlier in situation 2 only to 55 percent (where the likelihood in the case of total ignorance would, of course, be 50 percent). Correlations between scores on personality scales designed to measure a given trait and behavior in any particular situation presumed to tap that trait, moreover, rarely exceeded the .20 to .30 range. Virtually no coefficients, either between individual pairs of behavioral measures or between personality scale scores and individual behavioral measures, exceeded the .30 "barrier."

Mischel's response to the perplexingly low correlations found between objective behavioral measures was quite novel. Unlike previous commentators, he did not try to explain away the low correlations by suggesting flaws in methodology. Instead, he challenged us to entertain the possibility that those low correlations might be capturing an important truth about human behavior, that is, that cross-situational consistency might be the exception and behavioral specificity the rule. And he forced us to deal with the fact that neither our readiness to apply conventional trait labels nor the strong assumptions we make about behavioral consistency when we do so can be justified by the objective behavioral record. In doing that, Mischel explicitly issued two challenges. The first was to consider what perceptual, cognitive, and motivational factors might lead us to "see" high degrees of behavioral consistency and predictability where little or none exists. The second challenge was to find new ways of understanding the determinants of people's response to their social environment. Ultimately, Mischel insisted, the goal was to account for both response regularities and response specificities not in terms of traits but in terms of cognitive competencies, strategies for processing information, personal goals, subjective expectancies, and other "social learning" factors (Mischel, 1973; also Cantor & Kihlstrom, 1987).

We will describe the response Mischel provoked and take up the various challenges he offered. First, however, it will be useful to review the types of studies he cited as evidence of the lack of cross-situational consistency in behavior. Then the reader can appreciate the problem they posed to contemporary personologists, and continue to pose not only to personality theorists but also to laypeople who insist that their own everyday impressions of consistent and predictable actors are more than cognitive or perceptual illusions.

Empirical Studies of Cross-Situational Consistency

Newcomb and the consistency of extroversion. In 1929, Theodore Newcomb published a study of "problem" adolescent boys at a summer camp. His goal had been to examine the evidence for personal traits or dispositions falling under the general rubric of extroversion. These traits were talkativeness, seeking the limelight, energy output, ascendancy, interest in the environment, impetuosity, social forwardness, distractability, and preference for group as opposed to solitary activity. To pursue the question of behavioral consistency, Newcomb identified a broad range of behaviors occurring within the summer camp that would constitute evidence for one or another of these traits. These behaviors were selected in the same way that any layperson or personality psychologist would today. For example, talkativeness was defined in terms of the following behaviors: "telling of his own past, or of exploits he had accomplished," "giving loud and spontaneous expressions of delight or disapproval," "confining or not confining conversation with counselors to asking and answering questions," "spending quiet hour either alone or with others," and "amount of talking at meal times." These behaviors were reported on each day, on detailed rating forms, by the boy's counselor. For example, the counselor had to indicate whether the quiet hour was spent largely ignoring everyone else, talking quietly without moving about, or talking and laughing loudly. The counselor also had to estimate for each meal what percentage of the time each of the boys in his charge spent talking.

Newcomb averaged the daily records of behaviors for the odd days and correlated them with the daily records for the even days. Thus, for example, the association between talkativeness during the quiet hour with talkativeness during meal times was based not on the correlation between measures for single occasions, but on the correlation between the average of 24 quiet hours and the average of 72 (that is, 24 x 3) meal times. This "aggregation" of responses, as we will explain in more detail later, can be expected to yield a much higher correlation than would be the case if one were to examine individual occasions (because the mean of 24 observations is a much more stable and reliable measure than 1 observation and, as such, the relevant correlation is not attenuated by measurement error). Despite this, however, the average correlation that Newcomb found between ratings of any two behaviors intended to tap a given trait was only .14 – a level that any layperson facing a typical covariation-detection paradigm would be hard-pressed to discriminate from no relationship at all (Jennings, Amabile, & Ross, 1982).

There is a feature of Newcomb's study that a critic might seize upon in attempting to refute its central finding. His research subjects were children whose personal difficulties were such that they had been sent to a summer camp designed specifically for children with interpersonal problems – hardly a typical population. Indeed, as Newcomb himself noted, the atypicality of these subjects mostly involved extreme behaviors directly associated with extroversion and introversion (namely, aggression and extreme timidity). His answer to potential critics, however, was very simple: Because the variance in responses was apt to be greater than that in the population at large, the result logically should have been correlations that were *higher*, not lower, than those likely to be found for a nonselected "normal" population. As it happens, however, it is not necessary for us to push this defense of Newcomb's study. There have been other examinations of cross-situational behavior consistency using more representative subject samples, and the results they yielded were essentially the same as Newcomb's. Consistently, subjects' responses in one situation seemingly well chosen to tap a given personality trait have provided very little basis for predicting the same subjects' responses in a second situation designed to tap that same trait.

Hartshorne and May and the consistency of honesty. The earliest and still the most ambitious study of behavioral consistency actually was published a year before Newcomb's study. In 1928, Hartshorne and May examined the honesty of elementary and secondary school children in a wide range of classroom and nonclassroom situations. Their behavioral measures included willingness to steal some change left on a table in an empty classroom, willingness to lie to avoid getting another child into trouble, and willingness to cheat by adding false scores to a classroom test under circumstances where detection seemed impossible. Many of the specific behaviors they studied, furthermore, were examined more than once; for example, they measured children's willingness to cheat on each of several similar classroom tests. Thus, as in the Newcomb study, when the investigators came to examine the correlation between behaviors of different types, many of the scores they entered into the correlations were actually the average of several behaviors. Again, this aggregation of measures should have boosted the correlations beyond the level one might expect if only behaviors on single occasions had been considered. Nevertheless, the average correlation they obtained between any one type of honesty behavior and any other type was only .23.

Consistency research 1929-1968. The studies by Newcomb and by Hartshorne and May had been very expensive and time-consuming to conduct, and for over three decades there was no serious attempt to replicate or extend them. Few personality psychologists, however, were willing to concede the possibility that the predictability of behavior from one specific situation to another might truly be as low as these two empirical classics had suggested. Instead, they chose to dismiss the earlier studies on various methodological grounds, and without ever attempting to show that different results could be obtained by remedying the supposed methodological deficiencies, they turned to another, very different research strategy. Abandoning objective behavioral measurement, they focused instead on subjective paper-and-pencil self-reports and peer assessments. For example, people were asked how friendly they were under various kinds of circumstances (for example, "at parties" or "with coworkers"), or how assertive, or how conscientious they were. When questionnaires featuring many different self-report items of this sort were subjected to statistical analysis, low correlations became a thing of the past. Correlations between odd-numbered and even-numbered test items, or between alternate forms of a given test, or even between different tests measuring the same trait were high. So were correlations reflecting the "stability" of self-assessments over long periods of time (Block, 1971; Conley, 1984). Correlations in the .6 – .8 range were common, and reliabilities ran as high as .9. Also, correlations between different traits, at least when they were measured by paper-and-pencil tests, could also run reasonably high; and claims were made that such correlations, when subjected to sophisticated factor-analytic techniques, were beginning at last to reveal the structure of personality.

Some successes were also achieved with paper-and-pencil assessments made by peers. A particular assessor's ratings of a given individual across different situations showed consistency, and repeated measures taken over relatively long periods of time showed stability.

Some problems remained, however. Correlations reflecting level of agreement between different raters of a given individual were not very high. While the correlation coefficients sometimes reached the .50 level, much lower correlations were more typical. In the classic study by Norman and Goldberg (1966), the correlations between ratings for fraternity brothers, who had known one another for several years, were in the .20 range for most traits. Moreover, the correlations for any two people rating someone they had never met, but were only allowed to see, were not much lower; they averaged .13. Finally, the correlations between ratings by close acquaintances and selfratings rarely exceeded .50 and were more typically in the .30 range (Bem & Allen, 1974; Chaplin & Goldberg, 1985; Kenrick & Funder, 1988; Mischel & Peake, 1982a). In short, subjective paper-and-pencil assessment yielded higher correlations than the objective behavior studies; but consistently high correlations were to be found only in studies that examined consistency or stability of self-perceptions or stability in the perception of a target person by an individual rater.

But the proponents of paper-and-pencil assessment techniques faced an issue more troubling than modest agreement between different raters, that is, the *validity* issue. Simply stated, no amount of reliability in the assessments of a single rater (nor even agreement between different raters) proves that the consistency lies in the behavior of the person being rated. A rater can persist in beliefs or stereotypes that are unsubstantiated by objective response data or that are substantiated only by interpreting such data in the light of one's presuppositions. You may have decided that you are shy, sensitive, and conscientious, but who is to say that you're right? Similarly, two different raters, or a rater and an individual being rated, can agree on objectively unfounded personality assessments – provided that their assessments are guided by a shared set of implicit personality theories, stereotypes, or local reputations (for example, "people who wear glasses are brainy," or "short men are aggressive," or "all the Van Ormands are stuck-up"). Nevertheless, the ease of paper-and-pencil measures, and the often respectable correlations they yielded, left researchers with little inclination to return to the painstaking but unrewarding search for objective behavioral consistency.

Sears and the consistency of dependency. It was not until 1963 that another ambitious study of objective behavioral consistency was conducted. This was an investigation by Robert Sears on the dependency of nursery school children. Dependency in young children is an attractive trait to study because there are so many things children do that everyone would agree to be manifestations of dependency and that one can easily measure objectively. Sears examined such variables as touching or holding a teacher or another child, frequency of requests for reassurance, and frequency of attention seeking. He measured the children's dependency on their peers, on their teachers, and on their mothers, both in classroom situations and in the laboratory. Again, Sears' variables were not single observations of behavior in a single situation, but rather averages over many observations. Despite this statistical boost, the average correlation across behavior categories was only .11 – a correlation that was obviously too low to satisfy either the intuitions of the layperson or the requirements of conventional personality theory.

Implications of the Empirical Challenge

It was only five years after the Sears study that Mischel and Peterson launched their challenging assault on conventional assumptions about personal consistency. Essentially, what these theorists did was to clear away the accumulated underbrush of studies that had relied exclusively on agreement of subjective assessments and to refocus attention on the few studies that had employed objective behavioral measures. In giving priority to these objective measures, Mischel and Peterson noted the obvious objections to the use of reliabilities in subjective assessment as a means of demonstrating the existence (much less establishing the magnitude) of enduring individual differences in personality. They insisted that while agreement of measures and stability over time are interesting phenomena that are worthy of investigation, they do not establish the validity of the trait constructs in question. They also summarized the existing literature on information-processing biases and the other shortcomings of human inference that could compromise the validity of social perceptions and even self-perceptions – in particular, reliance upon stereotypes based on appearance, role, or reputation. Moreover, the two decades that followed saw an avalanche of research on biases in social perception and cognition, providing an even stronger foundation for the critique (Dawes, 1988; Fiske & Taylor, 1990; Kahneman, Slovic, & Tversky, 1982; Nisbett & Ross, 1980; Taylor & Fiske, 1978). Many of the biases that were demonstrated were of just the sort that would be expected to generate illusions of consistency. For example, large distortions of memory for "facts" in the direction of preconceptions of various kinds were the stock-in-trade of numerous research papers of the 1970s and 1980s.

It is important to note that Mischel did not argue that the absence of behavioral consistency across different situations proves that there are no measurable or predictable individual differences. On the contrary, he emphasized that individual actors might show responses that are very consistent within the same situation – that is, that *specific* responses to *specific* situations often might be very stable over time. In fact, some of the classic studies make this very point quite clearly. Stability coefficients – the correlation between two measures of the same behavior on different occasions – often exceed .40, sometimes reaching much higher. For example, Hartshorne and May (1928) found that the tendency to copy from an answer key on a general information test on one occasion was correlated .79 with copying from an answer key on a similar test six months later. Newcomb (1929) found that talkativeness at lunch was a highly stable attribute; it just wasn't very highly correlated with talkativeness on other occasions (see also Buss & Craik, 1983, 1984). Mischel insisted that strong differences between people were apparently limited to specific responses to specific situations, for example, friendliness in the lunchroom or willingness to confront one's employer, not broad, cross-situational, extroversion or assertiveness.

Mischel's assault on the underpinnings of personology did not end with his assertions about the lack of cross-situational consistency. He added to the personologists' discomfort by claiming that the correlations between trait scores derived from standard personality assessment scales and objective behavioral outcomes were also very low. Individual behaviors could rarely be predicted with correlations beyond the .30 barrier, and typical correlations were lower. He then went on to point out that personality scales employing indirect and subtle projective assessment techniques were rarely more successful at predicting actual behavioral responses (and generally were far less successful) than were simple self-reports.

Finally, and perhaps most provocatively, Mischel proceeded to demonstrate that subjects' willingness or ability to "delay gratification" (a trait dear to the hearts of psychoanalytically oriented personologists) might depend less on the dispositions of the person than on the specifics of the situation. Thus, while a child's success in delaying gratification in any one situation – that is, forsaking a small immediate reward in favor of a later, more substantial one – could be predicted only to a modest degree (again with correlations generally less than .30) either from personality measures or from the child's success in some other situation, the capacity of children in general to delay gratification successfully could be altered dramatically by manipulating some fairly subtle features of the situation testing that capacity. For example, in one study (Mischel & Ebbesen, 1970) it was found that most children quickly opted for the small but immediate reward when both rewards were made perceptually salient (a mean delay of one minute), but they managed to delay gratification (a mean delay of 11.3 minutes) when both rewards were hidden. Following up these results, Mischel (1974) and his co-investigators showed that any of several simple cognitive strategies that allowed children to divert their attention from the prospect of immediate reward could substantially enhance the capacity of virtually all children to delay gratification. In other words, such manipulations of context (and perhaps also of the meaning of that context to the children) could swamp the influence of any broad enduring differences in impulsivity, or patience, or any of the other individual differences among children that parents and professionals alike have in mind when they try to account for observed variability in the way different children respond to real-world opportunities and temptations.

PROFESSIONAL RESPONSES TO THE CHALLENGE OF 1968

Bem's Revival of the Nomothetic-Idiographic Distinction

Perhaps the most interesting early response to Mischel (and one that in some respects anticipates arguments to be made in more detail in a later chapter) was offered by Daryl Bem, a leading social psychologist (the father of self-perception theory, as discussed in Chapter 3), who was in transition to becoming a personality psychologist. Unlike most other critics, Bem did not disparage the existing behavioral data. Instead, he essentially conceded Mischel's basic contention about the degree of cross-situational consistency to be found when a random sample of people respond to some fixed set of trait-relevant situations. He maintained, however, that a rather more restricted trait theory might still be viable, one that held only that at least *some* traits appropriately can be applied to at least *some* people.

Reviving a distinction made almost 40 years earlier by Gordon Allport (1937), and one used heavily by Mischel's mentor George Kelly (1955), Bem and Allen (1974) proposed that personal consistencies of the sort implied by common trait labels can be found. But to do so, researchers must adopt an "idiographic" approach to personality as opposed to a "nomothetic" approach (that is, one focusing on the unique aspects of a given individual's personality configuration instead of assuming that each person can meaningfully be assigned a score on every dimension of personality).

The central feature of the idiographic approach is that one first identifies the particular traits that "apply" for the individual in question (or, alternatively, one first identifies particular individuals for whom the trait of interest is truly applicable). In other words, one must conduct one's search for behavioral consistency recognizing that only a subset of trait dimensions usefully characterizes any given individual, and that only a subset of individuals can be characterized in terms of any given trait dimension.

A second feature of the idiographic approach is the willingness, in defining the subset of particular situations within which response consistency is to be found, to look to the individual actor for guidance. There are two distinct ways in which this can be done. One can observe people's behavior in a substantial sample of situations to discover the particular consistencies shown by particular individuals (which presumably are likely to be shown by them again in a new sample of situations). Alternatively, one can use information about the person's personal history, needs, goals, interpretive schemas, or the like, in an attempt to *anticipate* the particular and unique sets of situations in which particular people will manifest their particular dispositions. In either case, the idiographic practitioner would not expect everyone to manifest a meaningful "score" on a fixed set of traits in a fixed set of situations. Instead, each individual would be expected to manifest his or her particular dispositions only in the particular subset of situations that were relevant for that individual.

Bem and Allen's theoretical departure point was the assumption that consistency will be shown only by people striving to meet personal standards or to convey a consistent impression to others, and it will be manifested only in the particular situations deemed relevant by those people. In other words, consistency will be manifested only by people who actively monitor their behavior and strive, at least within particular situations, to achieve the same consistency of performance predicted and sought by the researchers. For example, some people will monitor their behavior for the degree of friendliness or conscientiousness it displays because these personal attributes represent important values for them and are central to the impression they wish to convey to others. Other people will seek to be consistent in their displays of masculinity, intellectuality, ecological awareness, or patriotism for the same reason. But again, they will be consistent only across the particular situations that they personally deem relevant to the attribute in question.

Unfortunately, as Bem and Allen acknowledged, their methodology did not proceed very far in the direction suggested by their theoretical analysis. They did try to identify a subset of potentially "consistent" actors (whose behavior was to be contrasted with a subset of actors expected to be "inconsistent"), but they did not do so on the basis of behavioral observation or analysis of the individual actors' interpretive schemes or personal concerns. Nor did they try to choose the most applicable traits for their particular actors. Instead, they simply stipulated two specific traits – friendliness and conscientiousness – and then classified the population of available actors as high or low in consistency. In the case of friendliness, this classification depended on the subjects' global self-characterizations; in the case of conscientiousness, it depended on their self-reports of specific past behavior. Perhaps most important, and most at odds with the spirit of their own idiographic prescriptions, they made no attempt to choose their specific situations or measures idiographically. They simply selected a small number of situations and measures that they, the investigators, thought pertinent to the stipulated traits, and then exposed all their subjects to that same, fixed, set of situations. Finally, it should be noted that Bem and Allen employed only a very small number of discrete behavioral measures – two in the case of friendliness and three in the case of conscientiousness. Their other measures were all subjective, rather global, assessments by self, parents, or peers.

Despite the limited way in which the investigators put into practice the requirements for idiographic measurement, their results offered at least some initial encouragement for their argument. In the case of friendliness, the correlation between the two behavioral measures collected (that is, the quickness with which the subject engaged another individual in conversation immediately prior to participating in an experiment and the amount the subjects talked in a group discussion when the experiment began) proved to be very high among their "high-consistency" subgroup $(r = .73)$ but not among the "low-consistency" subgroup $(r = .30)$. Although the former correlation is impressive in magnitude, it is worth noting that the two behaviors in question hardly constituted independent manifestations of some global trait. Both behaviors reflected the individual's willingness to talk to strangers – in fact, the subject's willingness to do so on one particular occasion in one particular setting.

In the case of conscientiousness, the three measures employed – promptness in returning borrowed class readings, faithfulness in completing class assignments, and neatness of the students' appearance and living quarters – were more varied and more independent of one another. But Bem and Allen's data revealed that neither the consistent nor the nonconsistent group showed significant positive correlations for any pairs of these measures. (The average for the consistent group was –.04 and for the inconsistent group was –.19.)

Bem and Allen, however, responded to their findings with more enthusiasm than our summary of results might lead one to expect, largely because they did not buttress their argument with behavioral measures alone. Like earlier personologists, they relied heavily on self-assessments and on subjective assessments by peers and parents. And like previous investigators, they were rewarded for doing so. In the case of both friendliness and conscientiousness, they found that the high-consistency subgroup's peer ratings, parent ratings, and self-ratings correlated highly with each other (average $r = .61$ for friendliness and .48 for conscientiousness) and even with the relevant behavioral measures (average $r = .47$ for friendliness and .36 for conscientiousness), while lower correlations were obtained in the low-consistency subgroup.

The Bem and Allen paper, perhaps more because of the force of its general arguments than the strength of its data, soon provoked a great deal of controversy and criticism, both from personologists who argued that the investigators' approach had not been idiographic. enough and from Mischelians who once again insisted that correlations involving objective behavioral measures rather than subjective assessments were most relevant to the main point under contention. Also, the single high correlation involving behavioral measures that Bem and Allen reported apparently has not stood the test of replication. Mischel and Peake (1982a), after duplicating the main aspects of the Bem and Allen procedure and adding several additional measures of both conscientiousness and friendliness, found mean correlations between individual pairs of behaviors of .13 for conscientiousness and .05 for friendliness. Similarly, Chaplin and Goldberg (1985) performed a conceptual replication of the Bem and Allen study and found a correlation of .01 for conscientiousness behaviors and .00 for friendliness behaviors. More importantly, neither set of investigators found any more evidence of differentially high correlations for allegedly consistent subjects than for allegedly inconsistent ones, using either of the classification measures that Bem and Allen employed. In sum, then, Bem and Allen's initial steps in the direction of a more idiographic approach to personality did not solve the dilemma of behavioral inconsistency, despite the appeal of their basic argument. Their findings, and those of the follow-up studies they inspired, merely added behavioral data for two more traits, data featuring correlations of the same or even lesser magnitude than Mischel had noted in 1968.

Methodological Objections and Alternative Empirical Approaches

Aside from Bem and Allen's appeal for more idiographic assessment, the chief reaction to Mischel's assault, and the challenge it presented, was a mixture of stony silence, accusations of nihilism, appeals to common sense, and renewed insistence that the behavioral studies cited by Mischel were badly flawed. Critics maintained that the wrong types of situations and measures had been employed or that the wrong populations had been studied (for example, Alker, 1972; Block, 1977; Olweus, 1977; Wachtel, 1973). There was often an "ad discipline" ring to the defense. The social psychologists and other doctrinaire behaviorists, it was claimed, couldn't find the consistencies reflective of genuine individual differences because they had relied too much on simple-minded objective measures. By turning instead to more global and subjective personality assessments, and to ratings of behavior by the actors themselves or by peers who observed them in everyday contexts, the personologists insisted one could easily find the behavioral consistency that somehow had eluded Newcomb, Hartshorne and May, Sears, and all those who followed in their behaviorist footsteps. In other words, the personologists continued to insist that simple objective behavioral measures somehow obscured rather than clarified the important role that trait differences plays in everyday social life.

It is easy to empathize with the frustration felt by the personologists. Indeed, as we will make clear in Chapter 6, we believe that they were correct in their conviction that stable individual differences in social behavior are more than cognitive illusions. And we share their insistence that the people one encounters in the course of ordinary life show considerable consistency and predictability in the way that they behave and in the way that their behavior differs from that of their peers.

But we also believe that the personologists' curt dismissal of the behavioral evidence discouraged careful analysis of the sources of real-world behavioral consistency and inconsistency. In particular, the personologists did little to help us understand why lay intuitions about personality, and for that matter, why the research evidence marshalled by using global subjective reports, find so little corroboration when investigators go to the trouble of collecting objective behavioral data. If narrow traits like talkativeness or broader ones like extroversion, honesty, or dependency were the wrong ones to assess, then which traits would be the right ones? If talkativeness should not be measured by objective determination of the percentage of time individuals spent talking at the lunch table, then how should it be measured? If honesty should not be assessed by testing the willingness to cheat on a test or to steal money, then how should it be assessed? If neither "problem" boys in a summer camp, nor a broad cross-section of students in elementary and secondary schools, nor various samples of college students were appropriate populations to use in assessing personal consistency, then what populations would be appropriate? More generally, if the earlier behaviorist "failures" could be traced to unsophisticated methodologies, and if reliabilities and stabilities in more global and more subjective assessments captured the greater truth about behavioral consistency in the real world, why had there been no convincing empirical rebuttals using appropriate behavioral measures, procedures, and populations to show Mischelians the folly of their claims? In the absence of such empirical success stories, a rebuttal of a more conceptual nature was called for, one that explained both the seeming failures of Newcomb and company and the seeming successes of those who turned from objective behavioral studies to paper-and-pencil assessments. A decade after the initial challenge, one such rebuttal was offered by Seymour Epstein.

Epstein's Claims for the Power of Aggregation

Epstein's (1979, 1983) answer to Mischel's critique was one that appealed greatly to personologists. Essentially, he argued that in paying so much attention to low correlations between individual behaviors or outcomes, one overlooks the theoretical significance and potential practical benefits of *aggregating* observations. He pointed out that individual responses, like single items on a test of any kind, are highly unreliable and are likely to reflect the impact of many systematic and random factors other than the underlying personal disposition being measured. To obtain a reliable, accurate measurement of an actor's disposition, therefore, one must take the average of several different individual measures, or "items," so that random or extraneous factors influencing individual responses or items partially cancel each other out, and the signal becomes stronger relative to the surrounding noise. In other words, to find the consistency that had eluded the behaviorists, one need only make sure that the scores one correlates reflect a high proportion of the individual's underlying personal dispositions, or "true score," and a low proportion of "error." The payoff, Epstein maintained, will be relatively high correlations that in turn reflect genuine, stable, personal dispositions.

In a sense, Epstein's argument was purely statistical and beyond dispute. No one can disagree with the contention that multiple observations offer a more reliable measure, and a more accurate reflection of the "truth," than single observations. (Indeed, Mischel had made the same point in his 1968 book.) Moreover, in many familiar applied contexts, the importance of the aggregation principle is readily appreciated. The most accomplished students in a school will certainly miss an exam question here or there. They occasionally may even have an off day when they score relatively poorly on a particular test. But it is predictable that their end-of-term grades for particular subjects (each of which reflects the aggregate of many individual tests) and, even more, their grade point average (which reflects the aggregate of many individual grades) will be superior. Indeed, this is what we mean by "high academic ability"; and no sensible person would dispute the existence of individual differences in academic ability, or express despair about the possibility of measuring such differences, just because item-item, or even item-test, correlations are relatively low. By the same token, Epstein claimed, it would be foolish to answer questions about individual differences in honesty or friendliness by observing people's behavior in single situations and then calculating the relevant "item-item" correlations.

Epstein reminded his colleagues that there are simple, familiar statistical formulas that allow one to predict how *much* of an increase will be obtained in the reliability of measurement, and therefore how much of an increase can be expected in the correlations reflective of individual differences in personality, as one increases the level of aggregation for such measures. To illustrate the relevance of these formulas, and to show the magnitude of such "aggregation effects," let us consider a concrete example. That is, let us examine what would happen if one sampled a reasonably large number of behaviors presumed to tap the same trait and then averaged the relevant correlations obtained between all pairs of measures. More specifically, let us consider the case of a data set yielding a mean correlation of .16 for pairs of measures, a correlation level that is actually a little on the high side for empirical studies of the sort we have outlined.

Now a .16 correlation may seem unimpressive. Indeed, as Jennings, Amabile, and Ross (1982) showed, most observers are hard pressed to determine whether they are seeing a positive relationship or a negative one when they hear pairs of tones of differing durations, or see pairs of lines of differing lengths, that embody a .16 correlation. Nevertheless, it can be predicted, by use of the Spearman-Brown "prophecy formula" championed by Epstein, that if we took 25 independent behavioral measures of subjects' extroversion or honesty or dependency or conscientiousness (that is, measures of just the kind we reviewed earlier in our discussion of Mischel's challenge to the personologists) and correlated the average score of each subject for these 25 measures with the average score for another 25 independent measures of the same trait, the resulting correlation would reach .83 – a correlation that no one would call unimpressive and that no one could fail to detect. Indeed, averaging together even nine independent measures for each subject and then looking at their relationship to the average of nine new measures would yield a clear, and easily detectable, correlation of .63.

Epstein (1983) was not content to offer this argument in purely theoretical terms. He went to the trouble of demonstrating that, for at least some preferences and behaviors, the use of multiple measures really could boost correlations to the degree "prophesied." (What this showed, in effect, was that the requirement for independence of measures could be met or, more likely, that it could be violated without much cost in terms of the boost in correlation resulting from aggregation.) Traditional personology thus received a major lift. It had been shown, or so it seemed, that individual differences do exist along traditional trait lines, and that correlations reflecting these differences can be made quite large if one takes some perfectly reasonable psychometric precautions.

Epstein's argument was received with particular enthusiasm by personality test researchers because it seemed to explain why standard paper-and-pencil self-reports or peer evaluations generally show high levels of stability over time and sometimes show at least moderate levels of agreement between raters. Assessments of this sort, it can be presumed, are likely to be the product of many observations made on different occasions and in different situations. Accordingly, it could be argued, it is this aggregation of measures, rather than any influence of shared stereotypes or other biases in information processing, that accounts for the relatively high correlations that personologists are able to obtain using such assessments.

While Epstein's rebuttal freed personologists from the yoke placed upon them by Mischel's challenge and left them free to return to their development of techniques to measure individual differences, we believe his rebuttal may have misled uncritical consumers of the literature about both the practical and theoretical benefits achievable through aggregation. In the remainder of this chapter we will clarify the nature of, and the limits to, these benefits of aggregation.

MAKING SENSE OF "CONSISTENCY" CORRELATIONS

Let us suppose that Mischel and company are correct in their characterization of the evidence – that is, that individual responses by individual people to a fixed set of trait-relevant situations correlate with each other at roughly the level claimed by Mischel. And suppose, at the same time, that we accept Epstein's advice to rely upon aggregated rather than individual measures in making behavioral predictions. How much would predictions about individuals based on knowledge of their past behavior in many relevant situations differ from the predictions we would have made if we had known nothing about these individuals? And how accurate, on average, would such predictions prove to be when tested over the long haul? The answers to these questions can be linked to an even more basic set of questions to which we feel neither the personologists nor their critics have devoted sufficient attention. What does an individual's *distribution* of responses across many situations look like in a world where people show the degree of behavioral consistency that Mischel and Epstein both seem willing to agree on? For example, how frequently would an "extreme" individual show extreme behavior and how frequently would such a person look rather average? Conversely, how frequently would an "average" person look extreme?

To answer these questions, let us indulge in a research fantasy and assume that a variety of impossibly stringent methodological requirements have been met and a perfect data set handed to us for consideration – that is, let us assume that someone has measured the responses of a very large number of people in a very large number of situations, all well designed to tap the personality trait in question (for example, friendliness, conscientiousness, or honesty). Let us further assume that the simple, unaggregated responses collected in each situation have proved to be correlated with the responses in each other situation at a level yielding a Pearson r of exactly .16 – a level that our foregoing review of the literature suggests to be a generous estimate for most standard personality traits. Finally, let us assume that all the methodological requirements necessary to reap the full benefits of aggregation (principally, independence among the different observations) somehow have been met, and, while we are indulging in fantasies, let us suppose that all of the relevant response measures are distributed in a perfectly normal fashion, so that the relevant computational formulas can be applied without qualifications.

Now at last we are in a position to explore the real implications of the low correlations noted by Mischel and the higher ones that might be obtainable if we heed Epstein's advice and reap the benefits of aggregated measures. In fact, with a little assistance from some standard regression and aggregation formulas (and some coaching from statisticians more sophisticated than we are), we have performed the necessary calculations (Ross, Griffin, & Thomas, 1989). The results of these calculations have helped us sharpen our appreciation of both the potential value and the limitations – and in a sense, the very meaning – of the correlation levels that characterize the degree of cross-situational consistency to be found in trait-relevant behavior. Let us begin by outlining our basic conclusions.

1. By measuring a great number of trait-relevant responses for each individual, we can arrive at a reliable and accurate estimate of each individual's overall mean behavior, or "true score." Accordingly, we can predict with great accuracy the mean response that each individual will exhibit over a great number of future observations. Indeed, we can make accurate predictions about each individual's entire *distribution* of responses. But to the extent that the individuals' response distributions reveal them to be highly variable in their trait-relevant behavior – and that is exactly what *must* be revealed when the pertinent consistency correlations are all .16 – the uncertainty associated with predictions about any particular individual response by any individual actor cannot be reduced to any substantial degree.

2. Our behavioral samples necessarily will show that although individual response distributions differ somewhat in their central tendencies, all individuals will show a wide range of responses, and all will make responses close to the overall population mean much more often than they make responses that are at all extreme. (Again, if this were not so, the relevant consistency correlations would be higher than .16.) As a result, no amount of aggregation

will ever allow one to predict that even the most sociable, impetuous, or conscientious actors in our observational study will behave in anything like an extremely sociable, impetuous, or conscientious fashion in any particular situation. Conversely, when extreme behavior is displayed by someone on a particular occasion, we will never be able to assume that we are observing an individual whose overall mean or true score is extreme rather than average.

3. Examination of response distributions and mean scores for individuals nevertheless will serve us well for one type of prediction goal. Even on the basis of a correlation as low as .16 for individual responses, we will be able to make some pointed predictions about the *relative* likelihood that particular types of extreme responses will be shown by various specific individuals. Indeed, knowing that a particular individual has displayed an extremely "high" response on even a single occasion makes it safe to conclude that the person's response on some other occasion is much more likely to be extremely high than extremely low. And knowing that an individual's mean response over a great many observations is extreme makes these differences in the relative likelihood of particularly high or particularly low future scores reach dramatic levels indeed.

Predictions Based on Single Observations

Let us begin a more detailed consideration of our hypothetical study of behavioral consistency by examining a typical scatterplot (see Figure 4.1a) illustrating a .16 correlation between responses in two different situations relevant to a given trait such as extroversion. For example, the scatterplot might portray the sociability of each member of the sixth grade in a particular elementary school measured in the lunchroom on a particular day as well as sociability measured for each child several days later on the playground. We see a great deal of variability in the amount of extroversion being manifested by the various children in each situation and a weak relationship between responses in the two situations – a relationship difficult to distinguish, at least by simple inspection, from no relationship at all (see Figure 4.1b). Obviously, a relationship as weak as this means that knowledge of any individual's response in one situation gives us very little help in predicting that individual's response in the other situation. To be more precise, the conventional regression formula tells us that the best predictions we could make in such circumstances would reduce our average or "standard" prediction error by only a very small amount (in fact, only about 1 percent). The reason for this is

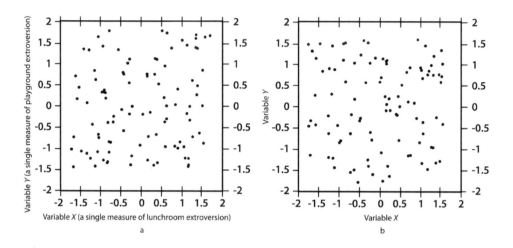

FIGURE 4.1
Scattergrams demonstrating (a) a correlation of .16 and (b) a correlation of .00.

straightforward. When the outcomes being predicted are highly variable, as is the case for our sixth-graders' displays of extroversion, the best predictions that we can make on the basis of knowledge of one previous response will, in virtually all cases, correspond to a level of extroversion very close to the average level manifested by the sixth-grade population in our study. In other words, the predictions we make generally will be similar to those we would have made if we had known *nothing* about that individual's past extroversion.

This point is conveyed graphically in Figure 4.2. The lower of the two distributions represents observations of behavior on one particular occasion, for example, the degree of aggression shown by 100 sixth-graders on the playground on Tuesday. The distribution is represented as a familiar bell-shaped curve in which the frequency of likelihood of a given response becomes smaller as the response in question becomes more extreme. Singled out for consideration are five children: a child who shows a degree of aggression corresponding to two standard deviations below the mean (a centile score of 2, indicating that only one other child showed less aggression), a child showing a degree of aggression corresponding to a standard deviation below the mean (a centile score of 15, placing the child roughly in the bottom sixth or seventh of the distribution of aggression scores), a child showing an average amount of aggression (a centile score of 50), and two children showing levels of aggression one standard deviation above the mean (a centile score of 85) and two standard deviations above the mean (a centile score of 98), respectively. The top distribution shows our best-guess predictions about the degree of aggression we expect to be shown by the same sixth-graders,

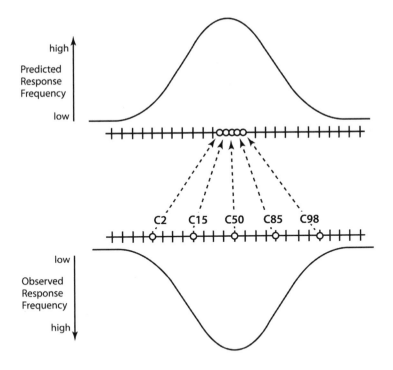

FIGURE 4.2
Best-guess predictions of next response (top distribution) based upon knowledge of single prior observations (bottom distributions) for five selected centile scores.

including the five individuals singled out for special consideration, on the field trip to the natural history museum on Friday.

It may be seen that the best guess we can make for any of the children is a level of aggressiveness close to average. Their *actual* responses, of course, will be highly variable, but given the .16 correlation, we can't predict *who* will show an extreme response and who won't. Thus even in the case of a child who had been one of the two most aggressive children observed on the playground – Billy, say, who pushed both Ellen and James to the ground and screamed "get lost" to shy Charlie – the best guess one can make is that he will be only a little more aggressive than the average child, perhaps doing only a little more jostling in line than the average child and grumbling about the boring exhibits loudly enough for one of the teachers to hear. Indeed, he is less likely to do something truly aggressive at the museum – for example, to start a fight – than he is to behave less aggressively than is average for his class. Conversely, and equally important, Jane, who yanked another girl's coat off the hook to put her own up and ran around the museum making enough noise that she had to be restrained by one of the teachers, thereby ranking as one of the two most aggressive children at the museum, is unlikely to have been one of the most aggressive children we observed on the playground visit. Instead, the level of aggression she is most likely to have exhibited on that earlier occasion is just a little more than the mean.

Predictions Based on Multiple Observations

Now, what are the benefits of aggregation? Suppose we had classified the children not on the basis of single observations but on the basis of 50, or 100, or even an infinite number of observations. To be sure, we would be able to predict very accurately the average level of shyness, aggression, or the like, that each child would manifest over a great many new observations. Indeed, we would be able to predict accurately each child's entire distribution of responses. That is, we could predict confidently that each child's distribution of future responses would closely resemble that child's distribution of past responses. But we still would not be able to reduce by much our uncertainty about individual children's behavior in individual situations. Specifically, knowing each child's long-term mean or "true score" for aggression, and making individual predictions accordingly, would allow us to reduce the average discrepancy between what we predicted and what we observed by only about 8 percent. That is, our average error would be 8 percent smaller than if we simply guessed that each child's behavior in each situation would correspond to the class average.

To understand why this reduction in error would be so modest, we must remember that all of the children – over the long haul – would show themselves to be highly variable, and virtually all would show averages rather close to the population mean. (Again, for this not to be so, the correlation in question would have to be higher than .16.) Accordingly, the best guesses we could make about responses by individual children all would still be close to the population mean. But, as the actual response distribution across different situations for each child is highly variable, these best guesses would often prove to be far off the mark. Figure 4.3 illustrates the nature of the response distributions for individual children who, overall, rank at various centiles in the population. Once again, we give special emphasis to the five children in our hypothetical study whose overall averages rank, respectively, at the 2nd, 15th, 50th, 85th, and 98th centile in the population. It will be immediately clear that even the most "extreme" children show decidedly average behavior more often than they show extreme behavior, and that even the most average children sometimes show behavior at the extremes. In short, when the relevant cross-situational consistency correlation is .16 the vast majority of the

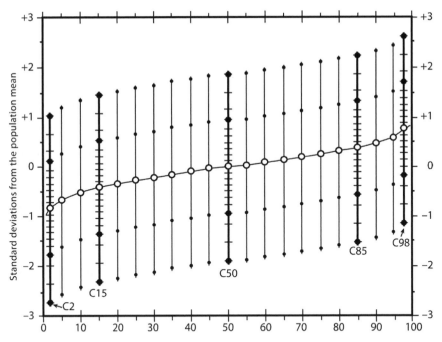

FIGURE 4.3
Personal response distributions for 21 individuals at various centile rankings in the population. Individual means are indicated with open circles. Scores one and two standard deviations above and below each individual's means are indicated with closed circles. Distributions for individuals at 2nd, 15th, 50th, 85th, and 98th centiles are emphasized, and cross-hatching is provided at every fifth centile on these distributions.

children show rather similar, and unexceptional, response distributions – the sort of distributions that would make one reluctant to use adjectives like "shy" or "aggressive" or even "average" without quickly adding some qualifications about variability.

Rank orderings of the children's past averages, to be sure, will be preserved in the future – assuming that the past and future behavioral samples are both sufficiently large and, of course, that the children remain unchanged in their dispositions. Thus the correlations between highly aggregated samples will be high, just as Epstein contended. The problem is that the distances between the children's new means, like the distances between their old means, will tend to be relatively small, and the variation individuals continue to show around those means will continue to be relatively large. The law of large numbers is a powerful principle, but it can neither wring blood from a turnip nor create certainty in the aggregate where variability reigns in the particular.

The Relative Likelihood of Extreme Behaviors

The variability in individuals' behavior captured in a simple cross-situational consistency correlation of .16 limits the degree to which uncertainty in prediction can be reduced, regardless of the level of aggregation. Nevertheless, a correlation of that level can prove to be quite useful for one type of prediction task that is frequently of concern in everyday social interaction. This task involves identifying people who are *relatively* more or less likely than their peers to score at either extreme of the distribution.

Predictions of this type clearly are very important for a variety of "screening" problems, where our primary concern is apt to involve either maximizing the likelihood of some extremely desirable outcome or response or minimizing the likelihood of some extremely undesirable one. Again, some specific computations drive this point home. Consider Tom, Dick, and Harry – three participants in a hypothetical study of the ideal type we have been discussing, but now dealing with extroversion of adults. Suppose we know that on a single randomly sampled occasion Tom scored two standard deviations below the mean, that is, at roughly the 2nd population centile (for example, while others were making merry at the office party, he retired to the library to peruse computer journals). And suppose we know that Harry scored two standard deviations above the mean, at the 98th centile (for example, at the same office party, he was observed wearing a lampshade and reciting ribald limericks). Given just these two "items" of information, we can make some rather striking inferences about their subsequent behavior. In particular, we can already estimate that Harry is roughly five times as likely as Tom (probabilities of 4.5 and .9 percent, respectively) to be doing something truly extroverted (that is, in the top 2 percent) when they are next encountered. Harry also is more than twice as likely to show a truly extroverted response than a randomly selected individual or than Dick, whose level of extroversion on the one previous time it was observed proved to be perfectly average. Tom, conversely, is roughly five times as likely as Harry, and more than twice as likely as Dick, to be doing something truly introverted (among the bottom 2 percent of those observed) the next time we sample their behavior.

At the risk of cooling the suddenly revived enthusiasm of the inveterate dispositionist, we should hasten to point out that, in absolute terms, such extreme behaviors remain unlikely for all three individuals (that is, about 4 percent for Harry, 2 percent for Dick, and less than 1 percent for Tom). Furthermore, Harry the extrovert and Tom the introvert are both about four times as likely to respond in a manner that ranks exactly at the population mean as they are to respond in a fashion that ranks exactly at the 98th centile (in Harry's case) or the 2nd centile (in Tom's case). But the fact remains that extreme observations – even single extreme observations – can be of practical value if we want to make "personnel selections" that maximize or minimize the likelihood that the chosen individual will show a particular type of extreme response or achieve a particular type of extreme outcome.

Of course, these differences in relative likelihood become greater when we are able to make our assessments on the basis of aggregated data. If ten prior observations have provided the basis for Harry, Dick, and Tom's respective 98th, 50th, and 2nd centile rankings, then we could presume that Harry would be roughly 35 times more likely than Tom, and roughly five times more likely than Dick, to earn an extroversion score in the top 2 percent of the population when the next observation is made. Moreover, if we have aggregated enough prior observations to eliminate all uncertainty about the three individuals' personal response distributions, and still found the same centile rankings, the ratios in question would be even more dramatic. Harry would be more than 100 times as likely as Tom to be the limerick-singing lampshade wearer. Conversely, Tom would be more than 100 times as likely as Harry to be the one retiring to read a computer journal. And both would be more than six times as likely to be showing these particular behavioral extremes as would "average" Dick.

With a little more calculation we can determine how likely we are to see some instances of extreme behavior from the relevant individuals within a specified number of observations. (See Figure 4.4.) We find, for example, that if extroverted Harry and introverted Tom have earned their reputations (and 2nd and 98th centile rankings) on the basis of a single past observation, then there is a 34 percent likelihood that Harry will behave in a manner that scores in the top 2 percent of the population at least once in the next 10 observations, but there is only an 8 percent likelihood for Tom. If their reputations were earned on the basis of 10 previous trials, the likelihood reaches 52 percent for Harry and drops to less than 2 percent for Tom. And if their reputations for extroversion and introversion were earned through very large, or infinite, numbers of past observations, the likelihoods in question reach 60 percent and less than 1 percent, respectively. In short, a modest sampling of future behavior might very well allow us to see Harry (but almost certainly would not allow us to see Tom) do something truly extroverted.

These degrees of extremity and probability begin to sound as if they are almost surely within the layperson's capacity to detect; and it may well be the case that lay trait terminology often is based less on notions about long-term "averages" than on notions about the relative probability of certain extreme behaviors occurring or not occurring within a reasonable period of time or over a reasonable sample of observations. The nature of lay beliefs about individual differences and about the limits of behavioral predictability will be explored in more detail in the next chapter. There we also will consider lay views about a central concern of this book, that is, the relative impact of person factors and situation factors in producing behavior.

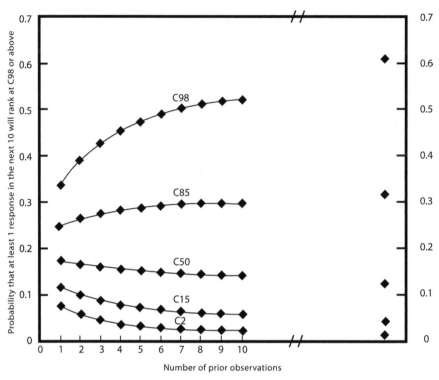

FIGURE 4.4
Probability that an individual will rank at or above the 98th population centile on at
least 1 of the next 10 responses as a function of the individual's centile ranking based
on varying numbers of prior observations.

CHAPTER 5
LAY PERSONOLOGY AND LAY SOCIAL PSYCHOLOGY

Throughout the last chapter, indeed, throughout the book to this point, we have made assertions about the layperson's implicit theories of personality and of social psychology. We have maintained that laypeople fail to appreciate the power and subtlety of the situational control of behavior and are guilty of a sort of naive dispositionism, seeing traits where there are none.

But how do we know what the layperson believes? How do we know that laypeople are not sparing and prudent in using the thousands of personality type and personality trait terms in our language? How do we know that they are not reasonably well calibrated for trait-based predictions, seeing predictability from one situation to another as low, and seeing high rank-order predictability (but small mean differences from person to person) over the long haul? How do we know that laypeople tend to underestimate the effects of situations on behavior? Perhaps it is only psychologists who are perennially surprised at the power of situational influences.

It is time now to look explicitly at lay psychological beliefs – to see what ordinary men and women believe about the existence and power of individual differences in personality, about the predictive utility of single versus aggregated measures of behavior, and about the role of situational versus dispositional determinants of behavior.

QUALITATIVE ASPECTS OF LAY PERSONALITY THEORY

We begin with the qualitative aspects of lay personality theory. Are people really the inveterate trait theorists we have claimed them to be? We know, from research as well as from everyday experience, that people rely heavily on trait terms when asked to describe each other. Park (1986, 1989) found that while behaviors, affiliative memberships, attitudes, demographic information, and physical descriptions were all used with some frequency, traits (such as kind, shy, self-centered, easygoing) were more than twice as common as the next most frequent form of description. Ostrom (1975) asked college students to list the items of information they would want to know about another person in order to form an impression. Trait information accounted for 26 percent of all items listed; behavior, affiliative memberships, attitudes, and demographic and physical information together accounted for only 19 percent. Livesley and Bromley (1973) have shown that the use of trait terms increases steadily over the course of development for children in our culture, eventually becoming the most frequent type of description in free-response characterizations of other people. The meaning of the trait terms that people within a culture end up with would appear to be remarkably uniform. Cantor and Mischel (1979) and Buss and Craik (1983) have asked people to rate various behaviors with respect to the degree to which they are representative of one or another of the standard trait terms. Their ratings show a level of agreement that is close to the level that they show when rating the degree to which various physical objects (for example, tables or sofas) are representative of relevant object categories (for example, "furniture").

It is instructive to compare the frequency with which people use trait constructs to explain behavior with the frequency with which they call on aspects of the situation or overall social context. Joan Miller (1984) asked people to "describe something a person you know well did recently that you considered a wrong thing to have done" and also to "describe something a person you know well did recently that you considered good for someone else." Immediately after describing each behavior, the subject was asked to explain why the behavior occurred. Half of the explanations offered by subjects for deviant behaviors invoked general dispositions (for example, "he is rather careless and inconsiderate"). This was three times the rate of offering situational context explanations ("it was hard to see, and the other bicycle was going very fast"). Similarly, for prosocial behaviors, one third of the explanations offered invoked general dispositions, and this was more than 50 percent higher than the rate for context explanations. Thus subjects showed themselves to be trait theorists, not situationists.

A pilot study by Ross and Penning (1985) makes a similar point. Subjects in this study first made predictions about the way particular target individuals would behave in an incompletely specified situation and then found out that their predictions were incorrect. Given such feedback, subjects were quick to make new assumptions about the actors' dispositions and slow to make new assumptions about the details of the immediate situation. For example, subjects were told that, contrary to their prior predictions, two Stanford students whom they had just judged to be very dissimilar on the basis of their pictures both had contributed to a "Gay Rights" ad. Such subjects were more apt to generate *dispositional* explanations (for example, the two students must have been gays or liberals) than *situational* ones (the students must have been asked in some manner that made it difficult for them to refuse).

Perhaps the most convincing line of work showing the layperson's reliance on dispositional constructs of a trait type comes from a series of investigations by Winter and Uleman (1984; Winter, Uleman, & Cunniff, 1985), who showed that trait interpretations are made at the very moment behavior is observed and, in fact, may be integral to the coding of behavior.

Winter and Uleman presented their subjects, via slides, with a number of sentences that described a particular action by a particular individual, for example, "The librarian carries the old woman's groceries across the street." Afterwards, subjects were presented with a "recall sheet" on which they were to write down as many of the sentences they had just seen as possible. To assist them in this task, two kinds of "recall cues" were provided. In some cases, the cue was the common trait or disposition label consistent with the action described in the relevant picture (for example, for the sentence above about the librarian who helped the old woman with her groceries, the word "helpful"). In other cases, the cue was a word that constituted a close semantic associate of the subject or predicate of the sentence (for example, "books" as an associate of "librarian").

Not surprisingly, the investigators found that subjects recalled substantially more sentences when cued by a relevant trait than they did in the absence of such cues. But trait cues also proved to be more effective than semantic cues even though the semantic cues were more closely connected to the specific words in the sentence in terms of assessed similarity or association strength than were the trait cues. Interestingly, subjects did not report having thought of the dispositional concepts when reading the sentence. In fact, they regarded it as implausible that thoughts about dispositions would have been helpful in recalling sentences.

The evidence to date thus suggests that people automatically – and unconsciously – provide a dispositional interpretation to behavioral information (see also Park, 1986, 1989; Lewicki, 1986). And it further suggests that the dispositions they favor are suspiciously similar to the trait constructs fabled in song, story, and personology texts.

QUANTITATIVE ASPECTS OF LAY PERSONALITY THEORY

What can be said of lay beliefs about the degree of predictability to be found for social behavior? Ideally, one would simply ask people to guess the relevant correlation coefficients, for example, the correlation for a group of campers between amount of talking at the lunch table and talkativeness during the "quiet hour." But the language of statistics is a foreign one for most people. Accordingly, investigators have been obliged to probe beliefs about consistency less directly, by asking subjects to make predictions or to furnish estimates of likelihood that could be translated into correlation coefficients.

In one such study, Kunda and Nisbett (1986) asked subjects for their beliefs about the likelihood that a pair of people would maintain their relative ordering with respect to the level of a given personality trait that they manifested across two situations. Such subjects read the following paragraph:

> Suppose you observed Jane and Jill in a particular situation and found that Jane was more honest than Jill. What do you suppose is the probability that in the *next situation* in which you observe them you would also find Jane to be more honest than Jill?

Other subjects were asked about the degree of stability to be expected over two sets of 20 occasions. They were asked about the probability that Jane would prove more honest than Jill over the next 20 situations (on average) given that she had been more honest over the preceding 20 situations (on average).

Similar questions were asked about the stability of honesty rankings. In all, cases, subjects were asked to make their estimates of likelihood on a scale running from 50 percent to 100 percent. These percentage estimates could be readily converted into correlation coefficients in order to compare them with the actual correlation coefficients characteristic for such behaviors.

Subjects were also asked comparable questions about abilities. They were asked the likelihood that a child who got a higher grade than another on a given spelling test would also do so on a second test and the likelihood that a basketball player who made more points than another in a given game would also do so in a second game. They were also asked comparable questions for sets of 20 spelling tests and 20 basketball games. Figure 5.1 shows the degree of consistency estimated by subjects

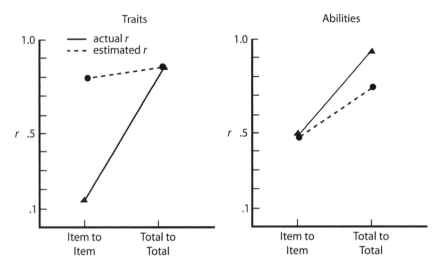

FIGURE 5.1

Estimated and actual correlation between individual behaviors (item to item) and aggregated behaviors (total to total), for traits and for abilities. (Kinda & Nisbett, 1986.)

for social traits and abilities. Also plotted are the actual correlations (derived from the literature reviewed in the previous chapter in the case of the social traits, and from studies by Kunda and Nisbett in the case of abilities).

The most dramatic aspect of Figure 5.1 is the degree of consistency expected at the level of individual social behaviors. Subjects seemed to think the consistency from one situation to another would be far greater than research has ever shown it to be. They estimated the likelihood that the rank order would be preserved over two occasions was 78 percent – a likelihood requiring a correlation in the range of .80, whereas research suggests the actual correlation to be about .10. Figure 5.1 also reveals that subjects showed little appreciation of the stability gained from aggregation of measures. Subjects thought that the consistency from one situation to another was only trivially less than the consistency from 20 situations to another 20 situations! We can express this failure to recognize the instability of single measures relative to aggregate ones quite precisely. Given that subjects estimated the item-to-item correlation to be .79, they should have estimated the 20-item-to-20-item correlation to reach 99. Alternatively, given that subjects estimated the total correlation to be .82, they should have estimated the item-to-item correlation to be only .23.

[Lest we be accused of picking on our statistically unsophisticated subjects, we remind the reader that we have emphasized throughout this book the continuity between lay and professional intuitions about behavior. In this spirit, Kunda and Nisbett asked professional psychologists, attending a convention symposium on statistical aspects of human judgment, to make the very same estimates as the college students whose data are shown in Figure 5.1. Some of these professionals would be describable as personologists, but most were social psychologists and experimentalists. The professional sample provided data that were essentially the same as those in Figure 5.1 – with one exception. The professional psychologists as a group were aware that traits are not very good predictors of behavior. (Or perhaps we should say they were *reminded* of that fact. Walter Mischel was seated prominently in the front of the room as they filled out their questionnaires!) In any case, the psychologists showed lower estimates of social trait consistency than did the lay subjects. Nevertheless, they still seriously overestimated the degree of consistency likely to be shown from one situation to the next. Moreover, like the lay subjects, they showed little recognition of the degree to which larger samples of observations enhanced consistency of rankings. As a result, they actually *underestimated* the degree of consistency likely to be shown for rankings based on 20 items and on balance performed no better, either empirically or mathematically, than lay subjects.]

Considered in isolation, these data might simply reflect subjects' difficulties with the specific metric employed or problems with the unfamiliar task of making hypothetical estimates about hypothetical individuals. Some additional lines of evidence, however, suggest otherwise. First, we should note that subjects' consistency estimates for ability measures were in much closer contact with the empirical evidence than were their estimates for trait measures. Subjects made estimates about the stability of rankings, over individual spelling tests and over individual basketball games, that were very close to the measured stabilities for these events. And, although they substantially underestimated consistency of rankings from one set of 20 ability tests to a second set, they did seem to recognize that the aggregated measures would be more consistent than the single-test measures.

It is thus only for behaviors reflective of personality, and not for behaviors reflective of abilities, that people dramatically overestimate the amount of consistency to be expected and seem oblivious to the advantages of aggregated behavioral samples over individual instances. The latter point is particularly important because it suggests that people will make confident trait-based predictions on a small evidence base and will be unmotivated to increase their evidence base before making predictions. For abilities, by contrast, they will be inclined to insist on a relatively large sample of behavior before rendering confident judgments.

Kunda and Nisbett argued that people are more accurate for abilities for several reasons. First, abilities are observed in fixed, highly repeatable situations. Second, ability-related behaviors are relatively easy to "code" unambiguously. Third, ability-related behaviors are often as sessed in numerical terms, which greatly facilitates application of the law of large numbers and thereby enhances recognition of the advantages of aggregation. Compare this state of affairs with the ambiguity of social behaviors. Joe's friendliness in class cannot be coded on the same dimensions as Jane's friendliness at a party. Even the unit to use for social dimensions is problematic. What is the appropriate unit for friendliness? Smiles per minute? Good vibrations per encounter?

A recent study by Brandon, Lawrence, Griffin, and Ross (1990) provided further evidence that laypeople expect levels of consistency and predictability in trait-relevant behavior that simply cannot be reconciled with the best available research evidence. This is true even when subjects make predictions not only about hypothetically described people but also about people they nominate themselves. Brandon and colleagues first asked subjects to indicate someone whom they believed likely to show high levels either of friendliness or shyness. They then asked subjects to offer a guess about that person's centile ranking relative to his or her peers with respect to friendliness or shyness, and to make a number of additional estimates about the distribution of that person's future responses in situations relevant to the trait. Their most important finding was their subjects' willingness to predict that the individuals they had nominated would manifest very high levels of friendliness or shyness in any particular situation in which those individuals were examined. They further estimated that their nominees would behave in a markedly shy or a markedly friendly fashion far more often than they would behave in a relatively typical or average fashion. In other words, they made predictions that would be reasonable and appropriate if, but only if, behavioral consistency from one situation to the next yielded correlation coefficients not in the .10 range suggested by the objective empirical studies, not even correlations in the higher ranges sometimes claimed by critics of those studies, but, rather, correlations very close to 1.0.

LAY DISPOSITIONISM AND THE FUNDAMENTAL ATTRIBUTION ERROR

Evidence regarding lay views of cross-situational behavioral consistency, while highly suggestive, is still rather new and in need of further critical scrutiny. But evidence that people are inclined to offer dispositional explanations for behavior instead of situational ones, and that they make inferences about the characteristics of actors when they would do well to make inferences instead about the characteristics of situations is far from new. It has been the subject of intense critical scrutiny. It is appropriate to review this literature now, including some recent and unpublished data. The evidence indicates that laypeople's vigorous personality theories are matched by only the most rudimentary and vestigial of social psychological perspectives. We will show that people (1) infer dispositions from behavior that is manifestly situationally produced, (2) overlook situational context factors of substantial importance, and (3) make overly confident predictions when given a small amount of trait-relevant information.

Inferring Dispositions from Situationally Produced Behavior

Failing to discount the implications of behavior in view of the constraints on it. The classic study demonstrating that lay perceivers fail to be appropriately sensitive to situational constraints was one conducted by Jones and Harris (1967). The study, ironically, was intended initially to show that subjects could make appropriate inferential use of information about situational constraints. Jones and Harris asked their college-student subjects to read essays or listen to speeches presumably written or spoken by fellow students. Subjects were told that the communicator had been assigned one side of the issue. For example, they were informed that the essay was produced by a political science student assigned to write an essay defending Castro's Cuba or that it was produced by a debater required to attack the proposition that marijuana should be legalized. Despite the fact that subjects clearly perceived the heavy constraints on the communicator in these no-choice conditions, their estimates of the true opinions of the communicator were markedly affected by the particular position the communicator had espoused. Subjects assumed that the target was sympathetic to Castro, or opposed to legalization of marijuana, if that was the position in the essay. The study indicates that observers are too willing to take behavior at face value, as reflecting a stable disposition (in this case, an attitudinal disposition), even when it is made abundantly clear that the actor's behavior is under severe external constraints.

Attributing volunteering to a disposition rather than to the compensation offered. A study by Nisbett, Caputo, Legant, and Marecek (1973) showed that even such an obvious, widely appreciated situational factor as financial incentive can be slighted in explanation and prediction if there is a possibility of explaining behavior in dispositional terms. The investigators allowed observer subjects to watch actor subjects participate in what all were told was a study on decision making. Subjects were female undergraduates. The experimenter announced, "Before we begin the study, I happen to have sort of a real decision for you to make." He explained that the campus "Human Development Institute" would be sponsoring a weekend for the corporate board and some of its prospective financial backers. The spouses of these people would need entertainment and campus tours for the weekend. If the subject could see her way clear to volunteering, she would be paid by the hour. Some subjects were offered $.50 per hour and some were offered $1.50. (Apply a multiplier of approximately 3 or 4 to make the values comprehensible for the 90s.) Only a fifth of the low-payment actors volunteered, while two-thirds of the high-payment actors volunteered. Volunteering was thus largely due to the sheer amount of money offered for doing so.

Both actors and observers were asked about their perceptions of the actor's reasons for volunteering or not volunteering. One item probed the extent to which the actor's behavior was considered an expression of a general disposition to volunteer or not volunteer for worthy activities: "How likely do you think it is that you (or the subject) would also volunteer to canvass for the United Fund?" Observers thought that volunteering actors would be substantially more likely to volunteer to canvass for the United Fund than nonvolunteering actors regardless of whether they had been offered $.50 or $1.50 for doing so. Observers were apparently misled by the actor's behavior, assuming it reflected a dispositional tendency to volunteer rather than a response to a suitably compensated "job opportunity."

Ignoring role determinants in favor of dispositional inferences. If people can fail to perceive the extent to which financial incentives rather than personal dispositions are determinative of behavior, then it is scarcely surprising to learn that they can also fail to perceive the extent to which subtler factors such as role relations can determine the nature of behavior. A deceptively simple demonstration of this point was made by Ross, Amabile, and Steinmetz (1977). They asked their subjects to play a brief "College Bowl" type of quiz game, in which one subject, selected at random, was to ask the questions and the other was to answer them. The questioner's role was to generate ten "challenging but not impossible questions," to which the contestant was supposed to provide answers out loud. Questioners, again and again, took advantage of their role to display esoteric knowledge in the questions they posed (for example, "What is the sweet-smelling liquid that comes from whales and is used as a base for perfume?") and in the answers they supplied (in this case ambergris) when contestants failed to answer correctly.

At the end of the session, both of the participants, and, in a subsequent reenactment, observers as well, were required to rate the questioner's and contestant's general knowledge. One might expect that it would have been clear to subjects and observers alike that the questioners' role advantage had been quite substantial. That is, the questioners' role guaranteed that they would reveal no area of ignorance, while the contestants' role gave no opportunity for such selective, self-serving displays. But the role advantage of the questioner did not prove to be sufficiently obvious either to the contestants or to the observers to prevent them from judging the questioners as being unusually knowledgeable. Both contestants and observers rated the questioner as far more knowledgeable than either the contestant or the "average" student in the university.

Can we generalize from subjects' blindness to the importance of questioner versus contestant "roles" in this study and assume that people will be comparably blind to the importance of more familiar social roles as well? That would be risky, but fortunately, a clever study by Humphrey (1985) allows us to do so. Humphrey set up a laboratory microcosm of a business office. Subjects were told that he was interested in studying "how people work together in an office setting." Some of the subjects were selected, by an ostentatiously random procedure, to be "managers" and to assume supervisory responsibilities, and some were selected to be mere "clerks" who followed orders. Managers were given time to study manuals describing their tasks. While they were studying them, the experimenter showed the clerks the mailboxes, filing system, and so on. The newly constructed office team then went about their business for two hours. The managers, as in a real office, performed reasonably high-skill-level tasks and directed the activity of the clerks, while the clerks were assigned to work on a variety of low-skilled, repetitive jobs and were given little autonomy.

At the end of the work period, managers and clerks rated them-selves and each other on a variety of role-related traits. These included leadership, intelligence, motivation for hard work, assertiveness, and supportiveness. In addition, they rated the leadership and motivation for hard work they would be likely to display in a future job of a specific type. On all these traits, managers rated their fellow managers more highly than they rated their clerks. On all but hardworkingness, clerks rated their managers more highly than they rated their fellow clerks.

The parallel of Humphrey's study to the simple demonstration by Ross and his colleagues is therefore complete and its generalizability to real-world settings and concerns is far greater. People find it hard to penetrate beyond appearances to the role determinants of behavior, even when the random basis of role assignment and the particular prerogatives of particular roles are made abundantly clear. (Presumably, in everyday life, where such matters are more ambiguous, even *less* allowance would be made, and the behavior in question would even more willingly be taken at face value.)

Slighting the Situation and Context in Favor of Dispositions

In our review of the evidence on lay personology at the beginning of this chapter, we repeatedly described the layperson as being overly inclined to see dispositions and apt to infer stronger dispositions than justified by the evidence. But perhaps we have taken people too literally. Perhaps when people say that *"Jane is generous,"* they merely mean that she is inclined to pick up the tab for her employees when they all go out to lunch, or that she is willing to spend a great deal of time with her children's activities, not that, in most situations in which one might plausibly assess generosity, Jane can be counted on to be well above average. It is possible, in other words, that people use trait terms narrowly, but simply don't bother to append to every trait utterance a list of the conditions that elicit the disposition in question. If so, their private beliefs about predictability might actually be quite in line with the facts. It will be recalled from our review of the consistency evidence in the previous chapter that the same data sets that show low consistency across different types of behavior and situations sometimes show rather high stability within similar types of behavior and situations. The average correlation between any two tests of honesty of school children studied by Hartshorne and May (1928) was quite low, yet the stability or reliability of the results of some tests was quite high. For example, the correlation between copying from an answer key on a general information test in March and copying from an answer key on a parallel information test in October was about .80.

Predictions about stability versus consistency. If people's trait ascriptions are implicitly conditioned on circumstances and context, then their beliefs might be more on target than Kunda and Nisbett (1986) gave them credit for. As a matter of fact, however, in a secondary study, Kunda and Nisbett asked one group of subjects to give their estimates of consistency for behavior of the same kind, in the same context, that is, estimates of stability. They asked another group of subjects to give their estimates of consistency for trait-related behavior of different types, in different contexts, that is, estimates of cross-situational consistency. What Kunda and Nisbett found was that subjects estimated both stability and consistency to be very high, and only very slightly different. In other words, there was no indication that subjects made much of a distinction between stability (which research often has found to be quite high) and consistency (which research has found to be almost uniformly low).

Taylor and Crocker (1986) performed an even more direct test of the hypothesis that people are insensitive to similarity of context when making predictions. They described targets' behavior along lines of either extraversion or independence in three different situations. For some of the subjects, the behavioral information was drawn from just one context, either three academic settings or three social settings. For other subjects, the behavioral information was drawn from both contexts, either two academic settings and one social setting or vice versa.

(Academic settings included "in class" and "with the professor"; social settings included "at a party" and "with friends.") Subjects were then asked to predict the target's behavior in an academic setting, a social setting, and an ambiguous setting.

If subjects' dispositional inferences are conditioned at all on context, then they ought to be more confident that targets would behave in a trait-consistent way in the specific setting for which they have past observations. Thus, if the target behaved in an extraverted way in three academic settings, then the subject ought to be more confident that extraverted behavior will occur in an academic setting than in a social setting. In addition, the trait-consistent inferences should be stronger for the ambiguous setting when the behavioral information came from academic and social settings alike than when it was confined to a single type of setting.

These predictions were not borne out. Subjects were just as likely to say that the target would behave in an extraverted way in academic settings when all three information items concerned extraverted behavior in social settings as when all three items concerned extraverted behavior in academic settings. Similarly, subjects were no more likely to predict extreme trait-related behavior in ambiguous settings when observations had been made across different types of settings than when made within a single type of setting. Taylor and Crocker thus found their subjects to be as willing to generalize across contexts to another as to generalize within contexts. This indicates that people do not possess a subtle recognition of the situational specificity that can sometimes characterize dispositions.

Pitting dispositions against situations. One study combines in a single demonstration both halves of the fundamental attribution error that is, an overeager dispositionism and an underdeveloped situationism. This is the classic Darley and Batson (1973) study of Princeton University theological seminary students, which we discussed at length in Chapter 2. A detail that we did not mention there was that their subjects were given a questionnaire intended to measure whether the basis for their interest in religion had to do primarily with assuring personal salvation or primarily with their concern for helping others. This fact means that Darley and Batson were able to compare the strength of a seemingly important dispositional variable with a "small" situational variable, namely, whether subjects believed themselves to be in a hurry as they passed by a person in apparent need of help. After filling out the questionnaire, subjects were instructed to go to a room in another building across campus where they were to give a sermon. It will be recalled that some of the subjects were told that their audience was already there and that the subject was unfortunately already somewhat late because the experimenter had fallen a bit behind schedule. Other subjects assumed that they had plenty of time. The route subjects were to follow to the other building was clearly marked out for them and they were set upon their way.

The parable of the Darley and Batson experiment is built upon another parable – the parable of the Good Samaritan. On the way to the new building, the seminary student was hailed by a man lying in a doorway, who asked for help. And did the seminary students offer their help? Did it make a difference what the nature of their religious orientation was? Did it make a difference whether or not they were in a hurry? The answers are, respectively: some, no, and a great deal.

Sixty-three percent of subjects who were not in a hurry stopped to offer help to the "victim." Only ten percent of subjects who were in a hurry offered help. In contrast, the dispositional measure concerning the nature of religious orientation played virtually no role in determining whether the subject stopped to help. The Darley and Batson experiment thus, in a sense, replicates but amends the lesson of the parable of the Good Samaritan. Their experiment invites us to surmise that all the priests and Levites who passed by on the other side of the road were simply running behind schedule!

But how do we know that people aren't properly calibrated for the Darley and Batson study? How do we know they don't think the hurry factor is very important and the religious orientation factor is unimportant?

Pietromonaco and Nisbett (1982) took the step of describing to subjects an experiment that was highly similar to that of Darley and Batson (substituting for the man lying in the doorway a woman who feigns a knee injury and asks the seminary student to call her husband). Subjects thought the great majority of seminary students would help, but that there would be almost a 20-point gap in the percentage helping in favor of those whose religion was based on a desire to help others. They also thought that whether or not the seminary student was in a hurry would make precisely no difference at all. They believed that "altruistic people" would help and "selfish people" would not, regardless of how much time they happened to have on their hands.

The entrenchedness of dispositionism. Pietromonaco and Nisbett, as it happened, conducted their study not just in order to establish the foregoing facts about people's biases, but also in order to test how difficult it would be to *change* those biases. They asked some of their subjects to actually read the Darley and Batson study before making their predictions about helping behavior in two different situations. One was the slight variant of the Darley and Batson study just described and one was a situation in which the target was not in an experiment but was on his way to visit a friend in the hospital. The victim was a pregnant woman in obvious need of assistance with her car. Some subjects predicted helping behavior for Princeton seminary-student subjects and some predicted helping behavior for a random sample of New Jersey males.

Informing the subjects by having them read about the Darley and Batson study had no significant effect on their predictions about the effect of the dispositional variable of religious orientation. It did have an effect on their estimates of the effect of the situational variable of being in a hurry; but the effect was a mere 18-percentage-point difference, far less than the 53-point difference reported by Darley and Batson.

A similar point was made in a study by Safer (1980) of students' tendency to attribute obedience in the Milgram experiment to dispositional tendencies rather than to the power of the situation. Safer showed the Milgram obedience film to students. Despite the film's emphasis on the extent to which it was the situational factors that compelled obedience, subjects substantially overestimated the amount of shock that would be administered when those factors were *absent*. Thus subjects continued to interpret behavior in terms of presumed dispositions, rather than recognizing the crucial role that Milgram's particular situation had played in producing his disturbing demonstration.

Preference for disposition-based predictions over situation-based ones. A recent study by Newton, Griffin, and Ross (1988) provides perhaps the most direct evidence of lay dispositionism. This study allowed subjects to pick the people, and the precise dispositions, that they deemed relevant for purposes of prediction. In a sense it allowed them to take their "best shot" at "idiographic" or person-based prediction. Newton et al., in a study inspired by the analysis of channel factors described in Chapter 2, gave two groups of subjects an opportunity to contribute to a campus food drive. The subjects in one group had been nominated by their peers as "least likely" among the peers' acquaintances at college to contribute; the subjects in the other group had been nominated as "most likely" to do so. Half the subjects in each group were given this opportunity under conditions where the compliance channel was facilitated in several subtle and not-so-subtle ways: The subjects were addressed in a letter by name and asked to contribute a particular food; they were given a map showing the location of the food collection box; and, perhaps most importantly, they received a follow-up phone call with a brief personalized reminder. Half the subjects were given the same opportunity in the absence of such channel facilitators. A letter was addressed "Dear Student"; no specific food was indicated; and there was no follow-up phone call and no map.

To determine lay beliefs about the predictive power of the situation versus the person, the nominators were asked specifically to estimate the likelihood of a donation by each subject in each of the two relevant conditions, that is, the condition in which the channel cues were particularly facilitory and the condition in which these channel facilitators were eliminated.

The results of the study by Newton and colleagues were straightforward. The nominators thought that the nature of the subject would be important and the nature of the situation trivial in determining whether the subjects would contribute. Specifically, they estimated that the "least likely" contributors would have a 17 percent likelihood of donating in the condition where channel factors facilitated doing so and a 16 percent likelihood of donating in the condition where channel factors did not facilitate doing so; they estimated the corresponding likelihoods for the "most likely" contributors to be 83 percent and 80 percent, respectively. In actuality, it was the nature of the situation that proved more decisive. Only 4 percent of subjects donated food in the nonfacilitory condition (0 percent of the "least likelies" and 8 percent of the "most likelies"), while 33 percent donated food in the facilitory condition (25 percent of the "least likelies" and 42 percent of the "most likelies").

In other words, nominators believed that their knowledge of peers' reputations and personality permitted them to make confident predictions, at least about *some* individuals, and that their designated altruists and nonaltruists would manifest their dispositions regardless of the situational factors involved. But they were wrong! The situational variables proved more important than the relevant actors' dispositions – more important, at least, than any dispositions salient to their peers.

The evidence thus highlights serious flaws in some central tenets of lay personality theory. The evidence, in fact, is consistent with an extreme version of the fundamental attribution error. People readily make trait ascriptions from data that permit only a situational interpretation or, at most, the interpretation that the actor behaves in a particular way in a particular type of situation. These trait ascriptions are then used as the basis for yet further predictions, which, again, are characterized by little attention to situational factors. As we will see, people often must pay very dearly, in terms of prediction accuracy, for their adherence to such dispositionist theories and for the suboptimal inferential strategies to which they give rise.

Overconfidence in Predictions Based on Dispositions

The foregoing hypotheses recently have been given some strong quantitative interpretations – both at the empirical level and at the theoretical level. In two separate series of studies, by Ross and his colleagues and by Nisbett and his colleagues, the costs of dispositionally based predictions have been examined.

In a study by Dunning, Griffin, Milojkovic, and Ross (1990), cited in Chapter 3, a number of situations, either of the laboratory variety or of the everyday-life variety, were described to observer subjects. The observers then were asked to make predictions about the behavior of target individuals in these situations. For example, subjects were asked to predict whether a target would call home at least once a week during the coming quarter, and they were asked to predict whether he would "comb his hair when we ask him for a picture" in the context of a laboratory study. In one set of conditions, information available to raters about the individuals whose behavior they were predicting was quite abundant: Raters were allowed to interview the target individuals in preparation for the prediction task. In another set of conditions, information was scarce: Subjects had to make their predictions working only from the target individual's name and picture.

The results were clear-cut. The average accuracy in high-information conditions (60 percent correct) was only trivially higher than it was under low-information conditions (57 percent correct). This means that whatever information the participants were able to garner about one another through an interview designed to help them in making behavior predictions proved to be of very limited value.

But perhaps people would not *claim* to be accurate about such oneshot predictions of behavior, even after an interview. Fortunately, the data of Dunning and his colleagues allow us to assess whether or not people think that knowledge about individuals helps them make predictions. The truth is that subjects actually believed that they could be rather accurate even when they had information only about the actor's name and appearance! In such low-information conditions, where subjects were right about 57 percent of the time, their expected accuracy had been 72 percent. In high-information conditions, where subjects were right about 60 percent of the time, their expected accuracy had been 77 percent. Thus subjects were overconfident of their ability to make predictions under both high- and low-information conditions. In addition, confidence was poorly calibrated with accuracy. Subjects were only modestly more accurate, and therefore the gaps between accuracy and confidence levels were greatest, when they expressed high rather than low confidence in their predictions. As a consequence, subjects were rather often wrong despite being very confident, or even nearly certain, that they were right – a dangerous epistemological stance.

In the studies by Dunning and colleagues, subjects sometimes made predictions that were consistent with their estimated base rates for the situations in question (or with base rates they were given by the experimenters) and sometimes not. An important aspect of the results is that subjects typically guessed at, or even below, the 50 percent (chance) level when their predictions went against the presumed (or known) base rate.

In one study, subjects who predicted with the base rate were right 75 percent of the time, while subjects who went against the base rate were right only 40 percent of the time. In this same study, subjects whose predictions contradicted the base rate were only slightly less confident than those whose predictions were congruent with the base rate, despite the fact that their predictions were far less likely to be accurate. The costs of going against the base rate were particularly dramatic when the base rates were extreme (and, by implication, situational factors were highly determinative). Subjects who went with the base rate when the base rate was at least 75 percent were right 85 percent of the time. Subjects who went against such base rates were right only 23 percent of the time. The latter subjects showed extreme miscalibration, thinking they were right 72 percent of the time!

The moral of these studies seems clear. For predictions of the kind studied by Dunning and colleagues, and by Newton and colleagues (where subjects were asked to predict who would be most likely and who least likely to contribute to a food drive), the base rate, whether known or presumed, is the best basis for prediction. When the base rate is extreme, one can oppose it in one's predictions only at one's dire peril. *And this* is *true even if the target is someone who the predictor knows well.* The base rate, it should be noted, essentially serves as the proxy for the power of the situation. When the situation is particularly powerful, the base rate is very extreme. It is risky, accordingly, to oppose the base rate for the same reason that it is risky to ignore the situation.

A similar set of studies by A. McGuire (1989) makes a similar set of points. She asked observer subjects to make predictions about target actors in two different helping situations. In one situation the target was asked to volunteer to be a subject in some psychology experiments, and in the other the target was placed in a rigged situation in which, as he or she climbed some stairs and began to overtake a woman on crutches, a book bag began to slip off the woman's shoulder. For some observers, the targets were unknown to them but were described by brief profiles telling of their year in school, what kind of organizations they belonged to, what kind of day they had been having, and so on. In other conditions, the observers had been identified by the targets as people who knew them very well.

Predictions in general proved to be only slightly more accurate than would be expected by chance. Observers, however, believed they were capable of substantial accuracy, especially in the conditions where they personally knew the target well. Moreover, observers who knew the targets well were no more accurate than those for whom the subject was described only by the brief profiles. The results are thus fully congruent with those of Ross and colleagues. Observers were less accurate than they believed, and they did not improve on their accuracy by adding their knowledge about the target to their presumed base rates for the situation, even though they *believed* that they had improved their accuracy by drawing on such knowledge. A little knowledge can be a dangerous thing, at least when it increases confidence far more than it increases accuracy. (See also Borgida & Nisbett, 1977; Nisbett & Borgida, 1975.)

Dispositionism and the Interview Illusion

The literature reviewed to this point is helpful in understanding what we have called the "interview illusion" (Nisbett & Ross, 1980). This is the assumption that one can learn a great deal of useful information about people's personalities from a brief get-acquainted interview. This belief may be called an illusion because the best available evidence on the predictive validity of unstructured interviews for estimating future college or graduate school performance, or job performance by blue-collar or white-collar workers, or professional success by executives, lawyers, doctors, or research scientists, indicates that the relevant correlations rarely exceed the .10 to .15 range. The majority of studies, in fact, produce correlations of .10 or less (Hunter & Hunter, 1984).

The research reviewed in the previous section shows that people are often quite confident that predictions they make based on limited information about a person are nonetheless accurate. The study by Kunda and Nisbett (1986) helps us see why this illusory belief can be sustained. The social behavior data in the interview are difficult to unitize and code, and the outcome data ("is a helpful coworker," "is a good leader of the unit") may also be hard to code. In addition, as Einhorn and Hogarth (1978) have pointed out, there is often blurred or even no feedback about job outcome. Notably, one usually doesn't know how the people who were *not* hired would have fared on the job!

These considerations suggest that it should be possible, using the metric developed by Kunda and Nisbett, to estimate exactly how far off people's estimate of the utility of the interview is, and to compare that estimate with their estimate of the utility of other kinds of information. In order to do this, they asked subjects to estimate the degree to which an interview would predict a trait-related behavior, namely success as a community organizer in the Peace Corps, and the degree to which an interview would predict an ability-related behavior, namely grade point average (GPA) at the University of Michigan. The anticipation was that subjects would overestimate both validity coefficients, but especially the trait-related validity coefficient.

The probability estimates requested of subjects were of the same sort that Kunda and Nisbett had sought with respect to behavioral consistency. That is, subjects were asked to indicate what fraction of the time it would be the case that one Peace Corps trainee rated higher than another trainee in an interview by a psychiatrist would also perform better as a community organizer. Other subjects were asked to indicate what fraction of the time it would be the case that one prospective college student rated higher in an interview by an admissions officer than another student would also subsequently get a higher GPA.

The actual interview validities, we should note, are below .10 in each case – .06 for the Peace Corps prediction (Stein, 1966) and probably about the same for predictions of GPA (see, for example, Klitgaard, 1985; Mayfield, 1964; Ulrich & Trumbo, 1965). Nevertheless, as can be seen in Figure 5.2, subjects thought the validity of the interview for predicting both outcomes was substantial. For Peace Corps success, subjects' estimated probabilities correspond to an interview validity of almost .60! For GPA, they correspond to a still respectable .32. This means that subjects think the interview would be a superb predictor for Peace Corps success, and would be a useful tool for predicting GPA.

The reader may be relieved to know that outcomes like academic performance *can* be predicted with some validity – certainly with more validity than that offered by the impressions of interviewers. But to do so, one must use measures that are based on behaviors or outcome samples that are truly relevant, and perhaps equally important, reasonably large and diverse. High school grades, for example, predict college grades with validities in the range .30 to .45. (It should be noted in Figure 5.2 that subjects *underestimate* the validity of high school GPA for prediction of college grades.) There are some valid predictors even of the trait-related outcome of success as a Peace Corps organizer, including the average rating assigned to letters of recommendation from people who know the

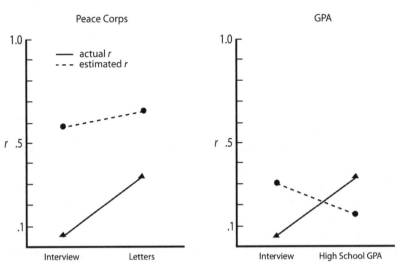

FIGURE 5.2
Estimated and actual predictability of Peace Corps success and of college GPA from interviews and from highly aggregated predictors. (Kunda & Nisbett, 1986.)

candidate well. This validity coefficient was found in one study (Stein, 1966) to be .35. It is important to note the difference, from a psychometric standpoint, between an interview and a letter of recommendation. The latter is typically based on many times the amount of information, often many hundreds or thousands of times the amount of information, that an interview is. Thus, from the purely psychometric standpoint of aggregation, the information available to referees would be expected to have much greater utility than that available to the interviewer. (In addition, it is often possible to increase the evidence base, as Stein did, by questioning multiple referees and aggregating their judgments.)

It is possible to speculate about the costs of letting low-validity interview data enter into judgments such as the decision to hire or not hire particular candidates (Hunter & Hunter, 1984). These costs go up as an inverse function of the size of the interview validity and as a direct function of the size of competing validities. Thus, we may say that most institutions that rely on interviews for selection pay for that practice twice – once when they go to the expense of interviewing candidates and, much more dearly, when they actually use the interview data in selection.

When Are Dispositional Data Useful?

As the above discussion indicates, sometimes one is better off by virtue of knowing dispositional information about individuals. We may now discuss the cases where the conventional wisdom turns out to be correct, at least in outline.

We hinted earlier at one case where individual difference information can be invaluable. This is where one has base rate information for the particular individual for the particular situation. Thus your prediction that Jack will talk a lot at the lunch table today, as in the past, is bankable, as is your prediction that your spouse will complain about the next party where people are standing around talking and drinking. It is entirely likely, in fact, that lay convictions about the utility of traits are in part based on an overgeneralization from successful predictions based on narrow, within-situation stability.

But even predictions made across different types of situations can have genuine utility. In the previous chapter we elaborated some special circumstances where trait-based predictions can be made with good prospects for accuracy. These include the following: (1) The prediction is based on a large, diverse sample of past observations, and pertains not to a single action or outcome, but to an average expected over the "long haul." (2) The prediction deals with the relative likelihood of extreme outcomes or events, and the actors have in the past shown themselves to be extreme relative to others. (3) The predictions are mindful of population base rates. In particular, extreme base rates and the situational pressures they reflect cannot be overlooked with impunity.

Given that there are actual individual differences in behavior, in other words, given that there is substantial variance in the responses of the population, trait information can in theory predict even to novel situations in which the observer has never seen the target. But you have to know the person fairly well, you have to be predicting behavior over the long haul, or the person you are making the prediction about has to be extreme on the predictor variable before this has any chance of being true.

As we have seen, laypeople accept no such qualifications. They seem to believe that they can predict the behavior of a wide range of people, little known to them, even in single, novel situations.

THE SOURCES OF LAY DISPOSITIONISM

How could people be so wrong in their fundamental construal of the causes of behavior? How could they prefer to base explanations and predictions on trait ascriptions of little or no predictive power for the task at hand, while being so insensitive to powerful situational factors and to individual difference data having real predictive utility, such as ability data and reputational data? In the remainder of this chapter we will consider sources of naive dispositionism that lead people to over-estimate the predictability of their peers' behavior. In Chapter 6 we will consider factors that make naive dispositionism less costly, and less a source of error, than one might presume from such an analysis.

Perception and the Dispositionist Bias

The explanation we prefer is a fundamentally perceptual one, owing originally to Kurt Lewin but first stated clearly by Fritz Heider.

> . . . behavior . . . has such salient properties that it tends to engulf the field rather than be confined to its proper position as a local stimulus whose interpretation requires the additional data of a surrounding field – the situation in social perception. (Heider, 1958, p. 54)

In short, and in the Gestalt terms that would have been congenial to Lewin and Heider, when we observe another person, an actor, it is the actor who is "figure" and the situation that is "ground." People are active, dynamic, and interesting; and these are the stimulus properties that direct attention. The situation, in contrast, is normally relatively static and often known only hazily. Nor does the observer normally spend much mental energy trying to figure out what goals the actor might be pursuing, what obstacles the actor might be confronting, what mood the actor might be in, and so on.

Why does the observer then go on to make a dispositional attribution corresponding to the form of behavior observed? Heider again was clear on this:

> . . . Man is not content simply to register the observables that surround him; he needs to refer them as far as possible to the invariances of his environment. . . . the underlying causes of events, especially the motives of other persons, are the invariances of the environment that are relevant to him; they give meaning to what he experiences. . . . (p. 81)

We need only add an explanation of why it is the dispositional properties of the person rather than those of the environment that people tend to infer when observing the person in the environment. To be succinct, what you *attend* to is what you *attribute* to. Indeed, there is no generalization coming from the Heider-inspired attribution literature of the 1970s that is better supported than this. For example, McArthur and Post (1977) found that the actor's behavior was attributed less to his situation when he was brightly illuminated or moving than it was when he was poorly illuminated or stationary. Similarly, Arkin and Duval (1975) showed that an actor's behavior was attributed less to his environment when the environment was stable than it was when it was in motion. Taylor and Fiske (1975) showed that when an observer watches actors A and B interact but can see A better than B, causal attributions about the outcome of the interaction are made more to A than to B.

Differing Causal Attributions for Actors and Observers

The preceding analysis, incidentally, implies that the actor and the observer will have very different understandings of the causes of the actor's behavior. The observer will be inclined to invoke dispositions of the actor, whereas the actor will be inclined to invoke situational opportunities and constraints. Jones and Nisbett (1972) argued that this is, in fact, generally the case. Actors tend to give fewer dispositional explanations for their behavior than observers do. For example, in the study cited earlier by Nisbett and his colleagues (1973), observers inferred that actors who volunteered for money were the volunteering type while those who didn't volunteer, for much less money, were not the volunteering type. But the actors themselves explained their behavior in terms of the sum of money they were offered. The same pattern was true for subjects asked to explain why they chose their college major and why they dated the person they did. The actor preponderantly explained such choices in terms of the properties of the stimulus ("I date her because she's a very warm person"), while the observer was more likely to invoke dispositions of the actor ("He dates her because he's very dependent and needs a nonthreatening girlfriend"). In addition, Nisbett and his colleagues found that actors believe that fewer trait terms are applicable to them than to their best friends, a new acquaintance, or even a well-known news commentator. Rampant dispositionism is kept in check when it is the self that is in question.

The contention that the divergence between the attributions of the actor and the observer is due at least in part to perceptual differences is supported by a study conducted by Michael Storms (1973). Storms had his subjects have a get-acquainted conversation while being videotaped. Also present during the conversation were two observers, one of whom was situated so as to be able to see actor A well but not actor B, and the other of whom was situated so as to be able to see actor B better. After the conversation, actors were asked to explain their own behavior and observers were asked to explain the behavior of the actor they could easily observe. Both actors attributed their behavior primarily to situational factors, such as the behavior of the other actor and the unusual situational context. Observers were more inclined to attribute the actors' behavior to inferred dispositions. However, when the observer was shown a videotape of the conversation that focused on the actor he could not previously observe well, that is, on the situation confronting his actor, he now gave attributions that resembled those of the actor himself. Even more remarkably, when the actor was shown a videotape of *himself,* he then made attributions that were similar to those of *observers!*

The results of Storms' study thus support the view that attribution is guided to a very substantial degree by one's focus of attention and that a primary reason that actors and observers have different casual interpretations is simply because actors and observers typically are attending to different things.

Construal and the Dispositionist Bias

The perceptual factors underlying the dispositional bias are undoubtedly aided and abetted by a variety of cognitive factors having to do with the way people construe social behavior. These will be noted briefly.

Linguistic factors. As Walter Mischel (1968) was among the first to note, people's dispositional attributions are probably hastened along by the fact that the same adjective that can be applied to the actor's behavior can usually be applied to the actor. Thus, "hostile" acts are perpetrated by "hostile" people, "dependent" acts by "dependent" people, and so on.

The language ordinarily does not allow us to make similar associations between acts and situations. (Consider the clumsiness of "a situation that promotes hostility.") A notable exception is the idea of a *difficult* task, that thereby disposes one to fail.

Impression perseverance. Once one has observed an actor's behavior or outcome and come up with a dispositional attribution, it can be difficult to alter one's hypothesis about that actor, even if one were to become privy to new information that challenged or invalidated the old information (Lord, Lepper, & Ross, 1979; Ross, Lepper, & Hubbard, 1975). There is evidence for a broad range of cognitive processes that would conspire to sustain initial impressions (Ross & Lepper, 1980). Subsequent acts are likely to be construed in terms that render them consistent with initial attributions; and confirmations are accepted at face value, while exceptions are readily explained away.

Theory and ideology. One's perceptually based inclinations are likely to be augmented with theories that capture them and justify them. The Western intellectual and moral tradition gives much support to the habit of dispositional explanations. Much of Western culture, from the Judeo-Christian insistence on individual moral responsibility to the intellectual underpinnings of capitalism and democracy in terms of the imperative of freedom of action, emphasizes the causal role of the actor and attributes actions of different kinds to actors of different kinds. The Marxist tradition is perhaps the major intellectual tradition to focus on situational explanations. Behaviorism, Lewinian field theory, and most sociological frameworks are traditions within the social sciences that take a situational perspective, but the impact of these on the larger society is, of course, rather slight. The possibility that nonWestern cultures may foster rather different psychological theories is a topic pursued in Chapter 7.

Statistics and the Dispositionist Bias

Finally, it should be noted that some commonplace statistical failings help sustain the dispositionist bias. First, people are rather poor at detecting correlations of the modest size that underlie traits (Chapman & Chapman, 1967, 1969; Kunda & Nisbett, 1986; Nisbett & Ross, 1980). Second, people have little appreciation of the relationship of sample size to evidence quality. In particular, they have little conception of the value of aggregated observations in making accurate predictions about trait-related behavior (Kahneman & Tversky, 1973; Kunda & Nisbett, 1986). The gaps in people's statistical abilities create a vacuum that the perceptual and cognitive biases rush in to fill.

The very factors that allow or encourage people to hold the personality theory that they do in the abstract, it should be noted, will tend also to lower the utility with which the theory is applied to individual predictions in daily life (Nisbett, 1980). Most importantly, people are likely to inflate the consistency values that they associate with particular traits for particular people. We can safely assume that they habitually will assign trait scores of greater extremity, with greater confidence, than is appropriate. This means that they readily will make predictions, with assurance, that a sophisticated personologist would recognize to be inappropriate.

How Could We Be So Wrong?

How could we make such serious errors about such important matters? The question here is often phrased in the terms of evolutionary theory: Judgments about other people are often important to survival and therefore we could not be expected to be terribly wrong about them. Such evolutionary arguments are extremely dangerous in psychology, as Einhorn and Hogarth (1978) have pointed out. The mere fact that some ability manifestly would be of great value to survival does not serve to establish that an organism must have it. The vervet monkey, for example, is constantly imperiled by leopards and pythons, yet experimental tests have shown that the most seemingly obvious signs indicating the nearness of leopards (such as the presence of a dead gazelle in a tree) do not alarm the vervet monkey. Similarly, the vervet monkey does not recognize the trail of a python, either by its sight or its smell.

And there is the question of whether personality judgments of the sort we have been discussing are really all that important to humans in the conditions under which they evolved. A critic of the social perception tradition has characterized it as "the social psychology of strangers" and has asserted that the errors that characterize our judgments about strangers may have nothing to do with judgments about intimates. It seems to us that there is a distinct possibility that both the characterization and the assertion are correct, or largely so. The lay personality theory discussed in this chapter may apply mostly to judgments about people we do not know well. Evolutionary pressures are more likely to have been applied to judgments about intimates in the early hominid and human troop than to judgments about strangers. Thus a simple reading of base rates for the individual for the particular, familiar situation would have been about all that was needed for quite accurate prediction in daily life. Most sophisticated analyses probably did not become important until people began to trade and travel and thus to meet individuals with unfamiliar behavior and construals.

Of course, many of us today spend most of our time with nonintimates and must constantly make judgments of some importance about near-strangers. So the errors of lay personality theory we have been describing are not mere foibles.

In the next chapter we will examine the implications of the predictive failures we have discussed in this one. Do these failures generate chaos for us in our attempts to coordinate our behavior with that of others? It would seem not, and thus there is a paradox. We deal with nonintimates all the time; we hold erroneous theories about the basis of their behavior; and yet we somehow seem to muddle through without an enormous number of prediction errors on a daily basis. What spares us? It is this question to which we next turn our attention.

CHAPTER 6
THE COHERENCE OF EVERYDAY SOCIAL EXPERIENCE

We begin this chapter with a personal confession. Despite all the evidence we have seen from objective studies of behavioral consistency (described in Chapter 4), and despite all we know about cognitive illusions and lay shortcomings in behavioral prediction (described in Chapter 5), we continue to believe that our own social world is inhabited by people who behave quite differently from each other in ways that are, for the most part, quite consistent. We would insist that Chuck, the ebullient clown of the freshman dorm; Norbert, the shy computer whiz who won a scholarship to M.I.T.; and Butch, the bully who long ago terrorized the entire third grade, really were distinct individuals who behaved in markedly different ways from each other and from their peers, not just in one situation but across many situations. We cannot be convinced, moreover, that our stereotypes and expectations about these individuals biased our interpretations of their behavior to such a degree that we saw distinctiveness and consistency where none existed.

We do not deny that our interpretations of people's actions frequently take into account our knowledge of their past behavior and our general impressions about their personality. We would concede, for example, that while we interpreted Chuck's bright red suspenders as a comic attention-getting device, we probably would have attributed the same suspenders on Norbert to a strange sense of fashion or a general lack of concern about appearance. Similarly, we remember that when Butch sat quietly off to the side of the playground during the lunch hour, we did not revise our view of his aggressiveness or see his standoffishness as evidence of any inconsistency in character or temperament. On the contrary, we attributed his behavior to sulkiness, and tacitly assumed he was sitting there planning new acts of intimidation. These are attributions we never would have made if the same standoffishness had been displayed by a child with a less aggressive reputation. But in conceding interpretation biases, we are not conceding that we have been guilty of any inferential folly. In fact, we would insist that we were *correct* to give weight to our prior experiences and more global impressions about people, and that completely "unbiased" interpretation would have led us astray more often than it enlightened us.

We would make similar claims about our performance as real-world prognosticators. While we recognize that we frequently have been guilty of overconfidence, we would insist that many of the real-world predictions we make with a high degree of confidence have an equally high degree of accuracy. We're sure that Coach Whiplasch will treat his team to some harsh language after their dismal first-half performance, that Aunt Edith will insist on singing at the next family wedding, and that good old Charlie will agree to drive us to the airport early on Sunday morning (and even accept our thanks with a wave of the hand and the assurance that it will be "no trouble at all"). And we insist that our own past experiences, more often than not, have justified our confidence in predictions of this sort.

In fact, the more one thinks about the realities of our day-to-day experiences with each other, the more difficult it becomes to accept the conclusions seemingly demanded by the "objective" studies of cross-situational consistency reviewed in Chapter 4. We do not dispute the charge that perceptual, inferential, and perhaps even motivational biases may lead us to see more behavioral consistency and predictability than any purely objective analysis would verify; but at the same time, we doubt that the objective behavioral studies captured the degree of consistency and predictability that exists in everyday social dealings.

Reconciling experience with the scientific evidence from objective studies demands that we reflect further upon the predictability of everyday social events – predictability we believe would be documented by even the most objective account of our experiences, and that we count on heavily in planning and conducting our lives. More specifically, we must try to understand how and why everyday social behavior may, in fact, be highly stable and highly predictable, even though appropriately designed empirical tests reveal cross-situational behavioral correlations fully as low as Mischel and company claim.

The resolution to this paradox, which will occupy most of the remainder of this chapter, rests on a pair of related arguments. The first and most basic argument is that real-world behavioral consistency need not be a reflection of personality traits. The second argument is that predictability need not depend on cross-situational consistency – at least not consistency of the sort that would be detected in any well conceived study in the tradition of Hartshorne and May, Newcomb, or Sears. Both arguments arise from a careful examination of the differences between the demands and constraints of well-designed, "fair" empirical studies and those of the messier, and in a sense "unfair" tests provided in everyday life. This examination, it will become apparent, highlights the ways in which person and situation factors may be confounded to produce the frequent regularities (and also the occasional surprises) that we all experience in our everyday attempts to understand, predict, and control each other's behavior.

We make no claim for originality in what follows. Great personality theorists from Gordon Allport to Gardner Murphy to Kurt Lewin, and great social theorists from W. I. Thomas to Robert Merton to Erving Goffman, have stated or anticipated every argument we now make. Our contribution is merely to organize these arguments for the specific purpose of bridging the gap between scientific evidence and everyday experience (see also Cantor & Kihlstrom, 1987; Snyder & Ickes, 1985).

SCIENTIFIC DISENTANGLING VERSUS REAL-WORLD CONFOUNDING

It does not take a great deal of thought to recognize that some of the consistency and predictability of behavior that we rely upon in planning and transacting our social affairs may have little to do with classically conceived individual differences. Such regularity sometimes can be yet another reflection of the power of the situation. The predictability of the physicians who examine us, the professors who lecture us, the coaches who exhort us, the colleagues who chat with us, and the assorted friends, neighbors, and family members with whom we intertwine our lives, owes much to the relative consistency of the situational forces and constraints that govern those particular individuals – or at least govern them when they interact with *us*.

In the course of ordinary experience, we rarely have a chance to observe the same people in radically different roles or situations in a way that would test fairly the cross-situational consistency of their geniality, generosity, or ability to delay gratification. Nor do we systematically vary our own behavior, or our status and circumstances, or the nature of our relationships with others, to determine how their responses to us might change as a result. Accordingly, we are not forced (indeed, not even given the opportunity) to appreciate the power of the relevant role demands and to disentangle dispositional influences from situational ones. Quite the contrary, we count on the fact that particular roles and relationships will render people's behavior predictable – despite the fact that broader, less "biased," and more "scientific" samples of behavior would reveal inconsistency and unpredictability of a sort and degree that would surprise us profoundly.

Scientific Disentangling of Person and Situation

The common real-world "confounding" of dispositional and situational influences is precisely why careful researchers go to such pains to define and measure individual differences in contexts that eliminate obvious role constraints and obligations. It is also why they hold their test situations constant for the different individuals being tested.

Few people would fail to recognize the lack of scientific rigor, indeed the *unfairness*, involved in deciding whether Jane was more aggressive or impulsive than Sally simply by counting how often each of them behaved aggressively or impulsively during a specified period of time. Suppose Jane spent the day driving a cab in Manhattan while Sally spent the same day helping the Reverend Fletcher's wife arrange flowers for an upcoming Easter service in a Long Island suburb. Suppose, furthermore, that Jane snarled twice, cursed half a dozen times, and once clenched her fist, while Sally emitted one sound that might conceivably be construed as a snort, muttered "oh fudge" on two occasions when she knocked some blossoms to the floor, and never clenched her fist during the entire time period. Such differences in objective responses could hardly be treated as unassailable evidence of personality differences. Nor would sensible laypeople be willing to resolve their doubts about the appropriateness of these personality tests simply by increasing the level of aggregation and reliability of their observations – for example, by observing Jane and Sally on a large number of separate days on which Jane continued to drive a cab through crowded city streets while Sally continued her bucolic existence as a suburban matron. More generally, sensible laypeople, like sensible researchers, would (or at least should) recognize the folly of deciding theoretical questions about personality by simply tallying the behaviors of different actors as they respond to the differing pressures and constraints of their very different lives.

Competent methodologists seeking theoretically appropriate, unconfounded tests of personality would recognize the need for a research design in which the target individuals could be observed responding to an identical, or at least fairly similar, range of situations. Sometimes this can be accomplished simply by selecting a population of individuals who, in some important sense, are all in the same global situation [for example, military recruits undergoing basic training or Newcomb's (1929) children at a summer camp] and then observing them in a variety of clearly defined circumstances that arise naturally in the course of their day (for example, at meal times, or during a long hike, or in the hour-long rest period). At other times, this objective can be accomplished by deliberately exposing people to a fixed set of situations under genuinely constant and well-defined circumstances (for example, Hartshorne and May's procedures that provided subjects with temptations to lie or cheat, or Mishel's procedures that obliged children to choose between a small reward now and large rewards later). The advantage of both of these methodologies is that they allow one to determine the extent to which people differ in their overall propensity to behave in particular ways, and to determine the consistency with which they show those propensities across different contexts, once role demands and other extraneous influences are eliminated or held constant.

Real-World Confounding of Person and Situation

Everyday social experience seldom if ever provides such pure and decisive tests of individual differences. We rarely get a chance to see the cab driver arranging flowers in church, or the flower arranger coping with the rigors of surly dispatchers, double-parked cars, and drunk passengers – much less a chance to see a random sample of people exposed, systematically, to both of these situations and to many more besides. (Though it is interesting to note that some provocative works of fiction, from Mark Twain's *Prince and the Pauper* to the Eddie Murphy movie *Trading Places,* offer "thought experiments" defending the same thesis that social psychological theory does – to wit, that clothes and the situation "make the man.") Of course, we sometimes do get to see familiar people in novel situations; and on such occasions, especially when the new situation differs radically in its opportunities and constraints from the ones in which we've had occasion to observe the actor in the past, we are apt to be surprised and enlightened. Just ask the seventh-grade youngster who comes upon her English teacher frolicking with his old college buddies on the beach, or the citizen who sees the tough traffic cop (the one who never misses an opportunity to ticket and lecture a speeder) comforting a lost two-year-old. Or remember what happened the last time you got to see one of your worldly and sophisticated adult friends interacting with her parents during a trip back home.

We also have this situationist lesson driven home to us when it is we ourselves who are being observed in an unfamiliar context – or at least in a context unfamiliar to the particular observer. The authors know all too well the surprised, even shocked look on the faces of students who have caught them in unprofessional behavior – slamming a racket after a missed volley on the tennis court, lining up for a ticket to a Grateful Dead concert, playing pinball at a hamburger joint, or shouting at their kids at the local Wal-Mart.

It is precisely the confounding of person and situation that allows people to be well served by their naive dispositionism. When we predict that the behavior of professors will be professorial, that the behavior of dictators will be dictatorial, or that the behavior of servants will be servile, it makes little difference whether we do so because we are aware of the impact of the respective roles, because we have made stereotyped judgments about the types of individuals who occupy such roles, or because we have taken role-prescribed behavior at face value and ascribed corresponding personality traits to the actor. In each case, the performances we observe more often than not will confirm our predictions and justify the relevant trait ascription – professorial, dictatorial, or servile – provided, of course, that we continue to observe the actors in circumstances where the privileges and constraints of their roles remain in effect, and provided that no other powerful situational factors suddenly intrude.

Misattributions can have similarly benign consequences in contexts where the immediate determinants of a particular person's behavior are less easy to detect. Thus our failure to recognize that Mrs. Jones' reclusiveness and secretiveness reflect the impact of an abusive, alcoholic husband (whom we may never even have met) will not undermine the accuracy of our predictions about Mrs. Jones' future behavior – unless and until she escapes from the situation that is constraining her. By the same token, we will suffer no adverse consequences from our failure to recognize how much a particular benefactor's consistent generosity owed to the tax code, or how much a particular congresswoman's consistently liberal rhetoric reflects the prejudices of her district – until we base our hopes on that benefactor's generosity continuing in the absence of tax advantages or on that politician's rhetoric being translated into political action when she becomes a member of the president's cabinet.

Audience-Induced Consistency and Predictability

If we were to spend a day following around a rock star, a captain of industry, or a star high school football player, we would soon discover some subtler, less direct, determinants of behavioral distinctiveness and consistency. In particular, we would discover the compelling influence exerted on these celebrated individuals by their audiences. A steady diet of adulation, coupled with relentless demands for attention and attempts to curry favor, would constitute a potent and consistent situational influence on *anyone's* behavior. Patterns of response that seemed suggestive of egotism or insensitivity, or of condescension and an air of noblesse oblige, would be quite unsurprising, even predictable. And such response patterns would not be a simple reflection of the actors' native dispositions. In particular, we would expect many previously modest and level-headed people to behave in a similar fashion. (An expectation that is nicely captured by the political saying that politicians who reach Washington "either grow or swell.") We would even expect celebrated people to fall so much into the habit of behaving like celebrities that they might continue to do so even when their customary audience is absent and their current audience is sparing them the usual pressures and demands.

Following around a member of the clergy or a respected academician, we suspect, would yield a similar insight. Their audiences would expect and generally reinforce displays of piety and concern from the cleric, and displays of intellectuality, absentmindedness, or even mild eccentricity, from the professor. Role and status are by no means the only source of such audience-induced effects on an actor's distinctiveness and consistency. An obvious racial or ethnic identity, a stigmatizing handicap, or even an unusual appearance or stature, can similarly alter – and in a sense homogenize – the nature of the social situations that the individual encounters. Indeed, most of us are likely to encounter such people only in situations where their audience is constraining their behavior, and only after repeated exposure to such audiences has led them to develop relatively rigid and predictable ways of responding.

The consequences of physical attractiveness offer a particularly interesting illustration of the interaction effect between audience and actor. No one would be surprised to learn that beautiful women are more likely to marry successful and accomplished men (Elder, 1969), thereby changing their own social status and altering the environment within which they function. But the benefits that come with physical attractiveness are by no means limited to matters of courtship and marriage. Several studies show that attractive youngsters, from the earliest years of school onward, are presumed to be more personable and socially accomplished than their less attractive peers, and also to be more intelligent and likely to succeed academically (Clifford & Walster, 1973; Dion, Berscheid, & Walster, 1972). Attractive people are further presumed to be happier, more sociable and extraverted, less socially deviant, and more likely to be successful in their personal and professional pursuits (Hatfield & Sprecher, 1986; also Albright, Kenny, & Malloy, 1988; Chaiken, 1979).

Given such differences in expectations and presumptions, it is hardly surprising that attractive people are more likely than unattractive ones to receive the "benefit of the doubt" from those who evaluate their actions. There is evidence, for instance, that playground transgressions are attributed more benignly, and that milder punishments are recommended, when the transgressor is a handsome child than when he is an ugly one (Dion, 1972; also Berkowitz & Frodi, 1979). Even people's products are affected by their appearance. When evaluating essays on "the societal consequences of television," male evaluators gave as much weight to the apparent attractiveness of the female author (whose photo accompanied the essay) as they did to the objective quality of the essay (Landy & Sigall, 1974).

A study by Snyder, Tanke, and Berscheid (1977) illustrates how such biases may lead the observer to alter the behavior of the favored or unfavored actor. Snyder and his colleagues contrived to have male subjects engage in a "get-acquainted" telephone conversation with a young woman whom they believed, on the basis of a photo, to be highly attractive or unattractive. The investigators subsequently required the callers to evaluate the personality of the young woman with whom they had just spoken. They also had raters separately evaluate the behavior of the caller and the personal attributes of the young woman – in each case hearing only one side of the conversation and possessing no information either about the woman's physical appearance or the male caller's beliefs about her appearance.

The experimental effects reported by Snyder and colleagues were not large, but they were very consistent across all measures. First, and perhaps not surprisingly, the male callers rated their partner to be more personally engaging when they believed her to be physically attractive. Second, and perhaps equally unsurprisingly, the male callers in such circumstances were rated as warmer and friendlier by the observers who heard only their part of the conversation. Finally, and most important in terms of our present discussion, the male callers in the different attractiveness conditions seem to have evoked different types of responses from the women with whom they conversed – responses that encouraged some erroneous personal inferences. Thus raters hearing only the woman's side of the conversation rated her to be more friendly and likable (and even a bit more attractive) when the photo seen by the caller had suggested she was beautiful rather than plain – even though the raters never saw the photos in question. Research may or may not bear out the truth of the parental admonition that "pretty is as pretty does," but the research of Snyder and his colleagues makes it clear that "pretty does as pretty is seen to be." Related research by other investigators makes it equally clear that racial stereotypes and other negative interpersonal expectations can produce similar confirmation biases (Cooper & Fazio, 1979; Word, Zanna, & Cooper, 1974).

Of course, people do not always respond to their "audiences" by confirming their hopes or expectations. (A steady diet of overly eager suitors, especially suitors whose enthusiasm seems all too obvious in its source, could lead to aloofness, distrust, or even manipulativeness.) But the general point should be clear. People's physical characteristics, no less than their roles and reputations, constitute important parts of the life space and important situational determinants of behavior. As a consequence, different actors – beautiful or ugly, rich or poor, big or little, black or white – may find themselves responding to different situations even when purely "objective" accounts of their situations (for example, attendance at the Sigma Chi party last Saturday, or being chided for laziness by Professor Fogarty, or asking Andrea for help in debugging a computer program) would fail to capture such differences.

The "homogenizing" effect of one's appearance, role, or status on others can lead us to see consistency and especially predictability in particular groups as well as in particular individuals. One of our favorite examples of this influence was provided over 20 years ago in a discussion of police demeanor between one of the present authors (then a graduate student) and a wealthy and influential Londoner (who at the time was president of the City of London Chamber of Commerce). The student's complaints of police brutality toward students in New York and London alike were dismissed with a wave of the hand and the smug but heartfelt assurance that "such reports of misbehavior are utter nonsense." The impeccably dressed middle-aged man went on to note that he had watched and even dealt with "our Bobbies" on many occasions ("Why, just last week they stopped me in the Rolls to tell me about a broken taillight") and had found them to be consistently courteous and helpful.

A less extreme example of this phenomenon is familiar. Parents are often surprised to hear accounts of their children's behavior at school, at a party, or in the home of a particular friend. Part of the surprise comes from the parents' failure to appreciate the impact of the various social contexts on children in general. But part of their surprise comes from the fact that whenever they personally observe their child, they themselves are an important element in the child's situation, producing more uniformity than would otherwise be the case.

More generally, people who behave in distinctive or extreme fashion may fail to appreciate how others act when they are not on the scene. Thus the person who monopolizes conversation at every social gathering, or constantly reminds everyone of the need to be nonsexist in word, thought, and deed, or who radiates animal magnetism, has enjoyed few opportunities to witness the behavior of people when they are free of that person's verbose, antisexist, or magnetic presence. Likewise, celebrities, clerics, or professors are likely to have biased notions about the way particular individuals, groups, or even people in general, characteristically behave.

Once again, insofar as we are concerned with problems of accurate social prediction, the implications of such audience-specific consistencies are mixed. On the one hand, predictions based on past experience will tend to be accurate so long as the source of confounding remains in place. On the other hand, predictions about how those people will behave in the absence of their customary audience can be expected to fare much less well.

WHEN PEOPLE CREATE THEIR OWN ENVIRONMENTS

Choosing and Altering Situations

"Fair" research designs for investigating personality not only eliminate sources of everyday consistency that are actually situational, they also reduce some sources that reflect genuine interactions between dispositional factors and situational ones. People in everyday circumstances do not just "happen" to face the particular situations that compel and constrain their behavior. They actively choose many of the situations to which they expose themselves, and they alter many situations they happen to encounter. (See Endler, 1983; Kenrick & Funder, 1988; Pervin, 1977; Snyder, 1981, 1983; and Swann, 1984, for more detailed discussions of person-situation interactions.) In particular, people play an active role in increasing the opportunities to develop, and then to display, the very characteristics that make them distinctive from each other. Again, the most obvious examples of this interaction and its effects on behavioral consistency and predictability would provoke little controversy. Physicians, clerics, entrepreneurs, and rock stars began by making choices that reflected their personal preferences and capacities. Their choices, in turn, placed them in social contexts that allowed, even compelled, them to further develop and display those preferences and capacities.

Such an "interaction effect" involving dispositions and situations can be seen with particular clarity in the case of people who are termed "intellectuals." By the academic and occupational choices they make, by the people with whom they pursue friendships, by the reading material they purchase (and maybe even by the decision they make to disconnect the television set because it is too tempting a situational influence to overcome), intellectuals effectively create their own environments. And the environments they create are ones that are relatively conducive to the continuing growth and display of intellectuality, and relatively free of pressures that would give rise to behavior inconsistent with intellectuality. (Although, we should reemphasize, a given intellectual's behavior generally will prove to be less consistent than the intellectual's customary audience supposes.)

People, of course, not only "choose" situations; they transform situations by their presence, their demeanor, and their behavior. The Reverend Fletcher no doubt avoids orgies and opium dens, and his audiences no doubt adjust their environment in anticipation of his goodly presence (both the guest list and the evening's entertainment tend to be somewhat more refined when Fletcher is among the invitees). And we suspect that the good Reverend also might take active steps to transform any opium dens or orgies into which he happens to wander. (Though we shouldn't be *too* confident in making such a prediction; for novel situations featuring strong situational temptations do have a way of transforming people, even people whose personal dispositions we thought we knew rather well from past observation.)

The capacity of people to make choices that both reflect their dispositions and alter their situations in ways that encourage the display of such dispositions is perhaps obvious in the case of occupations, hobbies, volunteer organizations, and even choices of friends and neighborhoods. But the same capacity can be seen even in the context of a well-controlled laboratory study. One particularly nice illustration was provided by the famous experiments of Kelley and Stahelski (1970) using a "Prisoner's Dilemma" paradigm. In their experiments, two subjects, unable to see or communicate with each other, had to choose whether to make cooperative or noncooperative responses on each of several consecutive trials. The relevant "payoff matrices" were presented to the participants: When both subjects chose the cooperative response, both received a modest payoff. When one chose the cooperative and the other the competitive response, the latter received a high payoff and the former suffered a large loss. When both chose the competitive response, both suffered a moderate loss. Different subjects, however, construed the situation in different ways. To some, it was obvious that the sensible strategy was to play the cooperative response as much as possible so as to settle into a pattern of modest gain along with one's partner. Such subjects (as would be expected from people's tendency to assume that others share their construal of situations, and from their resulting tendency to overestimate consensus for their own behavior) overwhelmingly estimated that other subjects would see the object of the game in the same way and play cooperatively. To other subjects, it was equally obvious that the situation would reward "defection" more than cooperation, and they played accordingly, assuming that their partner would see things the same way.

The interactive consequences of such perceptions quickly showed themselves. Subjects who cooperated tended to elicit cooperation on the initial trials and to encourage continued cooperativeness by their partners. Thus they tended to be correct in their predictions. Indeed, by cooperating they not only created a situation in which it was relatively easy for their partners to reciprocate (and not particularly tempting for their partners to switch to a competitive response); they also effectively created a situation that encouraged their own continued cooperation because sustained mutual cooperation allowed both partners to fare quite well.

Conversely, subjects who opted to make a competitive response on an initial trial also tended to have their prophecies confirmed. Such behavior both discouraged early-trial cooperators from continuing to cooperate (lest they continue to be exploited) and gave would-be exploiters little reason to switch to cooperation (lest they expose themselves to almost certain exploitation). Therefore those who elected to play competitively on early trials likewise found their predictions confirmed. More importantly, the noncooperators created an environment that encouraged, even obliged, them to continue in their noncooperative ways. For these subjects could anticipate (quite correctly) that switching to a cooperative mode of responding would merely leave them vulnerable to exploitative strategies on the part of the other participant – strategies encouraged, even provoked, by their own prior exploitation attempts and their fears of being exploited.

Few clearer demonstrations exist to show how actors' perceptions and assumptions (whether based initially on deep personal convictions or on relatively incidental differences in situational construal) dictate responses that change the environment so as to make those responses become situationally constrained as well. In the Kelley and Stahelski demonstration we have a "personality parable" that is less famous, but perhaps no less instructive, than the situationist parables of Chapter 2.

Responsiveness to Others' Needs for Predictability

One of the most important ways in which people transform social situations, and in so doing make their own behavior or that of a peer more predictable, is to offer or solicit a specific commitment. Our willingness to venture a confident prediction that Ms. Gentille will attend our dinner party tonight (and our willingness to expend resources and make other arrangements in service of that prediction) is only trivially based on our knowledge of her personal dispositions or even of her situation. We may know little about her overall gregariousness, her liking for dinner parties in general, or her fondness for our particular brand of dinner parties. We may also know little about any time pressures, conflicting obligations, attractive social alternatives, or other situational constraints acting upon her. And we certainly do not have the benefit of knowing exactly how she subjectively construes our invitation or what she imagines our party will be like. All these uncertainties could have made our prediction task very difficult – were it not for the fact that she accepted our invitation, that she mentioned this morning that she would bring along a couple of bottles of a nice Cabernet, and that she has not phoned to tell us of any change of plans. For, at least in our neck of the woods, people who have committed themselves in this way do not fail to show up as they are expected to do – certainly not without first letting us know that we should revise our expectations.

The broader point is that people are often sympathetic to the plight of those who must predict their responses. For social harmony depends, in part, upon our willingness and ability to help other people predict our responses correctly, and our willingness and ability to respond in a way that confirms other people's predictions about us. Accordingly, in many important domains of social conduct, we signal our intentions and generally avoid disconfirming each other's predictions.

Note again the contrast between the demands of everyday experience and the logic of research designs seeking to validate traits or test the accuracy of social predictions. In laboratory or field observation settings, competent investigators would take pains to ensure that the people whose responses were being observed were indifferent to those who were doing the observing, or better still, unaware that any observing was taking place. They would try to make sure that the observers communicated no hopes or expectations to the actors, and that the actors provided no guidance about their intentions to anyone making predictions. They certainly would permit no promises or commitments to be made, no contracts to be negotiated, and no other considerations introduced that either obliged the actors to be predictable or required them to warn all concerned when, for some reason, they were going to do something surprising. And once again, the absence of such "contaminating" real-world influences would serve to make the actors' behavior less predictable, and to make the performance of anyone offering confident predictions about them rather poor (Einhorn & Hogarth, 1978; also Swann, 1984).

It is important to recognize that the responses we most often are called upon to predict may be quite overdetermined. The roles people choose, the situational forces that are imposed upon any who choose such roles, the expectations that observers communicate to actors, and the commitments that actors make to observers may all serve to rein-force each other. It is this overdetermination that contributes to the consistency and predictability of behavior, and that generally allows us to make correct predictions even when we overlook or misconstrue important features of the evidence upon which we base our predictions. When this overdetermination of behavior is eliminated, either by a fair and careful researcher or by significant changes in the social context within which the actor operates, apparent inconsistencies in response, and uncharacteristically high error rates on the part of those who predict the actors' behavior, can be expected. On the other hand, as we will see next, when person factors and situation factors interact in a powerful enough fashion, the result may be a degree of continuity in social behavior and a degree of predictability of social outcomes that is sufficiently striking to challenge any situationists who are too simpleminded in their faith.

CONTINUITY OF BEHAVIOR OVER THE LIFESPAN

The analysis offered to this point speaks directly to the apparent behavioral continuity that we seem to detect over an individual's lifespan (Block, 1971). It is easy, of course, to see how biases in the way an individual's behavior is sampled and interpreted by a given observer could exaggerate that observer's impressions of stability and continuity. And it is clear that such lifespan continuities, real as well as perceived, can reflect the stability of environmental pressures and constraints rather than the stability of an individual's inclinations or dispositions. But it also is evident from our earlier discussion that the interaction between the person and the person's environment – that is, the cumulative or aggregated effects of the person's active choices and the social environment's response to that person's behavior and reputation – can produce important lifespan continuities in an individual's actions and outcomes (see Caspi, Bem, & Elder, 1989). It is further evident that these continuities would be more difficult to detect – indeed might be prevented from manifesting themselves – by any research design that carefully selected and held constant the stimulus situations to be faced by the subjects. In particular, one would never expose the subjects to situations in which their preexisting reputations lead people to view them very differently or constrain their behavioral options.

Several studies document these cumulative consequences of person-situation interactions. For example, we know that extremely aggressive children produce stormy family environments that, in turn, prompt further aggression (Patterson, 1982). We also know that aggressive children expect others to be hostile (Dodge, 1986), much as the competitive Kelley and Stahelski subjects expect others to be competitive. Accordingly, they may behave in ways that elicit aggression – thereby both confirming such children's beliefs and heightening their subsequent inclination to act aggressively. Similar processes could produce similar cumulative consequences for children who are unusually shy, dependent, or impulsive, or for children who have unusually high or low aptitudes for particular types of activities. Both through conscious choice of activities and peers, and through the effects of their behavior on the sentiments and responses of those around them, children possessing particular characteristics create environments that dictate their own subsequent actions and outcomes.

In one particularly provocative study, Caspi, Elder, and Bem (1987) analyzed the results of a longitudinal study of Berkeley youngsters, documenting the cumulative consequences of youthful "ill-temperedness." An initial set of analyses suggested that boys' "temper tantrum" scores at age 10 predicted ratings of irritability, moodiness, and lack of control made by judges 20 years later (with r values ranging from .27 to .45). Furthermore, analyses revealed that the ill-tempered youths also quit school earlier than their even-tempered peers (hardly surprising given the response of teachers and peers to irascibility and poor impulse control). They also achieved less prestigious jobs and suffered more downward social mobility (also not particularly surprising, if only because of their relative lack of education) and were twice as likely to have their marriages terminate in divorce (an outcome which no doubt both contributed to and reflected their continuing problems of temperament, and was probably linked to their job histories as well).

Caspi, Elder, and Bem (1988) provided similar findings for shyness and dependence. Their work duplicates and extends the early, very ambitious work of Block (1971) showing marked stability in life outcomes and consistency in observers' ratings over periods of many years for several traits. In each case, the investigators' analyses revealed stability in ratings of these characteristics over the individual's lifespan. They also illustrated how the child's characteristic patterns of behavior (and the reactions such behavior provoked from others) served to create environments that promoted such continuity of temperament and led to predictable consequences for the individual's occupational history and family relationships.

It is worth noting, in view of our Chapter 4 discussion of aggregation, that lifespan continuity results involve associations between predictor variable and outcome measures that clearly are reflective of multiple events. Children acquire reputations, and receive special attention, relevant to their ill-temperedness only after a history of surliness, punctuated perhaps by a few displays of extreme aggressiveness. Similarly, people are rarely fired or divorced for a single behavior but rather for an accumulation of behaviors that ultimately become impossible to ignore. As Caspi and his colleagues have noted, it is the cumulative *consequences* of behavior, rather than the cumulative nature of the measures alone, that are responsible for the impressive magnitude of the relevant correlations.

Ironically, Walter Mischel – the theorist whose critique of conventional personality theory we have considered in such detail – has reported his own evidence of lifespan continuity. Specifically, he found that four-year-olds who had "delayed gratification" successfully in some of his particular laboratory situations showed higher levels of social and cognitive compliance as adults and, in turn, achieved higher scholastic performances. Indeed, the simple correlation between preschool delay of gratification time and subsequent SAT scores was .42 for verbal scores and .57 for quantitative scores (Mischel, Shoda, & Rodriguez, 1989). It is easy to see how ability to delay gratification, even if rather weak and domain-specific, could serve to produce such dramatic consequences. In a child's life there is almost always something more exciting to do than to concentrate on the cognitive task at hand. Those children with a little greater capacity to sit still may be those who, in our book-ridden culture at least, gain the cognitive skills, and at the same time earn reputations and develop conceptions of themselves, that contribute to further scholastic achievement.

We have no doubt that peers who interacted with the grown-ups in these longitudinal studies of temperament would have shown at least moderate agreement in rating their aggressiveness, shyness, or bookishness. We suspect, furthermore, that these peers would have had success in making certain predictions about everyday behavior. At the same time, we think it would be relatively easy [in view of the "overconfidence" findings by Dunning and colleagues (1990) and by Vallone and colleagues (1990) discussed in Chapter 5] to show that such peers are relying on views of personality that are too strongly dispositionist, or at least too simplistic in their dispositionism. In particular, we suspect that the same peers would have fared less well, in terms both of accuracy and of overconfidence, if they had been required to predict how the individuals in question would respond in some "fair" test situations, that is, situations carefully designed to spare (or deprive) these adults most of the cumulative consequences of their youthful temperaments.

SITUATIONS, CONSTRUALS, AND PERSONALITY

Our analysis of complex real-world interactions between people and the situations that prompt and constrain their behavior narrows the gap between the valuable lessons offered by well-controlled research and the seemingly contrasting lessons offered by messy, confounded real-world observation. In concluding this chapter, we will offer some final thoughts about the strengths and limitations of conventional, intuitive lay personology. We will then consider the implications of our analyses for the ongoing attempts to develop a more satisfactory science of individual differences – one less congruent with the trait psychology of laypeople and the rather similar trait psychology designed by earlier personality researchers, but one with the potential, perhaps, to become more powerful and illuminating.

The Utility of Lay Personology Reconsidered

We have argued that lay personology generally proves to be quite serviceable for many everyday purposes, even though it may rest on overly simplistic, even erroneous, dispositionist assumptions. At the same time, naive dispositionism can lead to erroneous inferences and to ill-advised decisions in some specific contexts. Some of these inferences and decisions are relatively common and harmless, and some are relatively uncommon but potentially dangerous. Our discussion contrasting clean and fair research designs with messy real-world contexts should help clarify when it is that lay personology is likely to get its user in trouble.

The relation between lay personology and a more correct theory of personality is analogous to the relation between lay and scientific physics (Holland et al., 1986; Nisbett, 1980, 1987). Most of us manage to deal rather well with physical objects and forces in our environment, and some of us develop prodigious skills in particular domains (for example, hitting, catching, and throwing balls) despite some rather profound misconceptions about the laws of motion that govern the relevant physical events – misconceptions, incidentally, that were shared until a few hundred years ago by the most sophisticated of our thinkers (Champagne, Klopfer, & Anderson, 1980; McCloskey, 1983).

Most adults, for example, predict that an object being carried forward at a given speed (for example, a package they are carrying in their hands as they walk, or perhaps a small rodent being carried in the talons of a flying bird of prey) would drop straight downward if it were suddenly released. They are genuinely surprised to see the actual curved (in fact, parabolic) path that such objects trace to earth. This misconception and related ones (not addressed with scientific precision before the time of Galileo and Newton) had few consequences. Only recently in our evolutionary history have human beings had occasion to drop objects from fast-moving vehicles or to avoid objects being directed at them from on high. But the advent of aerial warfare early in this century quickly changed that. World War I bombardiers had to learn to curb their tendency to hold their bombs until they were directly over their targets (a problem ultimately solved, it is worth noting, by developing instruments that no longer relied upon "intuitive" calculation of the bomb's path). And World War I infantrymen had to learn to worry not about the bombs they saw being released overhead but, instead, about those currently being released from planes that were approaching them from a substantial distance away.

One of the most pervasive and important lay misconceptions about the physical world, mirrored in the thinking of early savants, bore an even more direct relationship to our discussion of lay personology. As Lewin noted:

> Aristotelian dynamics are completely determined in advance by the nature of the object concerned. In modern physics, on the contrary, *the existence of a physical vector always depends upon the mutual relations of several physical*

facts, especially upon the relation of the object to its environment. (Lewin, 1935, p. 28; italics in original)

In other words, in ancient physics the behavior of objects was understood exclusively in terms of the properties or dispositions of the object: A stone sinks when placed in water because it has the property of heaviness, or "gravity"; a piece of wood floats because it has the property of lightness, or "levity."

What is missing in such generally serviceable views about the behavior of objects is a *relational* view of the events in question. The relation must be considered between the mass of water and the mass of the object placed upon it, or in the example about falling objects, the relation between inertial movement and the force of gravity. The limitations and misconceptions of naive physics did not prevent the layperson from seeing a predictable and coherent world. Indeed, they served to enhance the predictability and coherence of everyday experience. These misconceptions did have some costs, however, for they made the layperson susceptible to potentially costly errors in judgment when new phenomena had to be dealt with. They also constituted intellectual baggage that had to be cast aside, at times reluctantly, before a far more powerful, but much less intuitive, way of looking at the physical world could be developed. (Of course, as our readers know, in the last century Newtonian conceptions of time, space, and motion gradually have given way to even less intuitive and even more powerful conceptions of the universe inspired by the genius of Einstein and other theoreticians.)

Psychology has had no Newton – much less an Einstein – to replace our naive, experience-based conceptions with a more precise and scientifically correct set of views to describe the relationship between the person and the situation. In fact, as we discussed in Chapter 1, one of psychology's most important lessons may be a deeper appreciation of the factors that make the development of powerful behavioral laws offering precise prediction so difficult, no matter how much we refine our methodological and conceptual skills. Nevertheless, we believe that the social psychological analysis of the relationships between people and their environments summarized in this chapter can help one sketch the outlines of a more powerful conception of personal distinctiveness and consistency.

The Search for More Powerful Conceptions of Personality

Suppose we sought to replace the traditional doctrine of traits with a different approach to the problem of individual differences, one inspired by the conceptual analyses offered in this chapter. Suppose, in particular, that we sought an approach compatible both with the low cross-situational consistency shown in well-controlled, fair, observational studies of the sort reviewed by Mischel and with the manifest regularities of everyday social interaction. The emerging outlines of such an approach can now be discerned, and we will sketch them.

We draw primarily on the social cognitivist tradition exemplified by George Kelly, Walter Mischel, Julian Rotter, and Albert Bandura, as well as younger theorists who have synthesized and augmented their work (for example, Cantor & Kihlstrom, 1987; Markus & Nurius, 1986). Like most of these cognitivists, we do not take for granted the existence of broad cross-situational consistency – either in overt behavior or in the cognitive and motivational processes that underlie behavior. Behavioral consistency and the lack of it both represent understandable if not always predictable consequences of the dynamic relationship existing between the particular individual and that individual's social environments. The approach that is called for, accordingly, must be idiographic in spirit – despite the burden this requirement places on the investigator and despite the limitations it forces us to acknowledge about the prospects for powerful, general-purpose, personality scales. That is, we will need to know different things about different people in order to appreciate the distinctiveness and coherence in their behavior and in order to anticipate when, and how, their behavior will prove consistent and predictable.

A related but perhaps more fundamental difference between conventional approaches to personology and a possible alternative approach concerns the perspective to be adopted in characterizing the behavior itself. An approach that seeks to make behavior explicable and predictable must take into account the subjective perspective of the actor, not that of the observer or researcher. Objective tallies of specific actions (for example, giving money to the panhandler, lowering the grade of the student who submitted her term paper late) or even types of actions (that is, generous actions, punitive actions, or the like) will be of limited value. The real coherence in a given person's behavior can be found only when one appreciates the person's intentions, strategic assumptions, self-perceptions, and inferences about relevant situations – that is, the person's own conception of the meaning of the behavior.

We will enlarge upon these issues and then offer a cautionary note about prospects for success.

1. Goals and preferences. Human behavior is organized around short-term, long-term, and even lifetime goals. People formulate plans to achieve these goals, monitor their progress, and maintain or change their patterns of behavior accordingly. Thus the coherence in Jill's on-the-job behavior may be understood in terms of the consistency with which she does and says very similar things across a range of related workplace situations, whereas the coherence in Jack's on-the-job behavior can be understood only by appreciating how he changes his behavior across situations with different demands, and in response to evidence that his goals are not being achieved. An anecdote from Cialdini's clever book (1988) on social influence makes the point well. Cialdini was interested in determining the best strategy for restaurant waiters to use in maximizing tips. He observed the highest-earning waiter in a particular restaurant for a period of time to find out what it was that he did. What was most notable about the waiter's behavior, it turned out, was that he didn't do anything consistently – except seek to maximize his tips. With families, he was warm and homey, winking at the children and anticipating their desires. With adolescents on dates, he was haughty and intimidating. And with older women eating alone he was solicitous and confidential. The "consistency" in these diverse behaviors lay only in the energetically and thoughtfully pursued professional goal of the waiter.

Individual differences in goals and preferences have long been seen as an important source of individual differences in behavior (Mischel, 1968). The personologist's approach, moreover, often has been idiographic, revealing that people differ from each other not only in their particular needs and values but also in the importance or centrality of those needs and values. Thus, esthetic concerns appear central and organizing for some individuals and of relatively little importance for other individuals. Recognition of social and political values similarly can provide the key for understanding some people's consistencies in behavior, but can be of little significance in understanding other people's behavior. Differences in the centrality and importance of achievement – especially career achievement – have been documented both in trying to understand individual differences within a culture and, as we will discuss in Chapter 7, in trying to understand differences between cultures (McClellard, Atkinson, Clark, & Lowell, 1953).

2. Competencies and capacities. To understand continuities and seeming discontinuities in behavior, we must know more than a person's goals and standards. We must also know something about the person's ability to achieve those goals and satisfy those standards. Accordingly, if our goal is prediction, we must discover as much as possible about the person's competencies and capacities. Cantor and Kihlstrom (1987), in a comprehensive discussion of this issue, explored the various dimensions of what they termed "social intelligence," including the skills and knowledge required to formulate short-term and long-term strategies for goal attainment as well as domain-specific differences in "expertise" (for example, getting along with peers, budgeting time and resources carefully, and mastery of cognitive strategies to help one successfully delay gratification).

These authors also emphasized that apparently similar situations may differ in the skill level required for attaining particular goals. Recent work by Wright and Mischel (1987) makes this point well. After studying boys with problems of aggression control, they came to the conclusion that the same situation placed different degrees of strain on the boys' capacity to restrain themselves. When the strain was less than a certain level, individual differences were neither apparent nor predictable. When the strain was greater, and the boys' social competence and impulse control were more sorely tested, individual differences in aggressiveness could be predicted with substantial reliability – well beyond the level of the standard personality coefficient discussed in Mischel's classic review. The message of this study seems clear. The personality tester who is looking for discriminability, like the ability tester, must employ tests that are appropriate to the individuals' particular level of overall competence, and ideally are also sensitive to their more specific strengths and weaknesses.

3. Subjective representations of situations. Since people's behavior in a given type of situation depends on their perception of that situation, progress in predicting and interpreting behavior may be limited until we make progress in mapping people's situational construals. Even during the decades when psychologists were preoccupied with the task of classifying people, there were a few lonely voices (Lewin, 1935; Murray, 1938; Brunswik, 1956; Barker, 1968) urging us to pay more attention to the task of classifying situations. Since the cognitive revolution of the 1970s the study of situational representation has come into fashion. (See reviews by Bem & Funder, 1978; Cantor & Kihlstrom, 1982.)

The emphasis to date has been on the characterizing dimensions that could be used to describe particular schools, psychiatric institutions, social gatherings, or the like, and to account for the responses they evoke from people in general (Forgas, 1982; Magnusson & Ekehammar, 1973; Moos, 1968, 1973; see also Cantor, Mischel, & Schwartz, 1982; Harré & Secord, 1973). But the notion of individual differences in construal also has begun to receive increasing attention. As Cantor and Kihlstrom (1987) note, differences in construal may reflect differences in immediate needs or goals; that is, a given dinner party may be a recreational situation for most guests, a social achievement test for the nervous host, and a self-promotion opportunity for the local politician in attendance. Such differences in construal may also reflect longer term, more idiosyncratic differences in personal history and temperament. Thus, family dinners and other commonplace social episodes may evoke warm and happy associations for some individuals but threatening or unhappy ones for other individuals (Pervin, 1976; 1985).

4. Attributional styles and perceptions of personal efficacy. While investigators have just begun to scratch the surface in exploring individual differences in construal, there is one difference in subjective interpretation, a difference closely related to the central concerns of this book, that has been extensively studied. This difference pertains to attributional style, and it has been given different names by different theorists, including "expectancy for internal versus external control" (Rotter, 1966), "self-efficacy" (Bandura, 1977a, 1977b), and "mastery versus helplessness" (Dweck, 1975). Some theorists have been heavily concerned with the origins of such attributional differences (for example, Seligman, 1975). Others have been more concerned with devising appropriate measures (Crandall, Katkovsky, & Crandall, 1965; Rotter, 1966) or with teasing apart different aspects of perceived control (for example, Collins, 1974; Lefcourt, 1972; Weiner, Freize, Kukla, Rest, & Rosenbaum, 1972). The important point, however, is that investigators have been able to show that people differ substantially in the pattern of attributional preferences they exhibit when they are called upon to account for their successes and failures or to explain other events affecting their happiness and well-being. As we will discuss further in Chapters 7 and 8, these differences in attributional style can have important motivational and behavioral consequences. Some individuals feel themselves in control of their own lives and responsible for their own happiness, success, and even health, and they act accordingly by taking steps to improve their fortune. Others feel themselves helpless pawns, unable to overcome environmental obstacles and the vagaries of chance; they too respond accordingly, by passively accepting their fate.

5. Conceptions of self. The more general notion that people are guided not only by their perceptions and beliefs about situations but also by their conceptions of themselves has received increased attention from cognitively oriented personality theorists. Hazel Markus and her colleagues (Markus, 1977; Markus et al., 1985) have shown that people have "self-schemas," or generalized understandings of the self, that serve to interpret both their own behavior and the behavior of others. Thus some people organize their understanding of behavior to a substantial extent around the concept of dependence and some around the concept of independence, while for others neither concept has much relevance. People who are "schematic" for dependence and independence can respond "me" or "not me" more readily to probes about particular traits semantically related to this dimension than "aschematics," they can provide more evidence when asked to defend assertions that they are dependent or independent, and they are highly resistant to information that seemingly contradicts their self-schemas.

In the same spirit, several investigators concerned with gender have explored the role of gender schemas. As Sandra Bem (1981, 1985) has demonstrated, some males and females monitor many aspects of their behavior for its degree of masculinity or femininity, whereas for others this is not a very salient dimension and they merely seek to respond to whatever opportunities or constraints exist in the particular situation (see also Markus et al., 1985; Spence & Helmreich, 1978). It seems apparent that similar individual differences in schema centrality are likely to exist with respect to ethnicity, occupation, political ideology, and other group identities.

Once again, the thrust of this work is highly idiographic. The self-schema investigators assume that different individuals will monitor themselves along different dimensions in different situations. But it should be noted that Snyder (1974, 1979) has shown that there are global differences in people's tendency to monitor their overt behavior and the reaction it may evoke from others. That is, differences in self monitoring, measurable with Snyder's simple paper-and-pencil scale, apparently reveal themselves across many behavioral dimensions and social contexts, with some people seeming to be consistently conscious of the impression they wish to create and their success in doing so, and others seeming to engage in such self-monitoring only rarely. It remains to be seen whether self-monitoring is best regarded as a general trait or as a tendency operating primarily in conjunction with important self schemas.

In an interesting paper, Markus and Nurius (1986) argued that people guide their behavior not merely with respect to the current conception of self but also with respect to "possible selves," that is, positive self-conceptions that they would like to earn by changed behavior and negative self-conceptions that they seek to avoid. Tory Higgins and his associates (Higgins, Klein, & Strauman, 1985; Higgins, Strauman, & Klein, 1986) have similarly explored the possibility that it frequently may not be the self *per se*, but discrepancies between actual and potential selves that dominate the individual's monitoring and construal of the social environment. (See also Cantor et al., 1987.)

The personality theory of the future will surely continue to stress the importance of understanding people's goals, competencies, strategies, construals, and self-conceptions. Research along these lines is likely to turn up a great many interesting facts about the determinants of human behavior and to tell us a great deal about the nature and degree of consistency to be expected of different kinds of people in different kinds of situations. But a cautionary note is in order. Even the most enthusiastic researchers in these traditions give us no reason to expect that behavior in particular situations, by particular (nonextreme) individuals, is ever going to be highly predictable. Indeed, the very multiplicity of individual difference factors leads us to that conclusion. Jane may behave as she does in a given situation because of certain goals she is pursuing and certain self-conceptions that she has. Alice may behave in a very different way, even though she has goals and self-conceptions that resemble Jane's, because Alice lacks some of Jane's competencies, or because she has different strategies. In order to predict the nonexceptional behavior of people in the full range of situations that show substantial individual variance, we simply would have to know too much, including all the situational and contextual dimensions that might be relevant as well as their weightings and their salience at the moment of action. The predictability of behavior for the scientist who deals with strangers, looks across a wide range of behaviors, and lacks detailed information about construals and commitments is bound to remain sharply limited. In contrast, a high degree of predictability may be attainable for most of us in our everyday experience, where we see the people we know in a restricted range of situations, where we can communicate with each other about our subjective perceptions, and where we make explicit or tacit agreements to enhance predictability. But there is no lesson of modern psychology that is clearer and more important in its implications than the message of the past three chapters: The predictability and coherence of everyday behavior are achieved in the face of lay psychological theories that are seriously deficient; and these deficiencies can lead to consequential errors in judgment in some very important personal and professional contexts.

CHAPTER 7
THE SOCIAL PSYCHOLOGY
OF CULTURE

In the last chapter we tacitly confined our discussion of behavioral predictability to cases where the participants are all members of the same culture and, for the most part, even of the same subculture and social class. If we were to extend our discussion to include a broader sample of humanity, however, issues of predictability would take on a very different cast.

Suppose, for example, we were called upon to predict whether a particular married woman would express pride, resignation, or embarrassment when we ask her about the wage-earning job she holds outside the home. Suppose we were asked to predict whether she would go to the market wearing a skirt and blouse, a pair of shorts and a halter top, or a modest full-length garment and a veil. Suppose we were asked to predict whether she will converse readily with the man behind her in line or refuse even to acknowledge his greeting. Suppose we were asked to predict whether a teenage girl would turn a deaf ear, protest vigorously, or submit meekly when her father insists that she stop seeing her new beau or that she change her diet, dress, or manner of addressing her elders.

Suppose our social predictions pertain to a male sitting in a local tavern. Will he be flattered or offended by inquiries about his crops, his real estate holdings, his love life, his increasing girth, or his views about capital punishment? And how much will it matter if the inquirer is a friend, coworker, or stranger, or if the inquirer is a man of higher or lower social status than the man in the tavern? Or suppose you are invited to a social gathering. Will your hostess expect a gift? How will she respond to a salutatory kiss on the cheek, or on the lips, or on the hand? Suppose you are going to pay your condolences to a recently widowed acquaintance. Will you find him shredding his garments, sitting impassively, or apologizing profusely for the absence of his wife as hostess?

The ability to make such predictions, and the ability to make appropriate inferences about behavior that confirms or disconfirms them, play a critical role in social functioning. But our success in such tasks may have little to do with our skills in the art of personality diagnosis. Rather, our success may reflect the fact that we are dealing with culturally dictated responses and that we are reasonably knowledgeable about the relevant culture or subculture.

An understanding of the role of culture is becoming increasingly important in a world where travel and commerce are leading people from markedly different societies to contact each other with unparalleled frequency, and where diverse ethnic groups are living side by side in modern nation-states like our own. Indeed, ethnic renewal, and ethnically based conflict, seem to be remarkably consistent themes in the chronicle of our times.

The topic of culture is deeply relevant to the specific theoretical concerns of this book. For ethnic, racial, religious, regional, and even economic subcultures are in an important sense the distillates of historical situations, as well as powerful contemporary determinants of individuals' behavior. They are, at the same time, important sources of the particular subjective meanings and construals we place upon the social events we observe. And ethnic cultures also constitute tension systems characterized by complicated balances of forces that generally resist alteration yet, paradoxically, can sometimes be the conduit of dramatic social change when new influences are introduced or old ones are removed.

In this chapter we will discuss the ways in which cultures affect behavior and the factors that influence the development, maintenance, and change of cultures. We will not attempt to be at all comprehensive in the discussion. Rather we will pay special attention to contemporary American society and to the particular ideologies and ethnic groups that have shaped its history and that continue to influence each other. For the most part, we will not have data from well-controlled laboratory or field studies to guide us. Instead, we will rely heavily on the observations and insights of seminal thinkers who have pondered the complex relationship between objective circumstances and subjective interpretation in the determining collective existence.

SITUATIONAL DETERMINANTS OF CULTURE

Effects of Ecology, Economy, and Technology

How do groups come to develop and to sustain the characteristics that make them different from each other? Many social scientists, most notably

Karl Marx, have answered this question in terms of external ecological or economic factors (LeVine, 1982; B. Whiting & J. W. M. Whiting, 1975). Thus hunter-gatherer societies, we are told, encourage individual initiative but also demand and reinforce values of group solidarity because the effective pursuit of game requires these qualities. Agricultural societies discourage independence and aggressiveness, and stress obedience and responsibility, because this combination of qualities is necessary for the predictability of resources and steady effort required to cultivate crops. By contrast, pastoralists, whose livelihoods depend on their herds, tend to be highly aggressive because stealing the neighboring tribe's livestock (and preferably wiping out the males of the tribe so as to avoid retribution) is a reliable route to wealth, and inability or unwillingness to fight is an invitation to more aggressive competitors.

This situationist thesis about the evolution of cultural practices and values is an attractive one. And some classic correlational studies have, in fact, found evidence of such associations between peoples' characteristic traits or values and their modes of producing food and acquiring wealth (for example, Barry, Child, & Bacon, 1959). But such correlational studies make it difficult to disentangle cause from effect, that is, to determine the extent to which societies' shared values and characteristic patterns of social behavior are truly consequences, rather than at least partial causes, of their particular economic circumstances. Accordingly, social scientists take particular interest in various "natural experiments" in which ecological demands and opportunities somehow have been manipulated by historical happenstance, allowing us to observe the nature of any resulting changes in cultural values, practices, and institutions. We will now examine two particularly intriguing such experiments in America.

The transformation of Plains Indian culture. The introduction of products and technology, whether by traders, military adventurers, colonizers, or religious missionaries, has provided a continuing source of external influence on the world's cultures. One technology-transfer experiment that was particularly dramatic in its consequences was the introduction of the horse to the hunter-gatherer peoples of the American West early in the seventeenth century. Within a half dozen generations, following initial contact with the escaped horses of the Spanish explorers, a distinct and complex culture of equestrian nomads was flourishing on America's Great Western Plain (Lowie, 1954).

The economic advantage of the horse lay in its facilitation of transport (previously, dogs had been relied upon) and the hunting of large game, especially the buffalo (which previously had been pursued far less effectively on foot). But the effect of the horse on Plains culture went far beyond the facilitation of existing practices. The possession of horses, and the ability to acquire them through raiding and to offer them in trade or ceremony, became the standard for prestige and power. Great discrepancies in wealth and status, within a given band and between different bands, became an important fact of social life. Moreover, the possession of large herds (often several thousand for a single village) demanded frequent movement to provide new grazing land for the herds, which thereby stimulated contact among previously isolated tribes. As a result, cultural leveling occurred over an immense territory. Tribes lost features of their earlier cultures as they acquired each other's tools and techniques for more effectively hunting the buffalo and using its products. The Crow, for example, lost the canoe, and the Cheyenne ceased to grow corn. They also developed a shared militarism and glorification of physical valor that made them increasingly distinct from Navajo, Hopi, Iroquois, and other non-Plains people.

The story to be learned from this cultural experiment is not a simple one of new technology inevitably transforming culture (Lowie, 1954). Not *all* tribes responded to the arrival of the horse by becoming aggressive equestrian nomads. The first tribes to acquire horses, tribes that already had an established farming culture, were not notably transformed. Indeed, these agriculturalists frequently were victimized by raiding parties from more aggressive tribes that acquired horses later but made them a more vital part of their culture. Nevertheless, the possibility of rapid transformation of cultural values and practices, in response to changes in external opportunities and constraints, was clearly demonstrated. This is a topic that we will discuss further when we later turn our attention to tension systems and cultural change.

Tocqueville on the evolution of American democracy and wealth. At about the same time as the culture of the Plains Indians was responding to the introduction of the horse, a very different cultural experiment was under way farther east in the New World. European colonists of diverse social backgrounds were confronting the challenges of a virgin land, and as they did so, they were beginning to lay the foundations of a new social and political system. Historians and social scientists long have pondered the connection between the opportunities and demands of this new land and the form of government that evolved. Why, they asked, did democracy come to America in the manner that it did?

The answer in elementary school textbooks is that the people in the New World grew accustomed to living free of the autocratic style of government characteristic of Europe at the beginning of the age of the nation-state. Having thrown off the yoke of the English monarchy, and lacking any hereditary aristocracy, the self-confident, independence-loving Puritan farmers and tradespeople settled on a form of government based on individual rights and popular representation. While there is nothing wrong with this story, it is incomplete. Notably, it does not explain why government in America never deteriorated into anarchy or into dictatorship (as it did rather quickly when Puritans, of essentially similar backgrounds to those of the American colonists, took power in England in 1649 under the leadership of Oliver Cromwell).

The answer offered by Alexis de Tocqueville, the great nineteenth-century observer of American society, was a decidedly situationist one. He argued that the physically demanding and socially primitive world of the colonists, coupled with the absence of any preexisting government institutions, required the citizenry to act cooperatively in ad hoc associations of their own construction. The habit of forming and using voluntary associations to pursue shared goals thus taught the skills and techniques of self-governance that are essential to democracy. Tocqueville believed it was no accident that

> ... the most democratic country in the world now is that in which men have in our time carried to the highest perfection the art of pursuing in common the objects of common desires and have applied this new technique to the greatest number of purposes. (Tocqueville, 1835/1969, p. 514)

This habit of "pursuing in common" had effects both internally on the members of organizations and externally on the wider body politic. Tocqueville described the internal effects in the following observation:

> When some view is represented by an association, it must take clearer and more precise shape. It counts its supporters and involves them in its cause; these supporters get to know one another, and numbers increase zeal. An association unites the energies of divergent minds and vigorously directs them toward a clearly indicated goal. (Tocqueville, 1835/1969, p. 190)

Organizing for the purpose of achieving many different goals eventually has quite general systemic consequences. The larger society becomes accustomed to responding to the interests represented by these associations, and the forms of government are affected by the skills that people develop through their membership in voluntary associations.

More recently, Tocqueville's argument has been extended by political economists to account for American economic development as well. Esman and Uphoff (1984) contend that associationism is important for the psychological and social understructure of developing economies.

> A vigorous network of membership organizations is essential to any serious effort to overcome mass poverty under the conditions that are likely to prevail in most developing countries for the predictable future. . . . While other components – infrastructure investments, supportive public policies, appropriate technologies, and bureaucratic and market institutions – are necessary, we cannot visualize any strategy of rural development combining growth in productivity with broad distribution of benefits in which participatory local organizations are not prominent. (Esman & Uphoff, 1984, p.40)

Thus both democratic forms of government and the wealth characteristic of highly developed economies have been attributed, in part, to the habit of working in voluntary associations and the resulting civic cast of mind – characteristics that, at least in the case of America, can be attributed to brute structural facts of ecological and economic necessity. There is, to be sure, an account of America's cultural and institutional development, and the development of capitalistic democracies elsewhere, that gives heavy weight to factors that are ideological rather than material in nature; and we will consider this account a bit later. But first we will consider some nonmaterial, yet still quite powerful, sources of ethnic attributes.

The Situation of the "Middleman" Minority

How does a group get for itself the reputation of being greedy, exploitative, disloyal, pushy, and intrusive, yet simultaneously clannish and exclusive? In Europe, and to a lesser extent in America, it is Jews who have long been vilified in these terms. Explanations for such antisemitic stereotyping generally center on unique features of Jewish history and culture and on traditional Christian teachings about the role played by Jews in the Crucifixion.

Yet a wider view shows that no such unique grounds are required for a group to attain the unattractive reputation just described. It is said that every country "has its Jews." Indonesia, the Philippines, and Vietnam have the Chinese; East Africa has Indians and Pakistanis; West Africa has Lebanese; Turkey has Armenians and Greeks; and Egypt has the Copts (who are Christian – thus making Egypt a country in which the "Jews" are Christians). These groups are called middlemen because they typically are much poorer than the ruling class but much richer than most natives and because they fill occupational roles that rulers are not interested in and that other natives lack the skills for. They are typically intermediaries in a market economy, acting as shop owners, brokers, moneylenders, and importers. They tend to reside in close-knit communities and to associate mostly with their own kind, with whom they share distinctive cultural characteristics such as dress, diet, and religion.

Members of such groups are often particularly hard-working and frugal and inclined to postpone gratification. But they are rarely popular because of these virtues. Instead, they are resented for their wealth and are scorned as parasites. If the middlemen try to break out of isolation, they are accused of pushiness and intrusiveness. If they remain in isolation in their own communities, they are accused of clannishness and disloyalty to the state. Not only the Jews in Europe but also the Armenians in Turkey, the Indians in Uganda, and the Chinese in Indo nesia and Vietnam (the boat people) have been expelled or murdered en masse by their resentful compatriots.

Consider in particular the fate of European Jews over the last several hundred years. Throughout most of that period, and in most places, Jews faced hostility and severe restrictions in the opportunities available to them. Often they were prevented from owning land, denied access to particular trades and professions, restricted to particular neighborhoods or ghettos, and faced with continual threat of expulsion or confiscation of any wealth they acquired. This state of affairs encouraged Jews either to forsake their identity entirely (that is, convert to Christianity and blend completely into the larger society) or else maintain a cohesive, protective, separate subculture that was unlikely to adopt the language, dress, or cultural preferences of the larger society. It also led them to earn their livelihoods only in those occupations that were left open to them and that were suited to the circumstances and priorities thrust upon them. Thus a few visibly successful members of the community might be moneylenders (a profession forbidden to Christians) or dealers in precious stones and metals (like moneylending, a highly suitable profession for individuals who were obliged to keep their assets liquid). Most simply were left to provide goods and services within the narrow confines of their own community, where acceptance by the larger society was not required and hostility from that society was less frequently experienced.

These characteristics – distinct dress, language, and cultural practices, and often disdained occupations – in turn constituted an incentive, or at least a justification, for further social exclusion and hostility, which in turn sharpened the Jews' sense of isolation and apartness and increased their cohesiveness. Jewish humor and folklore reflected and reinforced this feeling of apartness, continual threat, and the need to survive through one's faith or one's wits rather than through overt confrontation.

There is reason to believe that we are participating in an interesting natural experiment with respect to Jews in North America. Because they are members of already highly polyglot societies, which include many individuals and groups with skills overlapping or identical to those of Jews, they do not stand out in the way they did in more culturally uniform countries such as those of Europe. In certain countries (for example, Holland, Italy, Germany, Britain), at least for certain periods, hostility and restrictions were less marked and the distinctive features of Jewish ethnicity waned as Jews merged into the larger society. But it has been in North America, especially in the United States in the last half century, that Jews have found unprecedented acceptance and freedom of opportunity, and the result, in the authors' view, has been a remarkable blunting of Jewish identity. To people of the authors' generation, younger American Jews increasingly are recognizable only by their last names, not by any characteristic appearance, outlook, or practices. When the larger culture neglects to treat one's particular cultural identity as important, and different, that sense of identity can be hard to maintain.

The history of Jews in America is far from unique. Most ethnic groups, once they have learned English, produced a generation of children educated in public schools, and ventured forth into diverse neighborhoods and occupations, find their ethnic identity a less and less decisive factor in their social experience. But there are important exceptions to this pattern of "blunting" and assimilation. Racial groups whose identities are highly visible and continue to be deemed highly significant, most notably African-Americans and Hispanics, have had a very different cultural experience in America. Enough members of the larger culture continue to behave in distinctive ways toward members of these groups to ensure that their distinct ethnic or racial identities are salient on a daily and hourly basis. We noted in Chapter 6 that the situation confronting an individual includes the responses that the individual, by virtue of appearance, role, and behavior, provokes from others. By the same token, part of the situation confronting any ethnic group is the reaction it provokes and the reception it receives from the larger society. In a later part of this chapter we consider in some detail the way in which this situational aspect of ethnic group status affects the behavior of the individual and the relations of the group with the larger society.

CULTURE, IDEOLOGY, AND CONSTRUAL

Having reminded the reader of the good and present reasons for regarding culture as a consequence of objective situational pressures and constraints, we now switch our emphasis to the second leg of social psychology's tripod. It is time to consider the proposition that cultural values and beliefs can determine how people will interpret their circumstances and experiences. (Excellent recent treatments of this proposition can be found in D'Andrade, 1981; Shweder, in press; Shweder & LeVine, 1984; and Stigler, Shweder, & Herdt, 1990.) Our contention is not that cultural perspectives arise in a manner that is independent of objective situational forces. Rather it is that the values, beliefs, and modes of interpreting events that become characteristic of a given culture or subculture – whatever their origin – have a life apart from the situations that gave rise to them and can endure well beyond the demise of those situations. Indeed, as we will now discuss, at a given moment in history it is a group's beliefs and ideology, rather than immediate features of its objective circumstances, that may hold the key to its subsequent development.

The Protestant Vision and the Growth of Capitalism

The major figure associated with the view that shared cultural beliefs are sometimes the prime movers of history was the great nineteenth-century sociologist Max Weber, who deliberately framed his argument about the growth of capitalism as a rebuttal to Karl Marx's materialism. Marx had maintained that the mercantilism of the late Middle Ages led to a surplus of capital available for investment, and that this surplus offered opportunities for new means of production that in turn gave rise, inevitably, to the growth of capitalism. Weber, playing subjective social psychologist to Marx's objectivist economist, disagreed. In order to produce the new economic form, he argued, the objective circumstances in question had to be *interpreted* in line with a particular vision of the world, namely, the "Protestant ethic," which placed an unprecedentedly high value on worldly attainment.

Weber started his argument by noting the success of Protestant entrepreneurs in competing with Catholics, and the apparent thriftiness and discipline of young Protestant working women. He also noted that capitalism developed in the Northern European countries rather than in the Southern ones, which, at one point, were wealthier. Citing Montesquieu's observation that the English "had progressed the farthest of all peoples of the world in three important things: in piety, in commerce, and in freedom" (Weber, 1905/1984, p. 45), he questioned whether it is "possible that their commercial superiority and their adaptation to free political institutions are connected in some way with that record of piety which Montesquieu ascribes to them?"

Weber's answer was that the particular form that Protestant piety took in the fifteenth through the eighteenth centuries was highly conducive to the worker diligence, entrepreneurial activity, and accumulation of wealth that are characteristic of successful capitalism. He argued that the piety was fueled by the desire to show that one was among the "elect" – that is, one of those whom God had chosen or "predestined" to be among those who would enjoy salvation, rather than among those "non-elect" predestined for damnation. Though one could never know for sure whether one was among the elect, evidence of God's grace could be seen in the worthiness of one's life – that is, in the rejection of softness, luxury, and pleasures of the flesh, and in the faithful, energetic, and successful pursuit of one's worldly "calling."

> The elected Christian is in the world only to increase this glory of God by fulfilling His commandments to the best of his ability. But God requires social achievement of the Christian because He wills that social life shall be organized according to His commandments. . . . This makes labour in the service of impersonal social usefulness appear to promote the glory of God and hence to be willed by Him. (Weber, 1905/1984, p. 108-109)

Mere labor for the Lord was not enough, however. The pursuit of the common good had to be energetic and wholehearted so as to quell one's doubts about one's own election.

> On the one hand it is held to be an absolute duty to consider oneself chosen, and to combat all doubts as temptations of the devil, since lack of self-confidence is the result of insufficient faith, hence of imperfect grace. . . . On the other hand, in order to attain that self-confidence intense worldly activity is recommended as the most suitable means. It and it alone disperses religious doubts and gives the certainty of grace. (Weber, 1905/1984, p. 111-112)

The restless activity by itself probably would not have been sufficient to establish the new means of production underlying capitalism, however. This new system included the specialization of labor and the creation of mass markets through efficient production and consequent lowering of prices. Here the reception afforded the Calvinist "nonconformers" within the larger society became highly significant. Denied access to traditional Anglican schools, the middle-class Calvinists created their own institutions of learning, which, not surprisingly, emphasized the practical disciplines of science and technology. New inventions and production techniques thereby were developed, and spread, at an unprecedented pace.

Such innovation, however, was met by opposition from suspicious workers, who resented the new discipline to which they could be subjected, and from hostile traditional competitors who stood to lose their business. According to Weber, it was very difficult for such an innovator to be successful, and once again the sustaining role of ideology was all important.

> . . . it is only by virtue of very definite and highly developed ethical qualities that it has been possible for him to command the absolutely indispensable confidence of his customers and workmen. Nothing else could have given him the strength to overcome the innumerable obstacles . . . (Weber, 1905/1984, p. 69)

As even Marxists agree, the new rational economic forms also demanded equally rational political forms. In order to be effective, capitalism had to be free of arbitrary taxation and capricious action by government. In addition, the wealth of the new middle class gave its members the strength to demand the sharing of power. Thus laws and government came increasingly to favor the order and freedom required for maximal scope of action by the new class.

And so, according to Weber, the triple virtues of the English (and other Northern Europeans) were related to one another in a satisfying way. The piety is explained by a distinctive theology; the commercial superiority, by the energy and moral stature conferred by the piety; and the free political institutions, by the government reforms required for economic rationality.

Marxist analysis was thereby stood on its head. Rather than inexorable change in the objective situation defining economic possibilities, it was the subjective views about the causes and implications of worldly success that gave rise to a new material stage in human history.

This discussion of cultural values and their economic significance was extended by David McClelland, John Atkinson, and their colleagues (McClelland et al., 1953) in some of the most captivating and original work of the 1950s. They began with the demonstration that, in 1950, several hundred years after the Protestant Reformation, there was virtually no overlap in the per capita production of wealth of Protestant and Catholic countries in either the Old World or the New. They then went on to try to show the mediating influence of parental values, child-rearing techniques, and the cultural folklore to which children are exposed. One of the most striking demonstrations was that, historically, periods of economic development for a given culture (of all kinds, including non-Christian ones) can be predicted by increases in achievement themes in the children's literature of the generation before. They also were able to show significant correlations (albeit, generally rather weak ones) between the achievement imagery expressed by individuals, in their writings and in their responses to projective tests, and both the socialization practices to which they were exposed and their own actual achievement in various domains. There was, however, one weak link in the research evidence. Investigators were unable to establish that American Protestants show more achievement imagery than American Catholics (Veroff, Feld, & Gurin, 1962). Roger Brown, in his classic 1965 social psychology text, thought this a serious enough weakness to cast significant doubt on the entire enterprise. Whether this absence of a Protestant-Catholic difference is truly an embarrassment to Weber's thesis is a question to which we will return later, in light of some additional evidence.

Associationism and Economic Development

The debate between Marxists and Weberians about the rise of capitalism continues in remarkably spirited form today, almost 100 years after Weber cast down his gauntlet. One might suspect that the debate is not subject to empirical resolution, yet recent work by Putnam and his colleagues (Putnam, 1987; Putnam, Leonardi, Nanetti, & Pavoncello, 1983) suggests that it is possible at least to demonstrate that preexisting cultural differences can predict subsequent economic development.

Putnam (1987) begins his argument by citing Tocqueville on the importance of voluntary associations for creating the psychological infrastructure necessary for good government, and by citing Esman and Uphoff

(1984) on the importance of associations for creating the preconditions for wealth. He then argues that if such associations make an independent contribution to the development of wealth, then their existence at one point in time ought to predict wealth at some later point, even holding constant objective economic conditions.

To test this thesis, Putnam collected data on the degree of associationism characteristic of the 15 governmental regions of Italy in the period from 1860 to 1920. This was measured in various ways, including membership in mutual-aid societies, support for mass-based political parties, electoral turnout during the period, and percentage of contemporary cultural and recreational associations that existed prior to 1860. The state of economic development was measured primarily by agricultural versus industrial employment, with higher industrial employment considered evidence of greater economic development. Remarkably, current economic development is better predicted by the cultural facts of associationism existing a century ago than by the degree of industrialization existing a century ago.

> In fact, nineteenth-century associational traditions are such a powerful predictor of twentieth-century industrialization that when cultural traditions are held constant, there is simply *no correlation* at all between industrial employment in 1911 and industrial employment in 1977. . . . As between two regions of Italy in 1900 – one with a participatory tradition, but relatively backward, the other relatively more advanced (healthier, wealthier, wiser, and more industrial), but lacking that culture of participation – the former has advanced much more rapidly than the latter in socioeconomic terms during this century. . . . In short, the contemporary correlation between culture and structure reflects the impact of culture on structure, not the reverse. (Putnam, 1987, p. 18-19, italics in original)

A similar demonstration of the role of participatory experience is provided by work by Useem and his colleagues (Useem, Setti, & Kanchanabucha, 1988), who looked at the success rates for a participatory development project in different Thai villages. They found that the success of the different self-help programs they attempted to foster in the various villages was highly dependent on the percentage of inhabitants who were members of at least one village group and who had joined before in village problem-solving activities.

Such findings constitute significant support for the cultural position over the economic determinist position, since it is implausible that structural forces of a crass economic kind are driving the cultural differences in associationism either in the case of the regions of Italy or the different villages in Thailand. To the extent that such findings prove to be the rule rather than the exception, they may force a revision in the economic determinism that characterizes the social sciences today. At the very least, they serve to establish that cultural factors matter in the establishment of structural, economic facts, a point we will return to in the context of our later discussion of social change.

Collectivism Versus Individualism

Our discussion of ideology, achievement motivation, and associationism prompts consideration of a related, very important dimension along which the world's cultures and ethnic subcultures seem to differ – that is, the dimension of collectivism versus individualism. This dimension has been intensively studied by Harry Triandis and his colleagues (Triandis, 1987; Triandis, Bontempo, Villareal, Asai, & Lucca, 1988; also Boykin, 1986; Deutsch, 1982; Hofstede, 1980; Hui, 1984; J. M. Jones, 1983; Markus & Kitayama, 1991; Spence, 1985). The dimension is central to understanding a wide range of attitudes and behaviors. Collectivist societies, which include most traditional preindustrial societies and, to a large extent, the predominantly Catholic countries of Southern Europe and Latin America, as well as most Asian and African cultures, are characterized by an emphasis on family and community-based relations and values. The members of one's primary "in-group" – that is, one's kin, one's immediate neighborhood community, and in the case of modern industrial societies, one's work group – are the primary sources of demands and rewards, and the primary arbiters of what is desirable, what is permissible, and what is unthinkable. In short, in collectivist societies it is in-group norms and role relations that provide both the motivating force that drives the individual and the compass from which the individual takes direction.

Individualist cultures, which, not coincidentally, predominate in the nations of Western Europe that gave rise to the Protestant Reformation, as well as in North America, show opposite orientations. They are characterized by an emphasis on personal goals, interests, and preferences. Social relationships are dictated by commonality of interests and aspirations and are therefore subject to change as those interests and aspirations shift over time. In such societies the individual's choices, whether of dress, diet, friends, occupation, or spouse, are relatively free of the dictates of family, neighbors, or others to whom one might be linked in traditional role relations.

It is not the case, of course, that the individual in such societies is uninfluenced by his or her peers – as the long history of social influence research in America, cited in Chapter 2, attests. Rather, it is that the degree of social influence is less completely a product of preexisting, traditionally based group bonds. Thus in some circumstances people from relatively collectivist cultures may show *less* readiness to conform than people from more individualistic cultures. For example, research (Frager, 1970) suggests that Japanese subjects may be less inclined to conform to erroneous group judgments in an Asch-like paradigm than Americans – presumably because that paradigm does not expose the subjects to social pressures from a socially relevant in-group focused on a traditional topic of in-group concern. In a similar vein, a sample of Japanese subjects reported less inclination to give weight to the wishes of strangers or people from other countries than did a sample of Illinois subjects (Triandis et al., 1988). By contrast, the Japanese subjects indicated greater responsiveness to the wishes of their coworkers.

In traditional collectivist societies, the individual is likely to identify with a single all-important in-group that endures for a lifetime. Group members are connected to each other in a complex web of largely non-negotiable mutual obligations and expectations; and each member's accomplishments or misdeeds constitute an important source of pride or shame for the group as a whole. In more individualist societies, by contrast, people find it relatively easy and desirable to enter a succession of new social groups and to cultivate new acquaintanceships, and also relatively easy and acceptable to sever previous ties. Social linkages in individualist societies are also likely to carry fewer privileges and obligations, and in such societies the individual's well-being, psychic as well as material, is less tied to the approval and the fate of one's kin or community group.

In part, the individualist orientation is a legacy of the Protestant ethic and capitalism. The individual's relation to a traditional community and guild are replaced by relations of rational convenience and associations based on opportunity and self-interest. Child-rearing practices and goals also reflect this orientation. Parents from individualistic cultures are more likely to demand and reward independence and individual achievement and less likely to stress cooperativeness and approval seeking (Barry, Child, & Bacon, 1959; Hess, 1970; Laosa, 1981; and Rosen, 1959).

The individualist orientation is linked not only to the economic values and achievement needs conducive to modern capitalism but also to its egalitarianism. Collectivist societies seem able to accept inequality based on prerogatives of birth or social rank. The highly traditionalist caste system that still survives in contemporary India (and the supporting belief in reincarnation, by which relative privilege or deprivation is seen as the consequence of deeds in past lives) is an extreme manifestation of this collectivist feature. A less extreme example is provided by the deference shown to doctors, teachers, or aristocrats in the small villages of Southern Italy. There, we are told, traditional norms remain strong and the patrons waiting in line in a local butcher shop are apt to step aside at the arrival of their social superior and insist that the "gentleman" be served first. Contrast this practice with norms that exist in our highly individualistic, highly egalitarian campus subcultures, where the newest secretary or research assistant enjoys the same right to convenient parking places as the most distinguished full professor (and, to be sure, is expected to pay the same hefty fee for a parking sticker out of a far smaller salary).

Individualist cultures tend to be wealthier and more productive, on average, than collectivistic ones, although the recent emergence of Japan as a leading industrial power makes this correlation less compelling than it once was. (Markus and Kitayama, 1991, argue that the achievement motivation underlying Japan's economic advances may be linked not to individualist values, as in the West, but to collectivist values of family, honor, and group loyalty.) Whether individualist cultures are healthier or wiser is a different matter (Bellah et al., 1985). One interesting source of recent data on the costs of individualism comes from the field of health psychology. Anomie and loneliness are more characteristic of individualistic societies, and such social isolation exacts a heavy price, as indicated both by questionnaire studies and by statistics on homicide, suicide, and death from stress-related diseases (Triandis et al., 1988). One particularly compelling pair of related statistics relates to heart attack rates. First, whites in the United States have rates more than five times as great as Japanese living in Japan. Second, highly acculturated Japanese living in America (that is, those speaking English rather than Japanese in their homes, and relating to their children in an American rather than a Japanese fashion) have heart attack rates roughly five times as great as nonacculturated Japanese living in America – even after correcting for the influence of lifestyle variables such as diet, smoking, and exercise (Marmet & Syme, 1976). These findings suggest that the social support characteristic of collective societies is a stress buffer.

In general, then, collectivists pay a price in terms of economic and social restrictions but reap benefits in terms of social support in return. Individualists have more rights vis-a-vis their fellow humans, and more choice about which people to associate with, but cannot readily make demands on them in times of personal need. Psychotherapists fill the functions in individualist societies that kin, kith, and coworkers fill – or forestall – in collectivist ones. And lawyers in individualist societies fill the role of mediators in conflicts, which tend to be public and protracted. In collectivist societies the same functions tend to be performed privately, and often more quickly and painlessly, by elders or by clan or workplace authority figures.

The authors of this book, both hopelessly individualistic North Americans, nevertheless take delight in discovering some profound differences in their cultural heritages. Ross grew up in a secular working-class Jewish home, and Nisbett grew up in a middle-class Protestant home. Many of the differences between Jews and non-Jews regarding the role and influence of family are so well known through contemporary television programs, literature, and stand-up comics that they have become cultural clichés. But they still have the capacity to startle us. Ross once casually pointed out to Nisbett that he grew up in a family in which he was expected to show concern for the good opinion of his many great-uncles, all of whom his family could rely upon in time of need and all of whom he visited regularly. Nisbett shook his head and volunteered the information that he grew up not knowing who most of his great-uncles were and expecting nothing from them; that they would not be likely to know of any possible accomplishments or scandals involving him; that they would not be likely to care if they did know; and that he would not care if they did care. Such an anecdote helps explain, perhaps, why the distinguished personality psychologist and clinician George Kelly (1955), who stressed the importance of seeing social phenomena from the viewpoint of the individual, also emphasized the need to take into account a client's ethnicity in determining whether that client's perceptions and response were or were not evidence of pathology. Kelly observed, for example, that a Jewish client's seemingly excessive concern with family matters might be wrongly attributed to a pathological level of dependence – if the therapist were unaware of this collectivist aspect of Jewish life.

Social Context and Attribution in East and West

North American social psychologists have been preoccupied, over the last two decades, with attempts to describe strategies and biases in the way people make trait inferences and behavioral attributions. Recent cross-cultural work suggests that we may have been guilty of some ethnocentrism, or at least of a failure to consider variability across cultures and subcultures, in our efforts. Some contrasts between subjects showing the individualistic orientation of culture and those from more collectivist cultures provide an instructive starting point.

Importance of self relative to others. An interesting demonstration by Kitayama and his colleagues (1989) suggests that collectivist Japanese subjects may be less inclined than individualistic Americans to see themselves as the focal point of attention in their dealings with their peers. The evidence for this conclusion is a bit indirect, but ingenious in the way that it proceeds from a classic finding on similarity assessment.

In 1977, Amos Tversky reported the surprising finding that assessments of similarity between objects of judgment often are asymmetric – that is, that subjects tend to judge Madrid to be more similar to New York than New York is to Madrid, or judge jackals to be more similar to dogs than dogs are to jackals. The reason for this asymmetry apparently lies in the tendency for subjects to treat the more salient, important, and cognitively rich object as the implicit reference or standard of comparison, and thus judge the less salient and significant object to be more similar to the highly salient and significant one than vice versa. Consistent with this generalization, Holyoak and Gordon (1979) found that American subjects judged the similarity of others to themselves to be substantially greater than the similarity of themselves to others – that is, the relatively nonsignificant, nonsalient, cognitively impoverished other was deemed rather similar to the significant, salient, cognitively rich self, but not vice versa. What Kitayama and colleagues showed was a literal reversal of this pattern among Japanese – a result suggesting that the relatively collectivist Japanese may deem their peers more important and salient objects of attention and contemplation, and themselves less important and salient objects, than do individualistic "self-centered" Americans.

Generalized versus contextualized views of personal attributes. A related demonstration was reported by Cousins (1989), who used the "Who Am I" test to show that the collectivist Japanese are less inclined than Americans to claim that they possess broad, cross-situational, personal attributes. Thus, when a free-response version of the test stipulated no specific contexts, the Japanese listed only a fourth as many abstract, psychological attributes (for example, "I am optimistic") as did American subjects, but three times as many social roles and contexts (for example, "I am a member of the drama club"). When specific contexts were stipulated, however, it was the Japanese who were more likely to use psychological attributes to describe themselves (for example, "at home I am sometimes lazy" or "in school I am hard-working"). Cousins argues that this pattern makes sense in terms of the Japanese understanding that their behavior is dependent on social context. In contrast, Americans like to think of themselves as having a set of personal attributes that is independent of any particularized relations with other people or specified situational contexts.

No fundamental attribution error for Hindus? The weight that collectivist Asian subjects give to social context may also influence the way they account for social behavior. In particular, Joan Miller (1984) has shown that Hindus are more likely than Americans to explain events in terms of situational or contextual factors. As noted in Chapter 5 (where we discussed only the results for American subjects), Miller asked her subjects to describe, and then to account for, "good" or "wrong" things that someone they knew well had recently done. Their explanations were coded into broad categories of which the most relevant, in terms of our concerns, were those corresponding to general dispositions (for example, "generosity" or "clumsiness") versus context (for example, "there was no one else there to help" or "it was dark"). Individualistic, person-oriented U.S. subjects invoked general dispositions 45 percent of the time to explain negative or deviant behaviors, while Hindu sub-jects invoked them only 15 percent of the time. Similarly, U.S. subjects invoked dispositional explanations 35 percent of the time to explain positive or prosocial behaviors, while Hindu subjects invoked them only 22 percent of the time. In contrast, Hindu subjects invoked con-textual reasons 32 percent of the time for deviant behaviors, while U.S. subjects invoked them only 14 percent of the time; and Hindu subjects invoked contextual explanations 49 percent of the time for prosocial be-haviors, while U.S. subjects invoked them only 22 percent of the time. Miller also made use of an elegant control comparison to show that the differing American versus Hindu explanations were not the result of any differences in the actions to be explained. She asked her U.S. subjects to explain behavior generated by her Hindu subjects. Consistent with Miller's cultural difference hypothesis, the American subjects explained the Hindu-generated behaviors with virtually the same proportions of dispositional and contextual explanations that they applied to behaviors they generated themselves.

Does this mean that Hindus are free of the fundamental attribution error, thereby calling into question how "fundamental" the error really is? Perhaps, but Miller's study alone cannot establish this; for it is pos-sible that situational factors really do play more of a role in determining behavior in the East than in the West. Indeed, this is a basic assumption of scholars who contrast individualist and collectivist cultures. Accord-ingly, the Hindus may not be showing greater situationist insight, they simply may be explaining more situationally determined behavior. We suspect, however, that the truth involves both factors. That is, situa-tional influences, in non-Western contexts, may be both more powerful determinants of behavior and more salient explanations of behavior. Thus we suspect that Hindus and many other collectivist people really are less susceptible than Americans to the fundamental attribution error.

The studies just described represent some of the clearest evidence available that different cultures construe the world in ways that are truly different at base. And they suggest that marked cognitive differences may have fundamentally social origins.

Social Class and Locus of Control

Just as there is a "horizontal" dimension of difference among the world's cultures in preference for explanation, there is a cross-cutting and somewhat related "vertical" dimension of difference corresponding to social class. People of lower socioeconomic status (SES) are more likely to explain events pertaining to them by reference to external causes than are higher SES people (P. Gurin, G. Gurin, & Morrison, 1978). For example, lower SES subjects are more likely to believe that "many of the unhappy things in people's lives are partly due to bad luck," while higher SES subjects are more likely to believe that "people's misfortunes result from the mistakes they make." Lower SES subjects are also more likely to believe that "knowing the right people is important in deciding whether a person will get ahead," while higher SES subjects are more likely to believe that people will get ahead in life if they have talent and do a good job: "knowing the right people has nothing to do with it."

This explanation preference is correlated with a value preference. Higher SES people value autonomy and personal causation more than do lower SES people, probably for the good and sufficient reason that their livelihoods are more dependent on the efficaciousness of their personal decisions than are those of lower SES people (Kohn & Schooler, 1969). For example, higher SES subjects, more than lower SES subjects, value independent judgment, self-reliance, and being interested in how and why things happen. Lower SES subjects, more than higher SES subjects, value respectability and ability to get along well with people. In their child-rearing, higher SES parents claim to emphasize responsibility and self-control, while lower SES parents claim to emphasize good manners and obedience to parents.

Thus higher and lower SES people differ in the assumptions they make about causality and in their values related to locus of causality. Higher SES people assume that people's outcomes are primarily a direct reflection of their behavior, while lower SES people are more likely to assume that people's outcomes are beyond their control. To a substantial extent, of course, these explanation preferences are a reflection of reality. Higher SES people in fact have more control over outcomes, both in professional life and personal life, than do lower SES people. The values of the two groups can be seen as a response to their objective situation. Higher SES parents prefer inquisitiveness and control orientation in their peers, their children, and themselves, as befits managers and professionals. Lower SES parents prefer obedience and getting along with others, attributes that will be valued by employers and friends. (Though it should be noted that the differences between social classes are not large in any of the terms we have discussed in this book. Whether this is because the differences, in fact, are not great or whether the methodology of verbal survey responses mutes real differences is not clear. Participant observation work by Heath, 1983, suggests there are truly substantial social-class differences in socialization practices related to independence, self-reliance, and personal efficacy.)

The discovery of differences between the social classes in expressed ideology and values constitutes a victory for the situationist, economic determinism view of culture. The differences between classes, for the most part, are highly understandable in terms of the jobs that members of a class hold and for which they are tacitly preparing their children. Nevertheless, these differences in perspective, once established, may have objective as well as subjective consequences – creating additional constraints for lower SES people and additional advantages for higher SES people.

Regional Differences in the United States as Cultural Differences

Regional differences in explanation style. There is another cultural difference in explanatory style, one related to the type of national and class differences just discussed, that can be detected by comparing two different regions of the United States. Sims and Baumann (1972) have found that Southerners believe more in external control of events than do Northerners. To document and explore this difference, the investigators presented their subjects, all of whom were middle class, with sentence stems that they were to complete as they saw fit. Thus, for example, when subjects were given the stem "As far as my own life is concerned, God . . .," Southern informants were likely to provide the ending "controls it," while Northern subjects were more likely to write "watches over me." In other words, Southern subjects were assigning God an active role and effectively denying their own responsibility for their fate, while Northern subjects were assigning God a benign but essentially passive role and assigning primary responsibility to themselves. Similarly, Southern subjects were more likely to finish the sentence stem "I believe that luck . . ." with a phrase implying that luck holds great importance, (for example, "can make a man rich or poor"), while Northern subjects were more likely to finish it with a phrase denying its existence or significance ("there's no such thing"). And Southern subjects were more likely to finish the sentence stem "Getting ahead in the world results from . . ." with a view reflecting the importance of a moral stance or God's will, while Northern subjects were more likely to finish it with a view reflecting the importance of work.

What made Sims and Baumann's work particularly provocative, however, was their attempt to demonstrate how such differences in attributional stance can have life-and-death consequences. They began their argument by noting the puzzling fact that there are many more deaths from tornadoes in the South than in the North, a discrepancy that cannot be accounted for by any difference in the number or strength of tornadoes in the two areas, or by differences in the extent to which tornadoes' paths take them through densely populated areas, or by any other plausible physical explanation. They argued that the difference in death rates, which actually appear to be several times higher in the South, stems from differences in preventive measures taken by Northerners and Southerners – a difference fully compatible with the differing outlooks shown in their sentence completions. That is, Northerners, who are more likely to believe that their outcomes depend on their own actions, might be expected to pay attention to weather reports and to take cover when a tornado is in the vicinity. Southerners, who are more likely to believe that fate or God controls their outcomes, might be expected to pay less attention to weather reports and to be less likely to take cover when the reports are unfavorable.

To support these contentions, Sims and Baumann gave their subjects sentence stems directly relevant to tornadoes, for example, "During the time when a tornado watch is out, I . . ." Consistent with the investigators' hypothesis, Northern subjects proved more likely to say that they "listened closely" to the news media, while Southern subjects proved more likely to say that they "watched the sky." (Watching the sky is, of course, much less likely to reveal the real degree of danger, and to suggest appropriate precautions, than attending to news media.) Similarly, when they also gave their subjects such stems as "The survivors of a tornado...," Northern subjects were likely to offer endings indicating the survivors' need for assistance, Southern subjects to offer endings emphasizing the negative emotions the survivors would feel.

It should be noted that the stance characteristic of Southerners, like that characterizing collectivists, is a two-edged sword. Several investigators have examined what happens when disaster, for example, in the form of sudden infant death syndrome or a traffic fatality, strikes families. Those with a more external, religious orientation rebound more quickly and more readily return to productive lives (Bahr & Harvey, 1979; Bornstein, Clayton, Hlikas, Maurice, & Robins, 1973; McIntosh, Silver, & Wortman, 1989; Sanders, 1980).

Regional differences in the United States in homicide rates. Differences in cultural perspectives are of life-and-death relevance in more than one respect. It has long been known that homicide rates differ dramatically in different regions of the United States. Homicide rates are far higher in large cities than in small towns or in the countryside (and, for that matter, higher in the United States than in Canada or the rest of the industrialized world). But there is also a marked difference between Northern and Southern regions of the United States. In the old states of the Confederacy, and in the more southerly of the Western states, homicide rates are far higher than in the North.

How can one account for this regional difference? For generations, the opinion of most scholars who have addressed this question is that the difference is a cultural one. Unlike the Puritan founders of Northern society, the South was settled by the swashbuckling Cavalier class with roots in the aristocracy and landed gentry and by Scotch-Irish backwoodsmen. Neither of these groups had any allegiance to the sober Protestant ethic described by Weber. Weapons and fighting, in the tradition both of the English nobility and of the outback, were valued by these people. This difference in cultural heritage, Tocqueville argued, was intensified by the cultural consequences of slavery. White males in the South were freed of the obligation to work and therefore had time for hunting, weapons, and combat both of the mock and real varieties. In a clever natural experiment, Tocqueville compared slave Kentucky with free Ohio. The comparison was thus made between two states that did not differ in latitude (Kentucky being east of Ohio, not south of it).

> The white inhabitant of Ohio, obliged to subsist by his own exertions, regards temporal prosperity as the chief aim of his existence; and as the country which he occupies presents inexhaustible resources to his industry . . . he boldly enters upon every path that fortune opens to him . . . and his avidity in the pursuit of gain amounts to a species of heroism.
>
> But the Kentuckian scorns not only labor but all the undertakings that labor promotes; as he lives in an idle independence, his tastes are those of an idle man; money has lost a portion of its value in his eyes; he covets wealth much less than pleasure and excitement; and the energy which his neighbor devotes to gain turns with him to a passionate love of field sports and military exercises; he delights in violent bodily exertion, he is familiar with the use of arms, and is accustomed from a very early age to expose his life in single combat. (Tocqueville, 1835/1969, p. 378-379)

In short, Southerners owned firearms and used them for sport – including dueling and blood feud – basically to while away the weary hours while others were doing their work for them. Such behavior came naturally to those British descendants of a chivalric tradition where honor was everything and where an insult had to be repaid in blood.

Ever since statistics have been kept on national crime rates, it has been known that homicide is more common on a per capita basis in Southern states than in Northern States. But this does not establish that the difference is a cultural one. Other explanations, having to do with structural differences, are possible. Different states have very different fractions of their populations living in cities, for one thing. More importantly, different states have very different economies and ecologies. Agrarian or herd-keeping economies might require the ready availability of guns, thus creating a channel factor promoting their use. Even climate conceivably could make a contribution, for work by Craig Anderson and his colleagues (C. A. Anderson, 1987; C. A. Anderson & D. C. Anderson, 1984) has shown that higher temperatures are associated with higher rates of violent crime.

There have been two particularly interesting attempts to go beyond mere statistical comparisons to show that the homicide rate differences are, in fact, based in culture. One is by Gastil (1971), who showed that the degree of Southern influence on a state, as measured by the degree to which it has experienced immigration from the South, is a strong predictor of homicide for the state. The Western states in particular have high proportions of native-born Southerners and high rates of homicide. But, of course, this is not a completely satisfactory demonstration because it still allows all the aforementioned factors to vary across states. A similar effort has been made by Loftin and Hill (1974), who constructed an intriguing cultural measure of violence they called the Legitimate Violence Index. For each state, they calculated such indicators of preference for violence as per capita viewership of violent TV shows and readership of violent magazines, per capita production of football players, amount of corporal punishment permitted in the schools, and percent of homicide convictions that resulted in execution. They found that this index was correlated both with homicide rates for a state and with the southerness of the population of the state. Once again, however, this procedure does not control for all the necessary structural, that is, ecological and economic factors.

To provide a test less compromised by such extraneous influences, Nisbett and Polly (1991) undertook a more complex analysis. They reasoned that regional differences in homicide rates should be greatest in small towns and least for large cities, because small towns in a region are more alike in their culture and more distinguishable from small towns in other regions than are great urban centers. (Indeed, the very meaning of cosmopolitanism is that it represents a shedding of the provincial culture that characterizes a region's small towns). The investigators reasoned further that, if homicide rates are truly reflective of cultural factors, then it should be possible to show not only that regional differences are more manifest in small population centers than in large ones, but also that cultural indices (such as the Southerness Index and the Legitimate Violence Index cited earlier) can predict homicide better in small centers than in large. And, in fact, they found this to be the case. Homicide rates among non-Hispanic whites are about three times as high in the small cities of the South as in the small cities of the North. In contrast, homicide is only very slightly more common in the large cities of the South than in the large cities of the North. In addition, the correlation between the cultural variables and homicide rates is higher for small cities than for large.

These data are extremely suggestive of genuine cultural differences. They certainly rule out temperature differences, inasmuch as temperature differences are not importantly associated with city size. In order to further rule out ecological, economic, and ethnic differences as explanations of the differences, Nisbett and Polly performed a variation of Tocqueville's natural experiment by examining a region of the country where the ecology and economy are essentially the same, but which differ in Southernness. This region is the Great Plains, a vast agricultural region stretching from North Dakota through North Texas. The homicide rate for non-Hispanic whites in small towns in North Texas is several times that in small towns in more Northern states of the region.

One might wonder whether homicide-rate differences between regions could be due to differential rates of gun ownership. We should point out that if such differences in gun ownership did exist, we would have to decide whether they themselves reflected cultural influences rather than economic or ecological ones. But as it happens, no such decision is necessary. Under the guise of a consumer survey, Nisbett and Polly called several hundred people in North Texas and Nebraska, and found that roughly 70 percent of the non-Hispanic white males in both regions owned guns. Clearly, in the event of an insult or quarrel, most males in both regions have ready access to a gun. The males in North Texas are just much more likely to use it – because it is a part of their cultural knowledge that violence can be a solution to interpersonal conflict.

We regard these data as important for several reasons: (1) They establish to a high degree of confidence that a behavioral difference of some magnitude is driven largely by cultural factors. (2) They indicate that cultural differences can linger long after the structural and economic facts that gave rise to them are gone. (3) They suggest a methodological strategy for establishing that a difference is cultural rather than structural or economic: If the difference is cultural, it should be more pronounced, and more strongly associated with other cultural variables, in smaller, less cosmopolitan localities.

Enforcement of Cultural Norms

It is important to remember that shared cultural values and traditions, like most group norms, come to be valued and even actively defended. From Sherif's small groups judging the distances moved by a point of light, to the Bennington students faithfully hewing to a new party line about social issues, to the subjects in Schachter's discussion groups who confronted a "deviate" in their midst, the history of social psychology teaches us that people actively promote their beliefs and social construals and do not readily tolerate dissent from them. It follows that cultures, which have much more at stake than the informal groups studied by social psychologists, would be still more zealous in keeping their members in line with respect to beliefs and values. It is primarily for this reason that cultures can be so starkly and so uniformly different from one another.

Social psychology also tells us about the conditions that make it easy or difficult for a culture to enforce a monolithic view of social reality. The possibility of disagreement with the group depends heavily upon the degree to which outside sources of reference and support are available. Since isolation is the key to stability of cultural norms, the ever-increasing amount of communication and contact between different regions and cultures is bound to exert profound effects on such cultural stability. It has been argued that adjacent European villages in the Middle Ages may have been more different culturally than adjacent, or even relatively distant, European nations today. The peasants in the two villages were apt to have dressed differently, to have had different customs and traditions, and in some cases even to have spoken in dialects sufficiently different as to make understanding of one another difficult. By contrast, in today's "global village," the urban elite from London to Boston to Karachi to Buenos Aires have been exposed to similar information and ideas, and even to each other, to such a degree that differences in their outlooks and values may be difficult for the casual observer to discern. Similarly, the traveler to virtually any of the capital cities of the world is apt to see youth subcultures that more closely share tastes in music, clothing, and diet with similar subcultures a continent away than they do with the tastes of their elders or even those of other youths in the same community.

A consequence of the transportation and communication revolutions is that subcultures are constantly being swallowed up by the mainstream and losing their distinctive identities. Yet new subcultures are constantly being formed and old ethnicities are constantly being renewed and reinvigorated. In the next section we examine what social scientists have had to say about these drastic changes in identity and in group relations.

CULTURES AS TENSION SYSTEMS

Throughout this chapter we have discussed the intimate relationship between objective and subjective aspects of culture. We have indicated how ecological and economic influences on the one hand, and ideology and values on the other, can reinforce each other in a manner that preserves the status quo. At the same time we have indicated how changes in economic circumstances, or contact with new societies and ideas, can transform cultural norms and practices. In short, we have outlined the reasons why cultures constitute tension systems of the sort described throughout this book.

It is now time to flesh out this dynamic state of affairs in more detail. We begin by discussing the fates of two groups that have been transformed by their experience in America and have at the same time left indelible marks on the host culture as well. In both cases, we should note, we have relied heavily on two fascinating books on America's ethnic history by Thomas Sowell (1981, 1983).

Cultural Change in America

What group did a mayor of Boston have in mind when he said privately of them that they are "a race that will never be infused into our own, but on the contrary will always remain distinct and hostile"? As a hint, we will note the stereotypic traits held by many in the larger society to be characteristic of this group – dumb, lazy, violent, superstitious, and substance-abusing, though also happy-go-lucky, religious, musical, and having the ability to speak in an unusually colorful and powerful way.

Only those readers who guessed that the group the mayor had in mind was the Irish are correct. The year of the mayor's comment was 1840. It was alcohol that the Irish were held to abuse, and it was the sublime tradition of the Irish tenor that gave them their reputation for musicality. Although this description, of course, is similar to America's more recent stereotype of blacks, it is worth noting that blacks at the time were often preferred over the Irish as neighbors and as employees, not only by proper Bostonians but also by proper New Yorkers and Philadelphians (Sowell, 1983). As late as the great depression, help-wanted signs in those cities often bore the qualification "No Irish need apply."

Was the larger culture's attitude toward the Irish due simply to blind ethnic and religious prejudice? Not entirely. The great black historian and sociologist W. E. B. DuBois argued that the economic condition of the peasant in Ireland was worse than the condition of the American slave at the time of emancipation (cited in Sowell, 1983). Many peasants lived in conditions akin to that of the farm animals they tended. Indeed, in Ireland, in England, and in the United States, the Irish often kept pigs and chickens in their homes, even when they lived in urban areas – a practice unlikely to endear them to their neighbors. Nor were they likely to be the sort of workers who would appeal to employers. Sowell (1983) tells us that the rate of alcohol abuse among the Irish was very high, and that their reputation for violence was well deserved. (The phrase "fighting Irish" once referred to something more threatening than the athletic teams of Notre Dame, and the term "donnybrook," referring to a fistfight involving dozens of people, owes its origin to the name of a town in Ireland.)

The behavior that handicapped the Irish immigrants to America, Sowell (1983, p.63) points out, can be understood in terms of the economic situation the Irish peasants had long confronted in their homeland. The land the peasants farmed, the buildings that housed the animals they tended, and the homes they lived in were all owned by absentee English landlords. By law, any improvements to the property served to enrich only the landlord, who could then raise the rent because the property was more valuable. The impoverished farmers thus had little opportunity or incentive to show economic initiative of any kind. They had plenty of reason, however, to entertain themselves as poor people often do – with songs, storytelling, and strong drink – and they carried these features of their culture, along with their desperate poverty, wherever they immigrated. One notable consequence of the tradition of storytelling and verbal entertainment, in its public version, was the massive contribution of the Irish to the world's literature, from John Millington Synge and Sean O'Casey to James Joyce, George Bernard Shaw, and Brendan Behan.

And where are the Irish today, socially and economically? Well, combining their long-celebrated blarney and charm with their later-developed political acumen, they have long since been running Boston, with the acceptance, often with the votes, of the descendants of that earlier mayor. Furthermore, despite their failure to embrace the tenets, at least the *religious* tenets, of the Protestant ethic, they have attained a position in American society that is essentially indistinguishable from that of the mainstream. In fact, the Irish have incomes, levels of education, and IQ scores that are all slightly higher than average for Americans overall (Greeley, 1976, 1989; Sowell 1983, p. 192). Yet not all aspects of their earlier culture have been transformed. They still are prominent among America's leading writers – as the careers of Eugene O'Neill, Mary McCarthy, Flannery O'Connor, Mary Gordon, and countless other Irish-Americans attest. And when the Irish have problems, it unfortunately is still drink to which they often turn. The rate of alcohol-related illnesses among Irish-Americans is as much as 25 times what it is for Italian-Americans and as much as 50 times what it is for Jewish-Americans (Sowell, 1983).

The saga of the Irish ethnic group thus illustrates the dynamics of a tension system in several important senses. The group did not immediately prosper in America as the English, the Dutch, and the Germans had done previously. For a considerable period of time, they remained profoundly different from these other Northern European groups in their economic skills and cultural values. The visible effects of their poverty, their lack of economic skills, and some of their cultural values and practices – all born of dire economic circumstances in their native land – helped to fuel prejudice against the group, thereby further diminishing the economic opportunities available to them. Yet somewhere between the early nineteenth century and the late twentieth century, a combination of assimilation and changed objective economic reality took hold, driving before it the poverty of the Irish and many aspects of the distinctive culture to which that earlier poverty gave rise.

The Irish are not unique among immigrants from Catholic countries in having risen to an economic level above that of Protestants. By the 1970s, American Catholics had surpassed most Protestant groups in income and in the prestige of the occupations they held (Greeley, 1976, 1989). (This is true even when one controls for such facts as that Catholics live disproportionately in the wealthier states.) Whether Catholics have prospered because of assimilation to the achievement values of the original Protestant culture or because, like the Japanese and the Jews, their culture contained the seeds of other values and practices that are wealth-producing, we cannot know. But there is at least some evidence for convergence in the achievement motive. Recall that Veroff and colleagues were unable to show that American Protestants of 1960 had more achievement motivation than American Catholics. Given the economic progress that Catholics were making at the time, this result can now be seen as confirmatory of McClelland's general views, rather than disconfirmatory as it seemed at the time. Perhaps such convergence was also going on at the same time in Europe. At any rate, Montesquieu's observations about the English have long been out of date. His own country of France surpassed the per capita GNP of England almost a generation ago, and even the once-backward Italian economy passed that of the English in the mid-1980s. These facts are dramatic reminders of the transience of cultural differences that can seem written in stone to those who lack either the perspective of history or that of social science.

Blacks and Whites in the American South

The odyssey of Africans in America is even more dramatic and complicated than that of the Irish. Part of the story, the earliest part, is not as widely known as it should be, and we will sketch its outlines. We are indebted to Mechal Sobel (1987) for a brilliant account of the joint construction of the culture of the American South by Africans and Europeans, and of the dynamic relationship between their two subcultures.

The general assumption about Southern culture is that there were two symbiotic cultures – the dominant white culture, which was an adaptation of the English culture to Southern conditions, and the slave culture, which was an adaptation to the harsh conditions of servitude, with parts of the African culture remaining only in the form of a few speech practices, superstitions, and folk traditions of music and storytelling.

Sobel's book establishes convincingly that the culture of the South, as it was created in the eighteenth century, was a true blend of European and African culture. She notes first of all that blacks and whites were thrown together on a constant basis. Whites were often raised by black women who acted essentially as nannies. At least until they were teenagers, blacks and whites played together in fully integrated fashion. A white plantation owner was likely to spend more time with his black overseer than with any other person. It is extremely important, moreover, to note that in the early days, the separatist ideology of racial superiority had not yet developed. Blacks and whites worshipped together in the same churches, often with black ministers. As Sobel and other writers have shown, racist ideology was a later addition that served to ease the consciences of slave owners who found the institution of slavery increasingly difficult to justify in the face of religious and political challenges (van den Berghe, 1981).

In this situation of mutual contact, cultural influence inevitably was a two-way street, even though the nature and origin of the various African and English ingredients that found their way into the resulting stew of Southern plantation culture ceased to be apparent to the members of the dominant white culture. Sobel begins her account of this mutual influence by noting that the traditional English and African cultures were similar from the outset in some important respects. The versions of English culture that were predominant in the South, it will be recalled from an earlier discussion in this chapter, were variants of the precapitalist agrarian tradition that placed little value on work for its own sake and did not condemn idleness. As Weber pointed out, the traditional peasant works no more than necessary to put food on the table. In this respect the English culture was similar to African culture where the idea of work for its own sake did not play a role in the value system. Indeed, in most regions of West Africa, men worked only during the two months of the year when agriculture required it. The superstitions of the two cultures were also highly similar. Both believed in the power of witches and in the existence of trolls and other forest spirits. Finally, the religious beliefs of the two groups were congruent. The resurrection was a new idea to Africans, but the story of creation and of Adam and Eve was identical to the traditional West African account. These similarities facilitated mutual influence.

African influence on the emerging Southern culture was pronounced in several respects, especially in agricultural practices and architecture. Many of the techniques of Southern farming were adaptations of African ones. The practice of building houses on stilts to get them away from insects at ground level was an African one, and several other forms of house construction were taken directly from the more substantial types of construction in Africa.

Southern values were also influenced by African traditions. The Southern definition of kin from the outset was wider than in the North, and this was congruent with the definitions of extended family and clan that were common in Africa. The emotionality common to the American South, as compared with the taciturn North, Sobel attributes in part to African influence. This emotionality was particularly apparent in forms of religious expression. The so-called ecstatic approach to religion, consisting of vivid displays of emotion and even of possession, was a direct translation of African practices. The fundamentalist sects of the South, both black and white, display a version of this ecstatic approach. The notion of death as involving reunion with kin was a traditional African one, not part of the English tradition, that entered Southern religious ideology even in long-established Protestant churches. Many of the superstitions of the South also had specific African origins.

But perhaps the most important enduring contribution of the Africans was to the language of the South. Africans brought languages rich in proverbs, metaphor, and other figures of speech, and these were transferred directly to Southern English, as many scholars have noted (for example, Brooks, 1985). It is a commonplace observation that the greatness of Southern literature is in no small part due to the admixture of the African forms of language expression. That the contribution by blacks in this respect was indeed important is attested by recent work by Nisbett and Henderson (1991) indicating that contemporary black literary contributions (from Ralph Ellison, Langston Hughes, Richard Wright, and James Baldwin to Toni Morrison, Alice Walker, and August Wilson) are more substantial on a per capita basis than those of either Northern or Southern whites – despite the differences favoring whites in terms of higher education and socioeconomic status.

Finally, we note the universally acknowledged contributions of Southern blacks to the musical traditions first of Southern culture and ultimately of world culture. The collision of European melody with African rhythm in the eighteenth century resulted in a Big Bang whose celestial fallout, from the Negro spiritual, to ragtime, to jazz, to rhythm and blues, rock 'n' roll, soul, and rap, continues today.

Thus the Southern culture was from the outset a fusion of two cultures, already similar in many ways, in reaction to an ecology that was new to both, and an institution, namely slavery, that shaped both the constituent cultures.

The legacy of slavery, of course, had a continuing effect on black economic success similar to the effect that the original near-slavery conditions of the Irish had on that group. As Sowell (1983), Ogbu (1978), and others have noted, the conditions of slavery and the effective job ceiling enforced by the subsequent caste status created attitudes toward work and the acquisition of work-related skills that persist today, at least in the inner city. Those blacks who were well positioned at the time of the civil rights advances of the late 1960s, that is, those who had reasonably good jobs and educations, have moved briskly into the economic mainstream. Indeed, by 1980, college-educated black couples were earning almost as much as college-educated white couples (U.S. Bureau of the Census, 1981).

But those blacks who were badly positioned at the beginning of the civil rights era have actually worsened their situations. Certainly, rates of unemployment, incarceration, and family dissolution have escalated since the 1960s. Wilson (1987) attributes this state of affairs mainly to the loss from the economy of the blue-collar jobs that have long been the traditional entry point into the middle class. This loss is far larger than is widely realized, and is highly concentrated in the Northern urban areas that house large proportions of blacks. In any case, the diminished opportunity it entails for underclass blacks, and the persistence of social pathologies linked to that underclass status, helps perpetuate both white racism and black despair. Blacks still wait for the changes in objective circumstances, and subjective perceptions, that will permit their full and equal participation in American economic life, and in the social and cultural institutions that they have done so much to help shape.

Traditional Japanese Culture and Capitalism

Stories of dramatic cultural evolution can be told of most of the world's peoples. There are often two related themes to these stories. First, the situation changes in some profound way, and second, the original culture asserts itself to color the way in which the change is assimilated.

One of the most remarkable and timely of these stories concerns the introduction of capitalism to traditional Japanese culture in the 1870s. Japan was forcibly opened to trade with the West at that time. Early observers of Japan concluded that the country would never have any wealth. This opinion was based partly on the correct assumption that the Japanese islands had few natural resources and partly on the belief, common to observers of that time but no doubt ironic to more contemporary observers, that the Japanese were too indolent and pleasure loving ever to have a productive economy. Within 50 years, however, the Japanese proved themselves the masters of capitalist means of production and distribution. They built a dynamic and successful economy based on productivity and export that reached a peak in the period before World War II, and rebuilt it to even greater heights after the devastation wrought by that war. Even more dramatically, the Japanese changed the nature of capitalism within their own country and, increasingly, in the world at large. This change in the nature of capitalism has to do with a more cooperative relation between management and labor, a relationship that is congruent with, and may be attributable to, a traditional element of Japanese society, namely, the relation between a warlord and his vassal (Doi, 1971).

> In the traditional Japanese system there were no "rights" on the part of the subordinate. The only recourse for subordinates in the past, since they had no contractual relationships, was to hope to induce kindness and benevolence in their superiors. These feelings were induced by invoking potential feelings of nurturance and appreciation from them. This capacity to induce kindness and benevolence in superiors in a manipulative manner is called *amaeru* in Japanese. (De Vos, 1985, p. 160)

As a modern carryover of this type of relationship, the boss in Japanese companies is trusted to have parentlike feelings toward the employee.

> Indeed, the social expectations of his role often cause him to display overt behavior suggesting such feelings whether they are there or not. . . . He is to internalize the sense of responsibility for others under his authority. . . . For

example, business executives, foremen, or even higher executives in Japan will sometimes act as go-betweens in assuring a proper marriage for one of their subordinates. This is seen as a part of a parent-like responsibility and indeed a type of nurturant concern with the subordinate. (De Vos, 1985, p. 160)

The modern Japanese corporation thus resembles a family far more than does its Western counterpart. Managers are concerned with the daily lives of employees, who trust that managers will look after their interests. The fundamental conflict of interest between the two classes posited by Marx to be inevitable has been avoided to a remarkable degree in Japan. This turns out to have morale and efficiency advantages that have resulted in widespread imitation of Japanese management techniques in America – the very country, where, as we will discuss in Chapter 8, Kurt Lewin had pioneered techniques for reducing worker-employer conflicts (techniques that were based not on the Japanese "family" model but on the American ideal of democratic participation).

TRAITS, ETHNICITIES, AND THE COORDINATES OF INDIVIDUAL DIFFERENCES

What have we learned to this point? The following lessons seem the most important ones.

1. Economic circumstances, together with other objective facts of social life, such as the way one's group is treated by other groups, shape cultures in profound ways. The result is that cultures can differ profoundly in their values and habitual forms of behavior.

2. Subjective aspects of culture, including religious or ideological ones, affect the response to objective situations, and in some cases play a vital role in creating new social and economic circumstances.

3. Though cultures are tension systems that are generally conservative and resistant to change, they can also be powerful vehicles for change. When the objective pressures and constraints change, or when construals change because of contact with other groups, the culture can alter in sometimes profound and unpredictable ways.

4. Aspects of cultures can change powerfully and leave other aspects unaffected. The deferential *shtetl* Jews are not recognizable in their confident, socially accepted descendants on American college

campuses and corporate boards, yet the scholarly and pragmatic traditions established by Jewish religious and mercantile traditions of 2,000 years ago are recognizable in every group of Western Jews in the world today. The dirty, ignorant Irish are hard to find on either side of the Atlantic today, yet the traditions of language proficiency remain, and the culturally prescribed way of dealing with stress and unhappiness remains alcohol.

The emerging disciplines of "cultural psychology" and "cognitive anthropology" (D'Andrade, 1981; Shweder, 1991; and Stigler and colleagues, 1990) may ultimately help us account for, and predict, the dynamics of these processes in a more satisfying and systematic way. These new disciplines, lying as they do at the intersection of anthropology, economics, sociology, and psychology, are well situated to reap the benefits of the interdisciplinary spirit that has been revived in the social sciences. Traditional social psychology has an important role to play in the joint attempt to find some coherence in the chaotic pattern of cultural facts available to us.

Can Ethnicities Substitute for Traits?

The opening paragraphs of this chapter invoked the role of cultural sophistication in helping us anticipate and respond appropriately to the behavior we see in everyday social life. We hope, however, that neither those paragraphs nor the rest of this chapter have conveyed the impression that knowledge of ethnic or cultural differences can provide the royal road to prediction of individual differences that the study of traits failed to do. While knowledge of a culture or subculture can tell us a great deal about what is likely to be desirable, permissible, or prohibited in many domains of social life, it has limits. It cannot, for example, tell us much about the way in which Bill's behavior in a given situation will differ from Jacks, by virtue of knowing that Bill is a lower SES Southerner of Irish extraction now living in the Southwest while Jack is a middle-class Jew living in Los Angeles. However profoundly behavioral practices may differ across societies, the differences rarely are large or consistent within societies. The reason for this homogenization has a lot to do with social influence and with the fact that members of different groups within the larger society generally confront and are shaped by rather similar objective realities. Indeed, some of the cultural, ethnic, and class differences within our own society that we have discussed in this chapter tend not to be very large, at least by some traditional measures. The overlap in values and beliefs between upper and lower SES groups is substantial, for example. And it is only when examining the incidence of behavioral extremes, for example, incidence of alcoholism or homicide, or exceptional contributions to musical, artistic, athletic, or specific intellectual domains, that ethnic differences become especially noteworthy – a result that is consistent with our discussion in Chapter 4 of the statistics of individual differences.

It is important to recognize that while many ethnic differences map onto traditional trait dimensions (for example, the Protestant ethic maps onto lay conceptions of conscientiousness, and the Hispanic tradition of *simpatica,* or interpersonal responsiveness, maps onto friendliness), many ethnic differences are not well represented in lay psychology and do not seem to be part of the traditional structure of individual difference dimensions. For example, many aspects of collectivism, such as the importance of kin relations, and many aspects of social class differences, such as locus of control, do not correspond to dimensions that would be obvious to the casual observer. As a consequence, some interesting and important cultural differences may be overlooked or misunderstood by people who interact with one another. When differences in behavior occur as a result of behavioral norms or construal differences that have a cultural origin, they may be mistakenly mapped onto some conceptually related individual difference dimension; and the predictions made about behaviors in new domains irrelevant to those cultural factors will likely be erroneous, or at least made with unjustifiable confidence.

Why is Ethnicity an Increasingly Important Factor in Modern Life?

As the twentieth century draws to a close, two facts, one hopeful and one distressing, dominate the world landscape. The hopeful fact is that the economic and political systems of the developed world seem to be truly converging. The distressing fact is that ethnic divisions, both within and between nations, seem to be increasing. Such divisions can be seen in the form of conflict between the races on American college campuses, in the form of ethnic strife as the authority of the central government wanes in the Soviet Union, and in the continuation of tribal and religious animosities all over the world.

Is it possible that these facts are related? A connection can be drawn from the rationalism of the Enlightenment and the Reformation to the kind of economy that seems to work best in the modern world. It would seem to be an economy that is capitalist at base, but that finds some way to soften the dire predictions of Marx about the exploitive tendencies of capital – for example, by state reallocation of wealth on the Scandinavian model or by the paternalistic stance of Japanese-style owners. Such economies and the societies that sustain them are the most rational and humane the world has known.

But the very openness and rationality of these societies may sow the seeds of ethnic conflict. First, in societies where identifiable groups benefit differentially, whether because societal attitudes are prejudicial to some groups or because they are differentially positioned with respect to skills or work-related attitudes, the very freedom of these societies allows ethnic conflict to accelerate quickly. Second, few of the new economically advanced societies have provided ideologies that seem to satisfy the human need for meaning and community. Religion is a weak force in many of these modern societies; ethnicity is an attractive, though dangerous, alternative.

If the new facts about ethnicity are other than transient, and if our speculations about their roots have any merit, then there is a clear need for social scientists to identify ethnic differences, to explain them to different elements in the larger society, and to find ways to diminish their capacity to fuel conflict.

CHAPTER 8
APPLYING SOCIAL PSYCHOLOGY

When social psychologists apply their discipline to problems in our schools, workplaces, and communities, their efforts are heavily influenced by, and often are dramatic testimony to, the principle of situationism. Where conventional lay wisdom would hold the primary cause of a problem to be human frailty, or the weaknesses of particular types of individuals, the social psychologist is loathe to "blame the victim." Instead, in analyzing underlying causes and in suggesting potential remedies, the social psychologist looks to situational barriers and strategies for overcoming them. Those of us steeped in the Lewinian tradition, moreover, are apt to focus on the *immediate* environment – particularly the social processes that produce behavioral norms and the channel factors that mediate the relationships between attitudes and behavior.

While applied practitioners are bound to be situationists, their ultimate success may depend upon their appreciation of the other two fundamental insights discussed throughout this book – that is, the crucial role of subjective interpretation and the dynamic nature of cognitive and social systems. The first of these additional insights obliges the practitioner to take into account (and if necessary, to change) the actors' subjective appraisals of their particular situation and of any interventions designed to improve that situation. The second insight obliges the practitioner to recognize the dynamics both of the social systems within which people function and of the cognitive systems through which they process information. In particular, the sophisticated practitioner recognizes that social communities and belief systems alike are stabilized by potent forces, but that both types of systems can be changed profoundly when, by accident or design, those stabilizing forces are undermined.

As we discuss various intervention successes and failures in the course of this chapter, we will return again and again to these fundamental social psychological insights and to the lessons they offer, not only to intervention designers and practitioners, but to all of us who function in the social world, to children and parents, students and teachers, patients and physicians, workers and employers. These lessons have the power to transform the way we understand and respond to the events that constitute our social experience – the everyday social exchanges that we engage in and observe, the noteworthy happenings conveyed to us secondhand by our peers, and the more momentous events chronicled in the news media. First, however, we must spend some time on some lessons that have been learned not about social psychological theory but about methodology.

METHODOLOGICAL LESSONS FOR RESEARCH PRACTITIONERS AND CONSUMERS

Trained social psychologists show their expertise not only in the way they conduct their own research but also in the way they respond to commentary about social problems and remedies offered in the media. Most notably, an education in social psychology leaves one with a deep skepticism about pronouncements made solely on the basis of theoretical analysis or "clinical experience," in the absence of solid research evidence. To some extent, this skepticism comes from an awareness of the track record.

We've seen how often "expert" predictions about social trends and consequences miss their mark, and we've seen how often intervention programs that seemed sensible on theoretical or common-sense grounds proved to be ineffective or even counterproductive in the end. Our skepticism can also be linked to the same general theoretical insights that we noted earlier – insights about the subtleties of situational influence, the vagaries of subjective construal, and the complex dynamics of cognitive and social systems. Whether the question is the longterm social consequences of the AIDS epidemic, the costs versus benefits of legalizing cocaine, the best solution to the problem of homelessness, the relative merits of various types of child care arrangements, or even the benefits of an education at Stanford versus Michigan, the fundamental insights of our discipline oblige us to recognize the limited value of answers offered in the absence of direct evidence.

At the same time, research on informal inference (Dawes, 1988b; Kahneman, Slovic, & Tversky, 1981; Kunda, 1990; Nisbett & Ross, 1980) alerts us to various cognitive, motivational, and even perceptual biases that lead people to feel great but unwarranted confidence in their beliefs and predictions, biases that give experts and laypeople alike the illusion that they understand the meaning of past events (Fischhoff & Beyth, 1975; Fischhoff, Slovic, & Lichtenstein, 1977) and can accurately predict future ones (Dunning et al., 1990; Vallone et al., 1990). We've learned a great deal about methodological pitfalls and artifacts that can mislead us when we do applied research, and we've learned even more about the shortcomings of judgments and decisions made on the basis of intuition or ideology alone.

When it comes to matters of social policy, the lessons of our discipline prompt us to defend the value and cost-effectiveness of thoughtfully designed, carefully executed empirical research. We have seen how laboratory and field studies can be valuable in addressing issues that lie at the heart of our legal system (Ellsworth, 1985; Hastie, Penrod, & Pennington, 1983) and in testing the effectiveness of educational programs designed to improve public health and safety (Evans, 1982; Meyer, Maccoby, & Farquahar, 1980; Robertson et al., 1974). As a result, we become champions of formal experimental designs when they feasibly can be employed, and defenders of necessary methodological, statistical, and interpretive precautions when, as is more often than not the case, formal experiments cannot be employed (Campbell, 1969; Campbell & Stanley, 1963, 1966; Cook & Campbell, 1979; Cronbach, 1982).

The Value of "True Experiments"

Some of the most important and dramatic illustrations of the value of formal experimentation, and the dangers of more "clinical" assessment procedures, come from the annals of medicine. A classic illustration is provided by the history of research on the "portacaval shunt." In an unusual meta-analysis, Grace, Muench, and Chalmers (1966) compared the conclusions reached by investigators who had employed different research designs to evaluate this once-popular surgical treatment for cirrhosis of the liver. The treatment involved connecting the patient's portal vein directly to the vena cava. Table 8.1 summarizes the results of this comparison.

TABLE 8.1 A study of studies. The conclusions of 51 studies on the portacaval shunt are related to their designs. The well-designed studies show the surgery to have little or no value. The poorly designed studies exaggerate the value of the surgery.

	Degree of Enthusiasm		
Design	Marked	Moderate	None
No controls	24	7	1
Controls, but not randomized	10	3	2
Randomized controls	0	1	3

Summarized from Grace, Muench, and Chalmers, 1966, p.685, by Freedman, Pisoni, and Purves, 1978, p.8.

We see that a total of 32 studies, which represented the majority of the 51 published reports, relied on standard clinical evaluation procedures. That is, the investigators based their conclusions on the improvement or lack of improvement shown by a sample of patients after receiving the shunt (although the investigators presumably also made use of what they knew about the fate of cirrhosis patients who had not received the shunt). As Table 8.1 makes clear, virtually all these investigators reached positive conclusions about the shunt's effectiveness. In the second-largest group of studies, 15 in number, the investigators directly compared outcomes for shunt recipients and nonrecipients, although they did not assign patients to shunt versus no-shunt conditions *randomly*. This method of assignment again led most investigators to reach positive conclusions. Only four studies used the random assignment procedures necessary to qualify as a "true experiment." But this handful of studies permitted the physicians to reach what has proved to be the correct conclusion. That is, the portacaval shunt does not really benefit patients at all and, by implication, the positive results found using less formal procedures were the product either of "placebo effects" (to be discussed later in the chapter) or of biases resulting from nonrandom assignment of patients to the treatment conditions.

Some of the possible biases are pretty obvious, once they are pointed out. When only a subset of patients is to receive a new procedure or treatment, the ones chosen are likely to be "good candidates," that is, those patients with no additional illnesses to complicate treatment or evaluation, those who have positive attitudes and are likely to comply with the physician's instructions, possibly even those with highly supportive families eager to see their kin receive the latest and best treatment available. But when these good candidates prove to be in better post-treatment condition than patients receiving the standard treatment (or those not treated at all), the difference may have little or nothing to do with any therapeutic advantages of the new treatment. Instead, it may merely reflect the advantages enjoyed by the good candidates in terms of their prior health, their degree of medical compliance, or their family support. Comparable biases make their influence felt in social experiments when, for example, the recidivism rates for the "appropriate" or "deserving" prisoners assigned to a special rehabilitation program are compared with the rates for prisoners treated in more standard fashion.

While case studies and poorly designed comparisons have their shortcomings, they at least protect us from the folly of proceeding with no research evidence at all. A tragic case history of intervention based on common sense and good intentions alone can be seen in the "Tower in the Park" projects widely pursued as a means of "slum clearance" in the 1950s and 1960s. The logic underlying these projects seemed straightforward: Take a city block full of crumbling three- and four-story tenements and put the same number of people in a 20-story building in the middle of the block, converting the rest of the space into playgrounds and parkland. Then sit back and reap the social benefits bound to result from this environmental "upgrading."

What the urban planners failed to anticipate in their well intentioned but unsophisticated situationism was the finely balanced ecology of the old-fashioned tenement block. The objective physical conditions may have been deplorable, but at least everyone knew everyone in their own building and maintained relationships through frequent everyday contact. The good opinion of one's neighbors mattered, and social norms could be communicated and enforced in the way they are in any normally functioning community. Moreover, everyone had a good idea who belonged in front of the building and in its hallways, and mothers could glance out the window and see that their children were playing safely on the sidewalk or sitting on the stoop. In the pristine tower, this tension system was destroyed. Informal social pressures and group cohesiveness were greatly reduced because people had minimal opportunity to develop personal relationships or to monitor each other's behavior in the course of everyday life. Undesirable outsiders and criminals could not be told to depart the premises, both because they could not be distinguished from people who belonged and because the socially isolated residents were unlikely to feel responsibility for addressing collective problems. Youngsters had to remain cooped up in the apartment or run unmonitored through the building or in hidden corners of the park. Soon anomie, fear, and despair, to say nothing of vandalism, exacerbated the social and physical deterioration of neighborhoods that had long been poor, but nevertheless had been functioning social systems.

Twenty years after this bold but ill-fated intervention in the lives of the poor, governments began pulling down the ravaged towers. The financial costs of this folly can be measured in the hundreds of billions of dollars. The costs in terms of human suffering are less easily reckoned.

This ghastly toll could have been averted, one suspects, by building a half dozen such towers in various urban centers and then measuring the success of the experiment, that is, by monitoring the well-being of the residents and the surrounding neighborhoods for at least a few years, before deciding on the design of any slum eradication projects to follow.

We by no means wish to imply that the use of small-scale evaluation studies will invariably payoff with clear answers to guide social policy. On the contrary, many of the best-known intervention and evaluation studies conducted over the past few decades have prompted heated debates about the proper interpretation of the research results that were obtained. In each case, however, we believe the relevant findings served a valuable purpose in deflating rhetoric and sharpening the issues for subsequent debate and research, and the lessons learned have been worth many times their price (see Kiesler, 1980).

Consider the ambitious "negative income tax" or "guaranteed income" studies conducted between 1968 and 1978 (Moffitt, 1981). We learned, as one might expect, that experimental group participants, who received payments when their income fell below a stipulated "floor" level, averaged fewer hours of work per week than the control group participants (in part because they were unemployed more often, and longer). This difference was due mainly to the rather sharp reduction in hours worked by non-heads of household. For example, at the largest and best researched Seattle and Denver sites, there was a 20 percent reduction for wives and an even larger reduction for young unmarried men, compared with a 9 percent reduction for husbands (Robins & West, 1980). We also learned, contrary to the hopes and predictions of many program advocates, that rates of family dissolution proved to be not lower, but *higher* (for example 35 percent to 40 percent higher in the Denver and Seattle sites) among families receiving the income guarantee (Hannan, Tuma, & Groeneveld, 1977).

These results prompt some hard questions: Is it desirable or undesirable for married women, particularly those with dependent children, to work fewer hours (or, more accurately, for more of this population not to work at all)? Did the guaranteed income somehow increase rather than decrease family problems and conflict, or did it merely make it economically feasible for conflicted couples to separate? But such questions reflect a valuable narrowing of the parameters of debate. Critics cannot continue to claim that "no one" or "hardly anyone" will work in the face of an income guarantee. Proponents cannot continue to claim that decreased rates of family breakups will justify the costs of the experiment. And researchers and program planners alike have a much clearer understanding of what it is they might want to measure, or change, in any subsequent intervention.

By the same token, the "bail bond" studies conducted in the early

1960s (Ares, Rankin, & Sturz, 1963; Riecken & Boruch, 1974; Wholey, 1979) left us to debate whether it is desirable or undesirable to release criminal defendants without requiring them to make bail. But they did establish that such a policy would not lead to an unacceptably high rate of defendants failing to appear for their trial. The "no-show" rate among defendants benefiting from the no-bail policy was lower than 2 percent – *less* than the base rate for defendants in general. Similarly, as we will discuss later, the few well-designed evaluation studies of the Head Start programs of the 1960s could not end debate about the cost-effectiveness of such programs. But, 20 years later, they serve to limit both unrealistic promises by liberal proponents and unwarranted dismissals of the programs by conservative critics.

The Hawthorne Saga

As social psychologists have come to appreciate the value of formal ex-perimental designs, they also have become more sophisticated about the social psychology of experimentation. An important early chapter in this unfolding story began in 1924 in the Hawthorne Plant of the Western Electric Company in Chicago. A program of research had been initiated there by early devotees of "scientific management." These were the so-called efficiency experts, with their frequently satirized and much disliked "time and motion studies." To their great surprise and disappointment, these experts quickly found that they could not readily improve productivity by devising more efficient methods and then simply telling workers to change their behavior accordingly. The workers resented and distrusted these intrusions, which they found demeaning and felt had been designed to turn them into automatons. Consequently, they resisted – a result that our readers, now wise to the importance of subjective perceptions and to the workings of tension systems, should not find surprising.

One small study on the effects of lighting conditions provided the departure point for a very different approach to the productivity prob-lem, even though, in a sense, it offered negative results. Specifically, the Hawthorne investigators found that while improved illumination yielded an initial increase in worker productivity, no relationship between productivity and lighting conditions could be detected when lighting was systematically manipulated over an extended test period. This suggested to the investigators that factors having little to do with the physical environment, but everything to do with the perceptions and feelings of those being tested, might be playing a crucial role.

Further support for this interpretation was provided by a series of subsequent studies conducted with the assistance of social scientists from the Harvard School of Business Administration from 1927 to 1932. The best-known of these studies was a "time-series" experiment that focused on the productivity of five female assemblers who were housed in a separate test room and paid a piece-work rate that depended on their combined output. Over 23 time periods, ranging in duration from as little as three or four weeks to as long as 30 weeks, the group's productivity was monitored while the number and timing of this group's rest and meal breaks were systematically manipulated. The results of this experiment, or rather the human relations interpretation offered by the researchers who summarized these results (Mayo, 1933, 1945; Roethlisberger, 1941; Roethlisberger & Dickson, 1939), soon became the gospel for introductory textbooks in both psychology and management science.

The subjects, so the story is told, responded to virtually every change in conditions – whether it involved increases in the frequency and duration of rest periods and meal breaks, or decreases in them, or even their total elimination – with an increase in productivity. The net result was that over the 13 initial (and most commonly cited) test periods, worker productivity continually drifted upward, more or less independent of the particular rest schedule being employed, until it was roughly 30 to 40 percent higher than it had been during the preexperimental baseline period. In most accounts, the last two of these test periods received particular emphasis. In the twelfth period the workers lost their Saturday morning off and were deprived of the two work breaks that they had enjoyed during the previous period; nevertheless, the result was an 11 percent increase in total productivity. Then, in the thirteenth period, the two work breaks were restored and the company also began to furnish free lunchtime beverages; the result was a further 4 percent productivity jump.

In accounting for this pattern of results, the human relations advocates argued that the specific nature of the rest schedules and experimental manipulations employed during the 13 work periods had been inconsequential, and that productivity had increased solely because of changed social relations within the work group and improved relations between the workers and their supervisor. Mayo and his colleagues pointed out that the five assemblers, housed in a test room removed from other workers, were endowed with a special status that fostered increased group cohesiveness and esprit de corps. Just as importantly, the members of this small group suddenly found themselves receiving more and friendlier attention from their supervisor who, for the first time, actively sought their feedback and suggestions. These factors, along with a new pay schedule that based their earnings on the productivity of their own small group rather than the plant as a whole, led them to develop group norms favoring higher productivity, mutual assistance, and more positive attitudes toward management. Also, as the Lewinians of a generation later were to emphasize, this arrangement freed the five workers from the constraining effects of plantwide norms that suppressed productivity – norms whose enforcement by verbal and physical rebukes were observed in the Hawthorne Plant's "Bank Wiring Room" in a separate study conducted between 1931 and 1932 (see Homans, 1952).

In recent years, the Hawthorne studies have been justifiably criticized for a number of methodological shortcomings (including the absence of a control group in which working conditions remained consistent over the same time period) and for the unmistakable ideological bias that guided the initial reporting and continuing interpretation of results (Bramel & Friend, 1981; Franke & Kaul, 1978; Parsons, 1974). Notably, it has become apparent that the Hawthorne workers were more aware, and less childlike and subject to manipulation by kind words and managerial attention, than textbook accounts generally lead students to believe. We discover, for instance, that the workers were subject to implicit and at times explicit social pressures to keep increasing their productivity, both in order to retain the "privilege" of continued participation under the relatively attractive working conditions of the experiment and in the hope that the experiment's success would lead to factory-wide improvements in working conditions. We also discover that when two workers seemed hostile and noncooperative midway through the long series of experimental changes, they were replaced by two women more willing to contribute to the study's success. Indeed, we discover that over the entire 23 observation periods, the two biggest productivity increases came following this personnel change and, much later, following the onset of the Great Depression (an event that obviously increased the value and attractiveness of any job).

But such critiques, rather than diminishing the importance of the Hawthorne saga, point the way to an appreciation of its larger significance. Over the ensuing decades, the Hawthorne studies have come to serve as more than an object lesson about the importance of social relations and workplace morale and more than a reminder that control group and experimental group subjects should not differ in the degree to which they feel singled out for special attention and monitoring. Today, they help us to remember the more general lesson that we must always attend to the social dynamics of the interaction between researcher and subject. They oblige us to recognize that research participants, whether in the laboratory or the field, are not passive objects of manipulation but cognizant beings concerned with the consequences of the message that their actions will convey. Perhaps most importantly, the Hawthorne saga reminds sophisticated consumers of research to take a hard look at a study's methodology, and the possible influence of the various participants' motives, before accepting any conclusions offered.

WHEN "BIG" INTERVENTIONS FAIL

The methodological lessons learned from the Hawthorne studies make us wary when interpreting applied success stories. But, Hawthorne effects notwithstanding, many sensible and well-designed applied ventures do fail; and it is worth considering the scientific lessons to be learned and the social implications to be drawn from such failures.

Situationism, Liberalism, and the Politics of Intervention

Both the doctrine we have termed situationism and the tradition of applied social psychology are closely linked, in the minds of many people, to the political philosophy of liberalism. The connection is understandable. Over the past three decades, liberal pleas for school desegregation, food stamps, medicaid, prenatal health care, job training, drug education, and compensatory education are certainly situationist, both in their underlying assumptions and in their proposed remedies. But the equation should not be too simple-minded. Conservative proposals for harsher criminal penalties, heightened police surveillance, improved school discipline, and even tax incentives to encourage hiring of the "hard-core" unemployed, are similarly situationist in thrust (although most proponents of these measures probably would reject situationist explanations for the relevant problems). And, of course, many situationist interventions, including programs designed to increase seat belt use, decrease smoking, or improve diet, cannot reasonably be termed either liberal or conservative.

But we would be guilty of self-deception if we failed to note that the political climate of the past decade has been none too friendly to the types of analyses and remedies most often proposed by social scientists. We are popularly linked, with some historical justification, to social initiatives of the Kennedy/Johnson era that failed to fulfill the extravagant hopes and promises of many who lobbied for the necessary funds. We are similarly linked, at least in the charges of neo-conservative critics, to the view that juvenile delinquents, chronic truants, welfare cheaters, drug abusers, and sex offenders should be "coddled," that is to say helped or treated, without being held fully accountable for their behavior. We are also linked to the unpalatable argument that greater federal spending (and therefore higher taxes) will be required if we are to address our most pressing social problems. Indeed, many thoughtful and progressive people, speaking more in sorrow than in anger, claim that the intervention programs advocated by "well-meaning but naive" social scientists have had their test and failed.

There is no denying that ambitious situationist interventions often fail, or at least fall far short of promises and expectations (see Abt, 1976). Sometimes such failures are not particularly instructive, at least not from the vantage point of the theorist. Programs that look promising on paper can be implemented so ineptly and halfheartedly that their failure tells us virtually nothing about the soundness of the situational analysis that prompted them – just as the results of a failed laboratory experiment become uninformative when we discover that the experimental manipulation in question was botched. Other failures merely attest to our underestimation of the situational factors to be overcome. But some failures offer social psychological insights that are much less obvious, and much more relevant to the intellectual core of our discipline. Indeed, as we will now see, a thoughtfully conceived, welldesigned, and carefully implemented intervention program that fails can offer just as profound lessons, and raise just as provocative questions, as any of the successful laboratory experiments cited in our textbooks.

A Case History: The Cambridge-Somerville Youth Study

In 1935 Richard Clark Cabot established one of the most ambitious and exciting intervention programs ever conceived. It was designed to serve the needs of youngsters whose environments and past behavior made them prime candidates for delinquency and criminality (Powers & Whitmer, 1951). Approximately 250 boys from working-class families in a densely populated area of eastern Massachusetts, many of whom were specifically judged by schools, police, or welfare agencies to be "at risk," entered the program at ages ranging from five to 13 and then continued in it for an average of *five years*. During that time the intervention combined all the weapons in the liberal social scientist's arsenal. Caseworkers visited each child twice a month and provided whatever assistance seemed warranted, including, in roughly one-third of the cases, active involvement in family conflicts. For 50 percent of the boys, the caseworkers arranged for tutoring in academic subjects. Over 100 boys, or roughly 40 percent of the sample, received medical or psychiatric attention. Social and recreational needs were similarly addressed. Most of the youngsters were brought into contact with the Boy Scouts, YMCA, or other youth groups, and about 25 percent were sent to summer camps. In short, the program was the kind of multifaceted, long-duration intervention that many social scientists would love to see implemented today, but would concede to be too ambitious and costly to be a realistic possibility in the current political climate.

The most noteworthy features of the Cambridge-Somerville study, however, had nothing to do with the nature of the intervention itself; instead, they involved the exemplary quality of the research design. First of all, a true random assignment procedure was used so that the fates of the 250 youngsters in the treatment program could be compared with those of a like number of "matched mates" assigned to the control group. Second, and even more unusual, painstaking follow-up studies were conducted to investigate long-term effects – follow-ups that continued for 40 years after the intervention period and saw the successful collection of at least some basic outcome data for about 95 percent of the original sample (Long & Vaillant, 1984; J. McCord, 1978; J. McCord & W. McCord, 1959; W. McCord & J. McCord, 1959).

Both the scope of the intervention and the quality of the evaluation procedures employed in the Cambridge-Somerville project thus oblige us to take its results seriously. And these results were undeniably disappointing. Despite the positive impressions of the caseworkers and the equally positive survey recollections of many served by the program, the results of cold, hard, statistical comparisons revealed only failure. No differences between treatment and control groups were found with respect to juvenile offenses (about one-third in each group had "official" criminal records and an additional one-fifth had "unofficial" records). Nor did the treated subjects fare any better than the controls in terms of later adult offenses – roughly 15 to 20 percent in each group were found to have committed serious offenses against people or property. In fact, the small differences in adult crime rates favored the *control* group. And for at least one disturbing measure, that is, multiple offenses, this difference reached conventional levels of statistical significance. Other measures involving health and mortality, occupational success, and life satisfaction told the same story. On measure after measure, no evidence could be found to suggest that the treatment group had fared better than the control group; and on the few measures where a significant difference was found (for example, alcoholism rates and percentages achieving white-collar or professional occupational status), it was the control group that seemed better off.

Results like those from the Cambridge-Somerville study would prompt some politically conservative interpreters to justify cuts in social programs for disadvantaged youth, and to insist that it is personal values, capacities, and dispositions that determine who will become criminals and who will become honest citizens. More liberal or radical interpreters would be apt to respond in adamantly situationist terms, to insist that the environmental forces that drove so many youngsters to serious antisocial behavior were just too powerful to be combated with anything less than marked improvements in the youngsters' socioeconomic status and the quality of their neighborhood environments. Still other interpreters might insist that it is largely the vagaries of chance that place some youngsters but not others on the path to criminal behavior. But such rhetoric should not distract us from the perplexing but critical question raised by the

Cambridge-Somerville results: How could the various sources of assistance have failed to help at least *some* kids, and therefore to have produced at least some decrease in the relevant measures of social deviance?

We cannot answer this question with hard evidence; but we can offer some speculations that link the Cambridge-Somerville results to the three principal themes we have emphasized throughout this book. The relevance of the first theme, the power of situational influence, needs little elaboration. The situational factors manipulated by the Cambridge-Somerville intervention may have been trivial in their potential "effect size" – trivial, at least, relative to the influence of other situational factors that could not be manipulated. While this simple answer may be at least partially correct, it is not entirely satisfying – especially in light of the testimonials of so many participants that the interventions were potent and helpful to them. To find a more satisfying answer, we believe, one must proceed from the assumption that the intervention probably did help some individuals, and therefore that the lack of a net benefit (indeed, the hint on some measures of a net *detriment)* means that some youngsters somehow must have been *hurt* by it. Our search for possible sources of such detrimental effects, in turn, is guided by the two familiar themes we have considered so often – that is, the importance of subjective interpretation and the dynamic nature of the forces and constraints that operate in everyday social contexts.

Labeling and attribution. In the Cambridge-Somerville Program, as in any social intervention, we must be alert to the possibility that the meaning and message of the intervention – to the target population, and to those who dealt with them – were not entirely benign. The act of intervening implies the *need* for such intervention. The visit of a case-worker suggests that there is some deficiency to be remedied; it tells the world that negative outcomes are occurring and perhaps can be expected to occur in the future. Such a message can label or stigmatize the recipient of assistance in a way that changes the subsequent behavior of other people. ("I'd better not recommend John for a delivery-boy job at the grocery store; he's in some kind of program for delinquents." "That John Rocco who applied for a job today seems like a good kid, but wasn't he in trouble a while back? I know they've had some kind of social worker going to his house for years.") More importantly, the message may change the recipient's perceptions of his dispositions and of his capacity and responsibility to take action on his own behalf.

Comparison processes. Ironically, social interventions that address problems can increase rather than decrease the recipients' sense of deprivation, leaving them subjectively worse off than before. At least some of the Cambridge-Somerville youngsters may have been disappointed with the help they received or the outcomes they achieved, and they may have made comparisons not with their original situation, but with the type of assistance and outcomes they had hoped for or expected. Contact with the middle-class caseworkers, tutors, and camp counselors may have heightened their sense of relative deprivation and frustration about their own lives and prospects. More importantly, perhaps, the *end* of the intervention may have made them feel that they had lost something, and left them doubting their own resources and capacities to meet future problems in the face of that loss.

Unintended dynamic consequences of intervention. Acts of social intervention change not only perceptions and interpretations, they change the dynamics of social systems and relationships as well. Beyond bringing into play potent restraining forces (for example, pressures from peers who reassert and enforce antisocial norms), social interventions may serve to decrease some forces that otherwise would have exerted a constructive influence. In the Cambridge-Somerville context, intervention from outside agencies may have discouraged families from turning to a member of the clergy, a special teacher, or even a next-door neighbor who otherwise might have helped. Similarly, when "outside" help is clearly in evidence, individuals and communities may feel less inclination and responsibility to offer or develop their own forms of assistance. Such failures to provide resources can prove a particularly unfortunate consequence when, as in the Cambridge-Somerville case, the outside help will not last forever.

A note on trade-offs. In order to address critics who doubt whether the subtle detrimental effects that we have postulated could really have outweighed the obvious benefits of providing disadvantaged youngsters with much-needed counseling and encouragement, we need to look at the trade-offs between costs and benefits. Let us suppose that 10 percent of the target population would have manifested a particular problem or pathology (for example, a serious adult criminal offense) in the absence of any intervention. Let us also suppose that the treatment or intervention in question is highly effective, that is, it "saves" fully 50 percent of those who would otherwise show the problem. Now let us further suppose that the damage to those who would not otherwise have shown the problem is relatively small – let's say an 8 percent "casualty rate." A little simple calculation reveals that the net effect of the intervention will be negative, that is, an overall incidence rate for the problem in question of roughly 12 percent instead of 10 percent. (That is, .50 (10%) + .08 (90%) = 12.2%.) The point of this exercise, of course, is not to prove that interventions are doomed to produce more harm than good (on the contrary, unanticipated benefits may be more numerous and marked than unanticipated costs). It is just to emphasize again the difficulty of predicting long-term intervention consequences and, accordingly, the need for careful, well-designed evaluation research.

We hope our speculations about the reasons for the failure of the Cambridge-Somerville intervention have not obscured an overriding lesson of the study – that is, the depth of our ignorance about the relative importance of, and the interactions between, the various factors that promote healthy social development. Indeed, this lesson does not apply only to the external effects of intervention. Consider again the life-outcome results for the control-group youths in the Cambridge-Somerville study, cited in Chapter 2. At one extreme, some of the boys came from families where the parents were models of working-class rectitude, that is, father steadily employed, mother an effective home-maker, and so on. At the other extreme, some of the boys came from families beset with a whole complex of social pathologies, for example, father chronically unemployed and alcoholic, mother mentally ill, family history of dependency on multiple social agencies, and so on. Yet 40 years later, for a host of outcome variables including arrest and incarceration rates, incidence of mental illness, records of income and employment, and social class attainment, there was little or no difference between men who came from families that would seem to create the best prognosis and those that would seem to create the worst (Long & Vaillant, 1984).

Influences exerted by family conditions thus seem to have had scarcely more enduring effects on the control group youths than the ambitious programs of social scientists had on their peers in the treated group. Some were successful in their careers, valued as husbands and fathers, and content with themselves; some were criminals, unemploy-able, alcoholic, and abusive as husbands and fathers. But these outcomes were neither predictable from environmental measures nor deflectable by environmental interventions that the common wisdom of laypeople and social scientists alike holds to be very important.

This is not to say that we are completely ignorant about what affects people's most important life outcomes. We know, for example, that the intelligence of the control group adolescents was a valuable predictor of later life outcomes. We also know, from the studies by Caspi, Elder, and Bem (1987) cited in Chapter 6, that boys who have a problem with temper tantrums are more likely than their peers to be both underem-ployed and divorced in adulthood. Nor is it just early established, per-haps even genetically related, individual differences such as intelligence and temperament that predict life outcomes. Situationally based advan-tages and disadvantages associated with social class can outweigh intel-ligence and even early academic achievement. For example, middleclass children with poor grades in high school are substantially more likely to go to college than are working-class children with good grades (Sewell & Hauser, 1976); and the attainment of a college degree, in turn, proves in study after study to be one of the most powerful predictors of adult socioeconomic status.

What the Cambridge-Somerville studies remind us of (aside from the fact that some of our preconceptions about the causes and correlates of adult success may be in need of revision) is something very important about tension systems. Most normal human psyches are more robust and less subject to either early- or late-occurring trauma than our intuitions tell us (Kagan, 1984). Similarly, most normal communities like Cambridge-Somerville are more potent and stable in their influences on potentially deviant individuals than we recognize. By the same token, positive interventions, no matter how early they occur or how potent they seem, are not likely to have large or enduring effects, at least not on *average,* if the community ecology is allowed to work its influence on individuals.

WHEN "SMALL" INTERVENTIONS SUCCEED

While costly large-scale interventions often fail, relatively modest interventions sometimes prove to be remarkably effective, especially when they concentrate on potent channel factors and on the social influences that compel and constrain so much of human behavior. We begin with the classics in the field, the studies that were seminal to Lewin's development of group-discussion techniques, and that continue to exert an impact on our thinking almost half a century later.

Lewinian Discussion Groups and Democratic Procedures

A series of well-known field studies conducted during and just after World War II by Kurt Lewin and his associates (summarized by Lewin, 1952) demonstrated how entrenched patterns of behavior could be changed, in a relatively short period of time, by identifying and redirecting group influences. The starting point for one memorable study was the perplexing but well-documented difficulty that nutritionists had in trying to change wartime patterns of food consumption – specifically, in trying to persuade Americans to substitute underutilized sweetbreads, kidney, heart, and other organic meats for more traditional cuts that were then in short supply. As is so often the case, posters, pamphlets, and other media appeals proved ineffective. Even well prepared lectures delivered face-to-face to captive audiences, lectures that emphasized nutritional value and low cost, that suggested recipes and preparation techniques, and that appealed to patriotism by explaining the need to stretch food resources to aid the war effort, met with failure. Real and imagined resistance from family members, and entrenched cultural norms about the kinds of food that "people like us" consume and enjoy, proved too formidable an obstacle to be overcome with purely informational appeals.

Lewin's remedy – after careful observation and analysis of constraining forces and channel factors – was the use of small discussion groups with homemakers, who Lewin recognized to be the key "gatekeepers" determining which foods reached the family table. In these groups, a trained leader offered a brief introduction to the problem, and then encouraged the participants simply to talk about the ways that "people like you" could overcome whatever obstacles (principally, the anticipated objections of family members) stood in the way of using the new foods and available recipes. Later, at the conclusion of the discussion, the leader asked the women to indicate with a show of hands whether they intended to try some of these new foods before the group's follow-up meeting. The results were dramatic. Whereas an information-laden lecture presented in a control condition succeeded in getting only 3 percent of the audience to serve at least one of the new foods to their family, over 30 percent of homemakers assigned to discussion groups took the plunge. Follow-up studies showed that group discussion techniques could be employed to change a variety of similarly entrenched behaviors involving health practices and child care. For example, when rural mothers in a maternity hospital were individually advised by a nutritionist to administer cod-liver oil to their newborn infants, only about 20 percent complied within the initial test period. When the same information was introduced in the context of a six person discussion group, the rate of immediate compliance more than doubled, reaching 45 percent.

The simplicity of these studies should not blind us either to the insightfulness of the analysis that preceded Lewin's intervention or to the sophistication of some of the specific techniques employed (Bennett, 1955). By subtly introducing a new norm in the context of a newly created reference group, and by simultaneously communicating the consensus supporting that norm and inducing a behavioral commitment to it, via the show-of-hands procedure, Lewin was harnessing powerful social and motivational processes. His students and intellectual heirs were to pursue in their laboratories and training groups over the next two decades. The basic message of these early studies, however, is quite clear and remains just as relevant now as it was then. First, the provision of information, even highly relevant and seemingly persuasive information, often proves to be a disappointingly weak vehicle for achieving changes in feelings and behavior. Second, freeing individuals from an existing source of group pressures or constraints, especially if they are then exposed to new norms and subjected to new social influences, often proves to be a surprisingly powerful vehicle for accomplishing such changes.

One final group study in the Lewinian tradition deserves special mention, particularly in the light of our earlier account of the Hawthorne studies and the "human relations approach." Coch and French (1948) tackled a familiar workplace dilemma – the problem of inducing workers to accept changes in production methods without incurring resentment, lowered morale, and reduced productivity. The setting for this classic study was a pajama factory (owned, not coincidentally, by Lewin's former student and eventual biographer, Alfred Morrow). The factory employed about 600 workers, mostly rural women who were paid piece rates based on a careful assessment of the time required for different tasks. Coch and French constituted three comparable groups of workers for their study, each of which was called upon to make some seemingly very small change in the way the pajamas were sewn or boxed.

In the control group, the workers were simply assembled and informed about the relevant changes in production methods (and about the corresponding adjustment in the piece rate). As had been the case in the past, this group reacted unfavorably. There were expressions of hostility and resentment (17 percent of them soon quit their jobs) and an immediate sharp drop in the rate of productivity from which recovery was relatively slow and incomplete. In fact, eight weeks later only 38 percent of the workers had returned to their prior rate. In the second group, the required change was introduced in a rather different fashion. A group meeting first was held and the need to reduce product cost through more efficient production methods was presented in a vivid and concrete fashion (by showing the workers comparable garments manufactured at very different production costs). Representatives were then selected by the workers to meet with management and learn the new procedures, which they would later explain to the other workers and help implement. This *representation* procedure produced a far better result than the control condition. There was no apparent decline in morale or in relations between labor and management (no workers quit), and within two weeks the earlier rate of productivity had been regained. The third group initially was treated in a similar fashion except that *all* the workers became representatives, or "special operators," assigned to help implement the required production change. In this *total participation* condition the benefits were even more dramatic. The initial drop in productivity was shallow, and it lasted but a single day. Thereafter group productivity steadily climbed to a level roughly 15 percent higher than the previous rate. Also, morale remained high; there apparently were no worker complaints, and no one quit her job.

Once again, the simplicity of this demonstration experiment gives little hint of the sophisticated analysis that preceded it. Before designing their interventions, the investigators, in the best Lewinian tradition, carefully analyzed the motivational factors and group processes that restrained productivity in general and resulted in particular resistance to procedural changes. The specific techniques employed to increase productivity similarly incorporated a number of subtle features (for example, the manner in which the workers were encouraged to adopt the proposed changes and implementation details as their own group's norm, and not as something imposed upon them without their advice or consent). Moreover, it would be a misreading of the Lewinian message, to say nothing of the spirit of this text, to conclude that all problems in persuading people to change behavior can be overcome with group decision making. But the ultimate message of the study remains clear and timely as American industry today faces unprecedented challenges from competitors who seem to have taken that message to heart. Careful attention to group dynamics and the subjective life of the worker can be the key to improved productivity and performance; and the steps required to produce these benefits need not be drastic, costly, or aversive.

Forty years after Lewin pioneered the ideas of participatory management and work-group decision procedures, they were introduced to the United States as "Japanese" management techniques. They do deserve this label because the Japanese were the first to institute them on a widespread basis, but their origin was not entirely domestic. We have been told by the Japanese social psychologist Jyuji Misumi that Kurt Lewin visited Japan in the early 1930s and had a profound impact on industrial and academic circles there. Indeed, he was offered the Chair in Industrial Relations at the University of Tokyo. Wisely, given the global war that was soon to follow, Lewin came to the United States instead. Ironically, his ideas about industrial relations continue to have far more impact in postwar Japan than in the United States. Our Lewinian legacy lies primarily in the development, by Lewin's students, of consciousness-raising, encounter, self-actualization, and self-help groups that are so ubiquitous a feature of contemporary American life (see reviews by Back 1972; Lieberman, Borman, & Associates, 1979).

"Modeling" Effects on Prosocial Behavior

One of the most consistent effects demonstrated in both laboratory and field studies is the influence that one individual can exert on another. The presence of an appropriate social model can change the rate at which food or alcohol is consumed. It can alter the likelihood that an individual will laugh or cry, approach or avoid, delay or seek gratification, show or withhold affection, behave aggressively, altruistically, conventionally, or innovatively, or indeed show virtually any behavior (see reviews by Bandura, 1973, 1977a, 1977b, 1986). Not surprisingly, many studies demonstrate that the degree of social modeling is importantly influenced by the model's *characteristics* (for example, high versus low status, attractiveness, or power) and by the nature of the model's *outcomes* (for example, praise versus blame, and success versus failure in achieving some relevant goal). But what is perhaps most remarkable is the impact that social models can exert even when they have no particular distinguishing attributes and their behavior carries virtually no information about its consequences.

The presence of a salient social model appears to be a particularly potent channel factor in inducing people to engage in behavior that is socially desirable, that is, in facilitating the link between positive attitudes and positive actions. Effect sizes vary, but they are generally quite large both in absolute terms and relative to most people's intuitions. Thus, for example, Rushton and Campbell (1977) showed that face-to-face requests for blood donations that were successful 25 percent of the time in the absence of any model produced a positive response 67 percent of the time when a friendly peer complied with the experimenter's request. Even more impressive were the results of follow-ups to determine who ultimately showed up to give blood: None of the women in the no-model condition did, whereas 33 percent in the model condition did. Similar effects of an altruistic confederate were found by Bryan and Test (1967) who showed that motorists were much more likely to help a woman with a flat tire if they had seen a confederate 400 yards back pulled over and helping someone else.

A particularly powerful social modeling effect was demonstrated by Aronson and O'Leary (1983) at the height of the energy crisis in the early 1980s. Their setting was a field house shower room in which signs had been posted urging students to save energy by turning their shower off as they soaped themselves, and turning it on only to rinse themselves. Although virtually all students knew that the sign existed, and recognized that the recommended procedure would save energy, few students complied. Only 6 percent of those showering during a one-week "baseline" period actually turned the water off while soaping themselves. Making the message more obtrusive by attaching a larger sign with the same instructions to a tripod and placing it prominently in the middle of the shower area succeeded in boosting the compliance rate to about 20 percent. But the addition of appropriate social models that is, experimental confederates who drove home the sign's message by lathering themselves with their own shower turned off (but without saying anything to other shower users) produced a far more dramatic effect. In fact, the compliance rate reached almost 50 percent when one such model was present, and it jumped to 67 percent when two models were present. Again, the lesson is among social psychology's most important ones. When we want people to translate their positive intentions into equally positive actions, and when exhortations and reasoned appeals seem to be of limited effectiveness, a little social demonstration can be invaluable.

Interventions that Encourage Minority-Student Success

One of the most compelling social problems faced by the United States today is the lower educational and occupational success of certain ethnic minorities, including African-Americans, Hispanics, and Native Americans. The difficulties experienced by these groups are evident, from their first encounter with the educational system (where they are apt to be "streamed" into dead-end "special education" programs), through primary and secondary school (where they are more likely to fail or drop out) and even through college and graduate school. Similar difficulties are evident in the world of work, where minority unemployment and underemployment are rampant, and minorities are sorely underrepresented in managerial and professional positions. The authors know that even liberals are wont to shake their heads in pondering these facts and mutter about intractable problems, impassable structural barriers, and cultural differences that seem unlikely to change in the lifetimes of anyone now on the planet. So it is encouraging to note that there have been some remarkable successes in changing minority outcomes at every level of the educational system – success achieved through relatively "small" and very cost-effective interventions.

The first program we will discuss is that of Urie Treisman (1989), a mathematician at the University of California at Berkeley. In the 1970s, Treisman had noted the high failure rate of blacks taking introductory mathematics at his university. Most received such marginal grades in the course that their path toward a career in the physical sciences or medicine was effectively blocked. Worse than that, two-thirds of the black students who enrolled in introductory mathematics never graduated from Berkeley. Rather than bemoaning preparational disadvantages or musing about possible motivational deficits, Treisman turned anthropologist and literally followed black students around as they lived their lives. He did the same for another group noted for their success in mathematics and science at Berkeley, namely Asian students. The most striking difference that Treisman noted between black and Asian students was that the blacks studied alone, while the Asians studied in groups. The benefits of group study for mathematics seem obvious enough on reflection. Students do not have to endure demoralizing failure on problem after problem, since someone in the group is likely to have the solution. Moreover, group study allows each student the opportunity to see and incorporate the tricks and strategies of the others, to say nothing of the social support and reference group opportunities offered as the student interacts with others who need similar assistance.

Treisman next turned social psychologist and persuaded a large number of entering black students to enroll in a special "honors" program featuring group study of mathematics. (How he achieved this was no easy matter, since the students tended to resist anything that sounded like remedial assistance, and the group study procedure was particularly foreign to their experience.) Treisman apparently also offered students some systematic monitoring and encouragement. In any case, the results were dramatic. The black students who participated in the special group study program achieved grades in introductory math that were, on average, the same as those obtained by whites and Asians. More importantly, their college dropout rate plummeted to the same level as that for these other two traditionally high-achieving groups. It is difficult to say for certain which features – the seeming prestige of the special program, the group study procedures, or Treisman's monitoring and encouragement – were critical to the remarkable success of his program. But it is impossible to overpraise an intervention that makes such a difference in so many lives with such a modest outlay of resources.

Similar results have been obtained by Lewis Kleinsmith (Johnston & Kleinsmith, 1987), a biologist at the University of Michigan. Kleinsmith pioneered an interactive computer program designed to provide an instructional boost for introductory biology students. Black students taking the standard course finished far below whites, so far below that their careers in science, even their careers in college, were placed in jeopardy. Kleinsmith's interactive computer procedure improved the performance of all students nontrivially, but the effect on blacks was particularly dramatic. Their level of performance soared to that typical of whites in the new program and above that of whites in the old program. Again, the effect size in pragmatic terms was extraordinary. For many students it meant the difference between taking the fullest advantage of the college opportunity they had sought for themselves and either leaving college or taking a route through it that greatly restricted their future options.

Dramatic educational effects for disadvantaged students are not limited to blacks or to higher education settings. Jaime Escalante, the high school mathematics teacher of *Stand and Deliver* fame, has created a multifaceted program that produces a rate of advanced college placement among his mostly working-class Hispanic high school students that compares favorably with the rate obtained at many of the most privileged and well-regarded high schools in the country. Other educators working with both black and Hispanic populations have similarly developed successful, relatively low-cost ways to reach inner-city elementary school children and boost their performance up to or beyond national averages (Schorr, 1988). In short, relatively brief situational manipulations in our schools *can* succeed, thereby confounding the intuitions of those who argue that disadvantaged minority students are doomed to failure either by their personal limitations or by the social barriers and inequities they face.

Distal Versus Proximal Interventions

It is worth pausing to contrast the dramatic successes of these educational interventions with the results of programs of the Head Start type of the 1960s. These programs produced substantial early gains among inner-city preschoolers (that is, higher IQ scores in kindergarten, fewer children diverted to special education programs in first grade, and so on). But longer-term differences in IQ scores and academic performances in the higher grades were virtually nonexistent (Consortium for Longitudinal Studies, 1978). While we now know (Royce, Darlington, & Murray, 1983; Woodhead, 1988) that there *were* some very significant long-term gains in high school dropout rates, unemployment, and incarceration – gains that liberal and conservative political leaders alike now regard as sufficient justification for such programs – the initial disappointment in Head Start's academic results was both deep and destructive in its impact. Many critics, from all points on the political spectrum, became convinced of the intractability of the educational problem at hand. Critics on the left argued that the children's socioeconomic disadvantages could not be overcome without major structural changes in American society and education. Critics on the right insisted that the intellectual limitations of the children and/or deficiencies in the parenting they received made the expensive remedial programs a waste of money.

Few critics, however, recognized that some fundamental assumptions about the importance of early versus late (or "distal" versus "proximal") interventions simply needed re-examining. In particular, American behaviorists and Freudians alike, in emphasizing the importance of early learning experiences, had led us to exaggerate greatly the wisdom of the dictum that an ounce of prevention is worth a pound of cure. Nowhere, we believe, were the Freudians in particular more persuasive, and more misguided, than in their underestimation of the influence of immediate situational forces and constraints relative to formative childhood factors. Kurt Lewin, Freud's young contemporary and his intellectual opponent, vigorously attacked what he felt was the overly historical emphasis of psychoanalytic diagnosis and remedies. In a famous analogy, he considered the problem of determining whether the floor of an attic will be sufficiently strong to bear a given weight. One could, Lewin observed, determine the nature and quality of the construction material, investigate the plans and reputation of the architect and builder, and then attempt to predict how the resulting construction would stand up to the rigors of the passing years. Alternatively, and more profitably, one could design appropriate procedures to *test* the strength of the floor as it is, in its present condition.

Lewin, of course, did not deny the possible importance of historical facts in affecting the present situation. He simply emphasized the fact that most systems are highly subject to unpredictable change owing to the action of both external and internal forces. He also emphasized that when current situational influences are sufficiently powerful and "on target," they often can override the influence of the most potent historical factors. Thus the apparent contradiction between the disappointingly small effects of early educational interventions and the encouragingly large effects of later interventions serves to remind us again of two major principles of social psychology and two major themes of this book. Later, more proximal interventions can be powerful when they alter important features of the immediate situation – especially channel factors that facilitate the link between positive intentions and constructive actions. Early, distal interventions, by contrast, are likely to be less powerful, or at least they are likely to have difficult-to-predict effects, because human societies (and human psyches) are dynamic tension systems in a constant state of flux.

From the standpoint of the pragmatic proponent of social interventions, we can think of no more optimistic message. History need not be destiny. And though massive and expensive "early" interventions can have disappointingly small long-term effects (especially when we explore too narrow a range of outcome measures), smaller, cheaper, but more specifically targeted, "late" interventions can be powerful enough to restore the faith of the situationist.

LABELING AND ATTRIBUTION EFFECTS IN THE CLASSROOM

One of social psychology's most important and enduring contributions, as we have noted throughout this book, has been its theoretical explication and experimental demonstration of the profound role that subjective interpretation plays in human affairs. It is now time to document some applied contributions in this vein, focusing specifically on the role that social labels, self-perceptions, and attribution processes play in mediating educational outcomes.

Social Labels and Self-Fulfilling Expectations

Almost half a century ago Robert Merton (1948) made famous the concept of the self-fulfilling prophecy (see also Snyder, 1984). The basic notion underlying this concept is that what someone believes to be the case about a person or group may serve to create a reality that affirms the belief. In the absence of the belief, the reality might have been quite different. There are many different ways in which such a phenomenon can occur (see Darley & Fazio, 1980), some of which we already have mentioned at earlier points in this book. But perhaps the most dramatic illustration of the phenomenon itself was one provided in 1968 by Robert Rosenthal and his colleague Lenore Jacobson. These investigators gave IQ tests to children from several elementary school classes, and then shared the results of the tests with the children's teachers. At the same time, they identified to the teachers several children in each classroom who, they claimed, could be expected to show substantial IQ gains over the current school year. These children, in fact, had been randomly selected by the investigators, with no knowledge whatsoever about their potential for such gains.

The now famous result of this tiny intervention was that the targeted children tended to show the predicted IQ gains – gains large and consistent enough, in the case of first- and second-grade children, to be of practical as well as statistical significance. Scores of follow-up studies have verified Rosenthal and Jacobson's basic finding (Rosenthal & Rubin, 1978) and have begun to elaborate some of the mechanisms that produce this labeling effect. Most notably, teachers seem to treat the positively-labelled children differently from the other children, for example, by paying more attention to their behavior, giving them different verbal and nonverbal feedback, or simply exerting more effort (Harris & Rosenthal, 1985; Meichenbaum, Bowers, & R. Ross, 1969; Rosenthal, 1976, 1985; Zanna, Sheras, Cooper & Shaw, 1975). The significance of the finding that teacher expectations affect children's intellectual growth has not been lost on those concerned with minority education. Indeed, there is evidence that educators generally expect lower performance of minority children (Brophy & Good, 1974), and strong circumstantial evidence that these expectations can be a factor in the children's poor educational performance (Dreeben & Barr, 1983).

Labeling Versus Exhortation to Achieve Behavior Change

Most psychologists can cite at least a few research papers that they believe have received far less attention than they deserve. One such paper, in our opinion, was authored in 1975 by Richard Miller, Phillip Brickman, and Diana Bolen. It showed that children may be less responsive to communications urging them to change their behavior than to positive social labels and to the suggestion that they already possess the virtue in question. The specific behavior investigated in the first study by Miller and his colleagues was classroom littering. One classroom was assigned to a control condition in which the investigators simply measured the percentage of litter deposited in the classroom wastebaskets. A second classroom was assigned to a "persuasion" condition. In this condition, over an eight-day period, the children received various written and oral appeals – from their teacher, their principal, and even the school janitor – to keep their classrooms neat, to deposit all waste paper in the appropriate receptacles, and to pick up any litter they found on the floor. The third classroom was assigned to a "positive label" condition. In this condition, the same communicators, over the same eight-day period, never urged the children to change their behavior in any way; instead, they commended the children for *already* being neat. That is, each message, in one form or another, pointed out that their particular classroom (in contrast to some others in the school) was remarkably clean and commended the students for being so litter conscious.

The investigators then simply measured how much litter (including some litter deliberately created by the investigators) ended up in each classroom's wastebaskets in three different time periods. The first was a pretest period before any manipulation; the second was an immediate posttest period following the eight-day manipulation; the third and final one was a delayed posttest period following a two-week hiatus in which no mention of littering was made in any classroom. The results were very clear-cut. During the pretest period the percentage of litter deposited in wastebaskets was equally low (less than 20 percent) in all three conditions. During the immediate posttest period, the persuasion condition classroom showed a moderate decrease in littering (45 percent in wastebaskets), while the attribution condition classroom showed a very marked decrease in littering (roughly 80 percent of litter in wastebaskets). Even more significant, especially in view of the oft-noted difficulty of sustaining desirable changes in behavior, were the results for the delayed posttest. The persuasion condition students soon reverted to the high levels of littering characteristic both of their own pretest period and of the control condition classroom throughout all three periods in the study. The positively labeled students, by contrast, maintained the patterns of behavior congruent with that label by continuing to deposit most of their litter in the wastebaskets.

In a follow-up study, Miller and colleagues showed that mathematics achievements and corresponding changes in self-esteem were similarly responsive to attribution or labeling manipulations and similarly unresponsive, in the long run, to persuasion and other more conventional manipulations. Thus messages that commended students either on their current high levels of ability or on their current high levels of motivation produced elevations in test performance that were substantial and were sustained quite well over time. By contrast, neither persuasive exhortations nor the use of simple reinforcement techniques produced gains of similar magnitude and duration. The message of this study, like that of the littering study, again highlighted the importance of attribution and labeling processes, Positive changes in behavior were most apparent and most sustained when the target individuals were induced to attribute that positive behavior not to short-lived external forces but to their own (presumably enduring) values and abilities.

Motivational Consequences of Superfluous Inducements

In Chapter 3 we described an experiment by Lepper and his colleagues (Lepper et al., 1973) on the attributional and motivational consequences of extraneous or "superfluous" rewards. The critical finding from this experiment, it will be recalled, was that nursery school children who wielded their magic markers in expectation of receiving a "good player award" at the end of the experimental session subsequently played less with the magic markers – in a spontaneous, free-play session conducted two weeks later – than children who initially had used the markers without any such expectation of reward.

This basic phenomenon has now been well established in experiments conducted by many different investigators in many different laboratories using a variety of age groups, tasks, and external inducements (for example, Deci, 1971, 1972; Karniol & M. Ross, 1977; Kruglanski, Friedman, & Zeevi, 1971; Kruglanski et al., 1975; see reviews by Deci & Ryan, 1985; Kassin & Lepper, 1984; Lepper & Greene, 1978). The range of negative consequences demonstrated has also grown considerably. Indeed, it appears that the introduction of superfluous rewards can lead to a deterioration in many aspects of performance, including incidental learning, willingness to attempt more challenging problems, and even the overall quality and creativity of the product itself. There is also evidence that the availability of extraneous rewards can lead problem solvers to persevere on unproductive or inefficient rote strategies, rather than to "break set" by trying something new. Finally, there is now further evidence about response generalization and long-term consequences that follow once the reward or other inducements cease to be available: Children not only show less interest in and liking for the original version of the task, they also show a continuing preference for easier rather than more challenging versions of that task.

The applied implications of such studies were readily derivable from principles of attribution theory. One should avoid using strong, salient inducements to get people to do things that they would have done quite willingly in the complete absence of such external forces – or even done willingly in response to external influences that were weaker or subtler and more likely to leave them with the conviction that their responses reflected their own choices and preferences. The relevance of these studies to the much lamented motivational problems observed in our schools seemed equally evident. As education reformers and parents alike often have occasion to note, the same preschoolers who seemed blessed with intellectual curiosity and a thirst for learning before beginning their formal education seem to lose their enthusiasm for learning once it must take place subject to the contingencies and social controls of the typical American classroom.

But the publication of research and theorizing about the negative consequences of superfluous social control unleashed a firestorm of controversy and criticism. The reason for this hostile reception is that Lepper and company seemed to be calling into question a very popular, and apparently quite successful, behavior modification tool – the use of tangible rewards and the establishment of token economies (in which "points" could be earned and traded for various rewards and privileges). The issue, as Lepper emphasized, was not the immediate efficacy of such reinforcement techniques. This was not called into question by the results. Rather, it was long-term maintenance of change, and generalization to new situations in which the relevant external inducements would be absent, that were made to seem dubious.

There have by now been scores of pertinent studies on the long-term effects of reinforcement conducted by researchers of every stripe, school, and persuasion. The vast majority of them were designed either to show that the superfluous use of rewards or other inducement can have just the undesirable consequences that the attribution theorists warned us about (Condry, 1977; Lepper, 1988; Morgan, 1984) or to show that the judicious use of reinforcement can produce educational benefits without these undesirable consequences (Bandura & Schunk, 1981). We will not attempt here to summarize or organize the complex, and at times even conflicting, body of evidence and interpretation that now exists. But we will try to provide what we believe to be the important legacy of the theoretical and empirical confrontation – that is, a set of principles and caveats that offer guidance to the practitioner (parent as well as teacher) who seeks to maximize the potential educational benefits and to minimize the attributional and motivational costs of their influence attempts (Lepper & Hodell, 1989; also Harackiewicz, Abrahams, & Wageman, 1987).

Detrimental effects of extrinsic constraints are most likely to occur when initial interest is high, when extrinsic constraints are superfluous and salient, and when they provide a psychologically plausible explanation for one's engagement in the activity – when the reward, in short, can be easily viewed as a "bribe." Such effects are less likely to occur, by contrast, when any tangible rewards are based on quality of task performance (Harackiewicz, 1979), that is, when the rewards serve primarily to offer feedback and recognition of competence in a task that is intrinsically motivated already. Examples would include a handsome trophy to a tournament winner, or even a gold star for a child who finally succeeds in doing 20 simple multiplications in one minute. Detrimental effects are also less likely to occur when the rewards in question bear some integral relationships to the activity being rewarded – for example, a day off for an employee who burned the midnight oil to finish an important project. In short, rewards will leave intrinsic interest and motivation intact to the extent that the rewarded activity is seen not as a bribe but as a bonus acknowledging one's accomplishment.

Recently, Cordova and Lepper (1989) have begun to show benefits of techniques designed to *enhance* intrinsic interest and motivation. In this study, children undertook a problem-solving task, one similar to that posed in the popular board game "Clue." Their research design featured the presence or absence of an extrinsic reward contingent only on task completion (that is, the chance to choose a toy from the investigator's "mystery box") and a set of pedagogical embellishments to enhance the children's interest in the task (essentially, a comic book-style prologue that described a "crime" and invited the children to become detectives to solve it). The most impressive results reported by Cordova and Lepper pertained to the differences in the quality of intellectual performance and enjoyment shown by the children in response to the two types of inducements – differences not only in the initial task performance test but also in follow-up tests, conducted two weeks later, using a related but different task and offering neither external nor internal motivational enhancements. Rewards led children to use guesswork and unimaginative rote strategies and to achieve relatively poor performances. It also led them to rate their own performances and abilities more negatively, and to express a preference for easier problems in the future. By contrast, the use of embellishments to enhance intrinsic interest led children to more complex and efficient problem-solving strategies and to superior performances. It also led the children to more positive assessments of the task and of their own abilities, and to more ambitious preferences for future tasks.

Attributions for Classroom Success and Failure

All students experience academic failures and disappointments. The consequences of such events, however, may depend heavily upon the way they are interpreted, both by the instructors and by the students themselves (Nicholls, 1984, 1988; Weiner, 1974, 1979, 1985). The instructor who attributes a student's poor performance to low ability can be expected to console the student, assign easier work, or simply ignore the student in the future. The student who concurs in that attribution can be expected to avoid the relevant task, and to show relatively little effort or persistence when it cannot be avoided. If, on the other hand, a poor performance is attributed to factors that can be altered – to lack of effort or to inadequate teaching or learning strategies– very different consequences become likely. The student may try harder, try something different, or decide that the rewards for success in this particular context are simply not worth the effort. What the student is *not* likely to do in such a case, however, is to concede the impossibility of success, and make academic and career choices accordingly. Nor is the teacher likely to advise the student to adopt more "realistic" goals and plans.

Investigators have taken this question of attributional styles in several provocative directions. Carol Dweck and her colleagues have documented individual differences in the way that different children respond to increases in task difficulty and experiences of failure (which the investigators guaranteed by presenting some insoluble anagrams to children who previously had been unscrambling soluble ones). One response pattern, which the investigators termed "mastery," was characterized by increased effort in the face of failure, and renewed success when soluble problems later followed insoluble ones. The other response pattern, which they termed "helplessness," was characterized by decreased effort in the face of failure, and continued failure even after problems ceased to be insoluble (see Diener & Dweck, 1978, 1980; Dweck, 1975; Dweck & Leggett, 1988; Dweck & Wortman, 1982). Martin Seligman and his colleagues, in related work, have shown a similar association between explanatory styles and both academic success (Nolen-Hoeksema, Girgus, & Seligman, 1986; Kamen & Seligman, 1987) and sales performance (Seligman & Shulman, 1986).

Dweck went on to relate her particular findings to a puzzling pair of sex differences that long had been noted in the literature – first, the greater tendency for girls to attribute their failures to low ability rather than lack of motivation or effort, and second, the greater tendency for girls to respond to failure (or to threat of failure, or even heightened evaluation pressure) with motivational and performance decrements that seemed to reflect "learned helplessness." What made these sex differences puzzling was the fact that girls on average receive more praise, less criticism, and higher elementary school grades than boys. Indeed, girls are rated more favorably by teachers and other adults on virtually every type of personal assessment (Dweck & Goetz, 1978; McCandless, Roberts, & Starnes, 1972).

To shed some light on this seeming paradox, Dweck and her colleagues conducted a careful classroom observation of the interactions between fourth- and fifth-graders and their teachers (Dweck, Davidson, Nelson, &

Enna, 1978). The investigators noted first that although it was the girls who received the lion's share of the positive feedback from the teacher, the girls were far more likely than the boys to have such feedback pertain to nonintellectual concerns such as neatness (21 percent in the case of the girls versus only 7 percent in the case of the boys). The differences for negative feedback were even more striking. When girls received negative feedback, 88 percent of it pertained to intellectual quality and only 12 percent pertained to sloppiness or incorrect form. When boys received negative feedback, only 54 percent of it pertained to intellectual content and 46 percent pertained to matters of neatness or form. In short, the overall pattern of feedback encouraged boys more than girls to feel that their successes reflected their academic abilities, while their failures did not.

In a related line of work, Dweck and other investigators have tried to manipulate, rather than merely measure, the type of feedback presented to students. While it is still too early to tell how readily children, or adults, can be induced to adopt new attribution styles, some intriguing findings have been reported – notably evidence that "helpless" students of both sexes may benefit more from "attributional retraining" than from a set of consistent success experiences (see Dweck, 1975; Dweck et al., 1978; also review by Forsterling, 1985).

A very simple series of studies by Wilson and Linville (1982; also Wilson & Stone, 1985) offers further evidence that the consequences of academic disappointment can be manipulated by altering students' subjective interpretations and attributions. These investigators gave information to college freshmen who had scored in the bottom half of their class suggesting that the cause of low grades was "unstable"; that is, the students were assured that relatively low grades are common in the first year (and likely to go up as students become more familiar with their academic environment). In one study, freshmen in the experimental condition received relevant statistical information and also saw a videotaped interview with four relatively senior students who described their grade improvements in concrete terms. In another study, freshmen wrote essays (ostensibly for the benefit of high school students around the state) in which they were to incorporate information about some specific unstable factors unrelated to the students' academic ability (for example, poor course selection, unpleasant living conditions, and the like) that could lower new students' grades. The control group in each study, of course, received no such reassuring hints about the prevalence of poor freshman grades or the improvement that could be anticipated in subsequent years.

The attributional treatments introduced by Wilson and Linville proved to be effective in improving both the students' immediate performance on a sample of test items taken from the GRE and their grades in the following semester. (Interestingly, in view of Dweck's findings, these gains proved to be larger for male students than female students.)

While none of the gains in question were huge (even among the males the mean difference in long-term GPA was only half a standard deviation, or roughly the difference between the 40th and 60th centile of a normal distribution), it is encouraging, once again, to see that simple, inexpensive, one-time interventions can make a discernible difference in objective measures of academic performance.

SUBJECTIVE PERCEPTIONS AND OBJECTIVE HEALTH CONSEQUENCES

At the same time that researchers in education have been coming to recognize the importance of subjective labels, expectations, and attributions, researchers in the field of medicine and health psychology have been coming to an ever greater appreciation of the importance of these factors in matters of illness and health. Indeed, as society's healthcare concerns shift increasingly from the search for "magic bullet" cures for infectious diseases to strategies for helping people avoid health-threatening behaviors and cope with long-term illness, debilitating treatments, and the frailties of advanced age, social and psychological processes become ever more relevant (see Taylor, 1986). We cannot do justice to this vital area of application in the brief discussion that follows, but we can at least give our readers a provocative sample of some important issues and contributions.

Placebo Effects and Reverse Placebo Effects

Physicians have long been aware of "placebo effects," that is, the relief of suffering accomplished not by specific, demonstrably effective therapeutic agents but by the patient's *belief* that some kind of palliative or curative treatment has been administered. The casual reader of medical and psychological literatures may think of placebo effects as mere illusions, or as efforts by grateful or cowed patients to please the respected physician who has taken the trouble to treat them. It is important, therefore, to bear in mind that many studies show that placebos can have substantial, measurable effects, not only on subjective assessments of pain (for which a typical result is a significant analgesic effect in about one-third of patients) but also on more objective symptoms of organic illness. Furthermore, there is evidence that narcotics and tranquilizers, which *do* have well-documented specific effects, can become significantly less effective when patients are not aware that they have received such a drug (Beecher, 1959) or when patients receive the drug from a physician who doubts its effectiveness (Feldman, 1956).

Results like these have made psychologists, as well as physicians, take an increasing interest in the mechanisms by which placebo effects might operate. It has been estimated (Shapiro, 1978) that 65 percent of commonly presented symptoms are psychogenic in origin. To the extent that placebos engender optimism, relieve anxiety, or simply satisfy patients' needs for attention and nurturance, they can be expected to alter patients' subjective experiences of well-being and in turn relieve symptoms that are psychogenic.

Research over the last two decades has revealed a great deal about the negative effects of anxiety, stress, and feelings of helplessness on the endocrine and immune systems, so an objective, physiological basis for the psychological benefits of placebos seems likely. In fact, it now appears that there is at least one specific mechanism for placebo effects – the release of beta-endorphins, which serve as "natural" analgesics and mood-elevators in a manner similar to externally administered opiates. Evidence for this mechanism comes from a series of provocative studies (for example, Levine, Gordon, & Fields, 1978) suggesting that placebos may *lose* their capacity to reduce pain when their effects are opposed by the administration of naloxone – a drug that we know blocks the action of opiates, including, presumably, the body's own beta-endorphins. As we uncover such mechanisms, we begin to see the actual mechanisms by which purely subjective events can mediate, even dominate, objective material circumstances.

The problem posed by placebo effects in the evaluation of new drugs or treatments is widely recognized today, and ever more relevant as our society deals increasingly with long-term degenerative illnesses, and with controversial claims for biofeedback, acupuncture, vitamins, stringent diets, and other nontraditional therapies. The careful exploration of specific physiological mechanisms underlying placebo effects promises to pay increasingly important medical dividends. It is important, however, to consider the phenomenon of placebo effects in a broader, more historical, and more social perspective (Shapiro, 1960, 1964). For over three millennia, or until the practice of treating malaria with quinine began in the seventeenth century, most medicines (from the lizard's blood and crocodile dung favored by the early Egyptians, to the unicorn's horn, Egyptian mummy, viper's flesh, and other exotic concoctions employed by the physicians of the Middle Ages) and most medical treatments (including purging, bleeding, blistering, and freezing) likely owed whatever benefits they had to the nonspecific, psychologically mediated processes we now term placebo effects. Indeed, placebos and placebic treatments may have worked well enough, and often enough, to help sustain the good reputations of healers in all societies. As researchers continue to break down the distinction between "real" effects and "placebo" effects, medical scientists and practitioners will surely become increasingly sophisticated about the role that subjective processes play in the course of illness and treatment. We may hope that this increased sophistication will encourage the medical community to work toward the goal of enhancing the placebic benefits of the physician-patient relationship, helping them to better satisfy the social-emotional and psychological needs of patients.

Though placebo effects, or benefits of positive expectations about treatment, are very common, research by social psychologists shows that *reverse placebo effects* can also occur. That is, the erroneous belief that one is receiving an effective drug or treatment can exacerbate rather than relieve the patient's symptoms. The explanation for this paradoxical result can be found in attribution theory, particularly as it is applied to emotional experience and self-labeling (Ross, Rodin, & Zimbardo, 1969; Valins & Nisbett, 1972). To the extent that negative symptoms persist in the face of a treatment that "ought" to bring relief, one may be inclined to attribute such persistence to the seriousness and intractability of whatever it is that is producing one's symptoms. Such an "internal attribution" might be harmful if it produces worry and rumination that exacerbate one's symptoms. Indeed, one would be better off with some benign "external" attribution for one's symptoms – even if that attribution were *incorrect*.

Storms and Nisbett (1970) pursued this line of reasoning in a study in which insomniac subjects (students who reported lying awake at bedtime ruminating about their problems) were given a sugar pill placebo to take just before going to bed. One group was told that the pills would "calm" them; another group that the pills would make them "more aroused." As predicted, the "calming placebo" had a noncalming effect. That is, subjects reported that it took about 40 percent longer than usual for them to get to sleep. This reverse placebo effect occurred, the investigators contended, because the subjects found themselves experiencing their usual level of restlessness, then inferred that their insomnia (and the cares that kept them from sleeping) must be "worse than usual." By contrast, as the investigators further predicted, the "arousing placebo" had a paradoxical calming effect. The subjects reported that they fell asleep more quickly than usual, presumably because they could now attribute their arousal to the "pill" rather than to their problems, and could find some comfort in the fact that "even after an arousal pill" they were no more restless than usual.

Comparable findings have been obtained by Storms and McCaul (1976), who showed that stutterers' conditions were made better by telling them that they had been given an arousal agent and worse by telling them that they had been given a calming agent. At present, it is by no means clear when reverse rather than standard placebo effects will occur, or when "misattribution manipulations" can alleviate symptoms. One study by Brockner & Swap (1983) shows that it is only relatively introspective and thoughtful people who show the attributional effects found by Storms and Nisbett, and that other people may show no effect or even the opposite effects found by them. But it is becoming increasingly clear, as the remainder of this chapter will show, just how important a role subjective expectations and attributions can play in determining patients' responses to their "objective" condition (see Pennebaker, 1982).

The Beneficial Effect of Forewarning and Coping Information

While placebo and reverse placebo effects depend on misinformation, it is very often access to *correct* information, of a kind that physicians are sometimes reluctant to give, that determines the patient's well-being and speed of recovery. In 1958 Irving Janis reported an interesting survey result regarding stress and coping among surgery patients, one that was to pave the way for a major change in medical thinking and patient care. At that time, it was standard practice in many medical contexts for patients to be told a minimum about the exact procedures to which they would be subjected and about the specific aversive feelings and symptoms they were likely to experience. This reluctance to provide information may, in some cases, have reflected the physicians' indifference or unwillingness to "waste time on hand holding"; but it was also a practice that could be justified on the grounds that there was no point worrying patients prematurely since they would find out "soon enough" about any discomforts accompanying or following treatment. Indeed, a version of the placebo effect notion was sometimes used by physicians to justify the withholding of information. The claim was made that if patients are told too much about possible complications or side effects, they will experience them and thereby create problems for themselves and the physician. Janis's survey results rebutted this claim. He found that patients who had been relatively well informed about postsurgical sensations and reactions (either because the physician had provided more and clearer information or because the patient had understood and remembered the information better) showed better postoperative adjustment than patients who had been relatively uninformed.

While such a result might have surprised some physicians, it was not particularly surprising to contemporary psychologists. There was already a considerable experimental literature to suggest that when either animals or humans are subjected repeatedly to electric shock or other noxious stimuli, they suffer less distress and cope more effectively when they are forewarned by a distinctive signal (Glass & Levy, 1982; Reim, Glass, & Singer, 1971). Janis himself had anticipated his basic finding on the grounds that forewarning would help at least some patients to prepare themselves by "working through" the fear, anxiety, and sense of helplessness raised by the whole surgery experience. Other theorists, influenced by Schachter's work on emotional mislabeling discussed in Chapter 3, argued that forewarning reduced the tendency for patients to worry about the meaning of their symptoms and to wonder whether "something is wrong", or, worse still, to imagine frightening causes for their unexplained bodily symptoms, thereby creating a classic vicious cycle through which uncertainty and anxiety feed upon and worsen the physical symptoms. Still other theorists emphasized that preoperative information could stimulate patients to think about concrete ways to deal with aversive or embarrassing symptoms (diarrhea, vomiting, pain during urination) and to be prepared to discuss symptoms and possible coping strategies with their physicians or nurses.

The vast literature on forewarning that has developed over the ensuing decades does not really allow one to tease apart these differing explanations for what is by now a well-documented phenomenon. While study after study shows that both forewarning and specific advice about techniques for managing and reducing discomfort can benefit the patient, the studies do not always agree about which type of information is most important, which types of patients are best served by which type of information, or even which particular benefits are most likely to occur. But what the literature has made clear is the magnitude of the potential benefits to patients and healthcare providers alike. An evaluation study that followed shortly after Janis's correlational findings illustrates just how great these benefits can be.

The study was an unusually careful and well-designed one conducted by four physicians (Egbert, Battit, Welch, & Bartlett, 1964) who explored the recovery of patients following elective abdominal surgery. The patients were randomly divided into two groups – a control group in which patients received no specific information about the after-effects of surgery (beyond, presumably, the very minimal information customarily provided to all patients) and a "special-care" group in which patients received two different types of information from their anesthetists prior to surgery. The first type of information pertained to postoperative pain. The special-care patients were assured that pain after abdominal surgery was perfectly normal, and they were informed where they would feel pain, how severe it would be, and how long it would last. The second type of information pertained to coping strategies. The special-care patients learned that their postoperative pain is caused by spasm of the muscles under their incision and they could relieve that pain by relaxing those muscles. These patients were also taught deep-breathing relaxation techniques and given specific instructions about how to change their body position without tensing their abdominal muscles. Both types of information, furthermore, were reiterated when the anesthetist visited the special-care patients on the afternoon following surgery and on subsequent visits.

The first remarkable result from this study concerned the amount of narcotics requested by the patients and administered by ward nurses on the authority of the surgical resident. (Neither the nurses nor the surgeons, incidentally, knew whether the patient had been assigned to special-care or control conditions; nor were the patients ever informed that they were participants in an experiment.) On the day of surgery the two groups required, and received, roughly equal amounts of morphine. On the second day, however, the control group required roughly 50 percent more of the drug than the special-care group. Dosages declined thereafter for both groups, but on each of the four following days the control group required at least twice the dosage of the special care group. The investigators showed, furthermore, that this difference did not arise simply because the special-care patients were willing to endure more suffering. Subjective self-reports of pain, and "blind" observers' ratings of the patients' apparent comfort and their physical and emotional condition, indicated that the special-care group was suffering somewhat less than the control group.

The other significant result of these studies underscored the difference in the two groups' postoperative functioning. The surgeons, who it will be recalled were unaware of the patients' special-treatment or control group status, sent the special-care patients home an average of almost three days earlier than the control group patients. The savings in human suffering and money produced by a little bit of information is remarkable (see also Healy, 1968; Johnson & Leventhal, 1974; Leventhal, Brown, Shacham, & Engquist, 1979).

Like most powerful phenomena, the effects of forewarning and coping information may be multiply determined. Egbert and his colleagues thought of these presurgery information programs as attempts to produce "active placebo effects" – effects that owe their existence not simply to the patients' satisfaction that someone is noticing them and trying to help them, or to their optimism that relief lies at hand, but rather to the patients' conviction that they are no longer helpless and that they have information and techniques that allow them to help themselves. This change in the patients' outlook can be accomplished by making them more knowledgeable, and hence less dependent, vulnerable and subject to unjustified fears. It also can be accomplished by arming patients with specific ways of easing their pain, relaxing themselves while undergoing treatment, or even manipulating their bodies more comfortably. Finally, attribution processes also probably play a role. A patient who knows what to expect is not likely to believe that something has gone wrong when experiencing pain or unfamilar physical symptoms.

The Health Consequences of Perceived Efficacy and Control

Our discussion of placebo effects and the benefits of providing patients with coping information anticipates a major theme of contemporary health psychology and psychotherapy: the importance of attribution processes and feelings of control. In matters of health, as in matters of education, a sense of personal efficacy, even personal responsibility, generally seems to promote more adaptive responses than feelings of inefficacy or powerlessness. The ways in which control, perceived as well as real, can produce health benefits (see Rodin, 1986) include reduction of subjective threat or stress and changes in symptom labeling, as well as willingness to practice better health habits and, where necessary, to seek diagnosis and follow prescribed therapeutic regimens. There is also increasing evidence that the effects of control, both actual control and perceived control, may be mediated by physiological factors related to the functioning of the endocrine and immune systems.

The research literature has expanded at a great rate during the past two decades (see Bandura, 1989; Michela & Wood, 1986; Rodin & Salovey, 1989; Seligman, Kamen, & Nolen-Hoeksema, 1989) with findings too varied and too complex to permit simple summaries, much less definitive conclusions about theoretical and applied implications. But it is easy to see why researchers and practitioners have become increasingly convinced about the role that psychological factors in general, and attributional or coping style factors in particular, play in mediating health, illness, and recovery.

One source of this conviction has been the seminal work of Martin Seligman, Christopher Peterson, and their colleagues (Abramson, Garber, & Seligman, 1978; C. Peterson & Seligman, 1984; Seligman, 1975) relating depression to feelings of helplessness and hopelessness, and to a specific attribution style whereby negative feelings, outcomes, and life circumstances are attributed to uncontrollable personal or situational factors. Feelings of personal inefficacy and lack of fate control, furthermore, have been linked not only to prolonged negative mood states, but also to on-the-job stress and "burnout" (Maslach, 1982) and inferior health and high mortality rates (C. Peterson, Vaillant, & Seligman, 1985).

There are now literally hundreds of papers documenting links between subjective beliefs about the causes of one's illness and objective measures of mortality, rate of recovery, and adjustment to disability. Different types of illness (for example, cancer versus heart disease) or trauma (rape versus spinal cord injuries) seem to yield different correlations between attributions and prognosis. Moreover, there is a need to make careful distinctions with respect to causal attributions (for example, *blame* for the illness or trauma versus *responsibility* for subsequent coping; anticipated efficacy of potential *treatment* versus perceived efficacy of *self*). But it does seem increasingly clear that afflicted people seek meaning, or at least order, in their suffering (Taylor, 1983), and that they benefit from re-establishing feelings of personal efficacy and reducing feelings of victimization and vulnerability.

In this area of applied psychology most of the available evidence is correlational, and some problems of interpreting causal direction and anticipating the impact of relevant interventions are evident (see Rodin, 1986). Particular attributional styles may directly or indirectly produce better health and adjustment. But it is also possible that good health and adjustment may contribute to feelings of efficacy, or that third variables involving personal competencies, socioeconomic factors, or other life circumstances may be influencing both attributions and health. Researchers have shown considerable determination and ingenuity in trying to establish the causal pathway from attributional style to health outcomes (see Michela & Wood, 1986). Sophisticated statistical analyses have been used to disentangle causes from effects (see C. Peterson & Seligman, 1987). Also numerous physiological mediators – including neuroendocrine and immune system functioning – have been linked both to measures of attribution or coping styles and to medical outcomes (see Ader, 1981; Cohen & Williamson, 1991).

Experimental evidence based on manipulation of attribution processes rather than observed correlations, by contrast, has been slow in coming. However, there have been some intriguing hints and developments. Investigators concerned with the institutionalized elderly – a population particularly threatened with loss of personal autonomy and efficacy – have reported success in improving subjective and objective indicators of health through simple but theory-inspired interventions. Schulz (1976) accomplished such gains introducing a predictable positive event into the institutional patient's routine, namely a series of personal visits by an undergraduate. Langer and Rodin (1976; Rodin & Langer, 1977) did likewise merely by heightening the salience of choices and opportunities for control already available to patients.

Researchers also have made good use of "self-help" groups, which can play a significant role in shifting potentially destructive attributions of cancer patients, rape survivors, accident victims, and others forced to deal with catastrophic problems or losses (see Rodin, 1985). That is, patients see the similarity of their own problems and negative reactions to those of others, and thereby come to understand those reactions as normal, even appropriate responses to overwhelming situational challenges rather than reflections of personal inadequacy (Cohen & McKay, 1984; Gottlieb, 1983; Lieberman et al., 1979; Singer & Lord, 1984; Wortman, 1983). Such consensus information from peers proves much more valuable than pop-psychology interpretations and advice offered by well-meaning friends and family members ("you mustn't bottle up your anger," "you've got to fight this disease," "you've got to stop mourning and get on with your life"). There is now evidence that support groups for cancer patients actually prolong life to a very significant extent, perhaps by reducing stress and leaving the patient with more resources for coping with physical trauma (Spiegel, Bloom, Kraemer, & Gottheil, 1988).

Though attribution theory is relatively new, we should note that its influence is now widespread throughout American psychotherapy. Cognitively oriented and behaviorally oriented therapists alike recognize the importance of encouraging their patients' sense of personal efficacy. In fact, the psychiatric literature now urges therapists to downplay their own role, and stress the patient's responsibility, in determining the course and success of the therapy.

EVERYDAY APPLICATION OF SOCIAL PSYCHOLOGY

Despite the length of this chapter, we are acutely aware of all the many interesting and valuable uses being made of social psychology that we have *not* discussed – not only in the areas of industrial psychology, education, and medicine touched upon in these pages, but also in law, business, conflict resolution, and international relations (see Fisher, 1982; Oskamp, 1984). Nevertheless, we trust that our sampling has served to emphasize the utility of the more general theoretical insights and contributions that we have discussed throughout this book. We will close by reminding the reader of the applications of these ideas in daily life.

Social psychology's central principles, and examples of their application to pressing real-world problems, we argue, can serve to stimulate a kind of intellectual catechism to guide our responses to social events that we witness personally, and perhaps even more, to reports of events that we hear about secondhand. This catechism reminds us not to leap to premature conclusions about people or about the meaning of their behavior. Instead, even when confronted with words and deeds that seem at first consideration to offer evidence of great stupidity, great venality (or for that matter great virtue) – indeed, when we are confronted with behavior that seems to suggest exceptional personal attributes of any kind – we tell ourselves to pause and consider the situation. What were the details of the immediate context of behavior? How was the situation construed by the actor? And what was the broader social context or social system within which the actors were functioning? More pointedly, what objective situational features, or subjective construals, or tension system considerations, would make these seemingly exceptional actions less exceptional, and more congruent with what experience has taught us about the way ordinary people (ourselves included) generally behave? We are obliged to ask these questions when we see someone we love making seemingly foolish choices about jobs or relationships. We are even obliged to ask them when we see someone we despise acting in ways that seem characteristically despicable.

A social psychological perspective requires us not only to ask pointed and at times unpopular questions, but also to entertain tentative, sometimes conflicting "working hypotheses." Confronted with evidence that individuals or groups have been unresponsive to incentives and other seemingly potent situational factors, we are obliged to entertain a strong suspicion that our current information about the situation in question is erroneous or incomplete, or that we have failed to appreciate the discrepancy between our own views of the situation and those of the actors. When, as so often proves to be the case, people fail to change old ways of behaving in the face of evidence that seems amply persuasive, we are obliged to resist the temptation to attribute their intransigence to characterological stubbornness, stupidity, or dark ulterior motives. Instead, we are obliged to think more deeply about the dynamics that sustain the status quo. We need to consider the non-obvious functions served by existing patterns of behavior and the unseen forces that constrain change. By the same token, when seemingly minor incidents produce major changes in behavior, we must not look too quickly or thoughtlessly to characterological explanations for such volatility. Instead, we should look again to our familiar tripod, to unseen situational details, unappreciated differences in construal or subjective meaning, and disturbances in dynamic relationships among social forces that, without our full recognition, have hitherto helped to maintain the status quo.

The more specific results and theories that we have described provide further advice. The Lewinians continue to remind us that when positive changes in individual or collective behavior prove difficult to achieve, we should think about the role being played by preexisting group standards and other restraining forces, and also about channel factors that could be manipulated to facilitate the link between positive attitudes or values and positive actions. The dissonance and self-perception theorists continue to remind us that when "internalization" rather than "compliance" is our goal, we must be restrained and clever, and sometimes even devious, in our exercise of social control. They educate us about the benefits of providing Junior with piano lessons *after*, not before, he asks us for them; and the virtues of using "just enough" in the way of threats and inducements to get the job done. They also prompt us not to urge people to change their ways but rather to inspire and challenge them to act in accord with the most positive aspects of their beliefs, values, and self-definitions. The social-learning theorists remind us of the potential value (or cost) of providing those we wish to influence with concrete social models. And perhaps most important, the attribution theorists urge us to give a sense of mastery and control to the people who need our assistance – to offer aid in a manner that enhances rather than diminishes their sense of personal efficacy and self-esteem, and that encourages them to accept responsibility for their destiny.

The principles that social psychology has taught us over the past 60 years have broad social and political implications as well as personal ones. Economist and political theorist Thomas Sowell (1987) has argued that two opposing visions of human nature and society have struggled against one another across the centuries. He calls these visions "constrained" and "unconstrained." The constrained vision holds that human nature and the broad outlines of social life are relatively fixed and are very difficult to change, and that the effects of deliberate interventions to produce change are unpredictable and usually include unforeseen negative consequences that cancel or outweigh any positive ones. The unconstrained vision holds that human nature is highly plastic and malleable, and that we know the laws of individual psychology and social systems well enough to be able to plan interventions that will reliably improve the human condition. We believe that social psychology speaks in a clear voice to these questions – siding in part with the holders of the constrained view and in part with the holders of the unconstrained view.

The holders of the constrained view are surely right in their contention that the effects of interventions are hard to predict, and they are right about the reason for this: Our social sciences are not adequate (indeed we would go further and say they may *never* be adequate) to the job of foreseeing the consequences of novel interventions. Social psychologists personally experience, on a regular basis, something that was rare before the twentieth century – the opportunity to establish in a systematic way that their predictions about the effects of a given social situation were mistaken. As laboratory researchers, we are dead wrong in our hypotheses more frequently than we are dead right, and being half right is better than par. When we move from the laboratory to the applied setting, our track record does not improve and, if anything, it gets worse.

On the other hand, there is by now enough evidence to be able to side with the unconstrained view on the question of whether benign consequences of interventions are achievable. We have cited in this chapter just a small sampling of the successful interventions of social scientists. Though we cannot be confident in advance of the success of any given intervention, or even of the direction it will take, we know by now that it is often possible to intervene in unhappy lives or distorted social processes with felicitous results. The hard-won lessons of social psychology lessons about the importance of channel factors, reference groups, attributions of personal efficacy and responsibility, and the subtle dynamics of balanced forces in cognitive and social systems constitute a repertoire of strategies with which to supplement the guidance of common sense in constructing these interventions. As Donald Campbell eloquently argued in his 1969 paper aptly titled "Reforms as Experiments," so long as the initial intervention is carried out in an experimental spirit, with a serious attempt to gauge its effectiveness in a systematic fashion, our role as social engineers can consistently be a beneficial one. The pendulum of public opinion surely has swung too far against such experimentation. For, as we face the challenges of the last decade of the 20th century, and beyond, society has unprecedented need of the social scientist. Properly chastened by experience, slower perhaps to make rash predictions and promises, our discipline is equipped with theoretical and methodological tools that can make life richer and more fulfilling.

Afterword

Had we written *The Person and the Situation* two decades later, with the benefit of subsequent developments in the field, our emphasis now would be less on the relative influence of the person versus the situation and more on the way in which they interact. We would introduce the reader to the provocative new field of epigenetics (the activation or turning on or off of genes by particular experiences and environmental influences) a field that has made heredity/environment or nature/nurture debates of the past become increasingly passé.[1] But our larger focus would be on the concept of cumulative consequences, a topic we had touched on briefly in noting the work of Avshalom Caspi and Darryl Bem but not explored in the depth merited by its theoretical and applied significance. Like other social psychologists of our generation, we focused heavily on provocative "one-shot" experiments and immediate situational influences rather than more dynamic processes that unfold over time with ever greater impact.

In particular, it has become ever clearer that features of the person or the situation at one point in time can change subsequent experiences and interpretations of events, which in turn change both the actor and the opportunities and challenges that the actor will encounter. Gladwell's *Outliers* offers many striking examples of such upward and downward spirals, including the dramatic overrepresentation of professional hockey players whose birth dates made them older rather than younger than their peers in their earliest opportunities to play in organized leagues. As Gladwell explained, those so favored are bound on average to be bigger and stronger and more advanced in their skills than their team-mates, and as a result to get more playing time, have more successes, get more enthusiastic attention from coaches and parents alike, and thus be more eager to further develop their skills and come to define themselves as "hockey players."

Of course only those with some natural gifts and extraordinary motivation go on to professional careers. But the situational advantage or disadvantage conferred by a fortunate or unfortunate birthday acts as the multiplier of initial individual differences in talent and determination.

---

1 Masterpasqua, F. (2009) Psychology and Epigenetics, *Review of General Psychology*, 13, (3) September 2009, Pages 194-201. Here and elsewhere in this afterword, we give a couple of specific citations to ideas and to individuals who have taken the lead in particular areas of progress. But in this internet age the reader would be well served by "googling" the name of the concept or investigators or otherwise accessing information through the internet.

And for the relatively untalented youngster, it may dictate a fate of unremarkable mediocrity versus embarrassing ineptitude.

While Gladwell notes that birth dates may also create initial differences in readiness for schooling and resultant early experiences of success or failure, with predictable effects on social definition and self-perception, an even more important impetus for such upward or downward educational spirals may be individual differences that determine subjective interpretations of success and failure. Carol Dweck in particular has documented how a "mindset" that treats ability as something "fixed" leads to an avoidance of challenges that could offer growth and withdrawal of effort in the face of failure, whereas a mindset that treats ability as "malleable" and subject to growth through effort and learning leads to acceptance of challenges and ultimately new mastery.[2] Moreover, she has shown that a brief educational intervention designed to drive home the message of malleability can promote such a mastery orientation and willingness to persist in the face of difficulties on the part of students who would otherwise by limited by a mindset less conducive to growth.

The impact of more substantial situational advantages and disadvantages has also become increasingly evident. No one doubts the continuing impact of socioeconomic advantage or disadvantage, but one recent study by economist Raj Chetty and his colleagues has shown that, all things being equal, the value of a superior kindergarten teacher, in the flinty-eyed metric of the economist, may be as much as $1,000 a year when incomes are examined at age 27.[3] The value in terms of less easily quantifiable life skills, love of learning, and feelings about self, we suspect, may be even greater.

Ironically, another investigator documenting the cumulative consequences of individual differences has been Walter Mischel – the psychologist who had earlier been most influential in documenting the lack of cross-situation consistency in behavioral manifestations of classic personality traits. Most dramatically, just as we were reporting that classic work, Mischel and his colleagues were discovering that individual differences in nursery school children's ability or inability to "delay gratification" under controlled experimental conditions proved to be remarkably predictive of subsequent academic achievement.[4]

---

2   Dweck, C. S. (1999). *Self-theories: Their role in motivation, personality, and development.* Philadelphia, PA: The Psychology Press.

3   Leonhardt, D. (2010). The case for $320,000 kindergarten teachers. *New York Times.* Retrieved from http://www.nytimes.com/2010/07/28/business/economy/28leonhardt.html

4   Mischel, W, Shoda, Y & Rodriguez, M.L. (1989). Delay of gratification in children, *Science*, New Series, Vol. 244, No. 4907, 933-938.

Our discussion of the tripod of foundational insight would also be somewhat different today than in 1991. Situationism would surely continue to receive top billing; but we could now offer even more compelling real-world examples. Perhaps most compelling would be that offered by a comparison of Western European countries with a seeming small difference in the steps required of citizens who are willing to make their bodily organs available for harvesting and transplantation in the event of a fatal motor accident.[5] Some countries require would-be donors (as the US does) to affirm their willingness by inserting their signature on a line provided on the back of their drivers' licenses. Others require no such affirmation of willingness; instead the motorist who is unwilling to donate organs is required to so indicate with a signature in a designated space on the back of the license.

In the former countries – those with an "opt-in" system, in which the "default" is exclusion from the ranks of potential donors, the rate of opting-in was universally lower than 25%. In the latter – those with an opt-out system in which the default was inclusion, the percentage of potential donors was universally higher than 80%. For instance "opt-in" Germany saw 17% of motorists volunteer for potential organ donation whereas in "opt-out" Australia the rate was effectively 85%. Indeed a comparison of two Scandinavian countries revealed a rate of 5% for "opt-in" Denmark and 85% for opt-out Sweden. We suspect that the average reader would grossly underestimate the power of this "channel factor" and as a result make inappropriate attributions about the general altruism of the Swedish motorist who makes his or her organs available and the lack of such altruism of the Danish motorist who declines to do so. We also suspect that more than trivial differences in ease of "volunteering" account for this dramatic result. The "default" option signals behavioral norms, and thus the meaning of participating or not participating in such a program. In the opt-in case, the default and perceived norm is non-participation, "opting in" therefore is likely to be as an exercise of particular individual altruism or perhaps even as a lack of concern for desecration of one's body; in the opt-out case the default and perceived norm is participation, "opting out" therefore is likely to be seen as the product of misanthropy, bad citizenship, or perhaps eccentric religious beliefs.

Research on the second leg of the tripod, that is, the importance of subjective interpretation or construal, has been particularly productive and provocative. Most notable has been research on the effects of "framing" and "priming" on decision-making. Indeed, well before publication of *The Person and the Situation*, Barbara McNeil and colleagues showed that even experienced physicians were susceptible to variations in the way

---

5   Johnson, E. J., & Goldstein, D. (2003). Do defaults save lives? *Science, 302*, 1338-1339.

treatment risks and benefits were "framed." In particular, the marked preference the doctors attending a conference showed for the less risky but potentially less effective option of radiation over that of surgery that had been evident when the risk was described in terms of immediate mortality rates (i.e., 10% vs. 0%) vanished when the risks were described in terms of survival rates (i.e., 90% vs. 100%).[6]

In a more recent study designed to challenge convention economist wisdom Liberman and colleagues showed that the decision to defect versus cooperate in the Prisoner's Dilemma could better be predicted from the name attached to the game than by the reputation of the player. Indeed, players nominated by their dorm advisors as most or least likely to cooperate in the game did not differ in their likelihood of cooperating. But players in general were twice as likely to cooperate (66% versus 33%) when the game was referred to as the Community Game than as the Wall Street Game.[7] Other investigators, led by John Bargh and his colleagues, have shown that subtler, more implicit types of framing manipulations (a word contained in a seemingly irrelevant prior sentence-unscrambling task, or even words and pictures flashed on a screen too rapidly to be consciously processed and remembered), can also change expressed attitudes and actions.[8]

In describing the situationist tradition in social psychology we mentioned the "fundamental attribution error" which referred to the ubiquitous tendency for people to underestimate the impact of situational factors and overestimate the role of classic personality traits. If we were writing our book today we would emphasize a source of bias affecting inferences and judgments that we believe may be more truly "fundamental" – that is, the conviction that one's own perceptions, inferences, judgments, etc are a reflection of objective reality. This epistemic stance, which Ross & Ward termed naive realism, leads us to expect other reasonable and objective people to share our views. It also leads us to attribute disagreements in judgment to something about them – i.e., dispositions, idiosyncratic circumstances and experiences, and

---

6   McNeil, B.J., Pauker, S.G., Sox, H.C., & Tversky, A. (1982). On the elicitation of preferences for alternative therapies. *New England Journal of Medicine, 306,* 1259-1262.

7   Liberman, V., Samuels, S. M., & Ross, L. (2004). The name of the game: Predictive power of reputations versus situational labels in determining Prisoner's Dilemma game moves. *Personality and Social Psychology Bulletin, 30,* 1175-1185.

8   Bargh, J.A. (1997). The automaticity of everyday life. In R.A.S. Wyer, Jr. (ed.). *Advances in social cognition.* (Vol. 10, pp.1-61). Mahwah, NJ: Erlbaum. Also, Bargh, J.A. (Ed.) *Social psychology and the unconscious: The automaticity of higher mental processes.* Philadelphia, Psychology Press.

other distorting cognitive, motivational, or even cultural biases.[9]

The third leg in the tripod, that is, recognition of the importance of "tension systems" has also been evident, particularly in applied fields where Kurt Lewin's advice to focus not only on the steps one can take to induce desired change but also on the constraints or barriers that must be overcome to accomplish such change. Psychological barriers, including reference group attitudes, ego-defensiveness, loss aversion, dissonance, and reactance, stand in the way of progress in many areas of present concern, ranging from changing eating and exercise habits, to combating global warming, to resolving intergroup conflicts throughout the world. By addressing and overcoming these barriers rather than adding incentives, offering new persuasive arguments, or introducing coercive measures, change is not only facilitated but accomplished with less strain and conflict. Addressing those barriers as we attempt to initiate wise social policies promises to be an important challenge and opportunity for the next generation of social psychologists.

When we think about the most important developments in our field since 1991, we also think it is time to add another leg to the tripod, thereby making it a more solid platform. That extra leg would be recognition of the centrality of self in everyday social functioning. This recognition would go beyond the familiar idea that people defend the self against threats to positive self-regard, or that they strive for cognitive consistency and a sense of coherence and integrity in their beliefs and behavior. One important new idea about the self would be the role played by theories about the self – theories that guide behavior and dictate expenditures of effort and willingness to risk failure, and hence achievement and growth. As we noted earlier, Carol Dweck's work on the importance of beliefs about malleability of intelligence and academic ability has been particularly important in this regard, and it takes on particular significance because the evidence is mounting that beliefs in malleability of intelligence are not only adaptive but are in fact correct – as Nisbett documented in *Intelligence and How to Get it*.[10]

Two chapters in *The Person in the Situation*, the one on culture and the one on application, offered a portrait of areas that were just beginning to reach their potential. A glance at the list of authors in any contemporary journal will reveal an enormous increase in the ethnic and cultural diversity of contributors. This development reflects a lessening of the

---

9   Ross, L., & Ward, A. (1996). Naive realism in everyday life: Implications for social conflict and misunderstanding. In E. S. Reed, E. Turiel, & T. Brown (Eds.), *Values and knowledge* (pp. 103–135). Hillsdale, NJ: Erlbaum.

10 Nisbett, R. E. (2009). *Intelligence and how to get it: Why schools and cultures count*. New York: Norton.

parochialism of our field. By far the most notable development has been a growing awareness and documentation of the fact that American culture, for all its own diversity, represents the extreme end of a continuum in terms of its individualistic norms, values, and practice.[11] More collectivist cultures, including especially those of East Asia, not only show less focus on the self and more on family and other in-group members, they also are less dispositionist in their world view and in fact less prone to the fundamental attribution error. They focus less on the actor and more on the social situation surrounding the actor.

For many years the study of cultural differences was directed at documenting global differences in characteristics of thought, sentiment, and behavior. An important synthesis in research has come in the past few years as researchers in many laboratories across the world have demonstrated that culture itself can be "primed" – that is, made more cognitively available, and thus made to exert a greater influence on participants' responses, through subtle manipulations involving prior presentation of words or images. Another synthesis has come in the study of emotion and "positive psychology," as Jeanne Tsai and her colleagues have shown that members of American culture value and seek to maximize the experience of "high arousal" positive emotions such as excitement whereas members of East Asian cultures are more inclined to value and seek to maximize "low arousal" positive emotions like quiet contentment.[12]

When we consider our chapter on the application of psychology, we are struck by how much the optimism that "useful theories" were at hand and the promise that they could be employed to tackle some long-standing social skills has proven to be justified. Nowhere has this been more evident than in development of educational interventions, small and large, to assist racial minorities and members of other socially or economically disadvantaged groups in better realizing their academic potential. Claude Steele and his colleagues have documented the corrosive effects of stereotype threat, which can dissuade minority group students from undertaking academic challenges (and women from taking math courses of the sort necessary in many technical and scientific fields), and detracts from the test performance of those who do undertake such challenges.[13]

Steele and many other researchers across the country have also documented that wise policies and practices that defuse stereotype threat

11 Henrich, J., Heine, S. J., & Norenzayan, A. (2010). The weirdest people in the world? *Behavioral and Brain Sciences, 33*, 61-135.

12 Tsai, J.L. Knutson, B., & Fung, H. H. (2006). Cultural variation in affect valuation. *Journal of Personality and Social Psychology, 2*, 288-307.

13 Steele, C. M. (1997). A threat in the air: How stereotypes shape intellectual identity and performance. *American Psychologist, 52*, 613-629.

can yield dramatic improvements in performance. As noted earlier, Dweck has produced similarly impressive gains by altering students' mindsets so that they see academic ability and what we think of as global intelligence as malleable and therefore improvable through effort rather than fixed. Moreover, a new generation of younger researchers including Joshua Aronson, Geoff Cohen, Greg Walton, and their colleagues have demonstrated that interventions involving "malleability training," "affirmation," or "belonging" that have proven effective in the laboratory can be "scaled up" to close achievement gaps in ordinary classrooms and schools.[14] What remains to be seen is how successfully regular classroom teachers can implement these interventions on their own, without the assistance of researchers.

We cannot do justice here to the now flourishing field of applied social psychology, which is making its influence felt not only in education, but in efforts to promote health, to encourage individuals to save energy and curb CO_2 emissions. But we do want to comment on the extent to which central ideas in the social psychology we described in *The Person and the Situation* have been appropriated, augmented, refined, and spread not only by leading figures in behavioral economics such as Dan Arieli, and George Loewenstein, but also by skilled journalists, including most notably the author of the foreword of this volume, Malcolm Gladwell. A particularly noteworthy case in point is the highly readable and provocative *Nudge* by Richard Thaler, a leading behavioral economist, and Cass Sunstein, an eminent legal scholar.[15]

Thaler and Sunstein advocate a policy that they term "paternalistic

---

14 Aronson, J., Cohen, G., & McColskey, W. (2009). *Reducing stereotype threat in classrooms: A review of social-psychological intervention studies on improving the achievement of Black students.* U.S. Department of Education, Institute of Education Sciences (IES), National Center for Education Evaluation and Regional Assistance, Regional Educational Laboratory Program, Regional Educational Laboratory at SERVE Center UNC, Greensboro, No. 076 (July). Aronson, J., Fried, C. B., & Good, C. (2002). Reducing the effect of stereotype threat on African American college students by shaping theories of intelligence. *Journal of Experimental Social Psychology, 38,* 113-125. Cohen, G. L., Garcia, J., Apfel, N., & Master, A. (2006). Reducing the racial achievement gap: A social-psychological intervention. *Science,* 313, 1307-1310, Cohen, G. L., Garcia, J., Purdie-Vaughns, V., Apfel, N., & Brzustoski, P. (2009). Recursive processes in self-affirmation: Intervening to close the minority achievement gap. *Science, 324,* 400-403. Walton, G. M. & Cohen, G. L. (2007). A question of belonging: Race, social fit, and achievement. *Journal of Personality and Social Psychology, 92,* 82-96.

15 Thaler, R. H. & Sunstein, C. S. (2008). *Nudge: Improving decisions about health, wealth, and happiness.* New Haven: Yale University Press.

libertarianism" – a seemingly oxymoronic but nevertheless politically attractive combination of policies. These policies would give people great freedom in choosing how to invest their time, energies, and dollars, and how to ensure their long-term well being and that of their society, but would structure and characterize decision choice points in a manner that takes advantage of what we know about human motivation and decision-making (about things like "loss aversion," "reference points," "framing" and other influences and biases we have explored in the aftermath of Kahneman and Tversky's Nobel Prize-winning work).

We applaud and are heartened by such evidence of the growing, if not always fully acknowledged, influence of psychology in general and social psychology in particular. But we think that such contributors should take care not to lose touch with the roots of the ideas they employ and polish. Taking a social psychologist to lunch or for a cold beer is especially recommended. For the small price involved they will be reminded to consider the perspective of the actor whose behavior they are seeking to influence, and to consider the relevant balance of pressures and constraints. For the designers and implementers of social policy considerations of self-presentation and self-perception are particularly important. Beyond bottom line calculations of economic self-interest, they should think carefully about what policies and potential responses in light of those policies convey – what behavior is likely to be seen as normative, commendable, and a source of pride, and what behavior will be seen as counter-normative, blameworthy, and a source of embarrassment and shame.

References

Abbey, A. (1982). Sex differences in attributions for friendly behavior: Do males misperceive females' friendliness? *Journal of Personality and Social Psychology, 42*, 830-838.

Abelson, R. P. (1981). The psychological status of the script concept. *American Psychologist, 36*, 715-729.

Abelson, R. P. (1985). A variance explanation paradox: When a little is a lot. *Psychological Bulletin, 97*, 129-133.

Abramson, L. Y., Garber, J., & Seligman, M. E. P. (1980). Learned helplessness in humans: An attributional analysis. In J. Garber & M. E. P. Seligman (Eds.), *Human helplessness: Theory and applications*. New York: Academic.

Abt, C. C. (Ed.). (1976). *The evaluation of social programs*. Beverly Hills, CA: Sage.

Ader, R. (1981). *Psychoneuroimmunology*. New York: Academic.

Adorno, T. W., Frenkel-Brunswik, E., Levinson, D. J., & Sanford, R. N. (1950). *The authoritarian personality*. New York: Harper.

Albright, L., Kenny, D. A., & Malloy, T. E. (1988). Consensus in personality judgments at zero acquaintance. *Journal of Personality and Social Psychology, 55*, 337-348.

Alker, H. A. (1972). Is personality situationally consistent or intrapsychically consistent? *Journal of Personality, 40*, 1-16.

Allport, C. W. (1937). *Personality: A psychological interpretation*. New York: Holt.

Allport, C. W. (1954). The historical background of modern social psychology. In G. Lindzey (Ed.), *Handbook of social psychology* (Vol. 1). Cambridge, MA: Addison-Wesley.

Allport, G. W., & Odbert, H. S. (1936). Trait-names: A psycholexical study. *Psychological Monographs, 27* (Whole No. 211).

Andersen, S. M. (1984). Self-knowledge and social inference: II. The diagnosticity of cognitive/affective and behavioral data. *Journal of Personality and Social Psychology, 46*, 294-307.

Andersen, S. M., & Ross, L. (1984). Self-knowledge and social inference: I. The impact of cognitive/affective and behavioral data. *Journal of Personality and Social Psychology, 46*, 280-293.

Anderson, C. A. (1987). Temperature and aggression: Effects on quarterly, yearly, and city rates of violent and nonviolent crime. *Journal of Personality and Social Psychology, 52*, 1161-1173.

Anderson, C. A., & Anderson, D. C. (1984). Ambient temperature and violent crime: Tests of the linear and curvilinear hypotheses. *Journal of Personality and Social Psychology, 46*, 91-97.

Anderson, N. H. (1965). Averaging versus adding as a stimulus combination rule in impression formation. *Journal of Experimental Psychology, 70*, 394-400.

Anderson, N. H. (1974). Cognitive algebra: Integration theory applied to social attribution. In L. Berkowitz (Ed.), *Advances in experimental social psychology* (Vol. 7). New York: Academic.

Ares, C. E., Rankin, A., & Sturz, H. (1963). The Manhattan bail project: An interim report on the use of pretrial parole. *New York University Law Review, 38*, 67-95.

Arkin, R., & Duval, S. (1975). Focus of attention and causal attributions of actors and observers. *Journal of Experimental Social Psychology, 11*, 427-438.

Aronson, E. (1969). The theory of cognitive dissonance: A current perspective. In L. Berkowitz (Ed.), *Advances in experimental social psychology* (Vol. 4). New York: Academic.

Aronson, E., & Carlsmith, J. M. (1963). Effect of the severity of threat on the devaluation of forbidden behavior. *Journal of Abnormal and Social Psychology, 66*, 584-588.

Aronson, E., & O'Leary, M. (1983). The relative effectiveness of models and prompts on energy conservation: A field experiment in a shower room. *Journal of Environmental Systems, 12*, 219-224.

Asch, S. E. (1940). Studies in the principles of judgments and attitudes: II. Determination of judgments by group and by ego standards. *Journal of Social Psychology, 12*, 433-465.

Asch, S. E. (1948). The doctrine of suggestion, prestige, and imitation in social psychology. *Psychological Review, 55*, 250-277.

Asch, S. E. (1951). Effects of group pressures upon the modification and distortion of judgment. In H. Guetzkow (Ed.), *Groups, leadership, and men*. Pittsburgh: Carnegie Press.

Asch, S. E. (1952). *Social psychology*. New York: Prentice-Hall.

Asch, S. E. (1955, November). Opinions and social pressure. *Scientific American*, 31-35.

Asch, S. E. (1956). Studies of independence and conformity: A minority of one against a unanimous majority. *Psychological Monographs, 70* (9, Whole No. 416).

Back, K. (1951). The exertion of influence through social communication. *Journal of Abnormal and Social Psychology, 46*, 9-23.

Back, K. (1972). *Beyond words: The story of sensitivity training and the encounter movement*. Russell Sage Foundation.

Bahr, H. M., & Harvey, C. D. (1979). *The social psychology of religion*. London: Routledge & Kegan Paul.

Ball, D. W. (1972). The definition of the situation: Some theoretical and methodological consequences of taking W. I. Thomas seriously. *Journal of Theory in Social Behavior, 2*, 61-82.

Bandura, A. (1973). *Aggression: A social learning analysis*. Englewood Cliffs, NJ: Prentice-Hall.

Bandura, A. (1977a). Self-efficacy mechanism in human agency. *American Psychologist, 37*, 122-147.

Bandura, A. (1977b). Self-efficacy: Toward a unifying theory of behavioral change. *Psychological Review, 84*, 191-215.

Bandura, A. (1986). *Social foundations of thought and action: A social cognitive theory*. Englewood Cliffs, NJ: Prentice-Hall.

Bandura, A. (1989). Self-efficacy mechanisms in psychological activation and health promoting behavior. In J. Madden, IV, S. Matthysse, & J. Barchas (Eds.), *Adaptation, learning, and affect*. New York: Raven.

Bandura, A., & Schunk, D. H. (1981). Cultivating competence, self-efficacy, and intrinsic interest through proximal self-instruction. *Journal of Personality and Social Psychology, 41*, 586-598.

Barker, R. G. (1968). *Ecological psychology*. Stanford, CA: Stanford.

Barry, H., Child, I., & Bacon, M. (1959). Relation of child training to subsistence economy. *American Anthropologist, 61*, 51-63.

Barsalou, L. W. (1987). The instability of graded structure: Implications for the nature of concepts. In U. Neisser (Ed.), *Concepts and conceptual development: Ecological and intellectual factors in categorization*. New York: Cambridge.

Bartlett, F. C. (1932). *Remembering*. Cambridge: Cambridge.

Beecher, H. K. (1959). *Measurement of subjective responses*. New York: Oxford.

Bellah, R. N., Madsen, R., Sullivan, N. M., Swidler, A., & Tipton, S. M. (1985). *Habits of the heart. Individualism and commitment in American life*. Berkeley, CA: University of California Press.

Bem, D. J. (1967). Self-perception: An alternative interpretation of cognitive dissonance phenomena. *Psychological Review, 74*, 183-200.

Bem, D. J. (1972). Self-perception theory. In L. Berkowitz (Ed.), *Advances in experimental social psychology* (Vol. 6). New York: Academic.

Bem, D. J., & Allen, A. (1974). On predicting some of the people some of the time: The search for cross-situational consistencies in behavior. *Psychological Review, 81*, 506-520.

Bem, D. J., & Funder, D. C. (1978). Predicting more of the people more of the time: Assessing the personality of situations. *Psychological Review, 85*, 485-501.

Bem, S. L. (1981). Gender schema theory: A cognitive account of sex typing. *Psychological Review, 88*, 354-364.

Bem, S. L. (1985). Androgyny and gender schema theory: A conceptual and empirical integration. In T. B. Sonderegger (Ed.), *Nebraska symposium on motivation: Psychology and gender* (Vol. 32). Lincoln, Nebraska: University of Nebraska Press.

Bennett, E. (1955). Discussion, decision, commitment and consensus in "group decision." *Human Relations, 21,* 251-273.

Berelson, B. R., Lazarsfeld, P. R., & McPhee, W. N. (1954). *Voting.* Chicago: University of Chicago Press.

Berkowitz, L., & Frodi, A. (1979). Reactions to a child's mistakes as affected by her/his looks and speech. *Social Psychology Quarterly, 42,* 420-425.

Block, J. H. (1971). *Lives through time.* Berkeley, CA: Bancroft Books.

Block, J. H. (1977). Advancing the psychology of personality: Paradigmatic shift or improving the quality of research? In D. Magnusson & N. S. Endler (Eds.), *Personality at the crossroads: Current issues in interactional psychology.* Hillsdale, NJ: Erlbaum.

Borgida, E., & Nisbett, R. E. (1977). The differential impact of abstract versus concrete information on decisions. *Journal of Applied Social Psychology, 7,* 258-271.

Bornstein, P. E., Clayton, P. J., Hlikas, J. A., Maurice, W. L., & Robins, E. (1973). The depression of widowhood after thirteen months. *British Journal of Psychiatry, 12,* 561-566.

Boykin, W. A. (1986). The triple quandary and the schooling of Afro-American children. In U. Neisser (Ed.), *The school achievement of minority children.* Hillsdale, NJ: Erlbaum.

Bramel, D., & Friend, R. (1981). Hawthorne, the myth of the docile worker, and class bias in psychology. *American Psychologist, 36,* 867-878.

Brandon, E., Lawrence, A., Griffin, D. W., & Ross, L. (1991). *Lay views of crosssituational consistency and predictability for "simple" versus "aggregated" measures.* Unpublished manuscript. Stanford University.

Brickman, P., Coates, D., & Janoff-Bulman, R. J. (1978). Lottery winners and accident victims: Is happiness relative? *Journal of Personality and Social Psychology, 36,* 917-927.

Brockner, J., & Swap, W. C. (1983). Resolving the relationships between placebos, misattribution, and insomnia: An individual-differences perspective. *Journal of Personality and Social Psychology, 45,* 32-42.

Brooks, C. (1985). *Language of the American South.* Athens, GA: University of Georgia.

Brophy, J. E., & Good, T. L. (1974). *Teacher-student relationships: Causes and consequences.* NY: Holt.

Brown, R. (1965). *Social psychology.* Glencoe, IL: Free Press.

Brown, R. (1986). *Social psychology: The second edition.* New York: Free Press.

Bruner, J. (1957). *Contemporary approaches to cognition.* Cambridge, MA: Harvard.

Brunswik, E. (1956). *Perception and the representative design of psychological experiments* (2nd ed.). Berkeley: University of California Press.

Bryan, J. H., & Test, M. A. (1967). Models and helping: Naturalistic studies in aiding behavior. *Journal of Personality and Social Psychology, 6,* 400-407.

Buss, D. M., & Craik, K. H. (1983). The act frequency approach to personality. *Psychological Review, 90,* 105-126.

Buss, D. M., & Craik, K. H. (1984). Acts, dispositions, and personality. *Progress in Experimental Personality Research, 13,* 241-301.

Calder, B. J., Ross, M., & Insko, C. A. (1973). Attitude change and attitude attribution: Effects of incentive, choice, and consequences. *Journal of Personality and Social Psychology, 25,* 84-99.

Campbell, D. T. (1969). Reforms as experiments. *American Psychologist, 24,* 409-429.

Campbell, D. T., & Stanley, J. C. (1963). Experimental and quasi-experimental designs for research on teaching. In N. I. Gage (Ed.), *Handbook of research on teaching.* Chicago: Rand McNally.

Campbell, D. T., & Stanley, J. C. (1966). *Experimental and quasi-experimental designs for research.* Chicago: Rand McNally.

Cann, A., Sherman, S. J., & Elkes, R. (1975). Effects of initial request size and timing of a second request on compliance: The foot in the door and the door in the face. *Journal of Personality and Social Psychology, 22,* 774-782.

Cantor, N., & Kihlstrom, J. F. (1987). Personality and social intelligence. Englewood Cliffs, NJ: Prentice-Hall.

Cantor, N., & Mischel, W. (1979). Prototypes in person perception. In L. Berkowitz (Ed.),

Advances in experimental social psychology (Vol. 12). New York: Academic.

Cantor, N., Mischel, W., & Schwartz, J. (1982). A prototype analysis of psychological situations. *Cognitive Psychology, 14*, 45-77.

Cantor, N., Norem, J. K., Niedenthal, P. M., Langston, C. A., & Brower, A. M. (1987). Life tasks, self-concept ideals, and cognitive strategies in a life transition. *Journal of Personality and Social Psychology, 53*, 1178-1191.

Carlsmith, J. M., & Gross, A. E. (1968). Some effects of guilt on compliance. *Journal of Personality and Social Psychology, 11*, 232-239.

Cartwright, D. (1949). Some principles of mass persuasion: Selected findings of research on the sale of U.S. War Bonds. *Human Relations, 2*, 253-267.

Cartwright, D. (Ed.). (1951). *Field theory in social science*, by Kurt Lewin. New York: Harper.

Cartwright, P., & Zander, A. (1953). *Group dynamics*. (First Edition). Evanston, IL: Row, Peterson and Company.

Caspi, A., Bem, D. J., & Elder, G. H., Jr. (1989). Continuities and consequences of interactional styles across the life course. *Journal of Personality, 57*, 375-406.

Caspi, A., Elder, G. H., Jr., & Bem, D. J. (1987). Moving against the world: Lifecourse patterns of explosive children. *Developmental Psychology, 22*, 303-308.

Caspi, A., Elder, G. H., Jr., & Bem, P. J. (1988). Moving away from the world: Life-course patterns of shy children. *Developmental Psychology, 24*, 824-831.

Chaiken, S. (1979). Communicator physical attractiveness and persuasion. *Journal of Personality and Social Psychology, 37*, 1387-1397.

Champagne, A. B., Klopfer, L. E., & Anderson, J. H. (1980). Factors influencing the learning of classical mechanics. *American Journal of Physics, 8*, 1074-1079.

Chaplin, W. F., & Goldberg, L. R. (1985). A failure to replicate the Bem and Allen study of individual differences in cross-situational consistency. *Journal of Personality and Social Psychology, 47*, 1074-1090.

Chapman, L. J., & Chapman, J. P. (1967). Genesis of popular but erroneous diagnostic observations. *Journal of Abnormal Psychology, 72*, 193-204.

Chapman, L. J., & Chapman, J. P. (1969). Illusory correlation as an obstacle to the use of valid psychodiagnostic signs. *Journal of Abnormal Psychology, 74*, 271-280.

Cialdini, R. B. (1988). *Influence: Science and practice*. (2nd Edition). Glenview, IL: Scott, Foresman/Little, Brown.

Cialdini, R. B., Vincent, J. E., Lewis, S. K., Catalan, J., Wheeler, P., & Darby, B. L. (1975). A reciprocal concessions procedure for inducing compliance: The door-in-the-face technique. *Journal of Personality and Social Psychology, 21*, 206-215.

Citation World Atlas. (1980). Maplewood, NJ: Hammond.

Clifford, M. M., & Walster, E. H. (1973). The effect of physical attractiveness on teacher expectations. *Sociology of Education, 46*, 248-258.

Coch, L., & French, J. R. P., Jr. (1948). Overcoming resistance to change. *Human Relations, 1*, 512-532.

Cohen, J. (1965). Some statistical issues in psychological research. In B. B. Wolman (Ed.), *Handbook of clinical psychology*. New York: McGraw-Hill.

Cohen, J. (1977). *Statistical power analysis for the behavioral sciences*. (Rev. ed). New York: Academic.

Cohen, S., & McKay, C. (1984). Social support, stress, and the buffering hypothesis: A theoretical analysis. In A. Baum, J. E. Singer, & S. E. Taylor (Eds.), *Handbook of psychology and health* (Vol. 4). Hillsdale, NJ: Erlbaum.

Cohen, S., & Williamson, G. M. (1991). Stress and infectious diseases in humans. *Psychological Bulletin, 109*, 5-24.

Collins, B. E. (1974). Four components of the Rotter internal-external scale: Belief in a difficult world, a just world, a predictable world, and a politically responsive world. *Journal of Personality and Social Psychology, 29*, 381-391.

Condry, J. (1977). Enemies of exploration: Self-initiated versus other-initiated learning. *Journal of Personality and Social Psychology, 35*, 459-477.

Conley, J. J. (1984). Relation of temporal stability and cross-situational consistency in personality: Comment on the Mischel-Epstein debate. *Psychological Review, 91*, 491-496.

Consortium for Longitudinal Studies. (1978). *Lasting effects after pre-school.* Washington, D.C.: Department of Health, Education, and Welfare.

Cook, S. W. (1957). Desegregation: A psychological analysis. *American Psychologist, 12*, 1-13.

Cook, S. W. (1979). Social science and school desegregation: Did we mislead the Supreme Court? *Personality and Social Psychology Bulletin, 5*, 420-437.

Cook, S. W. (1985). Experimenting on social issues: The case of school desegregation. *American Psychologist, 40*, 452-460.

Cook, T. D., & Campbell, D. T. (1979). *Quasi-experimentation: Design and analysis issues for field settings.* Chicago: Rand McNally.

Cooper, J., & Fazio, R. H. (1979). The formation and persistence of attitudes that support intergroup conflict. In W. G. Austin & S. Worchel (Eds.), *The psychology of intergroup relations.* Monterey, CA: Brooks/Cole.

Cooper, J., Zanna, M. P., & Taves, P. A. (1978). Arousal as a necessary condition for attitude change following induced compliance. *Journal of Personality and Social Psychology, 36*, 1101-1106.

Cordova, D., & Lepper, M. R. (1991). *The effects of intrinsic versus extrinsic rewards on the concept attainment process: An attributional approach.* Unpublished manuscript, Stanford University.

Cousins, S. D. (1989). Culture and self-perception in Japan and the U. S. *Journal of Personality and Social Psychology, 56*, 124-131.

Crandall, V. C., Katkovsky, W., & Crandall, V. C. (1965). Children's beliefs in their own control of reinforcements in intellectual-academic achievement situations. *Child Development, 36*, 91-109.

Cronbach, L. J. (1982). *Designing evaluations of educational and social programs.* San Francisco: Jossey-Bass.

Crutchfield, R. A. (1955). Conformity and character. *American Psychologist, 10*, 191-198.

D'Andrade, R. G. (1981). The cultural part of cognition. *Cognitive Science, 5*, 179-195.

Darley, J. M., & Batson, C. D. (1973). From Jerusalem to Jericho: A study of situational and dispositional variables in helping behavior. *Journal of Personality and Social Psychology, 27*, 100-119.

Darley, J. M., & Fazio, R. H. (1980). Expectancy confirmation processes arising in the social interaction sequence. *American Psychologist, 35*, 867-881.

Darley, J. M., & Latané, B. (1968). Bystander intervention in emergencies: Diffusion of responsibility. *Journal of Personality and Social Psychology, 8*, 377-383.

Dawes, R. M. (1988a). *Rational choice in an uncertain world.* New York: Harcourt, Brace, Jovanovich.

Dawes, R. M. (1988b). *The potential non-falsity of the false consensus effect.* Unpublished manuscript, Carnegie-Mellon University, Pittsburgh.

de Charms, R. (1968). *Personal causation: The internal affective determinants of behavior.* New York: Academic.

Deci, E. L. (1971). Effects of externally mediated rewards on intrinsic motivation. *Journal of Personality and Social Psychology, 18*, 105-111.

Deci, E. L. (1972). Effects of contingent and noncontingent rewards and controls on intrinsic motivation. *Organizational Behavior and Human Performance, 8*, 217-229.

Deci, E. L., & Ryan, R. M. (1980). The empirical exploration of intrinsic motivational processes. In L. Berkowitz (Ed.), *Advances in experimental social psychology* (Vol. 13). New York: Academic.

Deci, E. L., & Ryan, R. M. (1985). *Intrinsic motivation and self-determination in human behavior.* New York: Plenum.

Deutsch, M. (1982). Interdependence and psychological orientation. In V. J. Derlega and J. Grzelad (Eds.), *Cooperation and helping behavior.* New York: Academic.

Deutsch, M., & Collins, M. E. (1951). *Inter-racial housing: A psychological evaluation of a social experiment.* Minneapolis: University of Minnesota Press.

Deutsch, M., & Gerard, H. B. (1955). A study of normative and informational social influence upon individual judgment. *Journal of Abnormal and Social Psychology, 51,* 629-636.

De Vos, G. (1985). Dimensions of the self in Japanese culture. In A. Marsella, C. De Vos, & F. Hsu (Eds.), *Culture and self.* London: Tavistock.

Diener, D. I., & Dweck, C. S. (1978). An analysis of learned helplessness: Continuous changes in performance, strategy, and achievement conditions following failure. *Journal of Personality and Social Psychology, 36,* 451-462.

Diener, D. I., & Dweck, C. S. (1980). An analysis of learned helplessness: II. The processing of success. *Journal of Personality and Social Psychology, 39,* 940-952.

Dienstbier, R. A., & Munter, P. O. (1971). Cheating as a function of the labeling of natural arousal. *Journal of Personality and Social Psychology, 17,* 208-213.

Digman, I. M., & Inouye, J. (1986). Further specification of the five robust factors of personality. *Journal of Personality and Social Psychology, 50,* 116-123.

Dion, K. K. (1972). Physical attractiveness and evaluations of children's transgressions. *Journal of Personality and Social Psychology, 24,* 207-213.

Dion, K. K., Berscheid, E., & Walster, E. (1972). What is beautiful is good. *Journal of Personality and Social Psychology, 24,* 285-290.

Dodge, K. A. (1986). A social information processing model of social competence in children. In M. Permutter (Ed.), *Minnesota symposium on child psychology* (Vol. 18). Hillsdale, NJ: Erlbaum.

Doi, T. L. (1971). *Amae no kozo: The anatomy of dependency.* Tokyo: Kobunsho.

Dreeben, R., & Barr, R. (1983). *How schools work.* Chicago, IL: University of Chicago Press.

Dunning, D., Griffin, D. W., Miojkovic, J., & Ross, L. (1990). The overconfidence effect in social prediction. *Journal of Personality and Social Psychology, 58,* 568-581.

Dweck, C. S. (1975). The role of expectations and attributions in the alleviation of learned helplessness. *Journal of Personality and Social Psychology, 31,* 674-685.

Dweck, C. S., Davidson, W., Nelson, S., & Enna, B. (1978). Sex differences in learned helplessness: II. The contingencies of evaluative feedback in the classroom and III. An experimental analysis. *Developmental Psychology, 14,* 268-276.

Dweck, C. S., & Goetz, T. E. (1978). Attributions and learned helplessness. In J. H. Harvey, W. Ickes, & R. F. Kidd (Eds.), *New directions in attribution theory* (Vol. 2). Hillsdale, NJ: Erlbaum.

Dweck, C. S., & Leggett, E. L. (1988). A social-cognitive approach to motivation and personality. *Psychological Review, 95,* 256-273.

Dweck, C. S., & Wortman, C. B. (1982). Learned helplessness, anxiety, and achievement motivation. In H. W. Krohne & L. Laux (Eds.), *Achievement, stress, and anxiety.* New York: Hemisphere.

Egbert, L. D., Battit, G. E., Welch, C. E., & Bartlett, M. K. (1964). Reduction of postoperative pain by encouragement and instruction of patients: A study of doctor-patient rapport. *New England Journal of Medicine, 270,* 825-827.

Einhorn, H. J., & Hogarth, R. M. (1978). Confidence in judgment: Persistence of the illusion of validity. *Psychological Review, 85,* 395-416.

Elder, G. H., Jr. (1969). Appearance and education in marriage mobility. *American Sociological Review, 34,* 519-533.

Ellsworth, P. (1985, July). Juries on trial. *Psychology Today,* 44-46.

Endler, N. S. (1983). Interactionism: A personality model, but not yet a theory. In M. M. Page (Ed.), *Nebraska symposium on motivation, 1982: Personality - current theory and research.* Lincoln, Nebraska: University of Nebraska Press.

Epstein, S. (1979). The stability of behavior: I. On predicting most of the people much of the time. *Journal of Personality and Social Psychology, 37,* 1097-1126.

Epstein, S. (1983). Aggregation and beyond: Some basic issues in the prediction of behavior. *Journal of Personality, 51,* 360-391.

Esman, M. J., & Uphoff, N. T. (1984). *Local organizations: Intermediaries in rural development.* Ithaca, NY: Cornell.

Evans, R. I. (1982). Determining smoking in adolescents: A case study from a social psychological research program. In A. W. Johnson, O. Grusky, & B. H. Raven (Eds.), *Contemporary health services: Social science perspectives*. Boston: Auburn House.

Eysenck, H. J. (1967). *The biological basis of personality*. Springfield, IL: Thomas.

Farr, R. M., & Moscovici, S. (Eds.). (1984). *Social representations*. Cambridge: Cambridge.

Feldman, P. E. (1956). The personal element in psychiatric research. *American Journal of Psychiatry, 11*, 52-54.

Festinger, L. (1954). A theory of social comparison processes. *Human Relations, 7*, 117-140.

Festinger, L. (1957). *A theory of cognitive dissonance*. Stanford, CA: Stanford.

Festinger, L., & Carlsmith, J. M. (1959). Cognitive consequences of forced compliance. *Journal of Abnormal and Social Psychology, 58*, 203-210.

Festinger, L., Pepitone, A., & Newcomb, T. (1952). Some consequences of deindividuation in a group. *Journal of Abnormal and Social Psychology, 47*, 382-389.

Festinger, L., Schachter, S., & Back, K. (1950). *Social pressures in informal groups: A study of human factors in housing*. New York: Harper.

Fischhoff, B., & Beyth, R. (1975). "I knew it would happen" - remembered probabilities of once-future things. *Organizational Behavior and Human Performance, 13*, 1-16.

Fischhoff, B., Slovic, P., & Lichtenstein, S. (1977). Knowing with certainty: The appropriateness of extreme confidence. *Journal of Experimental Psychology: Human Perception and Performance, 3*, 552-564.

Fisher, R. J. (1982). *Social Psychology: An applied approach*. New York: St. Martin's.

Fiske, S. T., & Taylor, S. E. (1990). *Social cognition*. (2nd Edition). Reading, MA: Addison-Wesley.

Forgas, J. P. (1976). The perception of social episodes: Categorical and dimensional representations in two different social milieus. *Journal of Personality and Social Psychology, 33*, 199-209.

Forgas, J. P. (1982). Episode cognition: Internal representations of interaction routines. In L. Berkowitz (Ed.), *Advances in experimental social psychology* (Vol. 15). New York: Academic.

Försterling, F. (1985). Attributional retraining: A review. *Psychological Bulletin, 98*, 495-512.

Frager, R. (1970). Conformity and anti-conformity in Japan. *Journal of Personality and Social Psychology, 15*, 203-210.

Franke, R. H., & Kaul, J. D. (1978). The Hawthorne experiment: First statistical interpretation. *American Sociological Review, 43*, 623-643.

Freedman, J. L., & Fraser, S. C. (1966). Compliance without pressure: The foot-in-the-door technique. *Journal of Personality and Social Psychology, 4*, 195-202.

Freeman, D., Pisani, R., & Purves, R. (1978). *Statistics*. New York: Norton.

Freud, S. (1901/1960). *Psychopathology of everyday life*. Standard Edition (Vol. 6). London: Hogarth.

Furstenberg, F. F., Jr., Brooks-Gunn, J., & Morgan, P. S. (1987). *Adolescent mothers in later life*. Cambridge: Cambridge.

Gastil, R. D. (1971). Homicide and regional culture of violence. *American Sociological Review, 36*, 412-427.

Gerard, H., & Miller, N. (1975). *School desegregation*. New York: Plenum.

Gilbert, D. T., & Jones, E. E. (1986). Perceiver-induced constraints: Interpretation of self-generated reality. *Journal of Personality and Social Psychology, 50*, 269-280.

Glass, C. R., & Levy, L. H. (1982). Perceived psychophysiological control: The effects of power versus powerlessness. *Cognitive Therapy and Research, 6*, 91-103.

Gleick, J. (1987). *Chaos: Making a new science*. New York: Viking.

Goffman, E. (1959). *The presentation of self in everyday life*. Garden City, NY: Doubleday-Anchor.

Gottlieb, B. H. (1983). *Social support strategies: Guidelines for mental health practice*. Beverly Hills, CA: Sage.

Grace, N. D., Muench, H., & Chalmers, T. C. (1966). The present status of shunts for portal hypertension in cirrhosis. *Gastroenterology, 50*, 684-691.

Greeley, A. (1976). *Ethnicity, denomination, and inequality*. Beverly Hills, CA: Sage.

Greeley, A. (1989). *Ethnic groups in the U.S.: Religious change in America*. Cambridge, MA:

Harvard University Press.

Griffin, D. W., Dunning D., & Ross, L. (1990). The role of construal processes in overconfident predictions about the self and others. *Journal of Personality and Social Psychology, 59*, 1128-1139.

Gurin, P., Gurin, G., & Morrison, B. M. (1978). Personal and ideological aspects of internal and external control. *Social Psychology, 41*, 275-296.

Hamilton, D. L., Dugan, P. M., & Trolier, T. K. (1985). The formation of stereotypic beliefs: Further evidence for distinctiveness-based illusory correlations. *Journal of Personality and Social Psychology, 48*, 5-17.

Hannan, M. T., Tuma, N. B., & Groeneveld, L. P. (1977). Income and marital events: Evidence from an income maintenance experiment. *American Journal of Sociology, 82*, 1186-1211.

Harackiewicz, J. M. (1979). The effects of reward contingency and performance feedback on intrinsic motivation. *Journal of Personality and Social Psychology, 37*, 1352-1361.

Harackiewicz, J. M., Abrahams, S., & Wageman, R. (1987). Performance evaluation and intrinsic motivation: The effects of evaluative focus, rewards, and achievement orientation. *Journal of Personality and Social Psychology, 53*, 1015-1023.

Harré, R., & Secord, P. F. (1973). *The explanation of social behaviour.* Oxford: Blackwell.

Harris, M. J., & Rosenthal, R. (1985). The mediation of interpersonal expectancy effects: 31 meta-analyses. *Psychological Bulletin, 97*, 363-386.

Hartshorne, H., & May, M. A. (1928). *Studies in the nature of character, I: Studies in deceit.* New York: Macmillan.

Hastie, R., Penrod, S. D., & Pennington, N. (1983). *Inside the jury.* Cambridge, MA: Harvard.

Hastorf, A., & Cantril, H. (1954). They saw a game: A case study. *Journal of Abnormal and Social Psychology, 49*, 129-134.

Hatfield, E., & Sprecher, S. (1986). *Mirror, mirror: The importance of looks in everyday life.* Albany, NY: SUNY Press.

Healey, K. M. (1986). Does preoperative instruction make a difference? *American Journal of Nursing, 68*, 62-67.

Heath, S. B. (1983). *Ways with words: Language, life, and work in communities and classrooms.* New York: Cambridge.

Heider, F. (1958). *The psychology of interpersonal relations.* New York: Wiley.

Helson, H. (1964). *Adaptation level theory: An experimental and systematic approach to behavior.* New York: Harper & Row.

Hess, R. D. (1970). Social class and ethnic influences upon socialization. In P. H. Mussen (Ed.), *Carmichael's manual of child psychology* (Vol. 2). New York: Wiley.

Higgins, E. T., Kline, R., & Strauman T. (1985). Self-concept discrepancy theory: A psychological model for distinguishing among different aspects of depression and anxiety. *Social Cognition, 3*, 51-76.

Higgins, E. T., Strauman, T., & Kline R. (1986). Standards and the process of self-evaluation: Multiple affects from multiple stages. In R. Sorrentino & E. Higgins (Eds.), *Handbook of motivation and cognition: Foundations of social behavior.* New York: Guilford.

Hofstede, C. (1980). *Culture's consequences.* Beverly Hills, CA: Sage.

Holland, J. H., Holyoak, K. J., Nisbett, R. F., & Thagard, P. R. (1986). *Induction: Processes of inference, learning and discovery.* Cambridge, MA: Bradford Books/M.I.T.

Holmes, D. S. (1968). Dimensions of projection. *Psychological Bulletin, 69*, 248-268.

Holyoak, K. J., & Gordon, P. C. (1979). Social reference points. *Journal of Personality and Social Psychology, 44*, 881-887.

Homans, G. C. (1952). *Group factors in worker productivity.* In G. E. Swanson, T. E. Newcombe, & E. L. Hartley (Eds.), *Readings in social psychology.* New York: Holt.

Hovland, C. I., Janis, I. L., & Kelley, H. H. (1953). *Communication and persuasion.* New Haven, CT: Yale.

Hui, C. H. (1984). *Individualism-collectivism: Theory measurement and its relation to reward allocation.* Unpublished doctoral dissertation, University of Illinois, Urbana.

Humphrey, R. (1985). How work roles influence perception: Structural-cognitive processes and organizational behavior. *American Sociological Review, 50*, 242-252.

Hunter, J. E., & Hunter, R. F. (1984). Validity and utility of alternative predictors of job performance. *Psychological Bulletin, 96*, 72-98.

Hyman, H., & Sheatsley, P. B. (1947). Some reasons why information campaigns fail. *Public Opinion Quarterly.* II, 413-423.

Isen, A. M., Clark, M., & Schwartz, M. F. (1976). Duration of the effect of good mood on helping: Footprints on the sands of time. *Journal of Personality and Social Psychology, 34*, 385-393.

Isen, A. M., Shalker, T. E., Clark, M., & Karp, L. (1978). Affect, accessibility of material in memory, and behavior: A cognitive loop. *Journal of Personality and Social Psychology, 36*, 1-12.

Jacobs, R. C., & Campbell, D. T. (1961). The perpetuation of an arbitrary tradition through several generations of a laboratory microculture. *Journal of Abnormal and Social Psychology, 62*, 649-658.

James, W. (1890/1948). *Psychology.* Cleveland: World Publishing.

Janis, I. L. (1958). *Psychological stress.* New York: Wiley.

Janis, I. L. (1982). *Groupthink* (2nd ed.). Boston: Houghton Mifflin.

Jennings, D., Amabile, T. M., & Ross, L. (1982). Informal covariation assessment: Data-based vs. theory-based judgments. In A. Tversky, D. Kahneman, & P. Slovic (Eds.), *Judgment under uncertainty: Heuristics and biases.* New York: Cambridge.

Johnson, J. E. (1984). Psychological interventions and coping with surgery. In A. Baum, S. E. Taylor, & J. E. Singer (Eds.), *Handbook of psychology and health* (Vol. 4). Hillsdale, NJ: Erlbaum.

Johnson, J. E., & Leventhal, H. (1974). Effects of accurate expectations and behavioral instructions on reactions during anxious medical examination. *Journal of Personality and Social Psychology, 29*, 710-718.

Johnston, J., & Kleinsmith, L. (1987). *Computers in higher education: Computer-based tutorials in introductory biology.* Ann Arbor: Institute for Social Research.

Jones, E. E. (1979). The rocky road from acts to dispositions. *American Psychologist, 34*, 107-117.

Jones, E. E., & Davis, K. E. (1965). From acts to dispositions: The attribution process in person perception. In L. Berkowitz (Ed.), *Advances in experimental social psychology* (Vol. 2). New York: Academic.

Jones, E. E., & Harris, V. A. (1967). The attribution of attitudes. *Journal of Experimental Social Psychology, 3*, 1-2.

Jones, E. E., & Nisbett, R. E. (1972). The actor and the observer: Divergent perceptions of the causes of behavior. In E. E. Jones, D. E. Kanouse, H. H. Kelley, R. E. Nisbett, S. Valins, & B. Weiner (Eds.), *Attribution: Perceiving the causes of behavior.* Morristown, NJ: General Learning Press.

Jones, J. M. (1983). The concept of race in social psychology. In L. Wheeler & P. Shaver (Eds.), *Review of personality and social psychology* (Vol. 4). Beverly Hills, CA: Sage.

Kagan, J. (1984). *The nature of the child.* New York: Basic Books.

Kahneman, D., & Miller, D. T. (1986). Norm theory: Comparing reality to its alternatives. *Psychological Review, 93*, 136-153.

Kahneman, D., Slovic, P., & Tversky, A. (Eds.). (1982). *Judgment under uncertainty: Heuristics and biases.* New York: Cambridge.

Kahneman, D., & Tversky, A. (1973). On the psychology of prediction. *Psychological Review, 80*, 237-251.

Kahneman, D., & Tversky, A. (1979). Prospect theory: An analysis of decision under risk. *Econometrica, 47*, 263-291.

Kamen, L. P., & Seligman, M. E. P. (1987). *Explanatory style predicts college grade point average.* Unpublished manuscript, University of Pennsylvania.

Karniol, R., & Ross, M. (1977). The effect of performance-relevant and performance-irrelevant rewards on children's intrinsic motivation. *Child Development, 48*, 482-487.

Kassin, S. M., & Lepper, M. R. (1984). Oversufficient and insufficient justification effects: Cognitive and behavioral development. In J. Nicholls (Ed.), *Advances in motivation and achievement* (Vol. 3). Greenwich, CT: Jai Press.

Katz, D. (1931). *Students' attitudes: A report of the Syracuse University reaction study.* Syracuse, NY: Craftsman Press.

Kazin, A. (1983, January). Anti-semitism: The banality of evil. *The Economist,* 286-291.

Kelley, H. H. (1967). Attribution theory in social psychology. In D. Levine (Ed.), *Nebraska symposium on motivation* (Vol. 15). Lincoln: University of Nebraska Press.

Kelley, H. H. (1972). Causal schemata and the attribution process. In E. E. Jones, D. E. Kanouse, H. H. Kelley, R. E. Nisbett, S. Valins, & B. Weiner (Eds.), *Attribution: Perceiving the causes of behavior.* Morristown, NJ: General Learning Press.

Kelley, H. H., & Staheiski, A. J. (1970). The social interaction basis of cooperators' and competitors' beliefs about others. *Journal of Personality and Social Psychology, 16,* 66-91.

Kelly, G. A. (1955). *The psychology of personal constructs* (2 Vols.). New York: Norton.

Kenrick, D. T., & Funder, D. C. (1988). Profiting from controversy: Lessons from the person-situation debate. *American Psychologist, 43,* 23-34.

Kiesler, C. A. (1980). Mental health policy as a field of inquiry for psychology. *American Psychologist, 35,* 1066-1080.

Kitayama, S., Markus, H., Tummula, P., Kurokawa, M., & Kato, K. (1989). *Culture and self-cognition.* Unpublished manuscript, University of Oregon.

Klitgaard, R. (1985). *Choosing elites.* New York: Basic Books.

Koffka, K. (1935). *Principles of gestalt psychology.* New York: Harcourt Brace Jovanovich.

Kohn, M. L., & Schooler, C. (1969). Class, occupation, and orientation. *American Sociological Review, 34,* 657-678.

Kruglanski, A. W., Friedman, I., & Zeevi, G. (1971). The effects of extrinsic incentive on some qualitative aspects of task performance. *Journal of Personality, 39,* 606-617.

Kruglanski, A. W., Riter, A., Amatai, A., Margolin, B., Shabati, L., & Zaksh, D. (1975). Can money enhance intrinsic motivation: A test of the contentconsequence hypothesis. *Journal of Personality and Social Psychology, 31,* 744-750.

Kunda, Z. (1990). The case for motivated reasoning. *Psychological Bulletin, 108(3),*480-498.

Kunda, Z., & Nisbett, R. E. (1986). The psychometrics of everyday life. *Cognitive Psychology, 18,* 195-224.

Landy, D., & Sigall, H. (1974). Beauty is talent: Task evaluation as a function of the performer's physical attractiveness. *Journal of Personality and Social Psychology, 29,* 299-304.

Langer, F. J. (1989). *Mindfulness.* Reading, MA: Addison-Wesley.

Langer, E. J., & Rodin, J. (1976). The effects of choice and enhanced personal responsibility for the aged: A field experiment in an institutional setting. *Journal of Personality and Social Psychology, 34,* 191-198.

Laosa, L. M. (1981). Maternal behavior: Sociocultural diversity in modes of family interaction. In R. W. Henderson (Ed.), *Parent-child interaction: Theory, research, and prospects.* Orlando. FL: Academic Press.

Latané, B., & Darley, J. M. (1968). Group inhibition of bystander intervention in emergencies. *Journal of Personality and Social Psychology, 10,* 215-221.

Latané, B., & Nida, S. (1981). Ten years of research on group size and helping. *Psychological Bulletin, 89,* 308-324.

Latané, B., & Rodin, J. (1969). A lady in distress: Inhibiting effects of friends and strangers on bystander intervention. *Journal of Personality and Social Psychology, 5,* 189-202.

LeBon, G. (1896). *The crowd.* London: Unwin. (Translated from *Psychologies des foules.* Paris: Oleon, 1895.)

Lefcourt, H. M. (1972). Internal versus external control of reinforcement revisited: Recent developments. In B. A. Maher (Ed.), *Progress in experimental personality research* (Vol. 6). New York: Academic.

Lepper, M. R. (1988). Motivational considerations in the study of instruction. *Cognition and Instruction, 5,* 289-309.

Lepper, M. R., & Greene, D. (1978). Overjustification research and beyond: Toward a means-end analysis of intrinsic and extrinsic motivation. In M. R. Lepper & D. Greene (Eds.), *The hidden costs of reward: New perspectives on the psychology of human motivation.*

Hillsdale, NJ: Erlbaum.

Lepper, M. R., & Greene, D., (Eds.). (1979). *The hidden costs of reward*. Hillsdale, NJ: Erlbaum.

Lepper, M. R., Greene, D., & Nisbett, R. E. (1973). Undermining children's intrinsic interest with extrinsic reward: A test of the overjustification hypothesis. *Journal of Personality and Social Psychology, 28*, 129-137.

Lepper, M. R., & Hodell, M. (1989). Intrinsic motivation in the classroom. In G. Ames & R. E. Ames (Eds.), *Research on motivation in education* (Vol. 3). New York: Academic.

Leventhal, H., Brown, D., Shacham, S., & Engquist, C. (1979). Effects of preparatory information about sensations, threat of pain, and attention on cold pressor distress. *Journal of Personality and Social Psychology, 37*, 688-714.

Leventhal, H., Singer, R. P., & Jones, S. H. (1965). The effects of fear and specificity of recommendation. *Journal of Abnormal and Social Psychology, 64*, 385-388.

Levine, J. D., Cordon, N. C., & Fields, H. L. (1978). The mechanism of placebo analgesia. *Lancet, 2*, 654-657.

LeVine, R. A. (1982). *Culture, behavior and personality: An introduction to the comparative study of psychosocial adaptation*. New York: Aldine.

Lewicki, p. (1986). *Nonconscious social information processing*. Orlando, FL: Academic.

Lewin, K. (1935). *Dynamic theory of personality*. New York: McGraw-Hill.

Lewin, K. (1951). *Field theory in social science*. (Edited by D. Cartwright.) New York: Harper.

Lewin, K. (1952). Group decision and social change. In G. E. Swanson, T. M. Newcomb & E. L. Hartley (Eds.), *Readings in social psychology*. New York: Henry Holt.

Lewin, K., Lippitt, R., & White, R. K. (1939). Patterns of aggressive behavior in experimentally created "social climates." *Journal of Social Psychology, 10*, 271-299.

Lieberman, M. A., Borman, L. D., & Associates. (1979). *Self-help groups for coping with crisis: Origins, members, processes, and impact*. San Francisco: Jossey-Bass.

Linder, D. C., Cooper, J., & Jones, E. E. (1967). Decision freedom as a determinant of the role of incentive magnitude in attitude change. *Journal of Personality and Social Psychology, 6*, 245-254.

Livesley, W. J., & Bromley, D. B. (1973). *Person perception in childhood and adolescence*. London: Wiley.

Loftin, C., & Hill, R. H. (1974). Regional subculture and homicide: An empirical examination of the Gastil-Hackney thesis. *American Sociological Review, 39*, 714-724.

Long, J. V. F., & Vaillant, C. E. (1984). Natural history of male psychological health, XI: Escape from the underclass. *American Journal of Psychiatry, 14*, 341-346.

Lord, C. C., Lepper, M. R., & Ross, L. (1979). Biased assimilation and attitude polarization: The effects of prior theories on subsequently considered evidence. *Journal of Personality and Social Psychology, 37*, 2098-2109.

Lowie, R. H. (1954). *Indians of the plains*. New York: McGraw-Hill.

Magnusson, E., & Ekehammar, B. (1973). An analysis of situational dimensions: A replication. *Multivariate Behavioral Research, 8*, 331-339.

Markus, H. (1977). Self-schemata and processing information about the self. *Journal of Personality and Social Psychology, 35*, 63-78.

Markus, H., & Kitayama, S. (1991). Culture and the self: Implications for cognition, emotion, and motivation. *Psychological Review, 98*, 224-253.

Markus, H., & Nurius, P. (1986). Possible selves. *American Psychologist, 41*, 954-969.

Markus, H., Smith, J., & Moreland, R. L. (1985). Role of the self-concept in the perception of others. *Journal of Personality and Social Psychology, 49*, 1495-1512.

Markus, H., & Zajonc, R. B. (1985). The cognitive perspective in social psychology. In G. Lindzey & E. Aronson (Eds.), *The handbook of social psychology: Vol. 1. Theory and methods*. New York: Random House.

Marmet, M. C., & Syme, S. L. (1976). Acculturation and coronary heart disease in Japanese children. *American Journal of Epidemiology, 104*, 225-247.

Marx, K. (1859/1904). *A contribution to the critique of political economy*. Chicago: Charles H. Kerr (translated).

Maslach, C. (1982). *Burn out: The cost of caring*. New Jersey: Prentice-Hall.

Mayfield, E. C. (1964). The selection interview: A re-evaluation of published research. *Personnel Psychology, 17,* 239-260.

Mayo, E. (1933). *The human problems of an industrial civilization.* New York: Macmillan.

Mayo, E. (1945). *The social problems of an industrial civilization.* Cambridge, MA: Harvard.

McArthur, L. Z. (1972). The how and what of why: Some determinants and consequences of causal attribution. *Journal of Personality and Social Psychology, 22,* 171-193.

McArthur, L. Z., & Post, D. (1977). Figural emphasis and person perception. *Journal of Experimental Social Psychology, 13,* 733-742.

McCandless, B., Roberts, A., & Starnes, T. (1972). Teachers' marks, achievement test scores, and aptitude relations with respect to social class, race, and sex. *Journal of Educational Psychology, 63,* 153-159.

McClelland, D. C., Atkinson, J. W., Clark, R. A., & Lowell, E. L. (1953). *The achievement motive.* New York: Appleton-Century-Crofts.

McCloskey, M. (1983, April). Intuitive physics. *Scientific American, 248,* 122-130.

McCord, J. (1978). A thirty-year follow-up of treatment effects. *American Psychologist, 33,* 284-289.

McCord, J., & McCord, W. (1959). A followup report on the Cambridge-Somerville youth study. *Annals of the American Academy of Political and Social Science, 32,* 89-96.

McCord, W., & McCord, J. (1959). *Origins of crime.* New York: Columbia.

McGuire, A. (1989). *Mistaken reliance on individual difference variables in predicting social behavior.* Unpublished manuscript, University of Michigan, Ann Arbor.

McGuire, W. J. (1986). The myth of massive media impact: Savagings and salvagings. In C. Comstock (Ed.), *Public communication and behavior.* Orlando, FL: Academic Press.

McIntosh, D. N., Silver, R. C., & Wortman, C. B. (1989, August). *Adjustment in bereavement: Religion, social support and cognitive processing.* Paper presented at the meeting of American Psychological Association, New Orleans, LA.

Mead, C. H. (1934). *Mind, self, and society.* Chicago: University of Chicago Press.

Meichenbaum, D. H., Bowers, K. S., & Ross, R. R. (1969). A behavioral analysis of teacher expectancy effect. *Journal of Personality and Social Psychology, 13,* 306-316.

Merton, R. (1948). The self-fulfilling prophecy. *The Antioch Review, Summer,* 193-210.

Meyer, A. J., Maccoby, N., & Farquhuar, J. W. (1980). Cardiovascular risk modification by community-based programs for life-style. *Journal of Consulting Psychology, 48,* 159-163.

Michela, J. L., & Wood, J. V. (1986). Causal attributions in health and illness. In P. C. Kendall (Ed.), *Advances in cognitive-behavior research and therapy* (Vol. 5). New York: Academic.

Milgram, S. (1961, December). Nationality and conformity. *Scientific American,* 45-51.

Milgram, S. (1963). Behavioral study of obedience. *Journal of Abnormal and Social Psychology, 67,* 371-378.

Miller, J. (1984). Culture and the development of everyday social explanation. *Journal of Personality and Social Psychology, 46,* 961-978.

Miller, R. L., Brickman, P., & Bolen, D. (1975). Attribution versus persuasion as a means for modifying behavior. *Journal of Personality and Social Psychology, 3,* 430-441.

Mischel, W. (1968). *Personality and assessment.* New York: Wiley.

Mischel, W. (1973). Toward a cognitive social learning reconceptualization of personality. *Psychological Review, 80,* 252-283.

Mischel, W. (1974). Processes in delay of gratification. In L. Berkowitz (Ed.), *Advances in experimental social psychology* (Vol 7). New York: Academic.

Mischel, W. (1984). Convergences and challenges in the search for consistency. *American Psychologist, 39,* 351-364.

Mischel, W. (1990, April). *Searching for personality: Toward a conditional analysis of dispositions.* Katz-Newcomb Lecture, Ann Arbor, MI.

Mischel, W., & Ebbesen, E. (1970). Attention in delay of gratification. *Journal of Personality and Social Psychology, 16,* 329-337.

Mischel, W., & Peake, P. K. (1982a). Beyond déjà vu in the search for cross-situational consistency. *Psychological Review, 89,* 730-755.

Mischel, W., & Peake, P. K. (1982b). In search of consistency: Measure for measure. In M. P.

Zanna, E. T. Higgins, & C. P. Herman (Eds.), *Consistency in social behavior: The Ontario Symposium* (Vol. 2). Hillsdale, NJ: Erlbaum.

Mischel, W., Shoda, Y., & Rodriguez, M. L. (1989). Delay of gratification in children. *Science, 24,* 933-938.

Moffitt, R. A. (1980). The negative income tax: Would it discourage work? *Monthly Labor Review, 104,* 23-27.

Moos, R. H. (1968). Situational analysis of the therapeutic milieu. *Journal of Abnormal Psychology, 73,* 49-61

Moos, R. H. (1973). Conceptualizations of human environments. *American Psychologist, 28,* 652-665.

Morgan, M. (1984). Reward-induced decrements and increments in intrinsic motivation. *Review of Educational Research, 54,* 683-692.

Moscovici, S., Lage, S., & Naffrechoux, M. (1969). Influence of a consistent minority on the responses of a majority in a color perception task. *Sociometry, 32,* 365-380.

Moscovici, S., & Personnaz, B. (1980). Studies in social influence: V. Minority influence and conversion behavior in a perceptual task. *Journal of Experimental Social Psychology, 76,* 270-282.

Murray, H. A. (1938). *Explorations in personality.* New York: Oxford.

Nemeth, C. (1986). Differential contributions of majority and minority influence. *Psychological Review, 93,* 23-32.

Newcomb, T. M. (1929). *The consistency of certain extrovert-introvert behavior patterns in 51 problem boys.* New York: Columbia University, Teachers College, Bureau of Publications.

Newcomb, T. M. (1943). *Personality and social change.* New York: Dryden.

Newcomb, T. M., Koenig, K. E., Flacks, R., & Warwick, D. P. (1967). *Persistence and change: Bennington College and its students after twenty-five years.* New York: Wiley.

Newton, F., Griffin, D. W., & Ross, L. (1988). *Actual versus estimated impact of person and situation in determining pro-social behavior.* Unpublished manuscript. Stanford University.

Nicholls, J. C. (1984). Achievement motivation: Conceptions of ability, subjective experience, task choice, and performance. *Psychological Review, 91,* 328-346.

Nicholls, J. G. (1988). *Competence, accomplishment, and motivation: A perspective on development and education.* Cambridge, MA: Harvard.

Nisbett, R. E. (1980). The trait construct in lay and professional psychology. In L. Festinger (Ed.), *Retrospections on social psychology.* New York: Oxford.

Nisbett, R. E. (1987). Lay personality theory: Its nature, origin and utility. In N. E. Grunberg, R. E. Nisbett, Judith Rodin, & J. E. Singer (Eds.), *A distinctive approach to psychological research: The influence of Stanley Schachter.* Hillsdale, NJ: Erlbaum.

Nisbett, R. E., & Borgida, E. (1975). Attribution and the psychology of prediction. *Journal of Personality and Social Psychology, 32,* 932-943.

Nisbett, R. F., Caputo, C., Legant, P., & Maracek, J. (1973). Behavior as seen by the actor and as seen by the observer. *Journal of Personality and Social Psychology, 27,* 154-164.

Nisbett, R. E., & Henderson, E. (1991). *Economic change and cultural achievements.* Unpublished manuscript, University of Michigan.

Nisbett, R. E., & Polly, G. (1991). *Homicide as a culturally-preferred form of conflict resolution.* Unpublished manuscript, University of Michigan.

Nisbett, R. E., & Ross, L. (1980). *Human inference: Strategies and shortcomings of social judgment.* Englewood Cliffs, NJ: Prentice-Hall.

Nisbett, R. E., & Schachter, S. (1966). Cognitive manipulation of pain. *Journal of Experimental Social Psychology, 2,* 227-236.

Nisbett, R. E., & Wilson, T. D. (1977). Telling more than we can know: Verbal reports on mental processes. *Psychological Review, 8,* 231-259.

Nolen-Hoeksema, S., Girgus, J. S., & Seligman, M. E. P. (1986). Learned helplessness in children: A longitudinal study of depression, achievement, and explanatory style. *Journal of Personality and Social Psychology, 51,* 435-442.

Norman, W. T. (1963). Toward an adequate taxonomy of personal attributes: Replicated factor structures in peer nomination personality ratings. *Journal of Abnormal and Social*

Psychology, 66, 574-583.

Norman, W. T., & Goldberg, L. R. (1966). Raters, ratees, and randomness in personality structure. *Journal of Personality and Social Psychology, 4,* 681-691.

Ogbu, J. (1978). *Minority education and caste: The American system in cross-cultural perspective.* Hillsdale, NJ: Erlbaum.

Olweus, D. (1977). A critical analysis of the "modern" interactionist position. In D. Magnusson & N.S. Endler (Eds.), *Personality at the crossroads: Current issues in interactional psychology.* Hillsdale, NJ: Erlbaum.

Orvis, B. R., Cunningham, J. D., & Kelley, H. H. (1975). A closer examination of causal inference: The roles of consensus, distinctiveness, and consistency information. *Journal of Personality and Social Psychology, 32,* 605-616.

Oskamp, S. (1984). *Applied social psychology.* Englewood Cliffs, NJ: Prentice-Hall.

Ostrom, T. M. (1975, August). *Cognitive representation of impressions.* Paper presented at the meeting of the American Psychological Association.

Park, B. (1986). A method for studying the development of impressions of real people. *Journal of Personality and Social Psychology, 51,* 907-917.

Park, B. (1989). Trait attributes as on-line organizers in person impressions. In J. N. Bassili (Ed.), *On-line cognition in person perception.* Hillsdale, NJ: Erlbaum.

Parsons, H. M. (1974). What happened at Hawthorne. *Science, 183,* 922-932.

Patterson, C. R. (1982). *Coercive family process.* Eugene, OR: Catallia.

Pennebaker, J. W. (1982) *The psychology of symptoms.* New York: Springer-Verlag.

Penrod, S., & Hastie, R. (1980). A computer simulation of jury decision making. *Psychological Review, 87,* 133-159.

Pervin, L. A. (1976). A free-response description approach to the analysis of person-situation interaction. *Journal of Personality and Social Psychology, 34,* 465-474.

Pervin, L. A. (1977). The representative design of person-situation research. In D. Magnusson & N. S. Endler (Eds.), *Personality at the crossroads: Current issues in interactional psychology.* Hillsdale, NJ: Erlbaum.

Pervin, L. A. (1985). *Personality: Current controversies, issues and directions.* In M. Rosenzweig & L. W. Porter (Eds.), *Annual Review of Psychology* (Vol. 36). Palo Alto: Annual Reviews.

Peterson, C., & Seligman, M. E. P. (1984). Causal explanations as a risk factor for depression: Theory and evidence. *Psychological Review, 91,* 347-374.

Peterson, C., & Seligman, M. E. P. (1987). Explanatory style and illness. *Journal of Personality, 55,* 237-265.

Peterson, C., Vaillant, G. E., & Seligman, M. E. P. (1988). Pessimistic exploratory style as a risk factor in physical illness: A thirty-five-year longitudinal study. *Journal of Personality and Social Psychology, 55,* 23-27.

Peterson, D. R. (1968). The clinical study of social behavior. New York: Appleton. Pettigrew, T. F. (1986). *Racially separate or together?* New York: McGraw-Hill.

Pettigrew, T. F. (1986). The intergroup contact hypothesis reconsidered. In M. Hewstone & R. Brown (Eds.), *Contact and conflict in intergroup encounters.* Oxford: Blackwell.

Petty, E., & Cacioppo, J. T. (1985). The elaboration likelihood model of persuasion. In L. Berkowitz (Ed.), *Advances in experimental social psychology* (Vol. 19). New York: Academic.

Piaget, J. (1930). *The child's conception of physical causality.* London: Kegan Paul.

Pietromonaco, P., & Nisbett, R. E. (1982). Swimming upstream against the fundamental attribution error: Subjects' weak generalizations from the Darley and Batson study. *Social Behavior and Personality, 10,* 1-4.

Pliner, P., Hart, H., Kohl, J., & Saari, D. (1974). Compliance without pressure: Some further data on the foot-in-the-door technique. *Journal of Experimental Social Psychology, 10,* 17-22.

Powers, E., & Whitmer, H. (1951). *An experiment in the prevention of delinquency: The Cambridge-Somerville youth study.* New York: Columbia.

Putnam, R. D. (1987). Institutional performance and political culture: Some puzzles about the power of the past. Paper presented at the meeting of the American Political Science

Association, Chicago.

Putnam, R. D., Leonardi, R., Nanetti, R. Y., & Pavoncello, F. (1983). Explaining institutional success: The case of Italian regional government. *American Political Science Review, 77,* 55-74.

Reim, B., Glass, D. C., & Singer, J. E. (1971). Behavioral consequences of exposure to uncontrollable and unpredictable noise. *Journal of Applied Social Psychology, 17,* 44-66.

Riecken, H. W., & Boruch, R. F. (Eds.) (1974). *Social experimentation.* New York: Academic.

Roberts, D., & Maccoby, N. (1985). Effects of mass communication. In G. Lindzey & E. Aronson (Eds.), *The handbook of social psychology: Vol. II. Special fields and applications.* New York: Random House.

Robertson, K., Kelley, A., O'Neill, B., Wixom, C., Eisworth, R., & Haddon, W., Jr. (1974). A controlled study of the effect of television messages on safety belt use. *American Journal of Public Health, 64,* 1071-1080.

Robins, P. K., & West, R. W. (1980). Labor supply response over time. *Journal of Human Resources, 15,* 524.

Rodin, J. (1985). The application of social psychology. In G. Lindzey & E. Aronson (Eds.), *The handbook of social psychology: Vol. II. Special fields and applications.* New York: Random House.

Rodin, J. (1986). Aging and health: Effects of the sense of control. *Science, 233,* 1271-1276.

Rodin, J., & Langer, E. J. (1977). Long-term effects of a control-relevant intervention with the institutionalized aged. *Journal of Personality and Social Psychology, 35,* 897-902.

Rodin, J., & Salovey, P. (1989). Health psychology. *Annual Review of Psychology,* 533-579.

Roethlisberger, F. J. (1941). *Management and morale.* Cambridge, MA: Harvard.

Roethlisberger, F. J., & Dickson, W. J. (1939). *Management and the worker.* Cambridge, MA: Harvard.

Rohrer, J. H., Baron, S. H., Hoffman, E. L., & Swinder, D. V. (1954). The stability of autokinetic judgment. *Journal of Abnormal and Social Psychology, 49,* 595-597.

Rosen, B. C. (1959). Race, ethnicity, and the achievement syndrome. *American Sociological Review, 24,* 47-60.

Rosenthal, R. (1976). *Experimenter effects in behavioral research* (enlarged ed.). New York: Irvington.

Rosenthal, R. (1985). From unconscious experimenter bias to teacher expectancy effects. In J. B. Dusek, V. C. Hall, & W. J. Meyer (Eds.), *Teacher expectancies.* Hillsdale, NJ: Erlbaum.

Rosenthal, R., & Jacobson, L. (1968). *Pygmalion in the classroom: Teacher expectation and pupils' intellectual development.* New York: Holt.

Rosenthal, R., & Rubin, D. B. (1978). Interpersonal expectancy effects: The first 345 studies. *The Behavioral and Brain Sciences, 3,* 377-386.

Ross, L. (1977). The intuitive psychologist and his shortcomings. In L. Berkowitz (Ed.), *Advances in experimental social psychology* (Vol. 10). New York: Academic.

Ross, L. (1988). Situationist perspectives on the obedience experiments. *Contemporary Psychology, 33,* 101-104.

Ross, L. (1990). Recognizing the role of construal processes. In I. Rock (Ed.), *The legacy of Solomon Asch.* Hillsdale, NJ: Erlbaum.

Ross, L., Amabile, T. M., & Steinmetz, J. L. (1977). Social roles, social control, and biases in social-perception processes. *Journal of Personality and Social Psychology, 35,* 485-494.

Ross, L., Bierbrauer, G., & Hoffman, S. (1976). The role of attribution processes in conformity and dissent: Revisiting the Asch situation. *American Psychologist, 31,* 148-157.

Ross, L., Greene, D., & House, P. (1977). The false consensus effect: An egocentric bias in social perception and attribution processes. *Journal of Experimental Social Psychology, 13,* 279-301.

Ross, L., Griffin, D. W., & Thomas, E. (1989). *Statistical considerations relevant to "simple" and "aggregated" cross-situational consistency: Computations from a thought experiment.* Unpublished manuscript, Stanford University.

Ross, L., & Lepper, M. R. (1980). The perseverance of beliefs: Empirical and normative considerations. In R. A. Shweder (Ed.), *New directions for methodology of behavioral science: Fallible judgment in behavioral research*. San Francisco: Jossey-Bass.

Ross, L., Lepper, M. R., & Hubbard, M. (1975). Perseverance in self-perception and social perception: Biased attributional processes in the debriefing paradigm. *Journal of Personality and Social Psychology, 32*, 880-892.

Ross, L., & Penning, P. (1985). *The dispositionist bias in accounting for behavioral disconfirmation*. Unpublished manuscript, Stanford University.

Ross, L., Rodin, J., & Zimbardo, P. (1969). Toward an attribution therapy: The reduction of fear through induced cognitive emotional misattribution. *Journal of Personality and Social Psychology, 12*, 279-288.

Ross, L., & Stillinger, C. (1991). Barriers to conflict resolution. *Negotiation Journal, 8*, 389-404.

Rotter, J. B. (1966). Generalized expectancies for internal versus external control of reinforcement. *Psychological Monographs, 80* (Whole number 609).

Royce, J. M., Darlington, R. B., & Murray, H. W. (1983). Pooled analysis: Findings across studies. In Consortium for Longitudinal Studies, *As the twig is bent*. London: Erlbaum.

Rumelhart, D. (1980). Schemata: The building blocks of cognition. In R. Spiro, B. Bruce & W. Brewer (Eds.), *Theoretical issues in reading comprehension*. Hillsdale, NJ: Erlbaum.

Rushton, J. P., & Campbell, A. C. (1977). Modelling vicarious reinforcement and extroversion on blood donating in adults: Immediate and long term effects. *European Journal of Social Psychology, 7*, 297-306.

Safer, M. A. (1980). Attributing evil to the subject, not the situation: Student reaction to Milgram's film on obedience. *Personality and Social Psychology Bulletin, 6*, 205-209.

Sanders, C. M. (1980). A comparison of adult bereavement in the death of a spouse. *Omega, 10*, 303-319.

Schachter, S. (1951). Deviation, rejection and communication. *Journal of Abnormal and Social Psychology, 46*, 190-207.

Schachter, S., & Singer, J. E. (1962). Cognitive, social and physiological determinants of emotional state. *Psychological Review, 69*, 379-399.

Schank, R., & Abelson, R. P. (1977). *Scripts, plans, goals, and understanding: An inquiry into human knowledge structures*. Hillsdale, NJ: Erlbaum.

Schein, E. H. (1956). The Chinese indoctrination program for prisoners of war: A study of attempted brainwashing. *Psychiatry, 19*, 149-172.

Schorr, L. B. (1988). *Within our reach: Breaking the cycle of disadvantage*. New York: Doubleday.

Schulz, R. (1976). Effects of control and predictability on the physical and psychological well-being of the institutionalized aged. *Journal of Personality and Social Psychology, 33*, 563-573.

Schutz, A. (1970). *On phenomenology and social relations*. Chicago: University of Chicago Press.

Sears, R. R. (1963). Dependency motivation. In M. R. Jones (Ed.), *Nebraska symposium on motivation* (Vol. 11). Lincoln: University of Nebraska Press.

Seligman, M. E. P. (1970). On the generality of the laws of learning. *Psychological Review, 77*, 406-418.

Seligman, M. E. P. (1975). *Helplessness: On depression, development, and death*. San Francisco: Freeman.

Seligman, M. E. P., Kamen, L. P., & Nolen-Hoeksema, S. (1988). Explanatory style across the life span: Achievement and health. In E. M. Hetherington & O. C. Brim (Eds.), *Child development in a lifespan perspective*. Hillsdale, NJ: Erlbaum.

Seligman, M. E. P., & Shulman, P. (1986). Explanatory style as a predictor of productivity and quitting among life insurance sales agents. *Journal of Personality and Social Psychology, 50*, 832-838.

Sewell, W. H., & Hauser, R. M. (1976). Causes and consequences of higher education: Models of the status attainment process. In W. H. Sewell, R. M. Hauser, & C. Featherman (Eds.), *Schooling and achievement in American society*.

Shapiro, A. K. (1960). A contribution to a history of the placebo effect. *Behavioral Science, 5*, 109-135.

Shapiro, A. K. (1964). Factors contributing to the placebo effect: Their implications for psychotherapy. *American Journal of Psychotherapy, 18,* 73-87.

Shapiro, A. K. (1978). Placebo effects in medical and psychological therapies. In S. L. Garfield & A. E. Bergen (Eds.), *Handbook of psychotherapy and behavior change: An empirical analysis.* New York: Wiley.

Sherif, M. (1937). An experimental approach to the study of attitudes. *Sociometry, 1,* 90-98.

Sherif, M. (1966). *In common predicament: Social psychology of intergroup conflict and cooperation.* Boston: Houghton Mifflin.

Sherif, M., Harvey, O. J., White, B. J., Hood, W. R., & Sherif, C. W. (1961). *Intergroup conflict and cooperation: The robbers cave experiment.* Norman: University of Oklahoma Book Exchange.

Sherif, M., & Sherif, C. W. (1953). *Groups in harmony and tension.* New York: Harper & Row.

Sherif, M., White, B. J., & Harvey, O. J. (1955). Status in experimentally produced groups. *American Journal of Sociology, 60,* 370-379.

Shweder, R. A. (1991). *Thinking through cultures: Expeditions in cultural psychology.* Cambridge, MA: Harvard.

Shweder, R. A., & LeVine, R. A. (Eds.). (1984). *Culture theory: Essays on mind, self, and emotion.* New York: Cambridge.

Siegal, A. E., & Siegal, S. (1957). Reference groups, membership groups, and attitude change. *Journal of Abnormal and Social Psychology, 55,* 364-366.

Sims, J. H., & Baumann, D. D. (1972). The tornado threat: Coping styles of the North and South. *Science, 17,* 1386-1392.

Singer, J. E., Brush, C. A. & Lublin, S. C. (1965). Some aspects of deindividuation: Identification and conformity. *Journal of Experimental Social Psychology, 1,* 356-378.

Singer, J. F., & Lord, D. (1984). The role of social support in coping with chronic life-threatening illness. In A. Baum, S. E. Taylor, & J. E. Singer (Eds.), *Handbook of psychology and health* (Vol. 4). Hillsdale, NJ: Erlbaum.

Snyder, M. (1974). The self-monitoring of expressive behavior. *Journal of Personality and Social Psychology, 30,* 526-537.

Snyder, M. (1979). Self-monitoring processes. In L. Berkowitz (Ed.), *Advances in experimental social psychology* (Vol. 12). New York: Academic.

Snyder, M. (1981). On the influence of individuals on situations. In N. Cantor & J. F. Kihlstrom (Eds.), *Personality and social interaction.* Hillsdale, NJ: Erlbaum.

Snyder, M. (1983). The influence of individuals on situations: Implications for understanding the links between personality and social behavior. *Journal of Personality, 51,* 497-516.

Snyder, M. (1984). When belief creates reality. In L. Berkowitz (Ed.), *Advances in experimental social psychology* (Vol. 18). New York: Academic.

Snyder, M., & Cunningham, M. R. (1975). To comply or not to comply: testing the self-perception explanation of the "foot-in-the-door" phenomenon. *Journal of Personality and Social Psychology, 31,* 64-67.

Snyder, M., & Ickes, W. (1985). Personality and social behavior. In G. Lindzey & E. Aronson (Eds.), *The handbook of social psychology: Vol. II: Special fields and applications.* New York: Random House.

Snyder, M., Tanke, E. D., & Berscheid, E. (1977). Social perception and interpersonal behavior: On the self-fulfilling nature of social stereotypes. *Journal of Personality and Social Psychology, 35,* 656-666.

Sobel, M. (1987). *The world they made together: Black and white values in eighteenth-century Virginia.* Princeton, NJ: Princeton.

Sowell, T. (1981). *Ethnic America.* New York: Basic Books.

Sowell, T. (1983). *The economics and politics of race.* New York: Morrow.

Sowell, T. (1987). *A conflict of visions.* New York: William Morrow.

Spence, J. T. (1985). Achievement American style: The rewards and costs of individualism. *American Psychologist, 40,* 1285-1295.

Spence, J. T. (1985). Gender identity and its implications for the concepts of masculinity and femininity. In T. B. Sonderegger (Ed.), *Nebraska symposium on motivation: Psychology and gender* (Vol. 32). Lincoln: University of Nebraska Press.

Spence, J. T., & Helmreich, R. L. (1978). *Masculinity & femininity: Their psychological dimensions, correlates, and antecedents.* Austin: University of Texas Press.

Spiegel, D., Bloom, J., Kraemer, H., & Gottheil, E. (1988). Effects of psychosocial treatment on survival of patients with metastic breast cancer. *Lancet, 2,* 889-891.

Steele, C. M. (1988). The psychology of self-affirmation: Sustaining the integrity of the self. In L. Berkowitz (Ed.), *Advances in experimental social psychology* (Vol. 21). New York: Academic.

Stein, M. I. (1966). *Volunteers for peace.* New York: Wiley.

Steiner, J. (1980) The SS yesterday and today: A sociopsychological view. In J. E. Dimsdale (Ed.), *Survivors, victims, and perpetrators: Essays on the Nazi holocaust.* Washington, DC: Hemisphere Publishing.

Stigler, J. W., Shweder, R. A. & Herdt, G. (1990). *Cultural psychology: Essays on comparative human development.* New York: Cambridge.

Stillinger, C., Epelbaum, M., Keltner, D., & Ross, L. (1990). *The reactive devaluation barrier to conflict resolution.* Unpublished manuscript, Stanford University.

Storms, M. D. (1973). Videotape and the attribution process: Reversing actors' and observers' points of view. *Journal of Personality and Social Psychology, 27,* 165-175.

Storms, M. D., & McCaul, K. D. (1976). Attribution processes and emotional exacerbation of dysfunctional behavior. In J. H. Harvey, W. J. Ickes, & R. F. Kidd (Eds.). *New directions in attribution research* (Vol. 1). Hillsdale, NJ: Erlbaum.

Storms, M. D. & Nisbett, R. E. (1970). Insomnia and the attribution process. *Journal of Personality and Social Psychology, 16,* 319-328.

Stouffer, S. A. (Ed.). (1950). *Studies in social psychology in World War II: Vol. 4. Measurement and prediction.* Princeton, NJ: Princeton.

Strack, F., Martin, L. L., & Schwarz, N. (1988). Priming and communication: Social determinants of information use in judgments of life satisfaction. *European Journal of Social Psychology, 18,* 429-442.

Swann, W. B., Jr. (1984). Quest for accuracy in person perception: A matter of pragmatics. *Psychological Review, 91,* 457-477.

Tajfel, H. (1970, November). Experiments in intergroup discrimination. *Scientific American, 223,* 96-102.

Tajfel, H. (Ed.) (1981). *Human groups and social categories.* Cambridge: Cambridge.

Tajfel, H., Billig, M. G., Bundy, R. P., & Flament, C. (1971). Social categorization and inter-group behavior. *European Journal of Social Psychology, 1,* 149-178.

Tarde, G. (1903). *The laws of imitation* (translated). New York: Holt.

Taylor, S. E. (1983). Adjustment to threatening events: A theory of cognitive adaptation. *American Psychologist, 41,* 1161-1173.

Taylor, S. E. (1986). *Health psychology.* New York: Random House.

Taylor, S. E., & Crocker, J. (1986). *Is the social perceiver a behaviorist or a trait theorist?* Unpublished manuscript, University of California, Los Angeles.

Taylor, S. E., & Fiske, S. T. (1975). Point of view and perceptions of causality. *Journal of Personality and Social Psychology, 32,* 439-445.

Taylor, S. E., & Fiske, S. T. (1978). Salience, attention and attribution: Top of the head phenomena. In L. Berkowitz (Ed.), *Advances in experimental social psychology* (Vol. 11). New York: Academic.

Tesser, A. (1980). Self-esteem maintenance in family dynamics. *Journal of Personality and Social Psychology, 39,* 77-91.

Thomas, W. I., & Znaniecki, F. (1918). *The Polish peasant in Europe and America.* Chicago: University of Chicago Press.

Tocqueville, A. (1835/1969). *Democracy in America.* J. P. Mayer (Ed.), George Lawrence, trans. Garden City, NY: Anchor Books.

Treisman, U. (1989). *A study of the mathematics performance of black students at the University of California, Berkeley.* Unpublished manuscript, University of California, Berkeley.

Triandis, H. C. (1972). *The analysis of subjective culture.* New York: Wiley.

Triandis, H. C. (1987). *Collectivism and development.* Paper presented at International Union of Psychological Sciences Conference.

Triandis, H. C., Bontempo, R., Villareal, M. J., Asai, M., & Lucca, N. (1988). Individualism and collectivism: Cross-cultural perspectives on self-ingroup relationships. *Journal of Personality and Social Psychology, 54,* 323-338.

Tversky, A. (1977). Features of similarity. *Psychological Review, 84,* 327-352.

Tversky, A., & Kahneman, D. (1981). The framing of decisions and the psychology of choice. *Science, 21,* 453-458.

Ulrich, L., & Trumbo, D. (1965). The selection interview since 1949. *Psychological Bulletin,* 63, 100-116.

U.S. Bureau of the Census. (1981). *Current population reports* (Series P-20, No. 366). Washington, DC: U.S. Government Printing Office.

Useem, M., Setti, L., & Kanchanabucha, K. (1988). Predictors of success in a participatory project in Thailand. *Public Administration and Development, 8,* 289-303.

Valins, S., & Nisbett, R. E. (1972). Attribution processes in the development and treatment of emotional disorders. In E. E. Jones, D. E. Kanouse, H. H. Kelley, R. E. Nisbett, S. Valins, & B. Weiner (Eds.), *Attribution: Perceiving the causes of behavior.* Morristown, NJ: General Learning Press.

Vallone, R. P., Griffin, D. W., Lin S., & Ross, L. (1990). Overconfident prediction of future actions and outcomes by self and others. *Journal of Personality and Social Psychology, 58,* 582-592.

Vallone, R. P., Ross, L., & Lepper, M. R. (1985). The hostile media phenomenon: Biased perception and perceptions of media bias in coverage of the "Beirut Massacre." *Journal of Personality and Social Psychology, 49,* 577-585.

Van den Berghe, P. L. (1981). *The ethnic phenomenon.* New York: Praeger.

Van Dort, B. E., & Moos, R. H. (1976). Distance and the utilization of a student health center. *Journal of the American College Health Association, 24,* 159-162.

Veroff, J., Feld, S., & Gurin, G. (1962). Achievement motivation and religious background. *American Sociological Review, 27,* 205-21.

Wachtel, p. (1973). Psychodynamics, behavior therapy and the implacable experimenter: An inquiry into the consistency of personality. *Journal of Abnormal Psychology, 82,* 324-334.

Waller, W. (1961). *The sociology of teaching.* New York: Wiley.

Watson, J. B. (1930). *Behaviorism.* New York: Norton.

Weber, M. (1905/1984). *The Protestant ethic and the spirit of capitalism.* London: Unwin (translated).

Weiner, B. (Ed.). (1974). *Achievement motivation and attribution theory.* Morristown, NJ: General Learning Press.

Weiner, B. (1979). A theory of motivation for some classroom experiences. *Journal of Personality and Social Psychology, 71,* 3-25.

Weiner, B. (1985). Attributional theory of achievement motivation and emotion. *Psychological Review, 92,* 548-573.

Weiner, B., Frieze, I., Kukla, A., Rest, S., & Rosenbaum, R. M. (1972). Perceiving the causes of success and failure. In E. E. Jones (Ed.), *Attribution: Perceiving the causes of behavior.* Morristown, NJ: General Learning Press.

Weiss, J., & Brown, P. (1977). *Self-insight error in the explanation of mood.* Unpublished manuscript, Harvard University.

White, C. M. (1980). Conceptual universals in interpersonal language. *American Anthropology, 82,* 759-781.

Whiting, B. B., & Whiting, J. W. M. (1975). *Children of six cultures.* Cambridge, MA: Harvard.

Wholey, J.S. (1979). *Evaluation: Promise and performance.* Washington, DC: Urban Institute.

Widom, C. S. (1989). The cycle of violence. *Science, 24,* 160-166.

Wilson, T. D., & Linville, P. W. (1982). Improving the academic performance of college freshmen: Attribution therapy revisited. *Journal of Personality and Social Psychology, 42,* 367-376.

Wilson, T. D., & Stone, J. I. (1985). Limitations of self-knowledge: More on telling more than you can know. In P. Shaver (Ed.), *Self, situations, and social behavior: Review of personality and social psychology.* Beverly Hills, CA: Sage.

Wilson, W. J. (1987). *The truly disadvantaged*. Chicago: University of Chicago Press.

Winter, L., & Uleman, J.S. (1984). When are social judgments made? Evidence for the spontaneousness of trait inferences. *Journal of Personality and Social Psychology, 47*, 237-252.

Winter, L., Uleman, J. S., & Cunniff, C. (1985). How automatic are social judgments? *Journal of Personality and Social Psychology, 49*, 904-917.

Wishner, J. (1960). Reanalysis of "impressions of personality." *Psychological Review, 67*, 96-112.

Woodhead, M. (1988). When psychology informs public policy: The case of early childhood intervention. *American Psychologist, 43*, 443-454.

Word, C. O., Zanna, M. P., & Cooper, J. (1974). The nonverbal mediation of self-fulfilling prophecies in interracial interaction. *Journal of Experimental Social Psychology, 10*, 109-120.

Wortman, C. B. (1983). Coping with victimization: Conclusions and implications for future research. *Journal of Social Issues, 39*, 195-221.

Wright, J. C., & Mischel, W. (1987). A conditional approach to dispositional constructs: The local predictability of social behavior. *Journal of Personality and Social Psychology, 53*, 1159-1177.

Zajonc, R. B. (1965). Social facilitation. *Science, 149*, 269-274.

Zanna, M. P., Sheras, P., Cooper, J., & Shaw, C. (1975). Pygmalion and Galatea: The interactive effect of teacher and student expectancies. *Journal of Experimental Social Psychology, 11*, 279-287.

Zimbardo, P. C. (1970). The human choice: Individuation, reason, and order versus deindividuation, impulse, and chaos. In W. J. Arnold & D. Levine (Eds.), *Nebraska symposium on motivation, 1969* (Vol. 17). Lincoln: University of Nebraska Press.

Index of Authors and Names

Subject Index

Active vs. passive processing of stimuli, 12
Actors vs. observers, differences in attribution
    for, 140-141
Adaptation level, 62-63
African-Americans:
    cultural contributions of, 198
    and culture of U.S. South, 190, 196-197
    economic position of, 198
    experiences of, 176, 194, 196, 199
Aggregation of measures:
    actual benefits of, 110-111, 114-118
    claims for power of, 107-109
    in classic consistency studies, 97, 98, 100
    Spearman-Brown "prophesy formula,"
    108
Alcoholism and Irish-Americans, 194-195,
    202
Altruism:
    effects of social modeling on, 49
    situational influences on, 130-131
    social modeling influences on, 49, 223-224
    (See also Bystander intervention)
Ambiguity resolution, 76
Asch, Solomon:
    conformity studies by, 30-35
    and construal notion, 12, 69-72
    and "object of judgment," 69-72
    vs. Sherif, 30-31
Asch conformity paradigm, 30-35
    historical-social context in, 32
    vs. real-world conformity, 32
    role of attribution and construal in, 34-35
Attitude change:
    in Bennington studies, 35-38
    and dissonance, 16, 45-46
    peer group influences on, 35-38
Attractiveness (see Physical attractiveness)
Attribution, 77-80
    for actors vs. observers, 140-141
    and Asch paradigm, 34-35
    attribution theory of construal, 79-80
    covariation principle in, 78
    and depression, 240-241
    discounting principle in, 79
    and educational outcomes, 232-235
    and emotion, 79-80
    and errors in interpreting behavior, 13
    and extreme behavior, 243

of failure to change behavior, 244
    lack of conservatism in, 88
    of own behavior, 80-81
    and psychotherapy, 240-242
    regional differences in, 188-189
    social class differences in, 186-187
    (See also Fundamental attribution error;
    Lay dispositionism)
Attributional style, 166, 232-235, 241-243
    and education consequences, 232-235
    and health consequences, 240-241
    link to sex differences, 232-234
    manipulation of, 234
    mastery vs. helplessness, 166, 232-233
Audience as source of behavioral consistency
    and predictability, 150-152
Authoritarian vs. democratic groups, 9
Autokinetic effect, 28-30
Awareness (see Self-awareness)

Bail bond study, 210
Banality of evil thesis and Milgram paradigm,
    52-53
Behavior:
    vs. attitudes and intentions, 10
    predictability of (see Predictability of
    behavior; Prediction of behavior)
    unpredictability of, 2-3, 6, 17-20
Behavioral consistency (see Cross-situational
    consistency in behavior)
Behavioral specificity, 92, 101
Behavioral stability over lifespan, 158-160
Behaviorism:
    and dissonance theory, 66
    resistance of social psychology to, 11
    and situationism, 59-60
    and subjectivism, 11, 60-62
Bennington studies, 35-38
Bias and partisan perceptions, 72-75
    in assimilation of evidence, 73
    as perceived in media, 73-74
Blacks (see African-Americans)
Blaming the victim, 204
Blood donations, 223
Burnout, 241
Butterfly effect, 18
Bystander intervention, 41-44, 48-50, 130-
    131

ABOUT PINTER & MARTIN

Pinter & Martin is an independent book publisher based in London, with distribution throughout the world. We specialise in psychology, pregnancy, birth and parenting, fiction and yoga, and publish authors who challenge the status quo, such as Elliot Aronson, Grantly Dick-Read, Ina May Gaskin, Stanley Milgram, Guillermo O'Joyce, Michel Odent, Gabrielle Palmer, Stuart Sutherland and Frank Zappa.

For more information, visit www.pinterandmartin.com